NEW LABOUR AND THE EUROPEAN UNION

To my mother, and in memory of my father

New Labour and the European Union

Political strategy, policy transition and the
Amsterdam Treaty negotiation

STEFANO FELLA

Routledge
Taylor & Francis Group

LONDON AND NEW YORK

First published 2002 by Ashgate Publishing

Reissued 2018 by Routledge
2 Park Square, Milton Park, Abingdon, Oxon OX14 4RN
711 Third Avenue, New York, NY 10017, USA

Routledge is an imprint of the Taylor & Francis Group, an informa business

Publisher's Note
The publisher has gone to great lengths to ensure the quality of this reprint but points out that some imperfections in the original copies may be apparent.

Disclaimer
The publisher has made every effort to trace copyright holders and welcomes correspondence from those they have been unable to contact.

A Library of Congress record exists under LC control number: 2002107424

ISBN 13: 978-1-138-73396-1 (hbk)
ISBN 13: 978-1-315-18697-9 (ebk)

Contents

Acknowledgements

First and foremost, I would like to express my gratitude to my PHD supervisor at the University of North London, Mike Newman, for his unstinting encouragement, support and patience, for his insightful comments and advice on the various drafts I presented to him, and for generally having faith in me. I am greatly indebted to a number of individuals who were involved in the Labour party's preparations for the Amsterdam IGC and who provided me with information and material on policy-making in this period and/or allowed themselves to be interviewed in the course of my research. Without their help, this book would not have been possible. I am not acknowledging them all by name for reasons of confidentiality. However, I will mention Sir Michael Butler, Richard Corbett MEP and Pauline Green who all provided me with very useful insights. Richard Corbett was also kind enough to read and comment on a couple of the draft chapters. Thanks are also due to James Cornford, the former director of the Institute for Public Policy Research (IPPR), who first suggested that I explore the possible positions on the IGC that the Labour party should adopt (albeit from the perspective of influencing policy rather than producing an academic analysis of it) in 1993. In addition, I would like to thank the European studies staff and students at the University of North London who contributed to a pleasant working environment while I was researching and teaching there from 1997 to 2001. I am particularly grateful to Peter Gowan, for ensuring I had enough teaching hours to finance myself and for commenting on a draft of my research, and to Mary Farrell for her words of encouragement. I would also like to thank the TMR network on political representation in the EU (financed by the fifth framework programme for research and development of the European Commission and co-ordinated by Herman Schmitt of the University of Mannheim) for funding my research fellowship at the University of Genova from July 2001 to May 2002, in the course of which I finalised the manuscript for this book. Thanks also to Kirstin Howgate and the editorial team at Ashgate for their help in bringing the book project to fruition. Finally, I would like to thank the close friends and family who kept me sane.

List of Abbreviations

BSE	Bovine Spongiform Encephalopathy
CAP	Common Agricultural Policy
CBI	Confederation of British Industry
CDU	German Christian-Democratic Party
CEE	Central and Eastern European States
CFSP	Common Foreign and Security Policy
CJD	Creutzfeldt-Jakob Disease
COREPER	Committee of Permanent Representatives to the EU
COSAC	Conference of Community and European Affairs Committees of the Parliaments
CSPEC	Confederation of Socialist Parties of the European Community
CSU	German Christian Social Union
DM	Deutschmark
DTI	Department of Trade and Industry
EC	European Community
ECB	European Central Bank
ECJ	European Court of Justice
ECHR	European Convention on Human Rights
ECOFIN	Council of Economic and Finance Ministers
ECSC	European Coal and Steel Community
EEC	European Economic Community
EFTA	European Free Trade Association
EMAC	Economic and Monetary Affairs Committee
EMS	European Monetary System
EMU	Economic and Monetary Union
EP	European Parliament
EPLP	European Parliamentary Labour Party
EPP	European Peoples Party
ERM	Exchange Rate Mechanism
ETUC	European Trade Union Confederation
EU	European Union
Euratom	European Atomic Energy Community
FCO	Foreign and Commonwealth Office
IGC	Intergovernmental Conference
JHA	Justice and Home Affairs
LWG	Leader's Working-Group on the IGC
MEP	Member of the European Parliament
NATO	North Atlantic Treaty Organisation
NEC	National Executive Committee
OEEC	Organisation for European Economic Co-operation

PDS	Italian Democratic Left Party
PES	Party of European Socialists
PES Group	Group of the Party of European Socialists
PLP	Parliamentary Labour Party
PS	French Socialist Party
PSI	Italian Socialist Party
PSOE	Spanish Socialist Workers Party
PVDA	Dutch Labour Party
QMV	Qualified Majority Voting
SDP	Social Democratic Party
SEA	Single European Act
SPD	German Social Democratic Party
TENs	Trans-European Networks
TEU	Treaty on European Union
TUC	Trade Union Congress
UKRep	United Kingdom Representation to the EU
UN	United Nations
UPE	Union For Europe
VAT	Value Added Tax
WEU	West European Union
WTO	World Trade Organisation

Chapter 1

Introduction: Britain and the European Treaty Review of 1996

The next Labour government, committed to radical, socialist policies for reviving the British economy, is bound to find continued membership a most serious obstacle to the fulfilment of those policies...British withdrawal from the Community is the right policy for Britain - to be completed well within the lifetime of the parliament (Labour Party 1983: 33).

We need therefore strong European political structures...so that the people of the Community can use their collective power to ensure that Europe moves in the direction they want and not solely in the direction determined by international commercial forces (Labour Party 1993b: 47).

Background

As the above quotations demonstrate, the official Labour party attitude to the EU inherited by Tony Blair when he became leader in 1994, was radically different from the position Labour had held just over a decade earlier, when Blair himself was first elected to parliament. This policy transformation reflected a wider re-evaluation of the Labour party's political strategy and its approach to the nation-state and to social and economic policy under the leadership of Neil Kinnock between 1983 and 1992. Labour's transformation into a modern European social democratic party was cemented under the leadership of John Smith between 1992 and 1994 (Hughes and Wintour 1990, Smith and Spear 1992, Jones, T 1996: 113-130, Davies 1996: 418-423, Anderson and Mann 1997, Ludlam and Smith 2000). The belief that the EU could be utilised as a mechanism for the realisation of Labour's policy objectives was integral to this new social democratic outlook (Tindale 1992, George and Haythorne 1996, Ladrech 2000: 73-75). For a young, modernising leader like Blair, Labour's new commitment to strong UK engagement in the EU would be unquestioned. Furthermore, Labour's involvement in a transnational European party confederation: the Party of European Socialists (PES), established in 1992, appeared to offer the Blair leadership a valuable mechanism by which to engage with the 'mainstream' EU agenda and pursue this social democratic approach in alliance with its European 'sister' parties (Newman 1996, Hix 1999, Ladrech 2000).

But a test to Labour's new found pro-Europeanism would be provided by the imminence of an intergovernmental conference (IGC) to revise the EU treaties, a partial agenda and start date for which was already set by the Treaty on European Union (TEU) agreed at Maastricht in 1991 (Corbett 1992, Dinan 1999: 169-170). Moreover, the IGC start date of 1996 was predicted to coincide with the likely date of a general election in the UK in 1996 or 1997. The new Labour leadership thus faced the prospect of fighting a general election in the midst of an IGC, in an increasingly Euro-sceptical[1] domestic political climate. Unlike his immediate predecessors, Blair was elected to the leadership of the Labour party at a time of genuine expectation that it would form the next government in the UK. Blair's own personal popularity added to this expectation (Dunleavy 2000: 130-132, Anderson and Mann 1997: 1-25). The positions that the Labour party adopted in relation to the 1996 IGC would therefore be of acute political sensitivity. The difficulties encountered by the Conservative government of John Major in ensuring the parliamentary ratification of the TEU, due to a concerted Euro-sceptical rebellion by a significant and vocal minority within his own parliamentary party, had contributed to a widespread feeling within the Conservative party that Maastricht represented the 'high water mark' of European integration (Baker, Gamble and Ludlam 1993, 1994, Garry 1995, Ludlam 1998, Young, H 1999: 435-471). Any further treaty changes that reinforced the supranational nature of the EU were deemed as highly undesirable by much of the Conservative party and politically unfeasible for the Major government. Nevertheless, the agenda for 1996 was likely to involve discussion of more supranational forms of decision-making in the areas of intergovernmental co-operation established by the TEU: i.e. the common foreign and security policy (CFSP) and justice and home affairs (JHA) policy, as well as proposals for greater use of qualified majority voting (QMV) in a number of policy areas to facilitate effective decision-making post-enlargement, and demands for an enhanced role for the European Parliament (EP) in order to address a perceived lack of democracy in EU decision-making (Edwards and Pijpers 1997, McDonagh 1998). Labour party documents produced prior to Blair's accession to the leadership had provided a strong indication that it might be prepared to support a number of the proposed treaty changes on the emerging reform agenda (Labour 1993b, 1994). But given the increasing unpopularity of the EU among sections of the British electorate it also seemed clear that an increasingly unpopular Conservative government would seek to regain public support by exploiting the political gap between it and the newly Europeanised Labour party on this issue and presenting itself as a patriotic defender of national sovereignty (Hix 2000: 59-62). The Labour party, in contrast, would be portrayed as 'soft' on Europe and likely to sell out UK national interests should it win power before the conclusion of the IGC.

Themes of Book

This book will provide a detailed examination of the process by which the Blair leadership sought to balance the Labour party's new found Europeanism with the conflicting requirements of the domestic political climate in the UK in order to develop a credible set of positions on the IGC in the run-up to the general election of May 1997. The book tracks the evolution of Labour's positions on the IGC from opposition to government, culminating in the successful completion of the IGC negotiations at the Amsterdam summit in June 1997. This examination will be placed in the context of the transformation of the Labour party in the late 1980s and early 1990s into a pro-European social democratic party and of its involvement in a transnational political formation, the PES, which brings together the socialist, social democratic and labour parties of the EU. The book will explore the extent to which Labour party membership of the PES, its consultations with other PES parties (many of whom were in government), and the mediating role played by Labour MEPs in the European parliamentary group of the PES, affected Labour's positioning on the IGC. Particular light will be shed on the relationship between the Labour party and its EU 'sister' parties in the PES, attempts at policy co-ordination made by the PES parties in relation to the IGC and the extent to which its interaction with the PES exercised a 'Europeanising' influence on the Labour party. However, policy-making will also be assessed in the context of a number of constraining factors conditioning Labour party EU policy, particularly domestic political factors - given the coincidence of the IGC and the 1997 general election in the UK - and bipartisan notions of national interest, pursued by UK governments irrespective of the party in power.

In examining the leader's working-group (LWG) on the IGC established by the Blair leadership in opposition, the book aims to shed light on both the nature of party policy-making processes and the general preparations for government undertaken by the Labour party prior to May 1997. In tracking the evolution of the party's positions once in government, it seeks to explore the influence of certain Whitehall and traditional 'national' interests on policy once in government. A detailed analysis will be provided of the role played by the Blair government in the final stages of the Amsterdam treaty negotiations in May and June of 1997. This will contribute to an understanding of the extent to which traditional 'structural' UK interests ensure certain continuities in UK government policy on the EU, irrespective of the party in office. Analysis of changes in positioning both prior to and following the entrance to government will be used to illustrate the extent to which the Labour party has shifted from a 'European social democratic' perspective on the EU (as elaborated under the Kinnock and Smith leaderships) to a more traditional economically liberal and politically pragmatic perspective under Blair. The book will thus draw attention to a distinctive 'New Labour' approach to the EU, which represents both continuity and change with previous UK and Labour party approaches. It will demonstrate that the broad lines of this New Labour approach to the EU would be established by the time of the Amsterdam summit and would be reflected in the later behaviour of the Blair government as regards European policy. In drawing attention to the shifts in policy on the EU, the analysis provided in the book will have a wider resonance in terms of illustrating the political and economic approach pursued by New Labour in opposition and government across a range of polices and the subtle (and sometimes not very subtle) shifts in policy undertaken in relation to policies championed in opposition in the fairly recent past.

Three distinctive phases in party policy-making on the Amsterdam IGC will be identified. The first of these covered the work of the LWG established by Blair in late 1994 shortly after he became party leader. The LWG had prime responsibility for formulating Labour party policy on the IGC and this work was reflected in the official party policy document, *The Future of the European Union*, which emerged from its deliberations in 1995 (Labour Party 1995). In addition to this, the LWG acted as a forum for ensuring the alignment of the public positions on the IGC taken by the Labour leadership in London, and those of its Brussels-based representatives in the EP. Furthermore, the work of the LWG was also influenced by the objective of seeking, wherever possible, to align Labour's positions on the IGC with those of its sister parties in the PES or, at the least, preventing joint PES positions from conflicting with its own. The effectiveness of these strategies will be examined, as will the general influence on IGC policy-making of the Labour party-PES relationship and the role played by Labour MEPs in the LWG, who acted as 'interlocutors' between the Labour party and the wider PES. The role played by various actors within the Labour leadership and the interaction among them is also of central importance to this study. Though Blair had overall control of the line adopted, significant contributions to party policy-making on the IGC were made by Labour's foreign affairs spokesman, Robin Cook, and by Larry Whitty, for whom a new post of European co-ordinator in the leader's office was created following Blair's decision to replace him as party general-secretary in 1994. Cook would play a particularly active role within the PES, representing the Labour party in the PES working-group on the IGC and at PES leaders' meetings. Whitty would assist in this PES-networking, while also playing the leading liaison role between the Labour leadership and the EPLP. Whitty would also have responsibility for drafting and submitting discussion papers for the LWG on most of the key treaty reform issues, while Cook contributed key papers on overall European strategy. The 1995 policy document would reflect the work of both Whitty and Cook. The roles played by these individuals reflected the interconnected relationship between the Labour leadership, the EPLP and the PES that contributed a 'Europeanising' influence on the party's IGC policy.

Nevertheless, Labour party policy-making on the IGC needs to be assessed in terms of the interaction between these 'Europeanising' influences and domestic political factors that would exert a conflicting pull on the direction of policy. The influence of domestic politics would become more clearly apparent in the second phase of IGC policy-making after the LWG stopped meeting in late 1996. In this second phase, electoral factors increasingly cast a shadow over policy as the general election drew nearer and 'Europeanising' influences on policy appeared to become more marginal. This phase would be particularly notable for the emergence of another principal actor in party IGC policy development, Sir Michael Butler, and the intensification of contacts between the Labour leadership and the Netherlands government which would chair the IGC negotiations in their crucial end period in the first half of 1997. The role played by Butler, a former UK ambassador to the EU, following his appointment as a special EU 'envoy' by the Labour leadership, will be of special interest in analysing the evolution of party policy and strategy in the run-up to the election. This strategy involved the discreet cultivation of contacts within other EU governments, the EU institutions and among UK government officials, and most critically the establishment of a confidential line of communication between the then Labour opposition in the UK and the Netherlands government. This provided the Labour leadership with detailed access to information on the IGC negotiations and ensured that the Labour leadership would be aware of the reform options being discussed within the IGC and the likely areas of compromise. It also facilitated the preparations by the Netherlands government of the final end-game of the IGC negotiations following the UK general election in May 1997. The significance of the line of communication with the Netherlands government will be assessed in the context of the opportunities for information sharing provided by the PES organisation, given that the Netherlands government was led by Labour's Dutch 'sister' party, the PVDA.

A third and decisive phase in policy-making on the IGC came with Labour's entry into government at the beginning of May 1997 and culminated in the conclusion of the IGC negotiations at Amsterdam in mid-June. In addition to comparisons with the positions taken by Labour in opposition, the extent of continuity between the EU policies of the Labour government and those of preceding Conservative administrations will be explored. In this light, the extent to which certain policies reflected a bipartisan consensus based on a perception of 'structural' UK national interests will also be examined (Bulmer 1992: 25-29). Related to this is the need to assess the influence of the official government machinery of Whitehall on the nature and direction of government EU policy (Buller and Smith 1998). Once in office, Labour party policy-making on the EU appeared to be submerged within the Whitehall machinery of policy formulation and government co-ordination. The effect this had on the positions on the IGC that Labour had developed in opposition requires particular attention. An analysis of the negotiating strategy and policy positions taken by the Labour government into the final negotiations, culminating in the Amsterdam summit, will also facilitate an assessment of the degree to which policy objectives, developed in opposition and refined in government, were reflected in the final treaty. The evolution of the Labour party's positions on the IGC in the run-up to the 1997 general election and following its election to government will be placed in the context of a broader evolution in the Labour party's approach to the EU under the Blair leadership. It will be argued that whereas Labour party documents in the early 1990s appeared to indicate a willingness to work with its PES 'sister' parties in pursuit of a social democratic re-orientation of the EU (Labour party 1993b, 1994, PES 1994) - reflecting factors in its recent pro-European conversion - further changes in the Labour party's general political and economic outlook under Blair would lead to a distancing from this approach.

The transformation of the Labour party into a pro-European social democratic party in the late 1980s and early 1990s and the European policy positions inherited by Blair in 1994 will be explored in the next chapter. However, before embarking on the examination of the three phases of party policy-making on the IGC identified above, it is also necessary to present a clearer picture of the political dilemmas confronting Blair when he became leader in 1994. The remainder of this introductory chapter will therefore outline the key issues on the IGC agenda and then explore the domestic political situation that made the treaty review such a delicate issue in the UK.

Why Was an IGC Necessary?

As noted above, a partial agenda for a treaty review and a start date of 1996 had been set by the TEU. Articles A and B of the TEU outlined general principles for revision, most importantly in the final paragraph of article B which referred to the 'pillar' based structure of the EU (Laffan 1997a: 291). The TEU had established two intergovernmental pillars, relating to the CFSP and JHA where co-operation would proceed on a consensual intergovernmental basis rather than the Community method that characterised previous European Community (EC) development. The initiating role of the Commission, the scrutiny role of the EP and the judicial role of the European Court of Justice (ECJ), all of which characterised the existing EC, were largely absent from these intergovernmental pillars, which operated alongside the 'first' EC pillar in the new European Union. In addition to the review of this structure, articles J.4 and J.10 of the TEU provided for the revision of the provisions relating to the CFSP and a possible framing of an EU defence policy and article 189b provided for a review of the codecision procedure, introduced by the TEU to give the EP an almost equal say with the Council in the determination of limited areas of EC legislation (Laffan 1997a: 293-295). The TEU also included commitments to give consideration to possible new treaty titles on civil protection, energy and tourism and to examine the hierarchy of Community acts (Corbett 1992: 286-88, 296, Edwards and Pijpers 1997: 4, McDonagh 1998: 37-38). These review provisions reflected the nature of the TEU itself: a compromise between those member states who sought the development of a more integrated supranational entity, with federal characteristics, and those (notably Britain) who wished to steer the EU towards a more intergovernmental method of co-operation, particularly in key areas of national sovereignty, as characterised by the intergovernmental pillars. A number of member states would seek the 'communitisation' of the intergovernmental pillars (or at least the JHA pillar), thereby bringing the areas of co-operation covered into the EC method of decision-making. The Major government had opposed an EC role in these areas of policy at Maastricht (Corbett 1992, Forster 1998) and was likely to remain steadfast in its opposition. Much the same could be said in relation to its attitude to the possible development of a European defence role within the ambit of the CFSP. It had strongly opposed this in the run-up to Maastricht, asserting the primacy of NATO in such matters (Forster 1998: 354-356).

Further additions to this limited IGC agenda would emerge in response to the Maastricht ratification crises in a number of member states and to the questions of institutional efficiency raised by accession of three new member states in 1995 and the commitment to enlarge the EU further. In addition to Britain, ratification problems had also beset Denmark, France and Germany. Indeed, the initial referendum rejection of the TEU by the Danish people had plunged the EU into crisis in June 1992 and acted as a trigger for the anti-Maastricht rebellion within the British Conservative party (though the Danish position would later be resolved by the negotiation of a number of derogations from the treaty and a second referendum in 1993, this time in favour). Furthermore, the treaty was only narrowly approved in a referendum in France, when a negative result would most likely have killed it, and in Germany, ratification was delayed by attempts to have the treaty declared unconstitutional (Edwards and Pijpers 1997: 1, Dinan 1999: 148-156, Criddle 1993). These difficulties helped to cultivate a growing awareness across the member states that the process of European integration as a project of political elites had become increasingly remote from the citizens of the EU. National governments had transferred policy-making in a number of areas previously subject to national parliamentary scrutiny to the EU level without any concomitant transfer of scrutiny to a European level representative body. Furthermore, not only was the Council, the legislature of the EU, in many policy areas unaccountable to any other democratically constituted bodies, but its deliberations and decision-making also took place in private. Such a state of affairs would be deemed unacceptable in the legislative bodies of the member states, much as some national executives might secretly crave it. Accordingly, a consensus developed that the treaty review would have to include measures to simplify the complex web of treaties and render EU decision-making more democratic and transparent, possibly through greater accountability to the EP (involving an extension of codecision) and greater transparency in the Council of Ministers. Further proposals to bring a closer identification with citizens' concerns also found their way onto the agenda, including more focused provisions for the protection of human rights, measures to combat racism and wider forms of discrimination and closer co-operation in addressing the high levels of unemployment in the EU (McDonagh 1998: 12-18).

Enlargement had implications for the efficiency of decision-making in the Council of Ministers and the allocation of weighted votes within it, together with the composition of the European Commission. The continuing prevalence of the unanimity requirement made decision-making difficult in an EU of 12 member states. Enlargement to 15 increased the problem. By 1995, 13 applications for membership were on the EU table, comprising Cyprus and Malta, with whom the EU was committed to commencing accession negotiations within 6 months of the completion of the IGC,[2] Turkey and ten applicants from the former Soviet bloc states in Central and Eastern Europe (CEE). The widespread requirement for unanimity should all or some of these applicants be admitted into the EU would be a recipe for institutional paralysis (Dinan 1999: 170). Hence, there were demands for greater use of QMV in Council decisions (McDonagh 1998: 155-156). Moreover, a continuation of the existing system of weighted votes, which disproportionately favoured the smaller states (in terms of ratio of votes to population size) was liable to lead to a situation whereby the larger states could be outvoted in those areas of decision-making where QMV did apply (even though combined they would represent a majority of the population even in an enlarged EU) This would be clearly unacceptable to the larger states which would accordingly seek a reweighting of votes to more accurately reflect their greater population size (McDonagh 1998: 156-157). Similarly, persistence with the existing situation whereby each member state could nominate one member of the European Commission (and the larger states two) was viewed as liable to render it increasingly unwieldy and unmanageable (Dinan 1999: 180). Hence, there were similar demands for a streamlining of the Commission and reform of the rules on its composition. The need to address these questions was recognised by the heads of government at the Brussels European Council of December 1993 which declared that, in the light of enlargement, the IGC would consider, together with the matters envisaged in the TEU: 'questions relating to the number of members of the Commission and the weighting of the votes of member states in the Council ...(and)...any measures deemed necessary to facilitate the work of the institutions and guarantee their effective operation' (European Council, December 1993). The spectre of enlargement would also lead to discussion of forms of variable geometry in order to prevent institutional paralysis, thus allowing groups of states to proceed with closer integration in particular policy areas without the participation of all member states. The emergence of this issue on the IGC agenda would also be related to the need to circumvent the unwillingness of certain member states, in particular Britain, to countenance closer integration in certain policy areas. Indeed, the two British opt-outs negotiated at Maastricht (from the protocol on social policy, and the provisions on economic and monetary union) had already formalised a variable geometry of sorts within the EU treaties (Fella 1999: 9-10).

One key issue that would not be on the agenda for the 1996 IGC was the central project of the TEU: economic and monetary union (EMU) culminating in the establishment of a single currency amongst its participating members. The monetary convergence conditions stipulated by the TEU for participation in the single currency (involving national targets on inflation and interest rate levels and limits on budget deficits) were seen by some critics as deflationary and thus linked to the high level of unemployment in the EU in the early 1990s. Moreover, in transferring control over key monetary decisions to a European Central Bank (ECB) independent of any political interference, the EMU process was seen by some as certain to compound the EU's democratic deficit. The notion that the convergence criteria needed to be broadened and that a political counterweight to the ECB was required did have support among French policy-makers. However, central bank independence and the tight monetarist convergence conditions had been a condition placed by the German Bundesbank on support for EMU. The German government therefore regarded the EMU provisions as non-negotiable and remained determined to keep EMU off the IGC agenda (Szukala and Wessels 1997: 82). A number of other member states were similarly far from keen on placing the EMU provisions back on the negotiating table for fear that the timetable for the single currency might slip back or that the German government might have second thoughts. For different reasons, the Conservative government in Britain would be unwilling to reopen the EMU provisions, given its general belief that its opt-out protected its position and the open divisions within its parliamentary party on the issue. EMU would therefore remain off the IGC agenda and would not be a major focal point of the Labour party's discussions in relation to the IGC. Accordingly, the development of Labour's position on EMU is not the main concern of this book, though it will be discussed in relation to the development of Labour's general positioning on the EU and in connection with specific IGC issues such as employment and the democratic deficit.

The Domestic Context: European Integration and British Politics in the 1990s

Though the exclusion of EMU from the IGC discussions would offer some comfort to the Major government given the antipathy towards the project within much of the Conservative party, the treaty review was still likely to involve discussion of a number of proposals which would be distinctly unwelcome for the British government. The wave of Euro-scepticism which began to engulf the Conservative party in the early 1990s would make agreement to further treaty changes in the direction of supranationalism very difficult, if not impossible, for the British government. Yet paradoxically, it was the Conservative party which had been viewed as the 'party of Europe' in Britain until the end of the 1980s, and historically, it had been Conservative governments which had initiated and agreed to each of the major steps taken to tie Britain closer into the European integration process. Indeed, it was the Conservative government of Harold Macmillan that reversed previous British isolation and launched the first application to join the then European Economic Community (EEC) in 1961. Furthermore, following the veto of this, and a second application by Harold Wilson's Labour government in 1967, by the French president, Charles de Gaulle, it was the Conservative government of Edward Heath that finally secured British entry in 1973. Moreover, the Conservative government of Margaret Thatcher enthusiastically embraced the Single European Act (SEA) of 1985, which significantly augmented the supranational nature of the EC, notably through considerable extensions of QMV, in order to provide the means to deliver a barrier-free European single market by 1992. Nevertheless, though the single market project had appeared at one with Thatcher's free market ideological approach, the SEA unleashed a new dynamic into the European integration process (viewed as moribund in the 1970s and early 1980s), which led to a series of proposals, notably for closer political union, EMU and a reinforced framework for European social protection, all of which were anathema to Thatcher's worldview. Many of the more 'integrationist' proposals would be personally associated with the dynamic leadership of the European Commission president Jacques Delors, who would become a prime focus of ire for Thatcher and her political allies. The re-launch of the European integration process in the late 1980s would trigger a Euro-sceptic reaction in Britain that would continue to convulse the Conservative party throughout the 1990s. Thatcher's attitude to the post-SEA proposals was famously encapsulated in her Bruges speech in 1988:

> We have not successfully rolled back the frontiers of the state in Britain only to see them reimposed at a European level with a European superstate exercising a new dominance from Brussels (Dinan 1999: 129).

Though the Bruges speech would later be cherished as a holy text by Conservative Euro-sceptics, and while the increasing stridency of Thatcher's discourse provided a signal of the direction that the Conservative party would travel in the next decade, her antagonism to further European integration was not shared by the majority of her cabinet colleagues at the time (Young, JW 2000: 143-149). Discomfort at the line that Thatcher was taking provided the pretext for her replacement by Major in 1990. Though Major promised a more constructive approach, he still found it necessary to negotiate the two British opt-outs on social policy and EMU at Maastricht a year later (Corbett 1992, Forster 1998). The opt-outs, the treaty avoidance of supranationalism in sensitive policy areas such as CFSP and JHA, the deletion of references in the treaty draft to the EU's federal goal and the new references to subsidiarity[3] earned Major the plaudits of the Conservative party and the right-wing press upon his return from Maastricht (Young, H 1999: 429-435). However, the general election and the events that followed in 1992 somewhat disturbed his calculations for a smooth ratification and transformed the nature of the domestic debate on Britain's role within the EU. The 1992 election left Major with a narrow majority of 21 MPs, causing him serious difficulties given the increasing number of Euro-sceptic MPs on the Conservative backbenches who were willing to defy his originally pragmatic line on EU policy. The government was reliant on the support of the Liberal Democrats and the abstention of Labour on key votes in order to ensure the parliamentary ratification of the bill incorporating the relevant aspects of the TEU into UK law. That Major could not rely on his own parliamentary party to muster sufficient parliamentary votes to ensure the passage was evident on the second reading of the bill in May 1992 when 22 Conservative MPs voted against. However, the situation was exacerbated following the Danish referendum rejection of the TEU on 2 June. This led the Major government to postpone the ratification process pending clarification of the implications of the Danish result, and emboldened a sizeable number of previously loyal Conservative MPs to call on the government to abandon the TEU. A total of 84 Conservative MPs signed a parliamentary motion calling for the government to make a 'fresh start' in respect of the future development of the EC (Baker, Gamble and Ludlam, 1993: 166).

Matters deteriorated further on 16 September 1992 when massive speculation forced sterling out of the exchange rate mechanism (ERM) of the European Monetary System (EMS) (Tsoukalis 1997: 152-162), blowing apart the central plank of the government's economic strategy.[4] Given that ERM membership was a precondition for the final stage of EMU, the events of 'Black Wednesday' (as the date of exit would be referred to) appeared to put paid to any prospect of the UK joining a single currency and seemingly destroyed completely the case for fixed exchange rates in the minds of sceptical opinion in Britain. The case for ERM membership had also suffered from its association with the severe economic difficulties endured in Britain in the period leading up to Black Wednesday. The severity of the economic recession and the high unemployment of the early 1990s were blamed on the need to maintain the exchange rate parity of sterling within the ERM, and the policy of high interest rates pursued to ensure this. Opponents of EMU would henceforth point to the economic problems caused by membership of this fixed exchange rate system in the early 1990s and the consequent economic recovery in Britain once sterling had departed from it as a concrete demonstration of the foolishness of any British pretensions to join the single currency. The ERM debacle further served to inflame anti-European, and in particular anti-German, feeling in Britain, with the Bundesbank attracting blame for not being prepared to give adequate support to maintain the parity of sterling and for pursuing a monetary policy which suited German domestic interests while creating economic imbalances among the fellow ERM members who were obliged to shadow this policy. The virtual collapse of the ERM a year later would further demonstrate the folly of fixing exchange rates in the eyes of the Euro-sceptics (Young, JW 2000: 160-163, Young, H 1999: 436-443).[5]

The Danish referendum and the ERM debacle emboldened the right-wing of the Conservative party, which had become increasingly hostile towards the EU, and had increased in numerical size and relative weight within the Conservative parliamentary party following the 1992 election, due both to the reduced size of the government majority and the entrance into parliament of a new and more stridently 'Thatcherite' intake of Conservative MPs. Unlike the older one-nation 'Heathites', these new MPs had 'matured' politically under Thatcher's leadership, and were more naturally Euro-sceptical and inclined to align themselves with their spiritual leader. In her new incarnation in the House of Lords, Baroness Thatcher stated her opposition to the TEU and openly incited her devotees in the House of Commons to follow suit. The Euro-sceptics pointed to the treaty extensions of QMV in the Council of Ministers, the introduction of EP codecision, the creation of EU citizenship and the closer co-operation envisaged on CFSP and JHA as evidence that the Major government had agreed to a further deepening of European integration. They also expressed fear that despite the opt-outs, Britain would at some point in the future be obliged to take part in EMU and the social provisions of the TEU. Following its reintroduction to the House of Commons, amid enormous political controversy in November 1992, a determined band of Euro-sceptic Conservative MPs conducted a guerrilla campaign against the Maastricht bill in its committee stage, drawing it out into 210 hours of debate over a four month period. 46 Conservative MPs rebelled on the third reading of the Maastricht bill in May 1993 (Young, H 1999: 388-397, Baker, Gamble and Ludlam, 1993, 1994, Garry 1995).

The increasing Euro-scepticism within the ranks of the Conservative party appeared to reflect a growing antipathy to the TEU among the British public at large and, indeed, increasing public hostility to the entire European project (Hix 2000: 53-58). This was spurred on by the virulent anti-EU campaign conducted by large sections of the predominantly right-wing British press (Wilkes and Wring 1998: 196-205). The hostility to the EU in the press, within the Conservative party, and across public opinion was, to an extent, mutually reinforcing. This political climate served to push the Major government towards a more openly antagonistic stance towards Britain's European partners.

Because of the size of the government's majority, the weight of Euro-sceptical opinion, and recognition that many of the loyalist Conservative MPs who supported the government during the ratification sympathised with the Euro-sceptics' arguments (as did a number of members of the cabinet and a swathe of junior ministers), Major adopted an increasingly Euro-sceptical tone himself. This was the price for unity within the government and across the Conservative parliamentary party and Major himself let it be known that he was 'the greatest Euro-sceptic' (Baker, Gamble and Ludlam 1993: 156). The stance adopted in the run-up to the Ioannina European Council in 1994 was one of two episodes in 1994 where Major isolated himself amongst his European colleagues by taking a hardline stance, in order to present to his own MPs and the wider public an image of government defence of British national interests in the face of the 'integrationist' inclinations of the other member states. This first dispute related to the adjustments of thresholds for adopting or blocking decisions conducted under the QMV rule in the Council of Ministers, deemed as necessary in advance of the accession to the EU of Austria, Finland and Sweden in 1995 (it was also presumed at the time that Norway would be acceding to the EU, but a negative result in the Norwegian referendum on accession later in 1994 prevented this). The view of the Commission and the general consensus among most of the member states was that the additional weighted votes of these new states required a slight increase of the blocking minority within Council (i.e. the number of votes required to block a decision) from 23 to 27. This would allow the ratio of votes required to remain roughly the same as a proportion of the new upwardly revised total weighted votes following enlargement. However, the Major government argued vigorously that the blocking minority should remain at 23.[6] Though an obscure issue, Major had, prior to the summit, presented it as one of tremendous importance to national sovereignty from which he would not back down, whipping up a frenzy of Euro-phobia on his own backbenches and within the right-wing press. However, his European colleagues refused to accede to the British demands at Ioannina and the blocking minority was agreed at 27 (George 1997: 110, Young, H 1999: 452-455, Young, JW 2000: 167-168).[7] There was agreement on a rather empty compromise designed to accommodate the British government whereby, should the blocking minority fall between 23 and 26, the Council would do all within its power within a reasonable period of time to achieve a consensual solution (this would not prevent an eventual decision, though it was already established practice to make a concerted attempt to find a consensual solution within Council before decisions were taken by QMV). There was also agreement that the question of the minimum number of votes required for a qualified majority would be re-examined at the forthcoming IGC (Laffan 1997a: 291). The acceptance of this compromise by Major and his foreign secretary, Douglas Hurd, despite the opposition of a number of cabinet members, led one prominent Euro-sceptic on the Conservative backbenches to openly implore Major to resign (Seldon 1997: 448-455).[8]

Major did get his way with his European colleagues in his second attempt to show he was a tough 'defender' of British interest against EU 'federalism' later in 1994. At the Corfu summit in June, Major was alone among the EU heads of government in vetoing the proposal that the then Belgian prime minister, Jean-Luc Dehaene, succeed Delors as European Commission president.[9] The Conservatives portrayed Dehaene as a federalist likely to continue Delors' work in pushing for deeper European integration and interfering in the rightful competences of the member states. There was also irritation that the Dehaene nomination had been agreed by French and German governments, who had then expected the rest of the EU to fall into line with their choice, and a consequent Conservative determination to combat this perceived Franco-German domination of the EU. Major's veto was sufficient to block Dehaene's appointment and he was thus able to claim a victory in his battle with the rest of the EU. The triumphant portrayal of this veto by the government's supporters and the right-wing press conveniently overlooked the fact that the compromise appointee, the Luxembourg president, Jacques Santer, who was backed by Major, held similar views to Dehaene on the direction of the EU. As Hugo Young astutely observes:

> This was pettiness by Britain - but pettiness with a domestic purpose: the invention of a defect, said to apply uniquely to the porky Belgian, for no better reason than the pleasure of being able to demonstrate, to a press and a party thirsting for continental blood, that nothing could cut more sharply than a touch of British steel (1999: 457).

This and the previous episode at Ioannina severely diminished Major's standing among his fellow EU leaders (Dinan 1999: 173).

Major's lurch towards antagonistic posturing within the EU could not save the Conservatives from a massive defeat in the EP elections of 1994, which left it with just 18 seats (on a rather lowly 28 per cent of the vote), in contrast to Labour's 62 seats (on 44 per cent of the vote).[10] Nor did Major's tactics succeed in uniting the Euro-sceptics under his leadership. In November 1994, Major was obliged to temporarily withdraw the Conservative party whip[11] from eight hardline Euro-sceptic MPs after they rebelled on a parliamentary vote confirming an increase in Britain's budgetary contribution to the EU despite Major's presentation of the vote as a vote of confidence. This group became the whipless nine when an additional backbencher resigned the whip in solidarity with the eight. In June 1995, in a bid to pre-empt a predicted leadership challenge from the Euro-sceptic right, Major himself resigned the Conservative party leadership in order to bring challengers out into the open. It was expected that the challenge would come from one of the backbench malcontents, possibly Norman Lamont, the former chancellor, who had been sacked from the cabinet in May 1993 and had subsequently taken up an openly hostile stance towards the EU. However, these expectations were confounded when one of the leading Euro-sceptics within the cabinet, John Redwood, resigned his post in order to take up the challenge. The backing for his campaign came primarily from the Euro-sceptic right. Major comfortably won the subsequent ballot of Conservative MPs by 218 votes to 89. But rather than settle the issue, a ballot in which a third of Conservative MPs voted against Major, abstained, absented themselves or returned spoilt ballot papers simply demonstrated the scale of disaffection within the parliamentary party (Young, JW 2000: 167-169, Young, H 1999: 457-459, Seldon 1998: 584-587).

Major would continue to cede ground to his Euro-sceptic MPs in the final years of his premiership, without satisfying their thirst for further demonstrations of his government's resolve to combat the 'federalist' tendencies of the EU. This involved adopting an increasingly antagonistic stance towards the rest of the EU which reached its nadir in May 1996, when the government declared a policy of non co-operation within the EU (involving vetoing all decisions requiring unanimity within the Council of Ministers), as a response to the EU decision to ban the export of British beef. This followed the government's own admission that British beef might be unsafe due to an outbreak of BSE.[12] Though non co-operation was ended a month later after a vague European Council compromise involving the gradual lifting of the beef ban subject to British measures to ensure beef safety, the dispute would leave the standing of the British government within the EU at a historical low (Young, H 1999: 460-463, Westlake 1997).[13]

The various displays of nationalistic posturing by Major could not detract from the two major issues which troubled his party's Euro-sceptic wing, i.e. the possibility of Britain being drawn into the final stage of EMU and the impending IGC. Major would make further concessions to the Euro-sceptics on EMU, for example promising a referendum prior to any attempt to seek the entry of sterling into the single currency in the lifetime of the following parliament. This would not be enough to satisfy the Euro-sceptics, many of whom would issue personal campaign statements for the 1997 general election opposing EMU membership categorically. Among those adopting these personal manifestos were a number of junior ministers, even though such a position was in contravention of the official government 'wait and see' line on EMU. With over a 100 of his parliamentary candidates in contravention of official party policy, Major would be forced to make an additional promise of a free parliamentary vote on EMU membership (should a government decision be taken to join) mid-way through the election campaign (Young, H 1999: 463-471, Seldon 1998: 720-727).

Greater success would be achieved in ensuring party unity on the question of further EU treaty reform. However, this was mainly because the strategy the government adopted in relation to this was almost totally negative. It was clear to Major and his cabinet colleagues that any further treaty changes which could be interpreted as deepening integration or enhancing supranationalism in the EU would be impossible to sell to a substantial proportion of his own parliamentary party. No further integration could be countenanced without risking a repeat of the Maastricht ratification difficulties. Indeed, the rising tide of Euro-scepticism within the Conservative party meant that the parliamentary party was unlikely to support such a ratification process, even if some of the more pro-European members of the government might personally be content to see certain reforms agreed. Many Conservative MPs who had remained loyal to the government during the Maastricht ratification had done so on the understanding that this was the end point in European integration as far as the government was concerned. Similarly, several members of the government, at junior and cabinet level, would oppose any such treaty changes. According to Hugo Young, the defence secretary, Michael Portillo, was pressing on Major a strategy of complete rejectionism as regards the IGC (1999: 458). The ructions caused by such a minor technical change as the increase in the 'blocking minority' (which as a percentage of the total weighted votes actually constituted a decrease) provided an indicator of the likely attitude of the British government to even minor changes that could be interpreted as increasing the scope of the supranationalism. In the light of this, communitisation of the intergovernmental pillars and support for further extensions of QMV appeared to be strictly off the agenda for the British government. The maintenance of the unanimity requirement in those areas where it still prevailed had become a totem of British government policy. The Conservatives and the right-wing press had popularised the unanimity principle as the right to exercise the national veto. So proudly wielded to prevent the appointment of Dehaene, it could be surrendered no further. Nevertheless, the Ioannina episode did suggest that the government would, if given the opportunity, be likely to support a reweighting of votes to favour the large states, as this would also enhance the ability of Britain, in alliance with other states, to block decisions where QMV already applied. Similarly, on the linked institutional issue of Commission reform, the British government had indicated that it might support the reduction of the number of Commissioners for each of the large states to one, but at the same time wanted to explore the possibility of removing the automatic right for each small state to have one Commissioner (George 1997: 111).[14] The Conservative government was not therefore opposed to all treaty changes, though its rejectionist discourse would sometimes imply this. Moreover, much of the party and elements within the government could be expected to heartily embrace any treaty reforms (though very unlikely to occur) that actually returned powers from the EU to the nation-states, particularly in relation to the jurisdiction of the ECJ. Nevertheless, aside from reforms that would enhance the prerogatives of Britain as a large state or repatriate EU competences, any significant treaty changes were likely to split both the government and the parliamentary party.

As Stephen George writes, Britain would go into the 1996 IGC as a 'status quo' state. He argues that the British government was 'generally satisfied' with the existing treaty apparatus whatever Conservative backbenchers and members of the House of Lords might say (George 1997: 108), though this does not quite take into account the clear indications that a number of members of the cabinet would have preferred it if Major had dropped the ratification of the TEU altogether (Young, H 1999: 444). In addition, George notes that, given the delay in TEU ratification, the British government viewed the IGC as too early to review the apparatus, particularly as three new member states had only joined in January 1995. Moreover, the British government felt that there were more important issues that the EU should be addressing, notably 'entrenching democracy' in the CEE states and 'increasing the competitiveness of the European economy' (George 1997: 108). The domestic political climate caused the government to accentuate the negativity of its position in its public statements on the IGC. The rejectionist nature of the government's stance was apparent in the position taken by David Davis, minister for Europe, and British representative on the Reflection Group of foreign ministers' representatives established to prepare the agenda for the IGC under the Spanish Council presidency in the second half of 1995 (Corbett 1996).[15] The negative government agenda would be confirmed by the publication of its White Paper on the IGC in February 1996 (FCO 1996). The policy of non co-operation adopted over beef later in 1996 would also stifle progress in the IGC and would further reduce expectations of a constructive British approach towards treaty change (Westlake 1997). Furthermore, controversy in Britain over the scope given by the European common fisheries policy to Spanish fishermen to buy up British fishing quotas led to government threats to veto all progress at the IGC unless a solution favouring British fishermen was agreed to by the rest of the EU (Duff 1997a: 185, 1998: 41).

While in the EU arena, the Conservative strategy was to reject treaty change, at the domestic level, the strategy was to depict the Labour party as soft on Europe and ready to 'sell out' Britain through treaty changes which would cede more power to the EU. The first part of this strategy was aimed primarily at the Conservative party itself and was intended to strengthen the internal party position of Major and his cabinet colleagues, though it was also hoped that a more aggressive and nationalistic stance within the EU would play well with public opinion. The second part of the strategy was more clearly aimed at the wider electorate. Opinion polls since Black Wednesday had generally indicated that the Conservatives were badly trailing Labour in electoral popularity and that a general election would result in a clear Labour victory. A body of opinion within the Conservative party was convinced that wrapping the party in the Union flag and making Europe and the defence of UK sovereignty (with the Conservatives as its guarantors and Labour as its betrayers) central to the political debate was the best way of turning the popularity ratings around and ensuring a fifth successive general election victory. Though some members of the cabinet, including Major himself, might have personally been prepared to accept further treaty changes, and most continued to favour a constructive British role in the EU, this would be sacrificed to wider domestic political considerations.[16] The theme of patriotism was itself a twin-pronged strategy which involved pointing to Labour's plans for devolved government within the UK as damaging to national unity, with the potential to combine with the threat to UK independence posed by its European policies to devastating effect on the fabric of the nation (Whiteley 1997: 551-552).

How then would the Labour party respond to the challenge posed by the IGC agenda and the rather unwelcoming domestic political environment in which it was developing? The late 1980s and early 1990s had seen the two main political parties in Britain exchange positions as regards the desirability of British engagement with the process of European integration. Despite its fractured history over the issue and a commitment as recently as 1983 to Britain's withdrawal from the European integration process, by the time Tony Blair took over the party leadership in 1994, Labour appeared to have taken over the Conservatives' former mantle as the 'party of Europe.' The chapter that follows will provide a brief historical overview of the evolution of Labour party attitudes to the European integration process, and then examine the process by which the more recent transformation into a broadly pro-European party occurred, placing it in the context of the wider ideological journey undertaken since the 1980s. This will enable an initial assessment of Labour party European policy and of the positions it could be expected to adopt on the main IGC issues as Blair assumed the leadership in 1994. This will set the scene for the thorough examination of party policy-making on the IGC that will follow in the remainder of the book.

Notes

[1] Throughout this book, whilst acknowledging that these are over-simplifications, I will use the terms Euro-sceptic and Euro-phile in their rather crude journalistic forms. Accordingly, Euro-sceptics are characterised by a belief that the existing level of European supranationalism should not be exceeded and/or should be reversed, while Euro-philes are characterised by support for the logic of supranational decision-making and/or a willingness to consider further advances in supranationalism. I will also use the terms 'pro-European' or occasionally simply 'European' as an alternative to 'Euro-phile.' Similarly, various actors or proposals will sometimes be described as supporting a more 'federal' EU or being more 'integrationist'. These descriptions will also be used to denote support for further advances in supranational decision-making.

[2] This was confirmed by the Cannes European Council of June 1995.

[3] Article B of the TEU referred to 'respecting the principle of subsidiarity' in achieving the objectives of the Union. Article 3b explains the principle thus: 'The community shall act within the limits of the powers conferred upon it by this Treaty and of the objectives assigned to it therein. In areas which do not fall within its exclusive competence, the Community shall take action, in accordance with the principle of subsidiarity, only if and in so far as the objectives of the proposed action cannot be sufficiently achieved by the Member States and can therefore, by reason of the scale or effects of the proposed action, be better achieved by the Community. Any action by the Community shall not go beyond what is necessary to achieve the objectives of this Treaty.' Although the principle of subsidiarity was not a new concept, the British government and other opponents of federalism seized on it after the signing of the TEU, as a reversal, or at least a brake on the EC's centralisation trend. Nevertheless, the concept could equally serve as a definition of how a federal system should operate: Different areas of policy requiring different level of government action, be it at a local, state or federal level (Duff 1997a: 5-7).

[4] The ERM was originally conceived as an adjustable system of exchange rates, whereby EC currencies would be permitted narrow margins of fluctuation against the strongest EC currency, the Deutschmark. However, the Delors report on EMU in 1989 recast ERM membership as the first stage in a process leading to the irrevocable fixing of currency rates and, in the final stage of EMU, their replacement by a single currency (Tsoukalis 1997: 143-152, 163-172). Although she had been opposed to British membership, Thatcher finally agreed to sterling's entry in October 1990, following persuasion from her then chancellor of the exchequer, Major.

[5] Following further currency turmoil, involving speculation against the French franc, the fluctuation bands of the ERM were widened to 15 per cent in August 1993, rendering the system virtually meaningless (Young, JW 2000: 163).

[6] The British position did have the support of Spain at Ioannina, but unlike Major, the Spanish government did not present the matter as a defining principle of national interest on which it could not compromise.

[7] This figure actually became 26 - the abandonment of Norway's planned accession meant a slight downward adjustment was required.

[8] The Conservative MP who called on Major to resign was Tony Marlow. The cabinet members who opposed the compromise were Michael Howard, Peter Lilley, Michael Portillo and John Redwood, the four most prominent Euro-sceptics within the government. Thinking he was speaking 'off the record' to a television reporter, Major inadvertently allowed himself to be recorded on tape referring to three of his cabinet Euro-sceptics as 'bastards' (presumed to be Lilley, Portillo and Redwood) in July 1993. Lilley and Portillo had both pressed Major to abandon the Maastricht bill after the Danish referendum rejection.

Redwood had not been in the cabinet at that point, but would presumably have taken a similar stance. It was clear that all four of these cabinet Euro-sceptics would oppose any further government concessions in the direction of greater European integration (Young, H 1999: 443-448).

[9] The then right-wing Italian government of Silvio Berlusconi had also initially expressed opposition to the proposed Dehaene appointment, but had relented from this position by the time of the Corfu summit (Young, JW 2000: 168).

[10] Of course, the British first-past-the-post electoral system considerably distorted the result. This distortion was even greater than it would have been if the voting percentages had been recorded in a national election, due to the vast size of the European constituencies.

[11] This effectively meant suspension from the parliamentary party

[12] A statement was made by the health minister, Stephen Dorrell, on 20 March 1996, suggesting that there may be a link between BSE (bovine spongiform encephalopathy) in cows and Creutzfeldt-Jakob disease (CJD) in humans (Seldon 1998: 639-640).

[13] Kirsty Hughes and Edward Smith describe this as 'one of the most damaging British foreign policy episodes in recent history' (1998: 94).

[14] This was linked to the British government view that there should be no further increases in EU competences and that therefore there would be no increase in policy portfolios to match the increase in Commissioners that enlargement would bring should the existing system of nomination continue.

[15] Agreement to establish the Reflection Group was reached at the Corfu summit in June 1994. The Group was chaired by the Spanish ministerial representative, Carlos Westendorp.

[16] Nevertheless, it can be noted that the existence of powerful pro-European figures within the Conservative government, notably Kenneth Clarke as chancellor and Michael Heseltine as deputy prime minister, tempered this strategy. This was notable in relation to British membership of the single currency: Clarke threatened to resign if Major ruled it out for the duration of the next parliamentary term (Young, H: 2000: 463-465).

Chapter 2

Labour's New Europeanism and the IGC Agenda

Labour and European Unity in Historical Perspective

The nature of Britain's relationship to the process of European integration has been a focus of controversy within both the Labour and Conservative parties since the first steps to establish supranational institutions were taken in the aftermath of the second world war. Governments of both parties have endured difficulties in coming to terms with Britain's post-imperial decline and in reassessing its external relationships in accordance with this fall from global power status (Gamble 1994, Northedge 1974, Barker 1971, Holland 1991, Clarke 1992, Frankel 1975). The weight of history has accordingly coloured the attitude of British governments, Conservative and Labour alike, on the question of European unity. The early steps to develop supranational institutions on the continent were met with a dismissive approach on the part of the post-war Labour government of 1945-51 and the Conservative governments that followed in the 1950s, born of a belief that attempts to develop supranational institutions on the continent were doomed to failure and that in any case Britain's global status was not compatible with membership of such a regional organisation. It was not until the beginning of the 1960s that this mind-set was replaced by a realisation that the maintenance of Britain's economic and political influence in the face of its apparent global decline required membership of the then EEC (George 1994, Greenwood 1992, Pilkington 1995, Young, H 1999, Young, JW 2000, Brivati & Jones 1997). However, when membership did finally come in 1973, this original self-imposed exclusion would come back to haunt British policy-makers, as they found that key tenets of the *acquis communautaire*,[1] particularly the common agricultural policy (CAP), the structure of the budget and the 'own resources' system for financing it, had been framed in a manner advantageous to the original six EC members and disadvantageous to British interests. The nature of this pre-defined EC framework, combined with differences of interpretation between Britain and the original six over the meaning and direction of the process of European integration would contribute to an 'awkward' relationship between Britain and its European partners (George 1994).

Although the recent historical experience of the 1990s presents a picture of the Conservatives as the political party most tormented on the question of Britain's relationship with the EU, an examination of the entire post-war period reveals that the Labour party has the greater history of division on the Europe question (Robins

1979, Newman 1983). It was the post-war Labour government of Clement Attlee that was faced with the initial decision over whether to take part in the negotiations that were to lead to the establishment of the European Coal and Steel Community (ECSC). The launch of the Schuman plan in 1950 with its proposal for pooled sovereignty in coal and steel, had come as a shock to a Labour government which had convinced itself that it had successfully thwarted attempts to build supranational institutions on the continent in the discussions which led to the establishment of the Brussels Treaty (defence) organisation, Organisation for European Economic Co-operation (OEEC) and Council of Europe at the end of the 1940s (Bulmer 1992: 5-6, Young, H 1999: 26-71). Although the Labour government's approach in this period came to be personified in the activities of its foreign secretary, Ernest Bevin, the views of the party mainstream were accurately summed up in the words of Hugh Dalton, who headed the government delegation to the Hague Congress in 1948 which led to the establishment of the Council of Europe

> It is no good denying that we are very much closer in all respects except distance to Australia and New Zealand than we are to Western Europe…(they) are populated by our kinsman…they speak our language, they have high standards of life and have the same political ideas as we have. If you go to these countries you find yourself at once completely at home in a way that you do not if you go to a foreign country…if the choice were put to us: 'Will you move closer to Western Europe at the cost of moving further away from the countries of the Commonwealth?' For my part, I would answer 'no' (Newman 1983: 130).

In addition, rejection of involvement in supranational schemes on the continent was linked to the need to pursue socialism in Britain, in contrast to the reactionary policies of the continent, as Dalton explained:

> We in Britain have fought through long years to win power for Socialism…We are not going to throw away the solid gains brought to us by a whole generation of political agitation and by the votes of our people and by three years of solid work in Parliament, in the Trade Unions and in the Government, upon the doctrinal altar of a federal Western Europe (Newman ibid).

Given the belief that Britain could continue to pursue its global power status through its ties to the English speaking world - through its leadership of the Commonwealth and its special relationship with the USA - the decision to reject participation in the negotiations which followed the announcement of the Schuman plan was not a difficult one for the Attlee government to make. Aside from the concerns held by some within the Labour party that ECSC membership would interfere with the socialist programme of its first majority government in Britain, Labour and the then Conservative opposition possessed a common faith in the capacity of the British nation-state, flushed by the success of war, to deliver on their party's political, economic and social objectives. This was linked to a bipartisan approach to Britain's external role, encapsulated by Winston Churchill's conception of Britain at the intersection of three concentric circles: 1) the relationship with the Commonwealth, with Britain exercising a leadership role through which it would retain global influence; 2) the Atlantic alliance and the special relationship with the USA; 3) lastly, and probably least, the relationship with the rest of Western Europe, towards which Britain would play a benevolent role whilst remaining free of any binding treaty constraints in order to pursue its global role (Bulmer 1992: 10-11, Young, JW 2000: 35-36)

When Churchill, deposed from office by the Labour party landslide in 1945, returned as prime minister at the head of a Conservative government in 1951, this bipartisan approach continued. Indeed, it was reinforced, given that most of the minority on the Labour left who had previously been sympathetic towards attempts to establish supranational European institutions had turned against the project by the early 1950s (Newman 1983: 138-147). Many of those on the left (including Michael Foot) who had previously seen in the European federalist movement the potential for a united socialist Europe, acting as a 'third force' autonomous of the superpowers, had become disillusioned with a movement for European unity dominated by pro-capitalist catholic conservatives (Anderson and Mann 1997: 124-125). Indeed, during the 1950s, the most vigorous opposition within the Labour party towards plans for political unity on the continent came from the Labour left (Anderson and Mann 1997: 126-128). The bipartisan approach continued when the Conservative government of Churchill's successor, Anthony Eden, declined to participate in the establishment of the European Economic Community (EEC) and the European Atomic Energy Community (Euratom), sealed by the Treaty of Rome in 1957. By the end of the 1950s, allegiances within the Labour party towards European supranationalism had switched somewhat, with a group on the revisionist right of the party, including George Brown and Roy Jenkins, in favour of British membership as a means of securing some kind of social democratic economic modernisation in the UK, while the left, with a few minor exceptions, were now viscerally opposed. Hence, when Eden's successor, Harold Macmillan, reversed official government policy and sought British entry to the EEC in 1961, Labour's then leader, Hugh Gaitskell after a period of vacillation, eventually came out strongly against membership, reflecting the majority view across the left and pragmatic centre of the party and horrifying his ideological allies on the revisionist right. Gaitskell famously described the desire of the EC's founding fathers to create a European federation as meaning 'the end of Britain as an independent nation state...the end of a thousand years of history' (Young, H 1999: 162-164, Robins 1979: 1-41, Newman 1983: 163-191, Anderson and Mann 1997: 128-129).

But Gaitskell's opposition to EEC entry was not as clear-cut as it seemed. Indeed, Hugo Young suggests that, had he become prime minister, Gaitskell would have quickly moved to resurrect Macmillan's failed application (1999: 168-170). The official party document on the EEC adopted by Labour's National Executive Committee in September 1962 indicated that membership might be acceptable provided that five (rather difficult to realise) basic conditions were met: 1) strong and binding safeguards for trade with and other interests of the Commonwealth; 2) freedom for the UK to pursue its own foreign policy; 3) fulfilment of the government's obligations to its partners in the European Free Trade Association

(EFTA);[2] 4) the right for the UK to plan its own economy; 5) guarantees to safeguard the position of British agriculture (Newman 1983: 173-178). Gaitskell's rather dramatic intervention had been designed to shore up his own position within the party following his disputes with the left of the party over his revisionist plans to replace the hallowed clause IV of the party constitution and his opposition to the left's attempts to commit the party to a policy of unilateral nuclear disarmament. Michael Newman suggests that though there was evidence of a softening of hostility towards participation in the EEC within the Labour leadership by 1960, in general its attitudes were a continuation of those expressed in government from 1945-51: 'a preference for Atlanticism, an emphasis upon the Commonwealth, and an anxiety to maintain important tools for economic intervention at the national level' (Newman 1983: 163). While Gaitskell's main preoccupation was with the damage that EEC participation would inflict on trading links with the Commonwealth, and to Britain's political status at the Commonwealth's head, the concerns of the left focused in particular on the intolerable possibility that the constraints imposed by membership might interfere with the socialist planning that they wished to introduce once in government. Although Gaitskell himself had no intention of introducing the kind of socialist programme favoured by the left if he became prime minister, his stress on the Commonwealth did appeal to the left given their preference for it as a framework for promoting third world development.

Among those who had raised the incompatibility of EEC membership with state planning at the time of the ill-fated Macmillan application was Harold Wilson (Newman 1983: 171-172). In 1964, a year after the sudden death of Gaitskell (occurring within days of General de Gaulle's first veto of British EEC membership), Wilson led Labour back into government with a programme of economic modernisation based upon national planning, harnessing the benefits of the technological revolution. Despite initially expressing strong scepticism towards the arguments for EEC entry, the failure of Wilson's national strategy for addressing Britain's economic decline led to a second British application for membership in 1967 (Young, JW 2000: 82-88). Like Macmillan before him, once in government and faced with the evidence of a decline of Britain's global political and economic influence, and a realisation that alternative strategies to arrest this decline were no longer viable, Wilson changed tack and sought British entry. As Newman writes:

> The bi-partisan agreement which had defined Britain's position as the centre of the world Commonwealth in the post-war period had now (temporarily) been reconstituted on a new basis, that is, in the assumption that membership of the EEC would bring about renewed political influence and economic modernisation (1983: 212).

Attempts to secure economic modernisation on a national basis whilst retaining global influence through British leadership of the Commonwealth, the special relationship with the USA, and the development of EFTA as an alternative to the EEC had not proved successful. Nevertheless, having chosen a new path to influence and prosperity, Wilson found this blocked by de Gaulle's second veto of a British application.

When Labour returned to opposition again after 1970, a mixture of political opportunism and party management led Wilson to oppose the entry terms successfully negotiated by Edward Heath's Conservative government. However, the votes of 69 Labour MPs, including Jenkins and John Smith, who rebelled against the line adopted by the Wilson leadership and voted for Heath's terms in 1971, proved critical to ensuring British entry to the then EC. Whereas Wilson had managed to convince a majority within the Labour party of the merits of EC membership in 1967, much of the party had swung against the idea by the time Heath had reactivated the application. The left, which in general had been consistently opposed to membership since the 1950s, became increasingly virulent in its opposition to membership in the 1970s, portraying the EC as a 'capitalist club', membership of which was incompatible with the pursuit of a socialist programme within Britain. In addition to this leftist critique, there were concerns across the party about the increase in food prices that application of the CAP would bring, the disproportionate size of the likely British budgetary contribution to the EC, the effect on trading patterns, particularly in respect of the Commonwealth, and the loss of parliamentary sovereignty that EC membership entailed. Nevertheless, a large grouping, mainly on the right of the party and led by Jenkins, continued to be strongly committed to British membership (Robins 1979: 77-92, Newman 1983: 219-227).

It was in order to paper over the increasingly damaging divisions within the Labour party on the European issue that Wilson staged a popular referendum on renegotiated membership terms in 1975, a year after Labour's return to government. By this point, it was clear that Wilson had not altered in his conviction, developed in government in the late 1960s, that Britain's future lied in Europe. Moreover, once in government again, many of the leading pragmatic centrists within the cabinet, such as the then foreign secretary, James Callaghan, had also become convinced that there was little alternative to membership. Hence, though the renegotiated terms were largely cosmetic, the majority within the government, led by Wilson and Callaghan, recommended and received public approval in the referendum on the 'renegotiated terms' despite the majority within the parliamentary party, the wider party membership and the affiliated trade unions being opposed (Daniels 1998: 73, Newman 1983: 235-240). The referendum campaign was notable for the spectacle of various members of the government campaigning on opposite sides, following the suspension by Wilson of the traditional convention of collective government responsibility on the question. Those cabinet members who campaigned for rejection of the renegotiated terms in 1975, mainly left-wingers such as Tony Benn, Michael Foot and Barbara Castle, though also some from the right of the party, most notably Peter Shore, remained largely unreconciled to membership. Hence, following its defeat in the 1979 general election, the capture of the party agenda by the Bennite left and the election of Foot as leader, the Labour party adopted a programme which promised withdrawal from the EC without further renegotiation, upon its return to government (Newman 1983: 244-245).

Alongside the campaign for unilateral nuclear disarmament, withdrawal from the EC, was by 1980 an article of faith for the Labour left.[3] The adoption of this left-wing agenda, which included increased constituency party control over Labour MPs and party policy, and the adoption of an alternative economic strategy involving widespread nationalisation (Callaghan 2000: 56-61), together with the promises on nuclear disarmament and EC withdrawal, prompted Jenkins, and a number of the other Labour MPs who voted for entry in 1971, to leave the Labour party and form the Social Democratic Party (SDP) in 1981. However, some on the pro-European right, including John Smith and Roy Hattersley, chose to stay within the Labour party and fight to have this leftist agenda overturned. The adoption of these positions in Labour's 1983 general election manifesto, famously described by the Labour MP Gerald Kaufman as 'the longest suicide note in history' (Anderson and Mann 1997: 17, Young, H 1999: 476), resulted in a landslide victory for Margaret Thatcher's Conservative government. Labour finished only narrowly ahead of the newly formed SDP-Liberal Alliance in terms of popular vote cast, recording its lowest percentage share of the vote (28%) since the 1930s.

The 'Europeanisation' of the Labour Party

Following the 1983 election debacle, Labour's newly installed leader, Neil Kinnock, wasted little time in distancing the party from the withdrawal platform. A policy document arguing that Britain should retain the option of withdrawal, but should remain within the EC for the duration of the 1984-89 European parliamentary term was adopted by the party conference, and in 1984, Labour fought the EP elections pledging to work within the EC to develop a pan-European reflation strategy (Anderson and Mann 1997: 119-121). While Labour's new deputy leader, Roy Hattersley, was a noted pro-European, both Kinnock himself, and his appointee as European spokesman, Robin Cook, had previously been strongly associated with the anti-EEC left. In June 1977, they had been among the 60 Labour MPs who had signed an appeal in the Labour newspaper *Tribune* declaring: 'Membership of the Common Market has been an unmitigated disaster for the British people. The Labour movement should commit itself to taking Britain out of the EEC' (Anderson and Mann 1997: 119). The move toward a more constructive stance on EC membership has often been presented as part of a wider strategy by Kinnock, once he became leader in 1983, to moderate both Labour's programme and its image, and to ditch Labour's more electorally unpopular policies, such as those on Europe and on extending public ownership. Though Kinnock had been previously associated with a soft-left loyalist grouping around Michael Foot, the result in 1983, and the corrosive effect of the splits between the left and right that had damaged the party's public image since the 1970s, convinced him that a more moderate and united image was required if Labour was to achieve success at the next election. Though the positions on EC membership adopted by Labour in the immediate aftermath of its defeat in 1983 were partly a recognition of a situation in which withdrawal was not a reality while Labour remained in opposition, by 1987 it was clear that the Labour leadership no longer regarded withdrawal as credible, electorally or otherwise. The 1987 general election manifesto made no mention of the withdrawal option. Instead it promised that a Labour government would work constructively with Britain's European partners in promoting economic expansion and combating unemployment (Anderson and Mann 1997: 132-33, Daniels 1998: 76).

Though the election was lost, Labour's improved performance under Kinnock was sufficient for him to retain the leadership for another parliamentary term, during which he would attempt to moderate the image of the party further and seek to develop a more constructive pro-European stance. Philip Daniels explains that after 1987, the development of a pro-European policy became a central element of the policy review exercise launched by Kinnock in order to effect a fundamental reappraisal of the party's programme. The reasons for Labour's conversion to pro-Europeanism quite clearly went beyond mere electoral politics. As Daniels suggests, this conversion could be attributed to 'pressures of domestic political competition, a change in trade union attitudes on Europe, the dynamics of the European integration process, and important changes in the party's approach to economic policy and the role of the nation-state' (1998: 78-79).

Both the domestic political context and developments within the EC during the 1980s were integral to the reversal of Labour's 1983 position. The abandonment of the alternative economic strategy meant that EC membership was no longer regarded as a threat to the implementation of Labour's economic policies. Faith in this kind of national centred statist strategy for economic renewal amongst the Labour left had in any case been severely undermined by the experience of the socialist government in France between 1981 and 1983 (Tindale 1992: 282-283). Under the political direction of its first socialist president, Francois Mitterrand (elected in 1981) the French government had embarked on a reflationary programme based on nationalisation, state intervention in the economy and labour market reforms, but had been forced to abandon this in the face of severe financial and balance of payments crises. The French strategy had been particularly precarious because other European governments were pursuing orthodox deflationary policies, as exemplified by those of the Thatcher government in Britain. Mitterrand was forced to perform a U-turn and follow suit (Callaghan 2000: 102-112). To many across the European left, this experience demonstrated the futility of attempting to pursue socialist policies on a national level, given the growing interdependence of national economies and the globalisation of capital (Ladrech 2000: 31).[4] While some on the Labour left continued to attack the EEC for seeking to institutionalise certain forms of free-market, deregulatory policies, others began to view the European institutions as a possible vehicle for developing the kind of interventionist policies at a European level which were now proving unsustainable at the national level, given these international economic changes. In a similar vein, the image in the 1970s of a Labour chancellor of the exchequer, Denis Healey, having to secure a loan from the International Monetary Fund, and implement a programme of budgetary austerity at its behest, in order to rescue the country's finances, had not been forgotten within the Labour party (Tindale 1992: 279). The limited room for manoeuvre that national governments had in relation to economic policy had become increasingly apparent.[5] Support therefore developed within the Labour left, and across the party, for a co-ordinated European economic strategy that could provide a protected space against the powerful and destructive tendencies of international capital (Callaghan 2000: 109-111). The Labour leadership thus became attracted to ideas such as the European reflation strategy mooted by the Labour MP and economist, Stuart Holland (previously an architect of the alternative economic strategy).[6] Indeed, when Kinnock and Cook visited the EP in 1984, and spoke to the socialist group of MEPs, Cook suggested that all the socialist parties of the EEC contest the European elections on a common manifesto arguing:

> We all face common problems in Europe and we must therefore offer the people of Europe common solutions rooted in our shared socialist values...Reflation in one country is no longer a viable strategy in the modern world. We will only build a sustainable sustained expansion if we work in co-operation with each other, not in competition against each other (Anderson and Mann 1997: 120).[7]

The attitudinal transformation as regards European policy could also be attributed to a fundamental re-evaluation within the Labour party of the traditional apparatus of the British nation-state, shaped by the long experience of apparently impotent opposition to Thatcherism (Tindale 1992: 285-288). Despite its sporadic lurches to the left on economic policy, the Labour party was, before 1983, in possession of a rather conservative approach to the apparatus of the British state. It was commonly believed within the party that the nature of Britain's uncodified constitutional apparatus, through which British governments, drawn from the majority party in parliament, could exploit their dominance in parliament to ensure the passage of any legislation they saw fit without constitutional check, could be harnessed productively to ensure the application of a socialist programme. David Marquand writes: 'old Labour was as committed to the doctrines and practices of Westminster absolutism as were the Conservatives' (1998: 20). However, when the Thatcher governments of the 1980s exploited this potential for 'elective dictatorship' to dismantle the social democratic consensus established by the post-war Attlee government in 1945-51, and adhered to by Conservative and Labour governments thereafter, Labour began to reassess its approach to the apparatus of the British nation-state. As Marquand continues: 'in the Thatcher years, when Labour found itself on the receiving end of a ferocious centralism, far exceeding anything it ever attempted itself, it underwent a death-bed conversion' (ibid).

In order to both secure its objectives and ensure their maintenance in the future, the Labour party turned its attentions towards a more pluralistic model of power. Such a model would acknowledge that democracy amounted to more than just 'majority-rule', but involved developing institutions which guaranteed the rights of all citizens and social groups and gave due recognition to the diverse regions and nations that make up the UK (Evans 1999: 73-78, Fella 2000: 65-66). Hence, a programme for constitutional reform was developed incorporating devolution to Scotland and Wales, and to the English regions, reform of the House of Lords, incorporation of the European Convention on Human Rights (ECHR) into British law, and freedom of information (Anderson and Mann 1997: 271-302). This pluralistic vision of political power also involved acknowledgement that in the face of globalisation, the fulfilment of certain policy objectives would require the increased 'pooling' of national sovereignties in international regimes, in particular the EC. The impotence felt by the Labour party, as the Thatcher governments emasculated local government, centralised political power, dismantled trade union power and vigorously pursued a programme of deregulation and privatisation, coupled with recognition of Mitterrand's experience in seeking to pursue 'socialist' policies in international isolation, led to a re-evaluation of the nation-state as an effective tool in securing and safeguarding Labour's political objectives (Tindale 1992: 282-288, Fella 2000: 74). Developments within the EC itself, notably the conscious attempt by the EC to develop a social dimension following the adoption of the SEA and the single market programme in 1985, were instrumental in crystallising this transformed approach.

Following the SEA, the development of a social dimension was championed by Mitterrand, with the support of other EC leaders, pursued vigorously by Mitterrand's former finance minister, Commission president Jacques Delors, and met with outright hostility by the Thatcher government in Britain. The British government was alone among EC governments in its refusal to sign up to the EC charter of social rights adopted as a 'solemn declaration' in 1989. However, the Labour party's affiliated trade unions, the majority of whom had opposed EC membership in the 1970s, were particularly attracted by the notion that they could win back at the European level some of the employment rights removed at the national level by the Thatcher governments (Rosamund 1993, 1998, Tindale 1992: 288-295). This sea change in attitude was demonstrated by the standing ovation and the serenading of '*frère Jacques*' bestowed upon Delors by the Trade Union Congress (TUC) in Bournemouth in September 1988 (Young, H 1999: 346).

In a similar vein, the Labour leadership, and the party at large, increasingly viewed the EC as an apparatus through which a basic framework of social rights could be developed and maintained (Tindale 1992: 292-295). A future Labour government could work constructively with its European partners, and use the EC institutions to secure and safeguard its objectives, installing a framework of social protection, enshrined in a legally superior system of EC law, which could not be overturned by a national government of a Thatcherite persuasion. The development of a social dimension in the EC, and Thatcher's growing isolation among European leaders, on this and other questions, also allowed the Labour party to exploit the political space increasingly vacated by the Conservative party, as the more pro-European of the two main parties. The image of extremism and division that had bedevilled Labour's approach to the European issue for several decades would increasingly be transferred to the Conservatives.

Labour and the Party of European Socialists

As the visit to the EP by Cook and Kinnock in 1984 indicated, Labour's conversion to pro-Europeanism involved a new willingness to co-operate with its 'sister' socialist parties in the rest of the EC. The Labour party did not participate in the establishment of the Confederation of Socialist Parties of the European Community (CSPEC) in April 1974 (Hix 1999: 204)[8] given its antagonism towards the EC and its boycott of the EP prior to the 1975 referendum. Though it did join this body in January 1976, its initial detachment and its 1980-83 platform of withdrawal cast a serious cloud over its relationship with its sister parties (Newman 1996: 7). Given the diverging approaches between Labour and the socialist parties from the original six EC member states, attempts to develop a common CSPEC platform for the first direct elections to the EP in 1979 failed, with Labour's then leader, James Callaghan, freshly deposed from prime ministerial office, proclaiming that each national party must pursue its own strategy (Hix 1999: 205). Labour's rapproachment with the EC after 1983, combined with the French socialist abandonment of its independent strategy in the same year, and the implication which many on the European left drew from it on the need for a common pan-European strategy, led to the adoption of joint socialist manifestos for the 1984 and 1989 EP elections (Hix 1999: 205).

Representatives of the various socialist, social democratic and labour parties had sat together in the one socialist group since the establishment of the assembly of the ECSC in the early 1950s (Ladrech 1996: 291-292). The first direct elections to the EP in the 1979 enhanced the importance of the socialist group, giving its members a direct legitimacy independent of the patronage of their national parties. However, the early 1980s saw this grouping divided, with most Labour MEPs remaining antagonistic towards the process of European integration. The majority of the 17 Labour MEPs elected in 1979, led by Barbara Castle, opposed EC membership. However, most of the new Labour MEPs elected in 1984 shared the Kinnock line that constructive engagement was required. Between 1984 and 1989, the European parliamentary Labour party (EPLP) was bitterly divided between these two different viewpoints, with the EPLP leadership passing backwards and forwards between the two opposing groups. However, the oppositionists were swamped following the 1989 EP elections by a swathe of new pro-European Labour MEPs (Anderson and Mann 1997: 138-139). Labour fought the 1989 EP election campaign arguing strongly for a 'social Europe', contrasting this to Thatcher's bitter antipathy towards a European social dimension, and was rewarded by winning 45 seats as compared to the Conservatives' 32.[9] Thereafter, the leadership and policy positioning of the EPLP remained firmly controlled by the pro-Europeans, and the EPLP increasingly began to play a more central role in the activities of the EP socialist group (Anderson and Mann 1997: 139-140). The increasing importance of the EPLP, itself a reflection of the enhanced role ascribed to the EP by the SEA (to be further developed by the TEU in 1991) was recognised by the Labour leadership in London, with the EPLP being accorded representation in the party's policy-making bodies. The EPLP leadership was represented on the 'Britain and the World' policy group established by Kinnock as part of the post-1987 policy review which cemented Labour's transformation into an actively pro-European party.[10] Then, in 1991, the Labour party conference gave the EPLP the same voting rights as the PLP in party leadership elections, introduced EPLP representation on the new party policy forum and set up a regular European conference (Martin 1992).

The development of closer co-operation among the European socialist parties, the increasingly influential role played by the socialist group in the EP reflecting the enhanced status of that institution, and the recognition granted by the TEU to the potential role of the European political parties as a means of channelling a European level of representation and political awareness,[11] all contributed to the establishment of the PES in November 1992. Although its name implied the creation of a new supranational party, the change was largely cosmetic (Newman 1996: 6, Hix 1996). The objective of the creation of the PES appeared to be improved policy co-ordination and organisation within what remained a confederation of national parties. Significant decisions continued to be based on unanimity amongst the national party leaderships and the PES remained financially dependent on its national affiliates (Hix 1999: 206).[12] Organisationally it would be dependent on the PES group in the EP, which under the new party statutes became the Group of the PES (PES group). Indeed, the PES headquarters would be based within the EP offices of the PES group. Official meetings of the national party leaders would become more commonplace - the practice of PES leaders meeting on the eve of the European Council would later be developed - and PES party working-groups, involving national leadership representatives, would be established in various policy areas, facilitating the adoption of party declarations by the leaders. The PES group would play a central role in the new party apparatus, and was accorded representation in the various PES party decision-making and policy formulation forums, including - at the highest level - involvement of the PES group leader at PES leaders' meetings. These meetings would also involve European Commissioners from the PES parties (Hix 1999: 207-213, Ladrech 2000: 92-95).

The developing engagement between the Labour party and its colleagues on the European mainland could be contrasted with the detachment of the Conservative party from other centre-right governing parties on the continent. The Conservatives had not taken part in the establishment of the Christian democrat EPP transnational confederation in 1976, but its MEPs joined the EPP group in the EP in 1992 while remaining outside the wider party grouping (Hix 1996: 320, Ladrech 1996: 298). This followed attempts to improve ties by Chris Patten, the Conservative party chairman between 1990 and 1992 (Young, JW 2000: 153, Bogdanor 1992: 295-298). Patten himself wanted to position the Conservatives as a pro-European Christian democratic party. This was rather a forlorn hope, particularly after Patten himself lost his parliamentary seat in the 1992 general election. The Euro-sceptic tide which swept through the Conservative party after 1992 would make a mockery of any hopes to align the Conservatives more closely with the EPP, as would the increasingly nationalistic tone that the government would adopt in response. While it can be argued that involvement in a transnational grouping contributed to a softening of Labour's stance on European issues (Hix 1999: 214, Newman 1996: 22-25), the looser links that the Conservatives had with other European centre-right parties would be rendered meaningless by the tide of Euro-scepticism which engulfed the Conservative party in the 1990s.

Labour and the Treaty on European Union

The opt-outs negotiated by Major at Maastricht provided the Labour leadership further opportunity to portray itself as firmly within the EC mainstream, in contrast to the Conservatives' semi-detached status (George and Haythorne 1996: 112). Kinnock pledged a future Labour government to reverse the social chapter opt-out. However, the position on EMU was less clear, though Labour's leading economic spokesmen at the time of Maastricht, John Smith as shadow chancellor, and Gordon Brown, then shadow trade and industry secretary, were both personally sympathetic towards the EMU project. Smith in particular (with support from Brown) had been instrumental in securing Labour's declaration of support for British membership of the ERM in 1989. Though this position appeared attributable more to a desire to establish Labour's 'credibility as a party of fiscal and monetary rectitude' (Anderson and Mann 1997: 70, George and Rosamund 1992: 181-182) it also had the effect of further demonstrating that Labour was now more pro-European than the Conservatives. [13]

The question of EMU membership posed a considerable challenge to Labour's new found Europeanism. A party policy document in 1991 suggested that while EMU 'could offer Britain considerable benefits, eliminating currency speculation within the Community and reducing business costs', Labour opposed a 'rigid timetable' for the establishment of a single currency without 'greater convergence between the different economies of the EC' (Anderson and Mann 1997: 136). Though this was a compromise position that could be interpreted as ruling out involvement for the foreseeable future, it did offer support for a single currency in principle. Hix argues that the consultations with other socialist parties in the CSPEC, which led to the adoption of a joint declaration on the Maastricht IGC, resulted in Labour reversing its previous opposition to EMU (Hix 1999: 214). On the eve of the Maastricht summit, the socialist leaders, with Labour's involvement, had adopted a declaration, calling for 'a progressive transition' to EMU, which was 'democratically accountable', promoted 'balanced development, sustainable and non-inflationary growth' and respected 'economic convergence, full employment, quality of life, (and) cohesion.' (Newman 1996: 16). Labour's manifesto for the April 1992 general election pledged that a Labour government would play an active part in negotiations on a single currency (Labour Party 1992, Anderson and Mann 1997: 72).

The Major government's surprise victory in the 1992 election condemned Labour to its fourth successive defeat and Kinnock to his second as leader, despite opinion polls in the run-up to the 1992 election which had pointed to a Labour victory or a hung parliament. Kinnock's speedy resignation was followed by the election of John Smith as his successor. [14] Though public attention would focus on the splits in the Conservative party, the Maastricht ratification process would also pose difficulties for Smith in relation to parliamentary tactics and party discipline. Despite his strong disapproval of the social chapter opt-out and his concerns about the democratic deficiencies of the TEU, Smith was not willing to see Labour oppose the ratification, even if there was the prospect that such a position might contribute to the downfall of the Major government. Smith's own pro-European pedigree had been clear since his act of pro-European rebellion in 1971, after which he consistently supported a constructive role for Britain in the EC and opposed Labour's lurches to leftist anti-Europeanism. Despite acknowledging the deficiencies of the TEU, Smith was not therefore prepared to preside over its destruction in the House of Commons, given the uncertainty this would create for the future of the European integration process and Britain's relationship with its European partners. Smith did, however, allow himself one act of political opportunism. Under his direction, Labour voted against the 'paving motion' to reintroduce the Maastricht bill in November 1992. Smith suggested that this position was justified as the government had previously stated that it would not reintroduce the bill until the Danish situation was clear but was now doing so before a resolution of the Danish position had been reached. Moreover, the Labour leadership chose to portray the vote as one of confidence in the Major government's conduct of European policy. The government won the vote by a margin of three votes, dependent on the support of the Liberal Democrats and some strong-arm tactics on the part of the government whips in order to ensure that some of their backbench waiverers returned to the fold (Young, H 1999: 395, Baker, Gamble and Ludlam 1993). If the vote had been lost, both the Maastricht bill and the government's survival would have been placed in jeopardy. The Labour leadership also conspired with the Conservative Euro-sceptic rebels to seek the passage of an amendment incorporating the treaty provisions on social policy into the bill, thus leaving the government with the choice of opting back into the social provisions (Labour's desired outcome) or abandoning the treaty altogether (the Euro-sceptics' desired outcome). In a series of complicated parliamentary manoeuvres, the government accepted this amendment in order to then hold a separate parliamentary vote reconfirming the social chapter opt-out after the third reading of the Maastricht bill, in July 1993. The combined forces of Labour and the Conservative rebels was enough to defeat the government on this latter vote, but Major then prevailed by holding a second vote in the form of a vote of confidence, thus forcing his rebels into line and securing the passage of the bill with the social chapter opt-out intact (Baker, Gamble and Ludlam 1994).

Though Smith was criticised by pro-Europeans in other parties for jeopardising the Maastricht bill through Labour's various parliamentary antics, the official position of the Labour leadership was that ratification of the TEU should not be prevented, and that its deficiencies could be addressed later, ideally under a future Labour government, i.e. through reversal of the social chapter opt-out and various democratic reforms. An imperfect treaty which made some progress towards political union and EMU and improved intergovernmental co-operation in certain policy areas was better than no treaty at all. However, Labour would not actively support the Maastricht bill by voting for it on second and third readings. Instead, it would signal its discontent with the treaty's deficiencies through abstention on the key votes. This line did not go down well with a significant minority within the party. Indeed, the tribulations endured on the government side of the House drew attention away from the fact that the number of Labour rebels was greater than those of the Conservatives. 59 Labour MPs voted against the Maastricht bill on its second reading (increasing to 66 on third reading).

Nevertheless, while this included a number of traditional opponents of the EC, including Benn and Shore, some of the rebels, most notably Peter Hain, acted from what they presented as a pro-European but anti-treaty viewpoint (Anderson and Mann 1997: 85). The latter group voiced particular concerns about the undemocratic treaty apparatus that the TEU would put in place, most prominently in relation to the unaccountable ECB, which would control monetary policy, and the damaging deflationary bias of the EMU provisions. Though it was sympathetic to these concerns, the official view of the Labour leadership was that rejection of the TEU would do even more damage and fatally undermine the credibility of the party's pro-European conversion. The 1992 Labour party conference resolution on the TEU thus stated: 'The Maastricht treaty, while not perfect, is the best arrangement that can currently be achieved.' Furthermore, the policy document on the EU adopted a year later stated: 'Labour sees Maastricht not as an end but as something to build on and improve' (Labour Party 1993b: 49).

In addition to the rather different nuances of Labour's divisions, pro-Europeans within the Labour party would, in differentiating their divisions from those of the Conservatives, point out that while those Labour MPs who opposed EC membership tended to be older and diminishing in number, within the Conservatives it was the newer and numerically increasing Thatcherite MPs who were the most hostile to developments within the EU (Daniels 1998: 89, Baker, Gamble, Ludlam and Seawright 1996). Moreover, the Conservatives' difficulties were compounded because they were in government, and the narrow parliamentary majority meant that a small and determined group of Euro-rebels could hold the government to ransom.

Smith did find it necessary to temper the Labour party's new Europeanism with a degree of caution. However, this was related more to the demands of the wider domestic political climate (i.e. increasing public antipathy towards the European integration process) than the particular requirements of party management. It was clear that the Conservatives were seeking to exploit this growing public antipathy to the EU by depicting Labour as 'soft' on Europe. This was evident when, following Smith's criticisms of Major's stance at the Ioannina European Council, Major childishly lampooned Smith as 'Monsieur Oui, the poodle of Brussels' (Young, H 1999: 454). Though this incident probably made Major look more foolish than Smith, some Conservative attacks did appear to have an effect on the Smith leadership's public positioning on the EU. For example, after the Conservatives seized on a number of radical sounding proposals in the draft PES manifesto for the 1994 EP elections (including significant increases in the scope of QMV and of EP powers and a suggested 35-hour working week), as evidence of Labour's 'sell-out' to the rest of the EU, the Labour leadership adopted its own more circumspect manifesto which emphasised the importance of maintaining the unanimity principle in certain key policy areas and promised that Labour would not seek to enforce a 35 hour week (Anderson and Mann 1997: 137-138, Labour 1994, PES 1994).[15]

Blair, New Labour and the IGC Agenda

Though Major's intertwined strategy for party unity, relations with the EU and electoral combat with Labour would gradually disintegrate around him, primarily on the single currency issue, the threat posed by this strategy was taken seriously by the new Labour leader, Tony Blair, in 1994. Blair's election to the leadership had been precipitated by the sudden death of Smith just prior to the EP election, rather tempering the party's jubilation at its stunning electoral victory. Blair would accelerate the modernisation of the party undertaken under the Kinnock and Smith leaderships, taking Labour beyond the moderate post-Keynesian European social democratic revisionism elaborated by Kinnock's policy review and cemented under Smith (Jones, T 1996: 113-130, Leys 1997, Ludlam 2000, Davies 1996: 418-423, Smith 1992, Tindale 1992).[16] Simply through repetition by the group of modernising MPs, policy advisers and communication strategists around Blair, the Labour party would be rebranded as 'New Labour' (Leys 1997: 19, Davies 1996: 440, Jones, N 1999) The qualitative leap would be symbolised by Blair's successful campaign to win party approval, in 1995, for the replacement of the once hallowed clause IV of the party's constitution with a modern statement of Labour's aims and values. Where the old clause IV referred to the 'common ownership of the means of production, distribution and exchange' and could be interpreted as implying state ownership of all aspects of the economy (even though this was not the practice of past Labour governments), the new statement positively embraced the 'enterprise of the market and the rigour of competition' (Anderson and Mann 1997: 33, Jones, T 1996: 135-148, Smith 2000: 263-264). Though the Kinnock leadership had shifted the party away from its 1983 espousal of widespread nationalisation to supplement Keynesian demand management of the economy, until 1994 there remained an emphasis on the role of the state in redistributing wealth towards the poorer sectors of society through a progressive system of taxation, involving greater taxation of high income groups to fund a strong universal welfare state, and the protection of key public services and utilities from the private economy. The state would actively intervene in the market economy to ensure a more egalitarian society (Smith 1992: 22-25). The privatisation programme undertaken under successive Conservative administrations was, in most cases, pragmatically accepted, but a line was drawn in the sand against its further extension, and new forms of 'social ownership' were advocated. However, under the Blair leadership, the Thatcherite inheritance of market liberalisation, deregulation and privatisation would be positively embraced and the previous emphasis on equality and redistribution would fade from official party discourse. New Labour would distance itself from the trade unions while actively seeking endorsement, financial backing and policy input from big business (Anderson and Mann 1997: 36-45, Taylor 2001: 245-252). The new emphasis in party thinking developed in the 1980s and early 1990s on a liberal agenda of radical constitutional reform, and the liberal positions on civil rights developed since the 1960s,[17] would also be toned down in the New Labour discourse.[18]

Though the central role of the EU in future British political and economic development would be an article of faith for the 'New Labour' politician, the precise direction that party policy on the EU would take under Blair was less than clear as he assumed the leadership in July 1994. If the creation of 'New Labour' had a clear defining goal, then it was in ensuring that the Labour party would finally exit from its political wilderness by winning the next election (Leys 1997: 21, Smith 2000: 262). Its policies had to be honed towards this goal, even where such a strategy conflicted with principles long held by the party faithful. In terms of European policy, the domestic political climate into which the Blair leadership was thrust appeared to suggest that caution was required.

How then could New Labour be expected to react to the emerging IGC agenda? Though his public pronouncements on Europe had generally paid lip service to the need for Britain to play a leading role in the EU, Blair's pro-European credentials were rather ambiguous when compared to the unabashed pro-Europeanism of John Smith (Anderson and Mann 1997: 24, Young, JW 2000: 176, Fella 2000).[19] However, party statements adopted prior to Blair's accession to the leadership suggested that Labour's approach to treaty reform would be considerably more constructive than that indicated by the Conservative government's behaviour. The discussion that follows will examine in greater detail the key IGC proposals and the reasons for their emergence on the agenda. The Labour party's likely responses to this emerging agenda will be explored in the light of its known public positions in the early 1990s and assessed in the context of the likely positions of the Conservative government and the governments of other member states.

Democracy and Transparency in the EU

Rather than the major extensions of treaty competences introduced by the previous two treaty reforms, leading to the SEA and the TEU respectively, the emphasis of the 1996 IGC appeared, from an early stage, to be on bringing the EU closer to its citizens, largely through reforms to make it more democratic and transparent, and also to improve the efficiency of the institutional framework in the perspective of further enlargement (Laffan 1997a: 289). Labour's approach to the treaty reform appeared to differ from the Conservative party most starkly in relation to the former. Indeed, a policy document adopted at the 1993 party conference, which elucidated Labour's constitutional reform programme, linked Labour proposals to democratise EU decision-making to its programme to modernise and democratise the UK constitution. The document, entitled *A New Agenda for Democracy* contained a section on democratising the EU (Labour Party 1993a: 34). It referred to a transfer of decision-making to the EC that had not been matched by new methods of holding this decision-making to account. This deficit in accountability, along with the various deficiencies in the UK constitution, was described as contributing to a seriously flawed democracy. The 'new constitutional settlement' elaborated by the Labour party would accordingly use the principles of 'subsidiarity, democracy and accountability' to remedy the problem of European institutions 'perceived as unresponsive, unaccountable...(and)...centralising' which had fuelled popular distrust of the European integration process. Among the proposals specified to put these principles into practice was one representing a significant departure from the Community method of decision-making: the document proposed that the right of legislative initiative enjoyed as the sole preserve of the European Commission be shared with both the EP and the Council of Ministers. It was also suggested that all EC legislation be subject to scrutiny, and a vote of approval, by the EP. These proposals would be within the context of strengthened national scrutiny of EC legislation, and more effective co-ordination of scrutiny between national parliaments and the EP, for example through joint committees of national MPs and MEPs which would meet to discuss proposals for new European legislation. The document also proposed greater democratic scrutiny of European Commissioners by the EP, and more openness to public scrutiny of the Council of Ministers, when performing its legislative function.

The proposals in *A New Agenda for Democracy* echoed the positions set out in Labour's policy document on the EU adopted in the same year: *Prosperity Through Co-operation - A New European Future* (Labour Party 1993b). This itself restated proposals made prior to the Maastricht summit in the 1991 policy document: *Opportunity Britain: Labour's Policy on Europe* (Labour Party 1991). These involved demands for more open decision-making in the Council, a review of the way in which the Commission and its president were nominally responsible to the EP, a shared right between the EP and the Commission to initiate legislation and the extension of the EP co-operation procedure[20] to social and environmental matters (Labour Party 1993b: 63-64). In restating these proposals, *Prosperity Through Co-operation* strangely made no reference to the codecision procedure introduced by the TEU, despite the treaty stipulation that its scope be reviewed in 1996.[21] However, in calling for EP scrutiny and an EP vote of approval on all EC legislation, *A New Agenda for Democracy* implied Labour party support for extending codecision across the board, going much further than the 1991 formulation. Though Labour's 1994 EP election manifesto did refer to codecision, it was more circumspect than the earlier documents, indicating support for its extension, but not making any precise commitment on its scope (Labour Party 1994: 22). This was a possible reflection of the closer attention paid by the Labour leadership to the detailed implications of some of its policy statements on Europe in the run-up to the 1994 EP elections, in the light of the Conservative election strategy of seeking to portray Labour as poised to sell out to Brussels. Nevertheless, the PES manifesto for 1994, which Labour had earlier endorsed, called for codecision to be the rule (PES 1994: 14). Though not contradicting this, Labour's own manifesto had downplayed this commitment.

Whatever the precise nuance of its position, Labour could be expected to have a positive approach to the proposals that were likely to be made at the 1996 to extend the usage of codecision beyond the limited scope defined by the TEU. The EP was itself in the forefront of demands to extend codecision to all legislative acts (Corbett 1992, Martin 1992). The need to extend codecision was supported by a number of member state governments, most importantly Germany, mainly out of a need to demonstrate to their citizens a greater appearance of democratic legitimacy in the EU institutions (Lightfoot and Wilde 1996: 14, Moravcsik and Nicolaidis 1998: 22, 1999: 81, Duff 1997a: 62, Dehousse 1999: 58).[22] In addition, the German constitutional court's opinion on the TEU had linked further transfers of authority to the EU with the need to address the democratic deficit, while some smaller states viewed a greater role for the EP as a way of redressing the dominant influence of the larger states in the Council (Duff 1997a: 18, Story 1997: 26, 34-35). Given the PES manifesto commitment on codecision, those member states with PES governments could be expected to be at the forefront of calls for its extension (Lightfoot and Wilde 1996: 9). However, as it would involve transferring a degree of control over decision-making from a body comprising national government representatives (the Council) to a more overtly supranational body (the EP), the proposal to extend EP codecision was likely to be firmly opposed by the Conservative government in the UK (Duff 1997a: 61-64). This opposition would be confirmed both by the negative position taken on the matter in the Reflection Group by David Davis and also the UK government White Paper on the IGC in February 1996 (Reflection Group 1995, FCO 1996).

In a similar vein, Conservative opposition to the EP demand that in order to improve the legitimacy of EU executive action, it (the EP) be granted the power to elect the Commission president could be virtually guaranteed. But, in any case, this was unlikely to win the support of many member states' governments. An alternative and more moderate proposal, which might be more likely to win support among the member states, was to give the EP a right of approval over the European Council nominee for the Commission Presidency (Duff 1997a: 65-66). This would build on the EP's power to approve the Commission as a whole, which was granted by the TEU. The restatement in *Prosperity Through Co-operation* of Labour's pre-Maastricht 1991 suggestion that the method by which the Commission and its president were responsible to the EP be reviewed was accompanied by a suggestion that this and its other demands on enhancing democracy had not been fully met by the TEU (Labour Party 1993b: 63). It appears therefore, that the Labour party in 1993 was prepared to support a further development of the EP's role in this area. However, no reference to this issue was made in Labour's 1994 EP election manifesto or in the PES manifesto. The omission from the former may have reflected Labour's increasing caution in 1994, while the omission from the latter was a probable reflection of the lack of consensus on the issue among PES parties.

Nevertheless, the Labour European manifesto for 1994 continued to stress its commitment to democratising the EU. Labour's consistent support in the early 1990s for measures to address the EU's democratic deficit reflected the anxiety expressed by the Smith leadership about the democratic deficiencies of the TEU. Reforms to democratise decision-making could also be expected to win the support of those pro-European backbench Labour MPs who had opposed the TEU ratification and rebelled against the party line because of these and other concerns. In a similar vein, there was widespread recognition within the Labour party of the need to make EU decision-making more transparent. Thus there was likely to be sympathy for the proposition, most firmly associated with the Nordic member states, that EU decision-making be made more transparent, for example through an obligation that the Council of Ministers deliberate in public when legislating, or at least that voting records be published. Though Labour's 1993 documents were rather vague in calling for more open scrutiny of Council decision-making, the 1994 EP manifesto was more precise in calling for all votes in the Council to be recorded and published, when it acted in its legislative capacity (Labour 1994: 22).

A connection could also be made between Labour's proposal for a freedom of information act in the UK establishing a general right of access to official information held by all levels of government and public authorities within the UK, as elucidated in *A New Agenda for Democracy* (Labour Party 1993: 42-43) and the demands emanating from the Nordic states for a general EU citizens' right of access to documentation relating to EU decision-making. The theme of openness had been pressed by the Danish following the initial referendum rejection of the TEU, which was partly attributed to concerns about the lack of democracy and transparency in EU decision-making. Indeed, in response to the Danish situation and concerns in other member states, the Edinburgh European Council of 1992 had committed the EU to greater openness and transparency (Peterson 1997: 170). The transparency theme was also picked up by the Swedes and Finns following their accession to the EU in 1995, with access to EU documents along the lines of Sweden's own freedom of information legislation becoming a prominent demand among Swedish politicians (Peterson 1997: 177).

The question of transparency also related to the comprehensibility of the EU treaties themselves, and citizen understanding of how decisions were made at the EU level, and indeed, on what basis. Explanations of EU decision-making and spheres of policy competence were dispersed across a series of complex and overlapping treaties. The decision-making procedures themselves were complex and numerous. Confusion was added by the existence of different forms of EU activities, i.e. the separate pillars, opt-outs and protocols to the EC pillar, and the existence of separate communities in the form of the EC, ECSC and Euratom. One radical proposal to remedy this confusion, supported by the EP and a number of pressure groups, was to draw up a constitution for the EU, building on the various constitutional provisions within the existing treaties that made up the EU's existing constitutional apparatus (Bertelsmann Foundation 1990, European Policy Forum 1993, European Parliament 1994, European Movement 1994). However, given the inevitable connections that would be made between the drafting of such a constitution and the construction of a federal European state, the difficulties that national ratification of such a constitution would bring and the generally far-reaching constitutional implications that such a move would have for the member states, there would be little enthusiasm for this idea among the key policy-makers in the member states. Many of those who backed this idea accepted it was unlikely to have many takers in the IGC and switched their pressure to the campaign for a reordering and simplification of the existing treaties, to provide a clear, coherent and accessible treaty framework based on democratic principles. This would itself represent a quasi-constitutional text. This view was evident in a 'reflection paper' written for the PES group by Richard Corbett, then its deputy secretary-general (and a Labour party member), in June 1994. Corbett's paper recognised that the concept of a constitution would provoke consternation among certain member states. Nevertheless, he argued that the case remained 'that the current set of overlapping treaties and amending treaties, three "pillars", and a dozen different legislative procedures should be replaced by a single, clear and concise document that spells out clearly the competences and powers of the European institutions and the limits thereof, and sets out a limited number of easily comprehensible decision-taking procedures' (PES Group 1994). The likely approach that the Labour party would take on this simplification proposal was not apparent from its various policy statements on the EU. However, the assertion made in *Prosperity Through Co-operation* that a 'fundamental overhaul of the Community's institutions' (Labour Party 1993b: 48) was required in order to bring the EU closer to its peoples and the suggestion in Labour's EP manifesto that 'all the Union's procedures should be simplified to make them understandable and open to review' (Labour Party 1994: 23) provided an indication that the Labour party might be amenable to the radical approach advocated by Corbett. Although the lack of democracy and transparency in the EU was one of the charges against it made by Euro-sceptics within the Conservative party, the emphasis placed by the Conservative government on the intergovernmental nature of the EU, its general unwillingness to alter the status quo in terms of the structure of the treaties and its weak domestic record on openness in decision-making all seemed to indicate that it would be unwilling to support reforms which would subject the complex negotiations between government representatives in the Council to greater public scrutiny, provide greater citizens access to EU documentation or alter the form of the treaties through a simplification or consolidation exercise.

The need to simplify decision-making also related back to another issue that the TEU had specified for review in 1996: the possible creation of a hierarchy of EC acts or norms. The Commission had raised this issue during the Maastricht IGC but no progress had been made apart from the commitment to return to it in 1996. The argument for a hierarchy derived from the situation in which the various EC legislative procedures involving the Commission, Council and EP applied for all forms of legislation in the EU, including acts of a highly technical nature which, if they were decided at a national level, would fall into the category of secondary or delegated legislation.[23] The Commission thus argued for a hierarchy of acts, distinguishing between constitutional acts (i.e. treaty provisions), legislative acts and implementing acts. The first two would be decided in the existing way, but the latter would be the responsibility of the Commission. It was argued that such a move would clarify the complex decision-making mechanisms of the EU, making them both more effective and transparent, identifying where responsibilities for decisions lay within the EC system (Laffan 1997a: 299, Duff 1997a: 67-69). Given that the establishment of such a constitutional hierarchy would transfer extra responsibility to the Commission, and would enhance the state-like character of the EU, British government opposition to the proposal was highly likely. However, probably because of the technical and slightly obscure nature of the issue, the Labour party position was not clear in the early 1990s. Neither *Prosperity Through Co-operation* nor Labour's 1994 EP manifesto made any mention of the proposal. Nor for that matter did the PES manifesto. Nevertheless, it seemed possible that Labour might be open to persuasion to support the proposal given its general presentation as part of the process of clarifying and simplifying the EU's complex and unwieldy decision-making processes.

Citizenship and Social Europe

The Labour party could be expected to adopt a favourable approach (and the Conservatives a negative one) to other more tangible proposals put forward to develop the EU's democratic character and demonstrate its relevance to its citizens. Although the EU treaties, in their existing formulation upheld some basic rights,[24] the coverage was far from comprehensive. The EP had elaborated a declaration of civil, political and social 'fundamental' rights in 1989, calling for it to be incorporated into the treaties (European Parliament 1989). This had not gathered much support among national governments. Some member states did support a proposal to incorporate the European Convention on Human Rights (ECHR) into EC law. However, the legal complexities of this option made it unlikely.[25] An alternative and more practical option that did gather support was to grant the ECJ jurisdiction to ensure that the EU respected the ECHR (Dinan 1999: 302-303). This would involve amending article F2 of the TEU which stated that the EU should 'respect fundamental rights, as guaranteed by the ECHR' but which had been placed within title I of the TEU, outside the EC pillar and therefore outside the jurisdiction of the ECJ (Duff 1997a: 53). In addition to this, there were suggestions that the treaty provisions on equality between men and women be widened into more general provisions to combat all forms of discrimination, for example, on basis of gender, race, religion, disability or sexual orientation (McDonagh 1998: 166-167, Duff 1997a: 132-133). The latter proposal in particular bore a strong echo of the Labour party position outlined in *Prosperity Through Co-operation*, which included a section on 'widening and extending equality rights.' This called for the EU to 'develop an equalities framework that is consistent with the best practices of international human rights legislation' in which the EC's approach to women's equality rights would be 'used as a model to tackle other forms of discrimination' (Labour Party 1993b: 56-57). The document described freedom from discrimination as a fundamental right, a commitment to which should be written into every EC policy. It also pledged Labour to work towards an EC framework to combat racial discrimination, harassment and violence. Labour's 1994 EP election manifesto continued in a similar vein as regards the need for European anti-discrimination legislation and action against racism and xenophobia (1994: 13-14). In relation to enhancing the general profile of the EU in guaranteeing fundamental rights, the section in *Prosperity Through Co-operation* on co-operation on home affairs provided a hint that Labour might be willing to support measures to ensure the judicial enforcement of fundamental rights standards within the EU. It underlined the 'essential' requirement that 'compliance with internationally recognised human rights standards is secured throughout the growing scope of European competence' (Labour Party 1993b: 62).

Though these various measures were presented as ways of bringing the EU closer to the citizens, the aspect of the TEU that had caused the greatest concern within the Labour party as regards it impact on both the democratic nature of the EU and the interests of its citizens was the EMU title. A number of backbench critics of the TEU within the PLP had focused their ire on the deflationary and monetarist bias of the EMU convergence criteria and the transfer of monetary sovereignty to an unaccountable ECB which would operate independently of any political interference

(Anderson and Mann 1997: 85). The Smith leadership had sympathised with these concerns, but argued that they should be addressed from within the new treaty framework. Hence *Prosperity Through Co-operation* suggested that the whole issue of accountability in the EMU process be reviewed at the 1996 IGC, and that there should be a strengthening of the existing treaty requirement that the ECB support the economic objectives of the EU. The economic objectives of the EU were laid down in article 2 of the TEU, which referred to 'harmonious and balanced development...a high level of employment and social protection...and economic and social cohesion and solidarity among member states.' *Prosperity Through Co-operation* therefore stated that it was 'crucial that the democratically accountable Council of Economic and Finance Ministers (ECOFIN) should be developed as the political counterpart' to the ECB. It was thus suggested that ECOFIN be given its own permanent secretariat and an enhanced role in the formulation of the EC's medium-term monetary policy. Furthermore, the ECB's responsibility to report to ECOFIN, the EP and national parliaments would be 'strengthened to provide greater openness and accountability to ensure that the Community's objectives as set out in article 2 are realised.' As regards British participation in EMU, the document again fudged the issue, restating Labour's belief in the need for 'real, rather than nominal convergence' as defined by 'the ability of all member states to sustain adequate rates of growth and employment without incurring unsustainable current account deficits' (Labour Party 1993b: 49-53). The Labour belief that the issues of EMU accountability and convergence could be reopened in 1996 could be interpreted as wishful thinking, as discussion of the EMU provisions was not formally on the IGC agenda and a number of member states had no wish to re-open the debate on them, given the exertion of political will and careful negotiation that had gone into their design.

An alternative option, which was more likely to win support in the majority of member states, was to keep the existing EMU provisions intact but simultaneously (and separately) develop the profile of the EU in combating the high unemployment that some critics had blamed, at least partly, on the deflationary EMU convergence conditions. The possibility of pursuing co-ordinated European action to combat unemployment had been one of the contributing factors in the conversion of some Labour party politicians to a constructive pro-Europeanism in the 1980s. The Labour party policy documents of the early 1990s had continued to push these themes. *Prosperity Through Co-operation* had restated the demand for a pan-European economic recovery and job creation strategy. The former Labour MP, Stuart Holland and the left-wing Labour MEP, Ken Coates had, in 1992, put forward a plan for a European counter-cyclical economic strategy, co-ordinated by the European Commission and utilising and expanding the lending facility of the European Investment Bank, in order to compensate for the deflationary effects of the EMU convergence criteria. Holland was also advising Delors on the formulation of a European recovery strategy, and many facets of the Coates-Holland plan found their way into a Commission white paper on growth, competitiveness and employment launched by Delors in November 1993 (Barrett Brown and Coates 1993, Lightfoot and Wilde 1996: 12-14). These ideas were embraced by the Smith leadership and Labour's EP election manifesto in 1994 continued to press the case for the Delors proposals and for greater economic co-ordination, better use of the European Investment Bank and a European recovery fund. It also continued to argue the need for real economic convergence in the establishment of EMU (Labour Party 1994: 9-10). However, the 1993 proposals on improving accountability of the ECB appeared to have been dropped by the time of the 1994 manifesto, possibly because the Labour leadership realised that the issue was a non-starter for certain other key member states.

The antipathy of the predominantly centre-right governments that prevailed in the EU in 1993 meant that the Delors white paper was met with an indifferent response by the EU member states (Anderson and Mann: 93-97). Nevertheless, a momentum did develop behind the more modest proposal, originally made by the Swedish government (Lightfoot and Wilde 1996: 13, McDonagh 1998: 84-87),[26] for an employment chapter to be inserted into the EU treaties, so as to provide for some form of co-ordination of EU action against unemployment and in order to demonstrate the EU's relevance to its citizens by focusing on an issue of widespread public concern. While support for the proposal came primarily from the PES parties, and could be expected to be shared by the Labour party, opposition came from the centre-right governments of Germany and (more predictably) Britain. This opposition was derived from a belief that an employment chapter would create unrealistic expectations, might lead to increased expenditure commitments, and that policy in this area should be the preserve of national governments (McDonagh 1998: 85).

One other key issue on which the Labour party could demonstrate its commitment to bringing the EU closer to its citizens and distinguish itself from the obduracy of the Conservative government was the social chapter. Labour had attacked the Major government for denying to British workers the framework of employment rights that the social chapter was intended to develop for the rest of the EU. Labour's pledge to reverse the social chapter opt-out negotiated by the Conservative government had been a central feature of its public statements on the EU since the Maastricht summit (George and Haythorne 1996: 112). It reflected a central demand of Labour's affiliated trade unions and could be expected to be popular with the wider public, at least those who stood to gain through improved rights in the workplace. Labour's position here could also be expected to win the universal approval of the other EU governments who generally resented the British opt-out, both because it undermined the legal uniformity of the EC and because it allowed British employers to undercut the labour costs of the continent through a lower level of employment protection (McDonagh 1998: 92-93).

The Pillar Structure and Effective Decision-Making

The differences between the Labour and Conservative approaches to the developing treaty reform agenda appeared to be less clear-cut on the second key IGC theme of making decision-making more efficient. Many of the issues raised by this theme would cause difficulty because the proposed solutions often involved increasing the scope of supranational decision-making. Here, Labour's approach in the early 1990s was more ambiguous.

The twin IGC themes of bringing the EU closer to its citizens and improving decision-making coincided when it came to the review of the treaty pillar structure deemed necessary by the TEU. The policy-making apparatus provided for in the intergovernmental pillars had come under criticism in some quarters for its secretive and unaccountable nature (Duff 1997a: 128-129, Justice 1996). This was a particular concern in the third pillar, given the implications of policy-making in justice and home affairs for the civil liberties of individuals. Though the EP had called for the extension of codecision to all EC legislation to address the democratic deficit in the first pillar, the situation in the intergovernmental pillars was different because actions undertaken within them could not be categorised as legislation within the EC legal framework. It was in the intergovernmental pillars therefore, that the absence of accountability in EU decision-making appeared most pronounced. While the EC pillar was subject to judicial review by the ECJ, Commission initiative and variable levels of EP scrutiny, the CFSP and JHA pillars operated by intergovernmental agreement with limited Commission involvement and a negligible level of accountability to the EP. This provoked less concern in relation to CFSP because of the general tendency of national executives to enjoy a degree of independence from their domestic legislatures when making major foreign policy decisions. However, the creation of the JHA pillar had resulted in a diminution of national parliamentary scrutiny over executive action in the areas of policy covered, without new mechanisms of pan-European scrutiny being established through the EP or otherwise. National governments had voluntarily transferred decision-making to intergovernmental bodies (the JHA Council and its various committees) that met in secret and were not subject to parliamentary scrutiny or judicial review by the ECJ. However, perhaps of greater concern to a number of the member states than the lack of democracy in these pillars was the perceived inefficiency of the intergovernmental decision-making apparatus, which some attributed to the absence of a central driving role for the Commission. There appeared to be widespread agreement (aside from Britain and Denmark) that, at least as far as the JHA was concerned, the structure was unsatisfactory. Indeed, a majority of member states (Belgium, Germany, Greece, Ireland, Italy, Spain and The Netherlands) had voiced opposition to the pillar structure in the run-up to Maastricht and had favoured the tree structure originally proposed by the Dutch, in which the EC institutional framework would apply throughout (Corbett 1992: 279).

Following the ratification of the TEU, there was little progress under the JHA pillar while the floundering of EU policy towards the former Yugoslavia appeared to demonstrate the limitations of the CFSP structure. A number of member states continued to press for the integration of the intergovernmental pillars. Support was more widespread for the partial communitisation of the JHA pillar in relation to immigration and asylum policy. Given that Germany was in receipt of over half of all immigrants and asylum-seekers and immigrants to the EU, the German government would take the lead in pressing for communitisation here as a way of strengthening co-operation on sharing this burden and tightening up policies on entry across the EU (Moravcsik and Nicolaidis 1998: 28-29). [27] However, Britain and Denmark remained opposed to this and the French also appeared reluctant given their contribution to the original design of the pillar structure (McDonagh 1998: 167-170, Szukala and

Wessels 1997: 92). Opinion on CFSP was more evenly divided between advocates of communitisation and those who preferred the existing intergovernmental structure, with Germany in the former group and France more clearly among the latter group (Szukala and Wessels 1997: 85-86). Having championed the pillar structure at Maastricht, and developed an even more Euro-sceptical public position since, it was clear that the Major government would seek to maintain the status quo. The likely position of the Labour party was less clear. *Prosperity Through Co-operation* actually made no mention of the pillar structure. However, its section on 'co-operating on home affairs' stated that it was 'essential that such co-operation measures should not merely be a function of intergovernmental agreement but should be brought fully into the community's legal system in line with Labour's commitment to ensuring transparency and accountability in decision-making.' Furthermore, it stated the need 'to ensure the increased accountability to both Westminster and the EP of the Trevi and Schengen groups' (Labour Party 1993b: 61). It seemed strange that the document should refer to the Trevi system of ad hoc intergovernmental co-operation in JHA matters that had existed outside the EC treaties prior to Maastricht but not to the JHA pillar introduced by the TEU that had superseded it. But presumably Labour's espousal of greater accountability would also apply to the new JHA pillar. The reference to Schengen may have betrayed a certain lack of understanding of the situation within the Labour leadership, given that the Schengen agreements (signed in 1985 and 1990) existed outside the EU treaties and that Britain was not part of the arrangements.[28] The document did not explain whether Labour favoured British involvement in Schengen or the integration of Schengen into the EU framework, as advocated by its signatories. Similarly, Labour's EP election manifesto in 1994 did not mention the pillar structure, but hinted that it might be in favour of some JHA communitisation by stating that the EU needed 'to move to increasing convergence and harmonisation of both migration and asylum policies' though it stressed the need to ensure that such policies recognised the 'specific needs of each individual member...ensuring that member states have full responsibility for administering immigration and asylum rules' (Labour Party 1994: 21). Labour was likely to be closer to the government line on the status of the CFSP pillar. *Prosperity Through Co-operation* made no mention of involving the EC institutions in CFSP decision-making. Rather it stressed the primacy of the member states in developing common policies, emphasising that 'the test of unanimity should be built in so that common action is taken only where it can be agreed by all member states' (Labour Party 1993b: 70) In a similar vein, Labour's 1994 manifesto stressed a CFSP 'based on agreed principles and objectives' (Labour Party 1994: 26) (see below for fuller discussion of Labour's attitude to NATO and European defence).

Assuming a rational calculation of the British national interest, both the Conservative and Labour parties could be expected to share a common approach to some of the institutional reform issues derived from a perceived need to maintain EU efficiency in the perspective of further enlargement. Although it would have preferred to have no treaty review and its rhetoric sometimes suggested that it would not support any treaty changes, the Major government could be expected to be supportive of proposals for Council vote reweighting and Commission reorganisation. Indeed, Britain shared a common interest with the other large states in pushing for a vote reweighting that increased the large states' share of the total weighted vote and a Commission reorganisation which guaranteed them a right to at least one Commissioner while removing this automatic right from the smaller states (Story 1997: 35). It was the large states, particularly the French government, which were pushing hardest for reform on these issues. They favoured a radical streamlining of the Commission, in which not all states would have a Commissioner at the same time (Dinan 1999: 180-181). Though the German government also favoured changes, particularly in the weighting of votes, Chancellor Kohl was more circumspect in pushing these questions lest Germany face accusations of over-assertiveness (Moravcsik and Nicolaidis 1998: 18, McDonagh 1998: 154).[29] On these issues, a cleavage would develop between the larger and the smaller states. The latter would generally seek to resist vote reweighting and removal of the automatic right to a have a Commissioner, as this would diminish their influence within the EU policy-making framework and increase the potential for dominance by the large states (McDonagh 1998: 156-160). Some of the small states, notably the Benelux, saw in the Commission's central role in EU policy-making a guarantee that common policies would truly reflect pan-European interests and not simply the interests of the large states (Pijpers and Vanhoonacker 1997: 123, 131). A great deal of importance was therefore attached to the need for each small state to be able to nominate its own Commission member. This view of the Commission as the guardian of pan-European interests was also a contributing factor to the support found among these states for communitisation of policy-making in the intergovernmental pillars. In *Prosperity Through Co-operation*, the Labour party acknowledged that enlargement would create a need for 'considerable changes in the way the institutions of the Community function' and that 'a set of rules designed originally for six members' could not be 'applied to a Community which might eventually number over 20 members.' However, the document did not commit the Labour party to supporting any precise reforms, and rather enigmatically pronounced: 'whether the Community should update the present rules, sticking to their main principles, or whether a whole new set of institutions is needed is still open to much discussion' (Labour Party 1993b: 63). Labour's manifesto for 1994 was also rather vague about the kind of institutional reform necessary in the light of enlargement, but was more circumspect, simply suggesting that the widening offered the EU the 'opportunity to modernise and reshape its institutions' (1994: 4). On the other hand, the joint manifesto with the PES was more forthright, arguing that the enlargement of the EU 'should be accompanied by a deepening of the EU' (PES 1994:11).

Many observers argued that the most important institutional change required to maintain efficiency in an enlarged EU was the extension of QMV to prevent decision-making getting bogged down by the need to reach unanimity in a wide range of policy areas, though it was notable that while all member states apart from the UK supported the principle of QMV extension, the precise areas where QMV was favoured differed from one member state to another (McDonagh 1998: 156). On this question, the Labour party was more likely to diverge from a Conservative government that appeared to have set itself on a course of rejection of any further QMV extension. Nevertheless, the Labour party remained cautious. Though it called for considerable institutional changes to cope with enlargement, *Prosperity Through Co-operation* made no specific mention of the need for further QMV extension. It did however welcome the provisions for QMV in environmental policy introduced by the TEU as a necessary way of bypassing obstructive national vetoes (which were described as 'usually British and Tory') on essential 'international pollution laws' (Labour Party 1993b: 49).[30] Labour's caution as regards QMV was evident in the run-up to the 1994 EP election. Although it had signed up to a PES manifesto calling for QMV in Council decision-making and codecision with the EP to be the rule, Labour's own manifesto for 1994 appeared to gloss over its position. While expressing support for QMV in social and environmental policy, it also stressed that Labour 'had always insisted...on maintaining the principle of unanimity for decision-making in areas such as fiscal and budgetary policy, foreign and security issues, changes to the Treaty of Rome, and other areas of key national interest' (Labour Party 1994: 22). The Labour party was thus stressing what it saw as exceptions to the QMV rule whilst avoiding presenting a clear contradiction of the line it had agreed within the PES. Conservative suggestions that Labour was willing to 'sell Britain out' by giving up the veto across EU policy and the generally Euro-sceptical domestic climate had contributed to Labour's caution in 1994 and would have a continuing effect on the party's consideration of the issue.

CFSP and European Defence

The Labour leadership could also be expected to proceed with caution on the third theme of the IGC: the capacity of the EU to project itself onto the international stage. As stipulated by the TEU, the treaty review would consider the CFSP provisions agreed at Maastricht, and, in particular, the potential development of an EU defence role. As with the debate on communitisation of the CFSP, opinion was divided as regards the development of a common European defence policy within the CFSP. However, the division did not fall between the same groups of states. France, while opposing CFSP communitisation and seeking to ensure the primacy of the national governments in decision-making, was a keen advocate of developing an autonomous European defence capacity (Anderson 1998: 135). One possible route in this direction, advocated ardently by Germany, was the incorporation of the West European Union (WEU) defence organisation into the EU (van Ham 1997: 317-318).[31] France and Germany had tabled a proposal for the development of an EU defence role in the run-up to the Maastricht summit in 1991, and support for this had come from most WEU members, including Italy, Spain, Belgium, Greece and Luxembourg (Anderson 1998: 136-136, Corbett 1992: 282). However, the Major government had taken an opposing view from most of its WEU colleagues and ensured that the TEU included only a vague reference to the possible eventual framing of a European defence (Anderson 1998: 136, Young, JW 2000: 154-155).[32]

The British government view was that the development of an EU defence role would undermine NATO and the Atlantic alliance, and it continued to insist on the primacy of the NATO alliance in European defence matters. This approach also had support from other Atlanticist EU-NATO members, notably Portugal, Denmark and the Netherlands (Anderson 1998: 135). This was an area of policy on which a bipartisan consensus existed in Britain between the Conservative and Labour parties

(Keohane 1992). This consensus, focused on the Atlantic alliance with the USA, had been temporarily vacated by Labour in the early 1980s as it lurched to the left and adopted a foreign policy characterised by neutralism, anti-Americanism and pacifism (Spear 1992).[33] This was encapsulated by the policy of unilateral nuclear disarmament, which remained official party policy up to the 1987 general election despite Kinnock's success in steering the party away from the anti-American isolationism of 1983.[34] Kinnock's policy review after 1987 resulted in Labour's reversion to an Atlanticist foreign policy firmly in the tradition of Bevin, Wilson and Callaghan, and the policy of unilateral nuclear disarmament was overturned at the 1989 party conference (Keohane 1993). This could be attributed to a mixture of electoral politics (the unilateralist defence policy had not been a vote winner) and new policy assumptions derived from changes in the Soviet Union that were leading to multilateral reductions in nuclear arsenals (Croft 1992). The return to a spirit of bipartisanship in foreign affairs was confirmed by the Kinnock leadership's support for British involvement in the US-led Gulf war campaign in 1991 (Spear 1992). This reaffirmed bipartisan approach was reflected in 1993 in *Prosperity Through Co-operation* which echoed the government line in asserting that 'arrangements for the foreseeable future should be based on NATO which is a proven and effective organisation and will have to retain its role as the principal defence structure for Western Europe' (Labour Party 1993b: 70) In a similar vein, while Labour's manifesto in 1994 expressed support for moves to establish the WEU as the European pillar within NATO, it stressed Labour's firm commitment to the NATO alliance as the principal bulwark of European security (Labour Party 1994: 26). Labour could therefore be expected to oppose proposals that the 1996 treaty review result in the development of an EU defence role. Opposition to this would also come from another NATO member, Denmark (which had declined to join the WEU), and the four neutral member states: Austria, Finland, Ireland and Sweden. Aside from the defence question, Labour could also be expected to extend this bipartisan approach to opposition to CFSP communitisation and to proposals for QMV in CFSP decision-making, as advocated by the German government (Szukala and Wessels 1996: 85).[35] Labour's position on the latter was made clear by the reference in *Prosperity Through Co-operation* to the need for unanimity to ensure CFSP actions were endorsed by all member states.

On other proposed modifications to the CFSP which would find their way on the IGC agenda, such as the creation of a high representative to give some continuity to the EU's external political representation and the establishment of a planning unit to better prepare the EU for emerging CFSP issues, Labour's position was less clear in the early 1990s. The latter proposal was relatively non-controversial and therefore might even be expected to win the support of the Conservative government in Britain. However, the former proposal, which was vigorously championed by the French government (Szukala and Wessels 1997: 85, Moravcsik and Nicolaidis 1998: 26), could be expected to arouse some suspicion in Britain, as it could be interpreted as detracting from the primacy of the national governments (acting through the rotating Council presidency) in the external representation of the EU.[36]

Differentiated Integration

The apparent British government intransigence on defence, institutional reform and a range of other questions, combined with the effect of its opt-outs, contributed to the emergence on the developing IGC agenda of proposals for some form of differentiated integration to allow those member states able and willing to proceed further with European integration to do so without Britain holding them back (Dinan 1999: 173, Hughes and Smith 1998: 94). Indeed, German Chancellor Kohl repeatedly suggested that it was not possible for the EU convoy to move at the speed of the slowest members (Duff 1997a: 14). Concerns on the continent about the intransigent British impeding progress were combined with fears that further EU enlargement would bring in a number of countries unable to keep up with the pace of integration and also heighten the risk of institutional paralysis, particularly given the prevalence of the unanimity requirement and the unwillingness of certain countries to depart from it. Thus in the late summer of 1994, leading politicians in both Germany and France put forward proposals for a form of two-tier Europe, in which those countries able and willing to do so, could form a more closely integrated inner core of the Union. The suggestion came in a policy paper of the ruling Christian Democrats (CDU)/Christian Social Union (CSU) in Germany and was echoed by the then French prime minister Edouard Balladur. The CDU paper, drawn up by Karl Lamers, the governing party's foreign policy specialist, proposed an institutionalised 'hard-core' Europe, with the Franco-German Alliance as the focus, and also including the Benelux countries and possibly Austria (CDU/CSU 1994, Duff 1997a: 16-18, Story 1997: 24). This core would deepen integration in the fields of monetary policy, fiscal and budgetary policy, and economic and social policy. It would also establish an effective common foreign policy and a common defence. The core would be open to all members capable and willing to join. Those who did not join would remain part of an outer circle of member states. It was suggested that such an institutional arrangement would become even more necessary with the accession of new member states, committed to European integration, but not able to meet the full criteria of joining the 'hard-core'. Balladur appeared to endorse this approach in an interview with the French newspaper, *Le Figaro*, published within days of the CDU/CSU paper, in which he suggested a Europe of three concentric circles to include: 1) an inner core for tighter integration in the economic and monetary sphere and defence and military matters; 2) a system of states based on the existing treaty arrangements; 3) a looser economic area and security agreement for the whole of Europe (*Le Figaro* 30 August 1994, Duff 1997a: 20, Szukala and Wessels 1997: 90-92).

Although these German and French proposals caused enormous controversy at the time and were subsequently watered down (Edwards and Pijpers 1997: 3), there appeared to be a general acceptance among the member states that some form of institutional flexibility would be required in the future. It was extremely unlikely that all member states, in an enlarged EU, would be willing or able to proceed at the same level of integration. While references to a 'two-tier' or 'hard-core' Europe were dropped, the notion of an inner group deepening integration would later be reformulated in terms of 'institutional flexibility' or 'enhanced co-operation.' Indeed, the debate was a recognition that differentiated integration already existed both within and outside the EU treaties, as reflected, for example, in the British social chapter opt-out (within the treaty framework) and the Schengen arrangements outside the treaty framework. The timetable and conditions for membership of the single currency also made it inevitable that further variable geometry would occur in the future, as not all member states would reach the necessary convergence in time while some might choose to remain outside irrespective of convergence (Duff 1997a: 183). Although the proposals for a two-tier Europe could be interpreted as a logical continental response to British obstruction and the Major government had made clear it did not wish to proceed in the direction of deeper integration, the official British reaction was to reject these proposals. In a speech in Leiden shortly after the publication of the CDU report, Major remarked that he saw 'real danger in talk of a hard-core, inner and outer circles, a two-tier Europe...in which some would be more equal than others' (Young, H 1999: 456-457, Young, JW 2000: 166). Though some observers suggested that this was a contradiction of Major's advocacy during the European election campaign earlier in 1994 of a 'multi-track, multi-speed, multi-layered Europe' (Young, H 1999: 456-457), the government position appeared to be that variable geometry with different groups of member states proceeding in different areas of policy was desirable, but that institutionalising different levels of integration with member states having to agree to a package of co-operation in various policy areas in order to belong to a particular tier of integration was not acceptable. The government position here reflected a recognition that an institutionalised two-tier Europe would leave Britain marginalised in an outer tier and shorn of influence in the EU. As JW Young comments, the British government was seeking 'the best of both worlds, minimising its EU involvement...whilst avoiding permanent exclusion from deeper integration' (Young, JW 2000: 166). Given the derision that the Labour party had directed at the Conservative government for placing Britain on the margins of the EU and the general feeling that the proposals for a hard-core or two-tier Europe were designed in order to bypass Britain, Labour could also be expected to oppose such proposals. Indeed, it was party policy to end the prime example of differentiated integration within the existing treaty framework, i.e. the social chapter opt-out. Further differentiated integration would undermine the party objective of taking Britain into the EU mainstream.

Conclusion: Blair's Inheritance

An examination of party policy statements in the early 1990s thus appeared to give credence to the view that Labour would approach the IGC under the Blair leadership with a more pragmatic and pro-European approach than that of the Conservative government. Furthermore, on issues related to the need to bring the EU closer to its citizens such as democratising decision-making, anti-discrimination, the social chapter and employment, the Blair leadership had inherited a set of positions that was close to the centre of gravity of political opinion within the EU, and the PES in particular, and which differed markedly from the Conservatives' negative approach. On a number of other IGC issues, particularly those related to improving the efficiency of decision-making, Labour's position in 1994 was less clear. However, Labour did not appear to be alone among the PES parties in this respect. The PES manifesto for the 1994 EP elections carried a similar ambiguity on a number of issues, omitting references to vote reweighting, Commission streamlining, CFSP and JHA communitisation, common European defence and differentiated integration. This appeared to be a reflection of the lack of consensus within the PES on these issues, where there was a tendency for the PES parties to reflect the traditional approaches and interests of their respective member states. Nevertheless, the general consensus that existed among the PES parties on the more 'ideological' issues relating to democracy, transparency, citizens' rights, social and employment policies and matters relating to general economic orientation was of considerable significance, as the pressure to place these issues on the IGC agenda tended to come from the member states where PES parties were in government (Lightfoot and Wilde 1996). However, these were generally the smaller states, the only exception being Spain, where the socialist PSOE held office until electoral defeat in 1996. Opposition to this progressive social democratic agenda tended to come from the centre-right governments who held sway in the major member states in the early 1990s. In particular, the British Conservatives were joined in their opposition to the employment chapter by the German government, while the French Gaullists, who had inflicted a crushing defeat on the Socialists in the 1993 National Assembly elections and would also regain the French presidency in 1995, shared British government reservations over greater transparency in decision-making and an enhanced role for the EP (Szukala and Wessels 1997: 93-94, Story 1997: 26-27).

The lack of consensus within the PES as regards some aspects of the developing IGC agenda would provide a political space for the Blair leadership to exploit in order to influence its common position. Labour's ability to do this was strengthened by its performance in the 1994 EP elections, the new relationship of mutual respect that had developed between Labour and its PES colleagues in the latter stages of the Kinnock leadership and under the Smith leadership, and the growing expectation in Britain and across the EU that Labour under Blair would win a British general election expected to take place in either 1996 or 1997. All these factors had led to an acceptance of the Labour party as a serious player in the treaty review. Labour's leverage within the PES group in the EP and within the EP overall had been considerably strengthened following the 1994 EP election. Its 62 MEPs made it the largest single national grouping in both the PES group and the EP overall. This was reflected in the election of Pauline Green, previously leader of the EPLP, to the leadership of the whole PES group. Her status within the PES would be of particular value to the Blair leadership as it formulated its IGC strategy.

Labour's position within the PES offered it opportunities for engagement with the developing IGC agenda, just as the Conservative government appeared to be disengaging from it. But in a number of areas, the Labour party's approach to the EU bore a strong resemblance to that of the Conservatives and reflected traditional British European or foreign policy objectives. Both parties placed an emphasis on the need for enlargement to the east to be an EU priority, for subsidiarity in policy-making and for radical reform of the CAP. Moreover, in stressing the primacy of NATO and the Atlantic alliance in European security and thus opposing proposals for a separate EU defence role, Labour seemed to be reflecting the traditional post-war assumptions of the British policy-making establishment (Bulmer 1992). Nevertheless, Labour's European policy documents in the early 1990s were imbued with a social democratic perspective on the EU which differed sharply from the traditional British and Conservative approach. This related back to one of the factors in the conversion of elements within the Labour party to a pro-European position in the 1980s: i.e. a recognition that certain socialist or social democratic objectives could no longer be realised at the national level and that the EC offered a potential framework for the necessary co-ordinated international action to achieve them. Thus *Prosperity Through Co-operation* referred to an internationalised world economy, in which 'the forces which should manage its operation and intervene to ensure competitive fairness, to control excess, and protect the vulnerable are not well organised.' Furthermore, it called for 'strong European political structures' to provide a 'means to ensure that transnational companies do not abuse their situation...to ensure that international economic success for some is not bought with monopolistic practices or at the price of a ruined environment, or an exploited workforce, or at the expense of those regions and people less able to fend for themselves...(and) so that the people of the Community can use their collective power to ensure that Europe moves in the direction that they want and not solely in the direction determined by international commercial forces' (Labour Party 1993b: 47). The emphasis that both *Prosperity Through Co-operation* and the 1994 EP election manifesto placed on European economic co-ordination and a European recovery programme with active policies to promote employment and the promotion of real economic convergence to ensure the sustainability of the EMU project reflected this social democratic conception of the EU, on which Labour occupied common ground with its PES colleagues (Ladrech 2000: 63-80).

Whether this radical social democratic approach to the EU would fit in with the new political approach pursued by Blair and his collaborators in the creation of New Labour was not certain in 1994. The Blair leadership would be characterised by a concerted drive to hasten the modernisation of the party's organisation and policy programme launched by Kinnock. The adoption of a more pragmatic and centrist policy approach under Blair would take Labour beyond the moderate European social democratic revisionism elaborated under his two predecessors. This would have clear implications for Labour's EU policy. Furthermore, the centralisation of policy-making that would take place under Blair, in which the formulation of party policy would become increasingly concentrated within the leader's private office, would also condition the development of the party's line on the IGC. The leader's office would seek to keep a tight rein over the formation of such a sensitive policy in the run-up to the expected general election of 1996 or 1997. Policy-making would increasingly be subordinated to the requirements of electoral politics as the Blair leadership constructed a political machinery ruthlessly devoted to ensuring electoral victory, and to which long-standing policy objectives would sometimes be sacrificed (Leys 1997: 20-21). Nevertheless, the transformation of Labour into a pro-European party in the 1980s and early 1990s appeared to be genuine, as did its willingness to engage positively with the emerging treaty reform agenda within the EU, in a spirit of co-operation with its PES colleagues. This climate of engagement and co-operation was at its strongest among Labour MEPs, who had gained a new influence within the Labour hierarchy in the early 1990s and were now in a position to play a central role in the PES (George and Haythorne 1996: 116-119). An understanding of the interaction of both these Europeanising influences and the electoral pressures which exerted a more pragmatic and negative influence on party policy, within the general context of the political transformation of the party effected by the Blair leadership, is central to an assessment of the development and nature of IGC policy by the then Labour opposition.

Notes

[1] The *acquis communautaire* refers to the entire weight of primary and secondary European legislation (i.e. the treaties and all regulations, directives and rulings deriving from them).

[2] EFTA was an intergovernmental organisation formed in 1959 with the aim of developing a free trade area amongst its members (Denmark, Sweden, Norway, Portugal, Switzerland, Austria and the UK). It had been promoted by the Macmillan government as a rival to the EEC and as a means to induce the EEC to liberalise its trade with Britain and the rest of Western Europe.

[3] Those left-wing MPs, such as Eric Heffer, who had previously continued to support EC membership as the first stage to a united socialist 'third force' Europe had by the early 1970s changed their mind. Heffer himself would cite the economic disadvantages of EC membership, and in particular the CAP, as the reason for his change of mind (see Robins 1979: 85n). Heffer would become a prominent figure within the anti-European Bennite faction that so influenced Labour's agenda in the early 1980s.

[4] Tindale cites Denis McShane (later to become a Labour MP and foreign office minister), who argued in 1988 that: 'to seek to implement policies without the fullest reference to what is happening beyond national borders (assuming one is not prepared to seal off the country in some authoritarian fashion) is to invite disaster, as the French discovered.' Alternatively, other anti-marketeers disputed the implications of the French experience. For example, Tindale cites Peter Shore, who argued that the wrong lessons were drawn: 'the French had expanded their economy too fast, and what had ruined their chances was the system of fixed exchange rates' to which he and other anti-marketeers were opposed (1992: 283).

[5] For example, one Labour left-winger, Brian Sedgemore (a member of the House of Commons Treasury Select Committee and formerly close to Benn) in explaining his conversion to pro-Europeanism stated: 'we don't want the next Labour Chancellor behaving like Denis Healey, waking up every morning sweating with fear lest international currency speculators were once again going to take him for a ride' (cited in Tindale 1992; 280).

[6] Stuart Holland was formerly an economist and adviser to Harold Wilson. He later resigned his seat to take up a professorship at the European University Institute in Florence, while working on a European recovery programme with Jacques Delors.

[7] Anderson and Mann cite Kinnock's economic advisor, John Eatwell, as summing up Labour's changed approach in 1992. He argued that it was no longer possible to have

Keynesianism in one country, and that rather, such macro-economic management should be replaced by a search for macro-economic stability as a framework for long-term investment while embracing the EC positively as the arena in which Labour's objectives could best be attained (1997: 72).

[8] This superseded the Liaison Bureau of the Socialist Parties of the EC formed in 1957 to coincide with the formation of the EEC.

[9] Labour's national share of the vote was 39 per cent to the Conservatives' 34 per cent - the first time since 1974 that Labour had recorded a higher share of the vote than the Conservatives in a nationwide election.

[10] The membership of the 'Britain and the World' group included in its membership David Martin MEP, a highly pro-European leader sandwiched between two highly Euro-sceptic leaders of the EPLP, Alf Lomas and Barry Seal, during the 1984-1989 EP term. Martin also authored a number of the reports adopted by the EP on the Maastricht treaty. He argues that following the policy review, the Labour party, in 1991, adopted the substance of his proposals in its European policy document: *Opportunity Britain: Labour's Policy on Europe* (Martin 1992, Labour Party 1991a).

[11] Article 138a of the TEU states: 'Political Parties at the European level are an important factor for integration within the Union. They contribute to forming a European awareness and to expressing the political will of the citizens of the Union.'

[12] In the discussions leading up to the formation of the PES, Kinnock disappointed Labour MEPs and colleagues in other European socialist parties by vetoing a proposal that decisions on policy in the new transnational party be taken by QMV where they related to an EC competence. Only the leaders of the Labour party and the Danish social democrats had opposed this proposal among the founding PES members (see George and Rosamund 1992: 183).

[13] Such was the desire of the Labour leadership to demonstrate its fiscal and monetary rectitude that it publicly supported efforts to maintain sterling at the parity at which it had joined in 1990: 2.95 Deutschmark to the pound - seen as high at the time and increasingly unsustainable by most economists. Thatcher had insisted on this high level after being persuaded to join in 1990. Both the Conservative government and the Labour opposition publicly refused to countenance a devaluation of sterling within the ERM up to Black Wednesday. Its acquiescence in this bipartisan position severely undermined the capacity of the Labour leadership to exploit this disastrous episode. Nevertheless, Anderson and Mann argue that while this was the official public line, had it won the 1992 election, Labour planned to seek a realignment of currencies within the ERM as soon as it took office (1997: 87).

[14] Smith defeated Bryan Gould by an overwhelming margin in the 1992 leadership election. Gould had been critical of aspects of Labour's pro-European policy, and in particular its support for membership of the ERM. Between 1987 and 1989, Gould had, as the party's trade and industry spokesman, been highly critical of the suggestion that Britain join the ERM. He was removed from this high profile economic role at the end of 1989, shortly after Labour declared for ERM membership, and replaced by Gordon Brown, previously Smith's deputy as treasury spokesman. Gould's anger at the refusal of the Labour leadership, and Brown (promoted to shadow chancellor in 1992) in particular, to acknowledge that this policy had been misguided, even with hindsight, led to his resignation from the shadow cabinet a few weeks after Black Wednesday (Anderson and Mann 1997: 82-88).

[15] Though Anderson and Mann suggest that Labour discarded the PES manifesto in 1994, this was not strictly true. It remained signed up to the PES manifesto and its own manifesto

did not contradict the positions in the PES manifesto. However, the Labour manifesto played up the pragmatism of its positions, and downplayed some of the more radical positions agreed within the PES.

[16] In an analysis of the Kinnock policy review in 1992, Martin Smith argued that the view it elaborated 'of the state, equality and the role of the market-place' was 'within the context of social democracy and not the New Right.' Labour had 'not adopted the position of the New Zealand Labour Party or some US Democrats of accepting a New Right economic policy within the framework of a liberal social policy' and was therefore 'ideologically closer to revisionism than Thatcherism' (1992:25). However, the positioning of 'New Labour' under Blair could be characterised as representing such a shift to this New Right economics plus liberal social policy position. Colin Leys suggests that although the modernisers around Blair saw themselves as carrying forward Kinnock's organisational initiatives 'in terms of ideology they represented something new.' Thus while Kinnock had sought to make the party electable, he 'never wholly abandoned the idea that capitalism was unjust.' Blair, on the other hand embraced capitalism as inevitable and beneficial and sought to make Labour 'the party of business' (1997: 19-20).

[17] The development of Labour's liberal position on civil rights was particularly associated with Roy Jenkins' two periods as Home Secretary (1965-67 and 1974-76) in the Wilson governments. Though the Callaghan government was severely criticised by the libertarian left of the Labour party for its lurch towards regressive measures on civil liberties at the end of the 1970s, the liberal approach was restored by Roy Hattersley as shadow home secretary and then deputy-leader in the 1980s (Anderson and Mann 1997: 231-242).

[18] The playing down of the significance of Labour's constitutional reform programme was exemplified by Blair's comparison between the tax raising powers of its proposed Scottish parliament with that of an English parish council (Anderson and Mann 1997: 287).

[19] Blair's European policy was described in a biography by John Rentoul as being 'as unsatisfactory as Major's, a rhetorical look both ways' (Rentoul 1995: 441).

[20] The co-operation procedure was introduced by the SEA for most single market provisions and granted the EP the right to put forward amendments to legislative proposals which, provided they had the support of the European Commission, could only be overturned by the Council of Ministers by unanimity. The codecision procedure introduced by the TEU for a limited number of areas granted the EP a stronger role, giving it the right to both amend proposed legislation, as in the co-operation procedure, and to ultimately veto legislation if it could not come to an agreement with the Council on its final form (Duff 1997a: 59-60).

[21] The 1991 Labour party conference had, however, passed a resolution in support of 'co-decision making between the European Parliament and the Council of Ministers' (Martin 1992).

[22] German political leaders generally viewed the extension of the EP's powers as part of a process of extending the German federal system to the EU as a whole. However, French politicians, who were reluctant to extend the EP's powers, suspected that Germany wanted to extend EP powers as a way of extending its own relative influence within the EU, given that Germany had a higher number of MEPs than the other large states and German political parties played a highly influential role in both of the main political groupings in the EP (i.e. the PES and the EPP). The German CDU was particularly dominant within the EPP, whereas the French governing Gaullist party sat in a smaller centre-right 'Union for Europe' (UPE) grouping detached from the EPP (Story 1997: 26-27). German representatives were not so dominant within the PES, given that the German SPD members were outnumbered by the EPLP members. The fact that the British electoral system gave a disproportionate number of EP seats to the Labour party, despite their having been voted for by a smaller

proportion of the EU population than the SPD, rankled with the latter, and was a factor in explaining Germany's strong support for a uniform (proportional) electoral system for the EP.

[23] Hence, the Council and the EP were often subjected to derision for the time they devoted to legislation on the noise level of lawnmowers, for example.

[24] These included the rights elaborated in the original Treaty of Rome to free movement of labour (art. 48), equal treatment for men and women (art. 119) and non-discrimination on the basis of nationality between EC nationals (art. 7). These had been further enhanced by the SEA, which bestowed a general right of free movement of persons (art. 8a), and the TEU, which established EU citizenship for all member state citizens (art 8), incorporating the existing free movement rights and introducing voting rights in EP and local elections for all EU citizens resident in a member state other than their own (O'Leary 1996).

[25] The ECJ ruled in March 1996 that the EC could not accede to the ECHR without treaty amendment and expressed concerns about incorporating a separate international legal order into the EU system (Dinan 1999: 302).

[26] The Swedish representative in the Reflection Group, the foreign affairs minister, Gunner Lund, presented a proposal for an employment chapter to the Reflection Group on 1 September 1995.

[27] Germany also saw stronger co-operation on policing to combat international crime as a potential means of increasing the popularity of the EU (Moravcsik and Nicolaidis 1998: 28-29).

[28] The Schengen agreements provided for the removal of internal frontier controls between signatory countries and the development of common external frontiers policies and flanking measures on internal security. The signatories of the initial agreement in 1985 were West Germany, France and the Benelux countries. By 1997, all EU member states except for Britain and Ireland had joined (Duff 1997a: 131-132).

[29] A reweighting would also raise the sensitive question of the need for Germany to have more weighted votes than the other large states if the system was to truly reflect differences in population size.

[30] The 1991 policy document, *Opportunity Britain* had, ahead of the Maastricht treaty, called for the extension of QMV in this area (Labour party 1991a, Martin 1992).

[31] The WEU built on the mutual defence alliance established by the Brussels Treaty in 1948 between Britain, France and the Benelux countries. The WEU was established following a British initiative in 1955, incorporating West Germany into the West European mutual defence arrangements, whilst providing a means to simultaneously provide for West German rearmament and assuage fears aroused by the prospect of this rearmament by locking West German forces into a broader West European military framework. Its tasks were effectively superseded by NATO during the cold war and it appeared to be an obsolete organisation until it was entrusted with the implementation of defence and military aspects of the CFSP by the TEU. With the exception of Denmark, the full members of the WEU were those members of the EU who were also members of NATO (see van Ham 1997).

[32] The Major government did form a tactical alliance with the Italian government in the run-up to Maastricht. The two governments submitted a joint paper stipulating the primacy of NATO in European security. The substance of this position was incorporated into the TEU. However, as with most of the other NATO members within the EU, the Italians were likely to support a further development of a European defence role provided that NATO primacy was respected (Tsakaloyannis 1997: 152, Young, JW 2000: 154-155). The position of France differed, as it had not taken part in NATO's integrated military structure since the 1960s and it had traditionally sought the development of a European defence identity which was autonomous of the North Atlantic alliance.

[33] Nevertheless, the support given by the Foot leadership to the British action to retake the Falkland Islands following the Argentinian invasion in 1982 demonstrated that Labour had not totally abandoned bipartisan consensus, nor had it fully embraced pacifism.

[34] Labour's commitment to unilateral nuclear disarmament in 1983 remained ambiguous. In addition to the closure of all American nuclear bases in the UK, the position involved entering the existing UK Polaris nuclear weapons system into arms controls talks, with a view to negotiating the system away within five years. However, Denis Healey, the party's foreign affairs spokesman and deputy-leader in 1983, suggested that if a Labour government was unable to obtain a bilateral arms control deal with the Soviets, trading off the UK arsenal for part of the Soviet one, then its nuclear weapons system would have to remain in operation. Contrary to this, Foot argued that the Polaris system had to be dismantled whether or not a deal was struck with the Soviets (thus rendering the British negotiating position in arms control talks meaningless). Labour's policy also involved working to turn NATO into a non-nuclear alliance, with the implication that a Labour government would withdraw the UK from NATO if this failed. Though the unilateralist commitment was retained in 1987, Labour's support for NATO was emphasised. Labour was also pledged to used the savings generated from the non-nuclear policy to reinforce spending on conventional forces. However, there were still ambiguities: Kinnock suggested that rather than remove American nuclear (cruise) missiles from UK bases immediately, a Labour government would make this commitment dependent on the progress of US-Soviet discussions on nuclear weapons reductions (Croft 1992: 203-208).

[35] Moravcsik and Nicolaidis explain that strengthening the mechanisms for co-operation in CFSP was of particular importance to Germany, as it had a far less viable unilateral foreign policy than France or the UK (1998: 24).

[36] External representation of the EU in relation to the CFSP was conducted through the Council presidency, which rotated between the member states on a six-monthly basis. A practice had developed whereby, in activities related to the CFSP, the member state holding the Council presidency would be assisted by the two member states holding the previous and next presidency respectively. This rotating 'troika' system had been criticised for providing a lack of continuity in external representation. Hence the French government suggestion that a high profile Mr/Ms CFSP be created to provide some continuity in external representation (Duff 1997a: 84-85).

Chapter 3

The Leader's Working-Group on the IGC

The Challenge Facing Blair

While the domestic political climate into which his leadership was thrust was the most visible difficulty confronting Blair in relation to the task of achieving a credible Labour party position on the 1996 IGC, he was also faced with separate and conflicting pressures on the framing of policy, which would have an effect both on the timetable in which policy decisions would need to be taken and the parameters within which the substance of policy would need to be defined. More specifically, a number of political actors connected to the Labour party would be exerting pressures on party policy to move in an opposite direction from that which the domestic political environment appeared to demand. Not only was an agenda for IGC reform fast developing across the EU institutions and member states, but these political actors were already developing their positions in response to this agenda, and indeed helping to shape it themselves. Of most relevance to the Labour party, was that its own MEPs were involved in the formulation of both the PES group position within the EP (and had a particular influence as the largest national grouping in the PES group) and the overall EP position (with the PES group particularly influential as the largest political group in the EP). Furthermore, Labour's sister parties in the PES, many of them in government, were formulating their positions on the IGC and pressure was developing for the adoption of a joint PES position. In addition, the Trade Union Congress (TUC) and its European counterpart, the European Trade Union Confederation (ETUC), were also in the process of adopting positions, which Labour's affiliated trade unions would accordingly feel obliged to adopt.

The risk for the Labour party was that its connection to these political actors would lead to the party being associated with the positions adopted by them and that these positions would be undesirable in the context of the domestic political environment. The priority for Blair, therefore, would be to develop a structure of policy-making which could respond rapidly to this developing agenda, allowing the Labour party leadership to take control of the development of the general policy line with which it would be associated, and to influence the development of the policy positions of these connected political actors to prevent them from developing in an 'undesirable' direction vis a vis the domestic political situation. A forceful top-down approach to policy-making was desired in order to avoid running the risk, should an absence of preparation continue, of policy positions being attributed to the Labour party (most likely by its opponents in the press and the government) based on statements by connected actors. This would most likely have led to the undesirable scenario of the Labour leadership being 'bounced' into either adopting these positions or conversely making a decision to renounce such positions and, in reaction, instead adopting a nationalistic policy (akin to that of the Conservative government) tailored simply to domestic political considerations.

Blair became acutely aware of these difficulties in the weeks following his assumption of the leadership. The development of a coherent and attractive European policy would be an integral element of Blair's long term strategy as he prepared the party for the next general election. This strategy involved presenting the Labour party positively as a party of government in possession of a credible set of policies as an alternative to those of the Conservative government. An incoherent or 'soft' position on Europe would severely jeopardise the potential success of this strategy. This was particularly the case given the imminence of the IGC and its likely coincidence with the general election. It would therefore become clear to Blair that one of the key, and perhaps most politically sensitive policy areas for the Labour party as it sought to present itself as a party of government would be the positions it would have to adopt in relation to the IGC. These positions would need to reflect a sensible and pragmatic Europeanism (in contrast to the destructive isolationism of the Conservatives) whilst also being robust enough to fend off Conservative attempts to play the national card for domestic political purposes.

The Establishment of the Leader's Working-Group on the IGC

The initial response of the Labour leadership to the conflicting pressures on policy development was to establish the leader's working-group on the IGC (LWG). This was based on a proposal outlined on 9 September 1994 in a letter from Jack Cunningham to Blair. Cunningham had held the post of shadow foreign secretary under John Smith's leadership and continued to do so until October 1994, when Blair allocated new roles to the shadow cabinet he had largely inherited. The letter proposed the establishment of a small working-group with the status of a 'leader's committee' responsible to Blair to examine how the party should prepare for the IGC.

A Labour party policy commission on foreign affairs, serviced by the international department at party headquarters, already existed and had co-ordinated work on previous party European documents. But Cunningham's letter proposed that the working-group have a remit separate to and a membership distinct from the foreign affairs policy commission, although membership would to some extent overlap. It was proposed that the party's international department would service the leader's committee, and that the committee would comprise representatives of the leader's office, the foreign affairs, treasury, home affairs and employment shadow ministerial teams and the EPLP and possibly staff from the PES group in the EP. Cunningham proposed that the leader's committee both agree the main principles of Labour's approach to the IGC and produce a series of clear policy proposals on the IGC issues. Although Cunningham's letter gave due recognition to the influential contribution that the EPLP and PES group in Brussels would make to the development of party policy and acknowledged the need for their close involvement in the work of the proposed committee, he also added a note of caution, emphasising the need for the party leadership in London to maintain control of IGC policy formulation:

> ...given that some members of the EPLP have in the past pursued a somewhat different agenda to our own, it is particularly important that our input into the policy development process is seen to be primary, and that the EPLP is seen to be working within our policy development structures. The European policy of the party clearly needs to be Westminster led and not Strasbourg led' (LP Cunningham, 9 September 1994).

While most aspects of the thinking outlined in Cunningham's letter on the structure of IGC policy-making would be pursued by Blair, Cunningham would not play a key role himself. Cunningham was moved 'sideways' to the trade and industry (DTI) brief in Blair's shadow cabinet reshuffle of October 1994. Indeed, Cunningham effectively swapped briefs with Robin Cook, previously DTI spokesman, who now assumed the post of shadow foreign secretary. Cook's appointment could possibly have been interpreted as a shift towards a more pragmatic stance on EU policy and away from the pronounced Euro-enthusiasm of the Smith leadership. Both Smith and Cunningham had been viewed as firm Euro-philes, and this had been reflected in the party statements on the EU between 1992 and 1994. Cook on the other hand was viewed as one of the more prominently Euro-sceptical members of the Shadow Cabinet. While Blair may have been partly motivated by the need for Labour to adopt a more pragmatic stance on the EU in the run-up to the general election in the light of the domestic political climate, the appointment of Cook was more likely motivated by reasons of party management, i.e. the need to place Cook in a post commensurate with his status in the party[1] while simultaneously keeping him away from the key economic briefs, given the antipathy of both Blair and his close ideological ally, the shadow chancellor, Gordon Brown, to Cook's 'soft-left' Keynesian views (Wickham-Jones 2000: 105-106).[2]

Another significant change made by Blair to the Labour party hierarchy was his decision to ask Larry Whitty to step down from the post of party general-secretary, after nine years in the job. Blair then assigned Whitty to the newly created post of European co-ordinator to the leader's office, working directly for Blair, and his deputy John Prescott, in the House of Commons. One of Whitty's key responsibilities would be to co-ordinate Labour's position for the IGC. The creation of a European co-ordinator directly responsible to his office was perhaps an indication of the importance that Blair attached to policy-making in relation to the IGC. It was also an important indication of the shift in policy-making in the party away from the policy directorate in party headquarters at Walworth Road (Cunningham had suggested that the working-group be serviced by the international department at Walworth Road) and towards Blair's private office. Blair's leadership would be characterised by the centralisation of policy-making in his own private office, which in terms of staff numbers would be unprecedented for a leader of the opposition.

It was intended by Blair that Whitty would work closely with Prescott in this new role. Amongst his other responsibilities, Blair had given Prescott the role of liaison with Labour's sister parties. Prescott would be the senior Labour party representative on the PES bureau, and would be appointed as a PES vice-president. However, in practice, much of the liaison with the PES and its component parties would be undertaken by Whitty, as Prescott's representative. One interpretation of the European roles given to both Whitty and Prescott (along with the role on the EU that Cook would obviously play as foreign affairs spokesman) was that Blair was deliberately giving European policy responsibilities to those senior figures within the party (i.e. Cook, Prescott, Whitty) whom he wanted to keep out of the way of the major reforms he intended to undertake of key aspects of party policy thinking, particularly on the economy, and of the internal Labour party structure. In the case of party reforms, it would be difficult to prevent Prescott as deputy-leader from having an influence, but in general, the new responsibilities given to Cook, Prescott and Whitty meant that they would be out of the country quite a lot, and also 'out of the loop' in relation to the adjustment of social and economic policy which was seen as central to Labour's success at the next general election.

Whitty's appointment as European co-ordinator was certainly seen by many as a consolation for being removed from the key post of party general-secretary. His appointment was viewed with cynicism by some who doubted whether it would amount to a real job. However, Whitty himself was treating his new post extremely seriously and quickly set about acclimatising himself to his new responsibilities and familiarising himself with the issues to be reviewed at the IGC, the tight constraints that the party had to work within, and the pressures that were likely to be exerted on policy-making. The speed with which Whitty came to grips with these matters was evident in the memo he sent to Blair, Cook and Prescott on 1 November 1994 recommending that a working-group responsible to Blair (i.e. the LWG) be established with immediate effect, along the lines set out in Cunningham's letter.

Whitty echoed Cunningham's concern that the party should avoid having its policy-making led by Brussels/Strasbourg, particularly through Labour's representatives in the EP, and also expressed alarm at the scope of the IGC positions that would have to be agreed upon by the party in a short space of time. In particular, he expressed concern at 'the speed with which developments are taking place in Parliament (EP), PES group and ETUC which could "lock in" the EPLP and/or leading members of it and affiliated trade unions to a position very early in 1995.' The memo expressed the fear that such a positioning could both pre-empt Labour's policy-making and/or differ from the position that the Labour party would wish to take politically in respect of a possible 1996 general election in which the Tories were likely to play the nationalist card. Indeed, Whitty emphasised his concern that both the TUC position via the ETUC, and the EPLP via both the PES group and the overall EP position, would be considerably more 'federalist' than the position the party would want to adopt, particularly in the run-up to the general election. Furthermore, he explained that his initial reading of documents from the PES group and from the TUC/ETUC had indicated that this was highly likely.

The tight timetable within which the LWG would have to work was outlined in a note attached to the memo. It explained that preparatory work by the governments of the EU member states would begin in July 1995, through the Reflection Group of foreign ministers' representatives. The Reflection Group would also include the president of the European Commission and two representatives of the EP. At this stage there was a possibility that given his status as vice-president of the EP and having been rapporteur for EP reports on the TEU, David Martin, a former leader of the EPLP and a vice-president of the EP,[3] could be one of the EP representatives. In addition, all the institutions of the EU had been asked to prepare a report on the functioning of the TEU in advance of the commencement of the work of the Reflection Group. The duration of the Reflection Group itself would be six months, reporting at the end of 1995. In preparation for the Reflection Group, the EP would be producing its report by around May or June of 1995. Again there was a chance that David Martin would be rapporteur, and consequently, the note warned, there was a possibility that the position of a highly federalist MEP would be identified with the Labour party. It would be important that, by then, the party was seen to have developed a clear and distinct position. When the time came, Martin did, as predicted, become co-rapporteur for the EP's report, but he did not become the EP's Reflection Group or IGC representative.

Partly in anticipation of the formulation of the general EP position, the PES group within the EP had already established a working-group on the IGC. This was chaired by the French socialist MEP, Elisabeth Guigou, who had been the French government minister for Europe at the time of the Maastricht negotiations. Pauline Green, as leader of the PES group, Wayne David, as leader of the EPLP, and David Martin would be members of this working-group (Guigou, rather than Martin, would later be put forward by the PES group as one of the EP representatives in the Reflection Group and IGC). A preliminary report to the PES group was expected to emerge from this working-group by December 1994. Therefore, there would be very little time left for the Labour party to influence the report. It was expected that the working-group report would form the basis of the position of the PES group as a whole. Thus, as with the EP position, the note warned that a British Labour MEP, Pauline Green as leader of the PES group, would be identified with a potentially federalist document. Discussion at the first LWG meeting would stress that it would be vital that all sides kept in touch and that potentially damaging differences were minimised.

The EPLP was also seeking to establish a working-group on the IGC and was calling for a Labour party/EPLP liaison group on the issue, but the LWG would take on this function. Furthermore, the PES Bureau meeting of 15-16 September 1994 had also agreed to establish a working-group on the IGC. It had been requested that each party leader designate a 'political representative' to be a member of it and Labour's European spokeswoman, Joyce Quin had been accordingly designated by the Labour party. Whitty suggested that he should also become a member of this working-group. A preliminary report was expected to emanate from it in time for the PES Congress in Barcelona on 6-8 March 1995, and would at the least, outline a number of strategic positions in relation to the IGC.

In addition to all these groups, Labour's unique organisational basis, involving the affiliation of the key trade unions in the UK, meant that the position taken by the individual trade unions, the TUC, and the ETUC, would be of special significance to the party. Whitty's note explained that the ETUC, as one of the 'social partners', would be consulted by the Reflection Group. Trade union input would also come through the report of the Economic and Social Committee[4] on the functioning of the TEU. The executive committee of the ETUC was aiming to produce a statement on the IGC and the functioning of the TEU by March 1995, in good time for the ETUC congress of May 1995. In order to input into this, the TUC would be putting forward an initial position by December 1994. It would also be producing a report for the annual TUC congress in September 1995. This meant that, in terms of influencing the TUC, there was little time available for the LWG. The note explained that there were difficulties in the TUC adopting an official position on the IGC, because Labour's affiliated trade unions would be tempted to identify with it, and put pressure on the party to do so as well. A TUC working-group on the IGC had already been set up in the summer of 1994, with Green, David and Nick Sigler (international officer at Labour headquarters) as members. Prescott and Whitty had also been invited to join. There were a number of organisational forums within which the Labour leadership could seek to influence TUC policy development on the IGC, most notably the 'contact group', set up in 1987 as a means of liaison between the Labour leadership and the most powerful trade union leaders (Anderson and Mann 1997: 313). Whitty suggested that given the advanced nature of TUC policy-making on the IGC, particularly when compared to that of the Labour party, the issue be given special attention through the 'contact group' (LP Whitty, 1 November 1994).

A picture thus emerges of a plethora of overlapping working-groups, formulating policy on the IGC, with the Labour party somewhere at their centre but not, as yet, in control. Most of these groups were well in advance of the Labour party in terms of formulating a position. The challenge for Labour was to develop a distinct position of its own and, rather than get locked in to the position of the other groups, establish a clear and coherent set of policies on the IGC and, given Labour's position in relation to each, exercise a hegemonic influence over the formulation of policy of each of these interconnected political actors. The establishment of the LWG with a broad membership, in which the views of the EP, the PES group, the PES, the EPLP and the TUC/ETUC could be reflected and through which a number of representatives could act as interlocutors, mediating between the Labour position and the position of these connected actors, was an attempt by Labour to assert a degree of control in this process. It was hoped that Labour would not only return to government in 1996 or 1997 and shape the final treaty outcome, but that it could indirectly influence the shaping of the IGC agenda while still in opposition through its connection to these other political actors, many of who were directly involved in the agenda-setting process.

Whitty as European co-ordinator would have the key role in implementing this strategy. The role given to Whitty in co-ordinating IGC policy-making on behalf of the leader's office was an important shift from Cunningham's original proposal that policy-making be co-ordinated by the international department at Walworth Road. A further subtle shift in emphasis from Cunningham's proposal can perhaps be discerned in the proposed membership of the LWG set out in Whitty's memo, which involved a greater degree of involvement for Labour's representatives in the EP. These Labour MEP's would act as valuable interlocutors between policy-making in the national party and the development of positions on the IGC in Labour's sister parties, the PES group and the EP in general. Their inclusion in the membership of the LWG indicated a recognition by the Labour leadership of this potential value. The proposed membership included Wayne David and Christine Crawley, leader and deputy-leader of the EPLP respectively, Pauline Green as leader of the PES group and David Martin as vice-president and institutional affairs rapporteur of the EP. The inclusion of the latter two would ensure that the views of both the PES group and the EP as a whole would be inputted directly into policy-making. The inclusion of all four was also useful for the Labour party leadership in ensuring that the party line, as it became formulated, would be fully understood and accepted by its representatives in the EP. Indeed, the inclusion of key EPLP figures in the working-group could be interpreted as a way of keeping them under the control of the party's policy development structure, as was Jack Cunningham's original concern.

The terms of reference and membership of the LWG were agreed at its first meeting on 5 December 1994 (LWG1 Minutes). The agreed membership would be Blair, Prescott, Cook, Gordon Brown, George Robertson (then shadow Scottish secretary but former European spokesman), David, Crawley, Martin, Quin and Tom Sawyer, Whitty's successor as party general-secretary. The paper on LWG membership approved by the meeting explained that due to her role as leader of the PES group, Pauline Green would not be a formal member of the LWG, though she would attend its key meetings (this was a minor technical point, as Green would attend and fully participate in all subsequent meetings and would be treated as a full member). It was agreed that other frontbenchers or MEPs with special responsibilities or experience would be called in as necessary, while Whitty and Geoff Norris from the leader's office would act as the LWG secretariat. Support would also be provided by Sigler and the chief executive of the EPLP, Dianne Hayter. David Lea from the TUC would be kept informed (LWG IGC1B). Reports would be made as necessary to the shadow cabinet and the National Executive Committee (NEC) - the ruling body of the Labour party (LWG IGC1A).

The terms of reference of the LWG would be to produce a series of policy proposals on the IGC as set out in both Whitty's initial memo and the Cunningham letter. Accordingly, the broad remit of the LWG would be to produce 'two levels of documents': 1) an overall statement of the Labour party's position; and 2) a 'below the line' position on the individual items before the IGC (i.e. more detailed positions which would not necessarily be stated publicly). More specifically, this would involve addressing the following issues:

1) the application and extension of subsidiarity and the closing of the democratic deficit;

2) the development and evolution of the role and powers of the Commission, EP, and Council of Ministers;
3) the relationship between the national parliaments and the EP and other EU bodies such as the Committee of the Regions;
4) the future of the pillar structure and JHA and CFSP matters in particular;
5) the extension of EU competence;
6) the institutional implications of enlargement and of the changing nature of the EU.

Whitty cautioned that even modest reforms in these areas might go further than what some in the party and the public at large would accept (LP Whitty, 1 November 1994).

In addition to these issues, Whitty's memo had suggested that the LWG would need to take into account parallel developments on EMU. This view was supported at the first LWG meeting, where there was general agreement that though discussion on the EMU matters would be deferred until later, formulation of policy on EMU would be tied to policy on the IGC (LWG1 Minutes).

Following the agreement of the terms of reference of the LWG, there was a preliminary discussion at the first LWG meeting in which Blair made suggestions about how its work should proceed. There was agreement in this discussion that a 'two-level approach' to the IGC process was needed: first, a 'broad and positive' positioning 'on the kind of things the electorate would want from Europe': this would include social protection, employment, real convergence of economic performance, CAP reform and the tackling of the democratic deficit. A public position on enlargement and 'real subsidiarity' would also be needed. Secondly, a clear and more detailed position on the institutional issues and the future shape of the EU (LWG1 Minutes).

The Work of the LWG

The LWG met twelve times, over a period of twenty months between December 1994 and October 1996, with meetings becoming more infrequent as time progressed, particularly after the Labour party policy document on the IGC emerged from the LWG's deliberations in September 1995 (after eight meetings). In agreeing the broad policy positions on the range of IGC issues, and in many cases, more detailed 'below the line' positions on the key reform questions, the LWG represented the critical phase in party policy-making on the IGC in opposition.

The method by which decisions would be adopted on the key issues of reform became apparent in the early LWG meetings. Blair chaired the meetings, broadly directing its deliberations. Whitty co-ordinated the work of the LWG on Blair's behalf. Whitty drew up the agendas for the meetings, though these agendas generally reflected suggestions made by other members of the LWG, particularly Blair and Cook. Furthermore, Whitty drew up the minutes of each meeting and provided a private 'chair's note' for Blair outlining the agenda for each meeting and making suggestions about the preliminary positions that Blair himself, and the LWG as a whole, might want to take. These chair's notes were usually copied to Prescott and Blair's chief of staff, Jonathan Powell. Moreover, while Cook would define the broad political approach that Labour would pursue, as encapsulated by his strategy paper (LWG IGC2A) submitted to the second LWG meeting, it was Whitty who generally produced the initial internal party documents on the detailed 'horizontal' institutional questions before the IGC, both in terms of the broad principles to be pursued on these questions and the 'below the line' details of Labour's position. Whitty would also produce commentaries and recommend a party line in response to external developments, such as the publication of positions in the EU institutions.

The papers produced by Whitty generally reflected the line that Blair wanted to take, as they were produced following consultations within the leader's office. Whitty's papers were usually cleared in advance with Cook and with Powell or Norris as the leader's representatives. Because they had already been cleared in advance with the key figures, these papers were generally broadly endorsed. Nevertheless, there was conflict on some contentious issues, though, with the exception of JHA communitisation, the differences were generally of degree rather than principle (Interview with LWG participant).

This policy-making process begun in earnest at the second LWG meeting on 9 January 1995. Although there had been agreement at the first LWG meeting to Blair's proposal that Cook co-ordinate work for it, setting out the key issues on both levels of the LWG's work, the organisation of the second meeting generally reflected the pattern of all twelve meetings. Thus Whitty co-ordinated the work of it, and while Cook set about defining Labour's broad political approach (the first level of the LWG's work), Whitty set out the party's tentative position on the second level of the LWG's work, i.e. the detailed positioning on institutional issues, as well as more general principles on institutional reform.

The work of the LWG would be guided by the broad political approach that Cook took the lead in defining. This broad European agenda reflected the agreement at the first meeting that a first-level position needed to be defined setting out a positive approach 'on the kind of things the electorate would want from Europe.' The second LWG meeting saw agreement that Cook's political strategy paper, *Labour's European Agenda* (LWG IGC2A) should form the basis of the party's positioning on European policy issues. Cook identified six priority areas on which Labour should focus, all of which represented a continuity with previously held positions. These were: 1) the social dimension (involving signing up to the social chapter); 2) employment; 3) radical CAP reform; 4) democracy (involving greater openness and accountability to the EP and national parliaments); 5) subsidiarity; 6) enlargement (including support for the necessary changes to facilitate it). In relation to the first three, Labour's support for the incorporation of the social chapter and the development of the social dimension had been well documented publicly since the Maastricht summit of 1991 (George and Haythorne 1996: 112-118, Young, JW 2000: 175-176, Daniels 1998: 78-82), while an employment recovery programme and CAP reform did not necessarily require treaty reform at an IGC. In elucidating the first two of these priorities, Cook's paper was also notable for its radical redistributionist and Keynesian tone. For example, in relation to the first priority, Cook suggested that Europe should 'belong to its people and...not become the property of businessmen' and that the wealth of the single market should be used to 'increase the quality of life of the working people who make the goods.' These remarks were interesting given that they came at a time of debate within the Labour party over the replacement of the old clause IV of the party constitution (which referred to securing for the workers the full fruits of their labour). In relation to employment, Cook emphasised the need for a 'co-ordinated reflation strategy' and a European reconstruction fund, and for EMU convergence criteria based on the performance of the real economy, rather than purely monetary criteria.

In addition, the paper was marked by a rather disparaging and impatient tone towards the detailed complexities of the debate on institutional reform. Whitty's chair's note had stressed that Cook's paper was a key political strategy paper intended to ensure that the party had 'clear political and electorally popular positions' in its European stance, putting clear water between it and the government, rather that getting 'obsessed by constitutional and institutional issues' (LWG2 Chair's Note). The paper itself lamented that the agenda for the IGC was not of the party's choosing and was of a technical institutional nature 'which does not connect with the lives of the citizen' (LWG IGC2A). This was slightly disingenuous as two of the priorities identified by Cook necessarily implied institutional reform, i.e. increasing democratic accountability in the EU and changes to facilitate enlargement, and the case for institutional reform being made across the continent was generally based largely on these two priorities (McDonagh 1998: 151-154). The other priority, subsidiarity, was an issue emphasised by both government and opposition in the early 1990s, although the Labour party sought to distinguish its position on the issue from that of the government by emphasising the link with Labour's domestic devolution agenda (Tindale 1992: 285-288, Fella 2000).

Cook had recognised that six priorities might be 'too numerous' for public consumption and that the party therefore focus on three or four of them for public statements. There appeared to be general agreement to this, although Whitty's chair's note had suggested that environmental policy be added to the definitive list of party priorities. Thus when Cook outlined Labour's broad policy agenda publicly in a speech to the European Policy Institute on 30 January 1995 he pinpointed three priority areas: 1) signing Britain up to the social dimension; 2) CAP reform; and 3) employment. The speech again reflected Cook's Keynesian political leanings in his discussion of the social dimension and employment and his attempts to provide a social democratic justification of the EU as a 'democratic parallel to the global character of modern capital' (LWG IGC3A). This also echoed the reasoning provided by Labour politicians in the late 1980s for the party's pro-European conversion (Tindale 1992: 279-285). Furthermore, Cook continued to show disdain for the debate on institutional reform whilst acknowledging that enlargement would necessitate such reform and also stating support for measures to make the EU more open and democratic, again implying institutional change. The speech was also notable for Cook's strong rejection of any dilution of the intergovernmental nature of the CFSP and of proposals for the development of a common European defence under EU auspices.

While Cook was setting the general tone of Labour's Europe policy, Whitty was doing much of the spadework in terms of fleshing out Labour's policies on institutional reform. This was a process he began with the drafting and submission of a paper to the second LWG meeting setting out a suggested overall approach to institutional change (LWG IGC2B) in the EU, together with more detailed papers exploring and making tentative recommendations on the sensitive issues of the structure of the EU treaties (LWG IGC2C), on the extension of QMV in the Council (LWG IGC2D) and on the role of the EP (LWG IGC2E). The Labour leadership was aware that on these key issues, as with the institutional reform agenda in general, the EPLP was likely to hold more Euro-enthusiastic positions than its London based colleagues. The London leadership was therefore eager to 'flush-out' these differences at an early stage, in the privacy of the LWG confines. Thus in his chair's note for the second meeting, Whitty suggested that Blair emphasise that the discussion on institutional reform was a preliminary one 'so that everyone feels free to put their views and we identify any conflict, particularly between Westminster and European colleagues' (LWG2 Chair's Note).

Nevertheless, although the understanding was that the discussion on institutional issues was a preliminary one, the second LWG meeting saw agreement on a number of broad positions as regards the party's approach to institutional reform, on the basis of recommendations made in the various papers submitted by Whitty. Thus the party's broad approach (IGC2B) would involve support for the following:

1) Rationalisation of the competences and procedures of the EU institutions;
2) Increased democratic accountability and control both through the EP and national parliaments;
3) Enlargement to the east and to Cyprus and Malta and institutional changes to facilitate this;
4) Rendering the whole European process more accessible and comprehensible to the electorate;
5) A clearer and more explicit approach to subsidiarity, by which national and regional or local governments would undertake their appropriate functions, rather than the European institutions.

On three of these issues, i.e. increasing democratic accountability, enlargement, and the institutional reforms necessary for it, and subsidiarity, the broad principles overlapped with the distinct policy priorities set out by Cook (LWG IGC2A), though it would be Whitty who would undertake the detailed work of identifying how such principles would be put into practice. This overall approach to institutional change would also involve opposition to any significant new shift in power or competence from national governments and parliaments to EU institutions, and to any form of two-tier Europe, while acknowledging, in the light of enlargement, that variable geometry might be necessary, in terms of opt-outs or derogations, or of differential timetables. As regards the form of the treaty (LWG

IGC2C), while rejecting proposals for an EU constitution, the party would advocate a consolidated treaty spelling out 'the relative powers of the institutions and the member governments.' However, the minutes record that while the LWG endorsed Whitty's recommendation that Labour support retention of a separate intergovernmental CFSP pillar, it did not back his recommendation that the party support JHA communitisation. Rather, it was agreed that this matter be subject to 'further discussion.' Although discussion of the possible extensions of QMV in Council and on significantly enhancing the powers of the EP also took place in the second LWG meeting, with Whitty's papers (LWG IGC2D, IGC2E) recommending both, decisions on these issues were deferred to further meetings following requests for more detailed position papers on the subjects (LWG2 Minutes).

A number of key principles guiding the Labour party's position on institutional reform were thus set in place almost from the beginning of the life of the LWG. The scope for policy-making within the LWG was accordingly restricted by the parameters set by these principles, although these were, in a sense, a continuation of the general positions held prior to the establishment of the LWG and developed in response to the TEU under the Kinnock and Smith leaderships (Labour Party 1992, 1993b, 1994). The domestic political climate meant that any movement from these inherited general positions in a more pro-European direction appeared politically unrealistic for the Blair leadership, although movements in the opposite direction were also politically difficult given the consternation they would cause in the EPLP, PES and TUC.

A number of decisions on the key institutional reform questions were taken in the first few LWG meetings. Indeed, after just four meetings of the LWG and four months of work, a clear outline of policy was beginning to emerge. This involved rejection of CFSP communitisation (agreed at the second meeting), acceptance of QMV extension, accompanied by a detailed formulation of the areas in which such extension would be supported (agreed at the third meeting)[5] and acceptance of a greater role for the EP with codecision generally applying in parallel to QMV in Council (agreed at the fourth meeting).[6] In addition, the LWG had agreed on measures to simplify and clarify the decision-making process, including simplification and reduction of procedures[7] and a consolidation of the various EU/EC treaties. The pattern of policy-making in these areas was clear. Discussion of horizontal questions of institutional reform, e.g. the pillar structure and the role and powers of the various EC institutions and decision-making procedures, would be based on positions papers submitted to the LWG by Whitty. However, Cook would then give his overall assessment of what the policy line should be, based on the recommendations in Whitty's papers and the consequent discussion, and Cook's conclusions would generally be reflected in the agreed policy line. While the final decision on these matters would ultimately rest with Blair, these decisions generally reflected the line that had emerged in discussion, echoing Cook's conclusions. Blair would generally sit back and take in the discussion, querying the occasional point, contributing positively in a 'responsive' rather than a 'leading' way. Nevertheless, Blair would make it clear when he wished a particular line to be ruled out, or if he felt a particular issue required further examination. Furthermore, he would be obliged to intervene on contentious issues where the discussion was finely balanced between different points of view. Where such conflict did occur within the LWG, the dividing line generally fell between the EP representatives and some within the London based leadership. However, within the leadership, both Whitty, partly due to his close contact with the EPLP in his role as European co-ordinator, and Quin (a noted Euro-phile and former MEP) were generally more sympathetic to the more Euro-phile position of the EP representatives. Moreover, Blair himself, while being acutely aware of the domestic constraints placed on policy-making, was also more sympathetic to the pro-EU position than some of his key shadow cabinet colleagues, such as Prescott, Brown and the shadow home secretary, Jack Straw, and in some cases, where the argument within the LWG was finely balanced, came down in favour of the pro-EU position.[8] Furthermore, Cook would also move away from his earlier Euro-scepticism as he became immersed in the key issues of EU policy, becoming a powerful advocate of a more pro-European position (Interviews with LWG Participants).

On areas of IGC policy where there was a clear departmental competence, the policy-making process was generally led by the relevant shadow spokesperson and Whitty played a lesser role than he did on 'horizontal issues.' Though Whitty would still co-ordinate the agenda for the meetings and make recommendations in his chair's notes when such matters were on the agenda, the initial 'agenda-setting' position paper was usually submitted by the shadow spokesperson concerned. Where the relevant spokesperson was not already a member of the LWG, then he or she would also be invited to attend. Accordingly, Cook would submit position papers on CFSP and defence, Straw would submit papers on JHA and related issues, Brown's deputy Andrew Smith would submit a paper on EMU and agriculture spokesman Gavin Strang would submit a paper on CAP reform.[9] These were areas where shadow spokespersons were likely to get 'territorial' in relation to policy-making being made by the LWG, although in most cases the overlap with policy-making in the LWG proved fairly unproblematic, particularly with respect to CFSP, given Cook's central role in the LWG. Of the other 'departmental' issues, EMU would not prove to be central to the IGC and Smith's paper (LWG IGC4F) on the subject - though echoing Cook's broad strategy in emphasising a social democratic rationale for European integration and the need for Keynesian counter-cyclical instruments at the European level - was submitted mainly for information purposes. In any case, the shadow chancellor, Gordon Brown, was a member of the LWG and certainly powerful enough to ensure that the line of the shadow treasury team was not tampered with. However, it was interesting that in spite of Brown and Blair's clear strategy of distancing 'New Labour' from old Labour Keynesianism as regards the UK economy, the Labour treasury team, headed by Brown, was continuing to endorse a pan-European Keynesian strategy.[10] As for the CAP, though it was an issue peripheral to the IGC, there was a consensus for radical reform across both the London leadership and the EPLP. But the one area that did cause severe difficulties was JHA policy, given that it was a key issue in the IGC and there was no leadership-EPLP consensus on policy. Further problems were caused by the fact that the shadow home secretary, Jack Straw, was not a member of the LWG.

Straw was particularly 'territorial' on this matter and steadfast in his opposition to communitisation of JHA issues.[11] He clashed publicly on this issue with the EPLP spokesman, Glyn Ford (another former EPLP leader) in early February 1995.[12] Such a public disagreement might have been avoided if the protagonists had been members of the LWG. It represented just the type of open dispute between the Westminster frontbench and the EPLP that the LWG had been designed to avoid. Nevertheless, the dispute made all the more apparent to the Labour leadership the need to maintain an agreed line on this and other sensitive issues, and perhaps more critically, the need to maintain clear lines of communication between the Westminster frontbench and the EPLP on the agreed party line with strong political direction from the former to the latter. The particular sensitivities aroused by the overlap between EU policy and home affairs policy resulted in policy-making on JHA issues being transferred to a parallel PLP-EPLP working-party on EU-UK immigration policy. The decision to do this was taken following a lengthy discussion of the dispute at the third LWG meeting on 20 February (LWG3 Minutes). This working-party was chaired by Straw, and would also include Ford in its membership, as well as David, Crawley and another MEP, Michael Elliot, who served with Ford on the EP civil liberties committee.

In allowing Straw to chair this working-party, the Labour leadership was confirming him in his lead role in policy-making in this area. However, JHA policy would not be fully classified as a matter of home affairs policy, as ultimately Straw would have to report on the conclusions of his working-party deliberations to the LWG, and it would be the LWG, and ultimately Blair, who would take the final decision on this crucial policy area. Furthermore, Whitty was also a member of the working-party (as was Quin), ensuring that the broader perspective of the LWG's work was not overlooked and that the leadership would have direct input into deliberations. Another IGC issue which was viewed as encroaching on Straw's home affairs remit (and for which Ford was the relevant EPLP spokesman[13]), was the proposal for an EU role in combating racism and other forms of discrimination. Following consideration of a position paper by Whitty on this issue at its fifth meeting, the LWG agreed to also transfer consideration of these issues to Straw's working-party (LWG5 Minutes).

An initial outline of policy on JHA and related matters such as action on racism, emerged from Straw's working-party in time for the seventh meeting of the LWG on 26 July 1995,[14] by which time positions had also been adopted on national parliamentary scrutiny of EU business and on proposals for new competences in energy, civil protection and tourism[15] (the three possible new competences identified by the TEU for consideration) as well as more detailed positions on CFSP and defence. In addition, policy developments elsewhere in the EU and among those political actors connected to the Labour party, had exerted pressure on the LWG to agree a clearer response to the proposals being made and, in some cases, attempt to influence their content. This was the case in relation to the development of the official positions on the IGC of the PES group, the EP as a whole and the ETUC (see chapter 4). However, one key policy development over which the Labour leadership had very little control was the publication of the Commission report on the functioning of the TEU on 10 May. Like the EP resolution it was intended to input into the Reflection Group prior to the commencement of its work in the second half of 1995. The chair's note to the fifth LWG meeting described the Commission document as a critical 'first bid to define an agenda for the IGC' and therefore likely to 'define the political agenda from now on' (LWG5 Chair's Note). Following his appointment to the Commission in 1994, the former party leader, Neil Kinnock (with whom Whitty had worked closely in his time as general-secretary), was well placed to keep the LWG informed of developments as regards the likely Commission position, although given his transport portfolio, he was unlikely to have been able to influence its formulation. However, Kinnock may have given his former colleagues in the Labour leadership advanced warning of the details of the Commission report.[16] The chair's note for the fifth LWG meeting (nine days prior to its publication) had warned that the report was likely to be 'far too federalist...particularly on CFSP.' Thus although the LWG did not consider Cook's detailed position paper on CFSP until the sixth LWG meeting, the need for the Labour party to be able to present a coherent public reaction to the Commission report resulted in the adoption of a line opposing any EU military competence at the fifth LWG meeting on the basis of Cook's verbal recommendations (LWG5 Minutes). The position on CFSP was fleshed out on the basis of the recommendations in Cook's paper at the sixth meeting (LWG IGC6E, LWG6 Minutes).

The Policy Document on the IGC: *The Future of the European Union*

By the seventh LWG meeting, policy-making had progressed to the point where Whitty was able to submit a draft interim report of its work (LWG IGC7D) for consideration by the LWG (this was drafted with the assistance of Geoff Norris from the leader's office).[17] This also incorporated the conclusions of Straw's working-party (LWG IGC7E) and a précis of the report on the CAP submitted by Strang (LWG IGC7C) to the same meeting. The interim report would form the basis of the policy document on the IGC, *The Future of the European Union,* adopted by the Labour party conference in September 1995, incorporating the positions so far adopted by the LWG, as well as positions implied by its reaction to developments elsewhere. The minutes of the seventh LWG meeting record that the report was discussed point by point by the LWG and a number of draft changes agreed. It was further agreed that Cook would co-ordinate the re-editing of the report over the summer, though the detailed re-editing was actually undertaken by Cook's adviser, David Clark, under firm instruction from Cook, before Cook himself made some slight refinements to it (LWG7 Minutes).

This re-edited final draft was submitted to the eight meeting of the LWG on 14 September 1995 before submission to the Labour party joint policy committee[18] and the NEC with a view to presentation at the conference at the end of that month (LWG IGC8A). The re-edited draft presented by Cook to the eighth LWG meeting was almost identical (with a few minor alterations) to the policy document on the IGC endorsed by the Labour party conference (Labour Party 1995), indicating that his draft had proceeded through the various approval stages practically unscathed.

Moreover, Cook's final draft itself was very close, both in form and content, to Whitty's initial draft. Much of the re-editing was stylistic, concerned with tidying up the wording and presenting the information in a more accessible style, given that this would be a public document.

In the various areas of IGC policy covered by the policy document, the Labour party position generally remained unchanged during the various stages of the drafting process, commencing with the submission of Whitty's draft interim report and culminating in the adoption of the IGC policy document at the Labour party conference in September 1995. In a number of policy areas, the line of argument employed to support the positions contained in the document echoed that put in the various position papers considered by the LWG. In all its drafting stages, the document was divided into two parts, the first outlining 'Labour's approach to Europe', the second setting out the detail of its position on institutional reform. The first section therefore contrasted Labour's positive and constructive agenda with the damaging isolationism of the Conservative government and also emphasised Labour's engagement with the European agenda as illustrated by its ties with other socialist and social democratic parties in government and colleagues in the EP (Labour Party 1995: 2-3). In spelling out this positive agenda, the document strongly echoed the line of Cook's initial strategy paper to the LWG (LWG IGC2A) in referring to the need to address issues of direct concern to the people of Europe rather than 'institutional tinkering' and identifying a number of objectives for action. Similarly, the document continued to pursue the rather social democratic Keynesian line employed by Cook's earlier document, with the need to create worthwhile employment for all, to achieve better redistribution of the wealth created by the single market, and to provide social and workplace protection without discrimination all identified as key policy objectives, alongside environmental protection, the achievement of peace and stability (through a more effective CFSP) and of an EU with the 'wholehearted' consent of its people (through more democratic decision-making). In addition to these objectives, the first section also highlighted the two vital issues related to the IGC: enlargement and EMU. In relation to the former, the document emphasised the need for radical reform of the CAP and the structural funds in order to sustain an eastwards enlargement and also proposed the creation of a European political area in order to involve the applicants in the political deliberations of the EU before full economic integration. As regards EMU, the document echoed the line set out in Andrew Smith's paper (LWG IGC4F) in signalling support in principle but referring to the need for long term 'real' convergence of the member states' economies and better political accountability (Labour Party 1995: 3-7). However, references in Whitty's initial draft which also echoed Smith's paper in expressing strong cynicism about the EMU convergence criteria and timetable and calling for stronger political direction and redistributive mechanisms (LWG IGC7D: 8-10) had been eliminated from the final document. The elimination of these references reflected a distancing from some of the critical discourse on the EMU process included in the 1993 EU policy document which had implied that a Labour government would only participate in the single currency if radical changes were made to the broader economic and political framework of EMU (Labour 1993b: 49-53).

The second section of the policy document, on institutional change, was divided into a number of sub-sections corresponding to what the party perceived to be the key issues on the IGC agenda. Although these were reorganised between Whitty's initial draft and the final conference version, the substance of the policy positions remained constant, with the exception of a few subtle alterations.[19] The policy document represented the most comprehensive public statement of the IGC positions agreed by the LWG. It restated the positions agreed at the early LWG meetings, such as rejection of a two-tier or *à la carte* EU, support for a consolidated treaty, rejection of CFSP communitisation, support for limited QMV extension (i.e. in social, industrial, environmental and regional policy), linked to a vote reweighting to more accurately reflect the population of member states, and a rationalisation of the EP's procedures involving a simplified codecision procedure applying wherever there was QMV in Council (Labour Party 1995: 9-12). The latter was one of a number of proposals to enhance the profile of the EP. The document also proposed unifying the EP's budgetary procedures, thus abolishing the distinction between compulsory and non-compulsory expenditure, thereby granting the EP full powers over all parts of the EC budget. This was a position that appeared to have been taken following the adoption of Strang's recommendations on CAP reform at the seventh meeting. In addition to proposals to radically reappraise the objectives and operation of the CAP, Strang's paper had argued that the distinction between these different forms of expenditure, with CAP classified as compulsory and thus escaping full EP scrutiny, should be abolished 'not only as a matter of democratic justice' but as a catalyst for CAP reform (LWG IGC7C). These were arguments echoed by the document, though it was the latter argument that was the key to persuading the Labour leadership to adopt this position. The other proposed measures to strengthen the EP's role involved giving it a binding mandate to request that the Commission make a legislative proposal and granting the EP a right of approval over the Commission president and individual Commissioners. The former proposal represented a slight toning down of the suggestion made in the 1991 and 1993 policy documents that the EP and the Commission should share the right to initiate legislation (Labour party 1991a, 1993b, Martin 1992), though the outcome would be quite similar and the proposal thus remained quite a radical one both in terms of the domestic debate in Britain and existing practice within the EU. The same could be said in relation to the final document's proposal in relation to the nomination of the Commission president. The re-edited version of the policy document (approved by conference) built on the proposal in Whitty's initial draft that the EP approve both president and Commission by also advocating that the EP, along with the member states, be able to nominate candidates for Commission president as well as give final approval (LWG IGC7D: 20-21, Labour Party 1995: 12). However, the LWG stopped short of supporting proposals that the EP elect the Commission president. This was generally seen by the Labour leadership as going too far in shifting the balance of power within the EU in favour of the supranational EP (Interview with LWG participant).

The document was more conservative as regards the size of the Commission: while advocating greater discretion for the president in allocating Commission portfolios, all versions of the document emphasised that the legitimacy of the Commission required the maintenance of the existing formula of one Commissioner per member state and two for the large states (Labour Party 1995: 12).[20] In relation to improving democratic accountability, the role of national parliaments was also emphasised. The document echoed the line recommended by Whitty at the fifth LWG meeting that there be 'closer co-operation between committees of the EP and national parliaments in the preparation and consideration of European legislation' though it suggested that proposals for a new 'second chamber' of national parliamentarians should be rejected (LWG IGC5E, LWG5 Minutes, Labour Party 1995: 13). In addition, the sub-section on EC legislation and subsidiarity called for 'more circumspect' EC legislation setting out minimum standards with national legislatures fleshing out the details based upon them (Labour Party 1995: 10).

On all these horizontal institutional issues, there was a continuity with the lines pursued by the Labour party prior to Blair's assumption of the leadership in 1994. However, whereas previous policy documents (Labour Party: 1993b, 1994) had been rather vague, the 1995 document was more precise in specifying the institutional reforms favoured. Thus whereas the general principle of support for an enhanced EP role had been clear before, the 1995 document made more precise commitments on the EP relationship to the Council (with codecision applying wherever the Council legislated by QMV), to the Commission (involving a vote of approval on the presidential candidate) and as regards the budget (with its full amending powers applying in all categories). The role of the EP proved a 'surprisingly uncontentious' issue for the LWG in that the proposal for codecision extension was approved 'relatively cleanly'[21] (Interview with LWG participant). There had been a general consensus within the Labour party leadership and the wider party since the end of the 1980s that the development of the EP's role was a desirable objective. This view was derived not only from concerns about democracy but also broader political and strategic calculations: Labour's performance in the 1989 and 1994 EP elections had been rare bright spots during its years of opposition. Particularly since 1994, when it became the largest national grouping within both the PES group and the EP as a whole, and with its representatives holding a number of key positions within it, Labour's stature and influence within the EP was considerably higher than at Westminster. Thus developing the power of the EP was seen by Labour, in the early 1990s, as a way of exercising some of the power and influence denied to it in Britain during its long wilderness in opposition. Blair had publicly stressed Labour's support for an EP 'right of codecision wherever the Council makes a decision by QMV' a 'right to initiate legislation though not to determine it' and a 'right to scrutinise all aspects of the Community budget, including the CAP' in a keynote speech on the EU made to the Friedrich-Ebert Stiftung in Bonn in May 1995 (Blair, 30 May 1995).

The clearest progression in policy within the LWG appeared to have occurred in relation to QMV extension. Though previous documents had acknowledged the benefit of QMV in limited areas, the only areas specifically mentioned were social and environmental policy and, in the 1994 EP manifesto, Labour had preferred to emphasise those areas where it favoured the retention of unanimity. Even QMV in environmental policy created problems for the Labour leadership, as it was anxious to ensure that the issue of environmental taxation be excluded from QMV and be classed as indirect taxation, for which unanimity would be retained (LWG3 Minutes, LWG IGC3D). This was a particularly sensitive issue domestically, given Labour's campaign against the Conservative government's imposition of VAT on fuel in 1993 and 1994. Nevertheless, though the issue of environmental taxation was a cause of a disagreement with some of the other PES parties, the overall list of policies proposed for QMV extension did not create significant divisions within the LWG. Cook played a particularly positive role in the argument for QMV extension, seeking to go further than others within the leadership on the issue and generally winning the argument (Interviews with LWG participants). It appears then, that Cook's conversion from moderate Euro-scepticism to positive pro-Europeanism came rather earlier than has been suggested by some observers (Anderson and Mann 1997: 142-143, Young, JW 2000: 176).

The position on QMV elaborated in the 1995 conference document reflected the decisions taken at the third LWG meeting, based on discussion of the paper submitted by Whitty (LWG IGC3D). Just as the Thatcher government had, in 1985, recognised the benefit of QMV in order to ensure the necessary decisions were taken to secure its key European objective, i.e. the realisation of the single market (Dinan 1999: 115-120, Young, JW 2000: 138-141), the Labour leadership had accepted the argument that QMV was both necessary and desirable to ensure the achievement of its policy objectives in the EU. Thus QMV was supported for social and environmental policy to ensure the adoption of decent EU level frameworks of protection in these areas. In industrial and regional policy, QMV was supported both 'to give effect to the single market and to allow growing help to badly hit sectors and regions' (LWG IGC3D). However, the policy document also emphasised that in areas of vital national interest, such as treaty changes, budgetary policy, taxation, external border controls and foreign affairs and security issues, Labour would support the retention of unanimity (Labour Party 1995: 11). On these issues, the appeal of institutional efficiency was outweighed by the unacceptability of a British government being outvoted and therefore having a decision imposed on it in sensitive areas of national interest. Moreover, if it had advocated QMV in these areas, the Labour party would have increased the scope for Conservative attacks focused on its willingness to surrender British national interests by giving up the veto. Thus, electoral politics and reasons of national interest combined to limit the number of areas in which the Labour leadership was prepared to publicly support QMV extension. In defending its position on QMV, the Labour leadership would point to the record of the Thatcher and Major governments in agreeing significant extensions of QMV through the SEA and TEU respectively. In his Bonn speech, Blair had outlined Labour's support for QMV in social, environmental, industrial and regional policy, but pointed out that the largest QMV extensions agreed to by Britain had come under Thatcher and Major (Blair, 30 May 1995). This Conservative record was also emphasised in the policy document (Labour Party 1995: 11).

In listing a number of new areas where Labour would support QMV extension, the 1995 document went considerably further than previous policy documents and, together with the commitments on extending the EP's powers, presented a clear distinction from the negative position on institutional reform being displayed by the Conservative government. However, the positions presented by the document on the treaty pillar structure bore a closer resemblance to those held by the Conservative government. In relation to CFSP, the relevant sub-section on CFSP echoed the line set out in Cook's paper submitted (LWG IGC6E) at the sixth LWG meeting. Both opposition to communitisation (as agreed at the second LWG meeting) and to any dilution of unanimity (as agreed at the third LWG meeting in the context of the general discussion of QMV and unanimity) were stressed, alongside rejection of an EU military competence or EU/WEU merger (agreed at the fifth LWG meeting). In a change to the drafts considered by the seventh and eighth LWG meetings, the final version of the document approved by conference, in stressing the need for unanimity also added that the Labour party opposed proposals to allow member states to opt out of some joint CFSP actions (Labour Party 1995: 14). All versions of the document did, however, indicate support for a 'more substantial secretariat and analytical support structure', better mechanisms for EP consultation and the development of the WEU's role (though separate from the EU), as recommended in Cook's position paper (LWG IGC6E). The document's emphasis on national control of CFSP decision-making and the primacy of NATO represented a continuity with the positions elaborated under the Kinnock and Smith leaderships, following Labour's return to a bipartisan approach to foreign policy (Labour Party 1993b: 70, 1994: 26, Spear 1992).

In a similar bipartisan spirit, the sub-section on JHA, which reflected the deliberations of Straw's working-party as presented to the seventh LWG meeting, rejected the option of communitisation. It echoed the line of Straw's report (LWG IGC7E) that such policy should remain an intergovernmental matter in accordance with the principle of subsidiarity, though recognising the need for greater transparency and EP accountability.[22] There was, however, a notable change made in the re-editing process supervised by Cook over the summer of 1995, with a reference in the initial draft interim report submitted by Whitty and Norris to a role for the ECJ in tightly limited circumstances (i.e. in relation to decisions made intergovernmentally not to national legislation) being dropped. In addition to rejection of JHA communitisation, all versions of the document stressed that a Labour government would not sign the UK up to the Schengen arrangements (LWG IGC7D: 15-16, LWG IGC8A: 5, Labour Party 1995: 15-16). It was in JHA policy that the greatest divisions emerged between the London leadership and the EPLP representatives within the LWG. While the latter pressed for some JHA communitisation, both within the LWG and Straw's working-party, this was strongly resisted by both Straw and Blair (Interview with LWG participant). This appeared to represent a hardening of Labour's position under the Blair leadership, given that the documents produced under the Smith leadership had provided a vague hint that communitisation might be acceptable to Labour (Labour 1993b: 62, 1994: 21). Nevertheless, there were differences between Straw and the EPLP over the interpretation of the vague wording of the 1994 manifesto. Ford and other Labour MEPs, including Glenys Kinnock, had argued that the reference to 'increasing convergence and harmonisation of both migration and asylum policies' implied support for communitised policies in these areas (*The Guardian*, 16 February 1995), but Straw maintained that the reference that followed the need to 'recognise the specific needs of each individual member state and ensuring that member states have full responsibility for administering immigration and asylum rules' implied intergovernmental co-operation and national control over policy (LP Straw, 23 February 1995). The switch to a tougher stance on JHA policy could be linked to the general 'toughening' of the Labour party position on home affairs policy under Blair's leadership, with Straw building on the foundations laid by Blair during his stint as shadow home secretary under Smith's leadership from 1992 to 1994. This involved supporting hardline measures on crime and policing and distancing New Labour from the liberal positions on civil rights promoted by the former deputy-leader, Roy Hattersley, in the 1980s (Anderson and Mann 1997: 239-242). In seeking to establish his credentials as a 'tough' home secretary in waiting, Straw would increasingly ape the hardline positions adopted by the highly Euro-sceptical Conservative home secretary Michael Howard. This involved opposing any interference by Brussels in the UK's right to retain its frontier controls and to pursue its own immigration and asylum policies (Anderson and Mann 1997: 255-266, Newman 1996: 24).

While Straw's tough line was reflected across the leadership on the JHA and Schengen, he appeared to be over-ruled by Blair in favour of the more progressive position being advocated by the EPLP representatives in the related area of anti-racism provisions. The policy document stated that Labour would press for a treaty amendment to ensure that persons 'legally resident in one member state' were 'protected against discrimination and harassment on grounds of race when travelling within the EU' (Labour Party 1995: 16). The paper from Straw's working-party, in contrast, would have confined such protection to those travelling in the rest of the EU 'in the course of their employment' (LWG IGC7E). Furthermore, Straw sought to confine action to combat racism to the intergovernmental mechanisms of the third pillar. He also seemed to be over-ruled here as the policy document argued for discrimination on the grounds of race to be tackled in the first pillar, on the same basis as it was on the grounds of sex (at least as it related to employment). Whitty had joined the EPLP in arguing for a first pillar anti-racism provision, and had written a note to Straw reminding him that this had been Labour's position in the 1994 European manifesto. He also pointed out that, unlike in other areas where Labour differed from the 'European federalist vanguard', should it now oppose this, Labour would be isolated within the PES (LP Whitty, 16 June 1995). In its final version approved by conference, the policy document went further than the two earlier drafts presented to the LWG in also emphasising Labour's commitment to appropriate EU action to end other unnamed forms of discrimination (possibly a reference to a broader anti-discrimination provision, encompassing discrimination on the basis of disability or sexual orientation). Moreover, the document made the explicit link to Labour's own progressive tradition on the issue of race relations, referring to the 1968 and 1976 race relations acts passed by past Labour governments in the UK and arguing that such an approach needed to be applied across the EU (Labour Party 1995: 16).

The LWG and the Launch of the IGC

Following the approval of the policy document on the IGC, there appeared to be a degree of complacency about the need for further LWG meetings, possibly based on a feeling that the task of agreeing a coherent line on the key issues had been completed. Henceforth, the work of the LWG appeared to carry less urgency about it and the meetings became more infrequent. The biggest gap occurred between the eighth meeting in September 1995, when Cook's re-edited draft interim report was presented, and the ninth meeting, five months later, in February 1996. The work of the LWG, in these latter stages, also became more reactive, both in relation to developments in the IGC agenda, and new stages in the IGC process. Indeed, the ninth meeting was called to assess the IGC situation in the light of the Reflection Group report submitted to the Madrid European Council in December 1995 and of the imminent launch of the IGC.[23] It was agreed at Madrid that the IGC would be launched under the Italian presidency on 29 March 1996 (McDonagh 1998: 55). Thereafter, IGC personal representatives (appointed by the member governments) would meet weekly and foreign ministers would meet monthly to carry the negotiation forward (McDonagh 1998: 61). Henceforth, the focus of the LWG would be on co-ordinating the Labour party response to developments in the IGC and ensuring a common party line within the party leadership, Westminster frontbench and EPLP. Indeed, the chair's note for the ninth LWG meeting noted that the party 'had managed quite well so far...to hold a line' but emphasised that this needed to be 'sustained as the IGC unfolds'. It therefore proposed that henceforth the LWG meet every two months to consider developments (this would be kept up for the next two meetings). Thus Whitty would continue to provide briefings on IGC developments while Cook would give his 'overview' of what the party position should be.

The Reflection Group report submitted at Madrid and the subsequent European Council declaration elaborated on the basis of it had indicated a clearer and more limited initial IGC agenda than had been expected within the LWG (LWG9 Chair's Note, Reflection Group 1995, McDonagh 1998: 40-41). Moreover, ahead of the Madrid summit, the French President Chirac and German Chancellor Kohl had, on 6 December 1995, sent a letter to the Spanish Council presidency setting out what they saw as the priorities for the IGC. These included an improvement to the mechanisms of the CFSP (involving a more clearly defined EU-WEU relationship), the creation of a free movement area (involving common immigration and asylum policies and closer co-operation to combat international crime), more effective institutions (involving extensions of QMV, a reweighting of Council votes and a review of the composition and appointment of the Commission) and consolidating democracy (including a stronger role for the European parliament and national parliaments and firmer application of subsidiarity). The joint letter also referred to the need to facilitate differentiated integration through a general enabling clause to allow those member states with the will and capacity to do so to develop closer co-operation in certain policy areas within the EU institutional framework (Chirac and Kohl 1995).

The Chirac-Kohl proposals in many respects coincided with the agenda outlined by the Reflection Group report, which divided the work of the IGC into three broad headings: 1) making 'Europe' more relevant to its citizens; 2) enabling 'Europe' to work better and preparing it for enlargement; 3) giving the Union greater capacity for external action. The report set out the views taken within the Reflection Group on the range of issues grouped under these three headings. However, it avoided identifying specific member states, simply referring to issues where there was a majority in favour of a particular proposition, or a division between different groups of states. In a number of areas, it referred to issues where only a small minority or just one member state opposed a reform proposal (Reflection Group 1995, McDonagh 1998: 40-41). From known public positions, it could be clearly deduced that the latter category usually referred to the UK. This is confirmed by accounts given by individuals present in the discussions (Corbett 1996, McDonagh 1998: 41, Dehousse 1999: 4). Indeed, Richard Corbett, as adviser to Elisabeth Guigou, one of the two EP representatives, provided the Labour party with a presence in the Reflection Group discussions and was thus able to furnish Whitty with a detailed report of the positions taken by David Davis, the British government representative.

On the basis of the information provided by Corbett, Whitty was able to submit a report to the ninth LWG meeting, demonstrating that in a number of areas where the British Conservative government was in a minority (sometimes of one), a Labour government would have been in the majority within the Reflection Group (LWG IGC9A).[24] The difference was at its most stark in relation to the extension of QMV[25] and of EP codecision, and, of course, integrating the social protocol into the treaty proper, all of which the Conservative government had been alone in opposing and which Labour favoured. Furthermore, a Labour government would have been with the large majority in supporting a clearer elaboration of citizens' rights, anti-racism provisions, new treaty provisions on employment, improved environmental provisions, developing the WEU, and greater transparency in Council meetings, while the Conservative government was in a small minority in opposing these within the Reflection Group.[26] Whitty also referred to two areas where the Conservative government party was in a majority in opposing a reform proposal, and where a Labour government would be in the minority in favour. These were proposals for improved co-operation on tourism, which the LWG had agreed to endorse at its fifth meeting, and the proposal to abolish the distinction between compulsory and non-compulsory expenditure and give the EP full scrutiny of the budget. Whitty noted that Labour had not included a reference to the tourism proposal in the conference document and that therefore the party should 'quietly forget about it.' However, he recommended the position on the budgetary procedure be maintained.

Whitty referred to a third category in which the Conservative government was in a small minority and where a Labour government would share the same position. This appeared to apply solely to JHA policy, where the UK representative had been alone in explicitly opposing communitisation and other proposed changes (though some of the UK reservations were shared by Denmark). Whitty noted that in 'supporting the government (Labour could) neutralise Tory attacks (and) antagonism on this from the electorate but of course maximise our isolation in the PES.' Labour also shared Conservative government opposition to the communitisation of the CFSP pillar, although here UK isolation was not as pronounced, as opinion was more evenly divided within the Reflection Group on CFSP and related defence questions.

Leaving aside the similarities of Labour's positions to those of the Conservative government on the pillar structure, the LWG was in a position to indicate satisfaction at its ninth meeting that the party's positions were in the 'European mainstream' at least in terms of first pillar issues, in contrast to the Conservatives' largely isolated position in the Reflection Group (LWG9 Chair's Note). However, the Reflection Group report had raised a number of issues on which the LWG had yet to develop a clear position. Indeed, in a paper submitted to the ninth meeting, Whitty noted that in the course of the work of the Reflection Group and in the discussions at Madrid, both amongst the PES leaders and within the European Council, and also through 'soundings around the European scene and from pressure groups and others', a number of issues had emerged (and were likely to be on the IGC agenda) which had either not been touched upon by the LWG, or on which it had not agreed a clear line in the deliberations leading up to the production of the party conference document. These included the issues of EU citizenship, public services, anti-discrimination,[27] employment and animal rights, some of which had the potential, according to Whitty, to be of 'significant political and presentational importance' (LWG IGC9H).

This paper therefore tentatively recommended positions on these issues to be communicated to all party spokespersons, though the chair's note (LWG9 Chair's Note) stressed that these positions would not be for publication. The recommended positions included support for the proposals, which had majority support in the Reflection Group, to incorporate the ECHR into the treaty and list existing EU citizenship rights at the beginning, and for broader anti-discrimination provisions.[28] Whitty also suggested general sympathy for a proposal to guarantee a universal access to public services, while expressing caution about the detailed implications. On employment, which had been classed as a new issue probably because the LWG had not given any consideration to the details despite the interim report indicating support for the general principle of an employment chapter, Whitty suggested a reiteration of support for the principle while seeking to avoid a whole new range of competences. Animal welfare had not been covered by the Reflection Group, but Whitty suggested that the recent public outcry in the UK concerning the export of live calves in veal crates (McLeod 1998) pointed to the need for some kind of EU provision classifying farm animals as sentient beings rather than simple farm produce (LWG IGC9H).

In anticipation of the launch of the IGC, a number of other important reports on the IGC were published in early 1996 including, in the UK, reports of the House of Lords EC committee and the House of Commons select committee on European legislation, and most importantly the White Paper on the IGC produced by the Conservative government. As with the reports on the IGC published by the European Commission, by the EP and other bodies in 1995, the general pattern was for a summary and analysis of the reports to be drafted, usually by Whitty, for consideration by the LWG. While the less politically sensitive reports would simply be 'noted' by the LWG, some required response due to their authorship and the sensitivity of the proposals therein, in which case Whitty's commentary would be accompanied by recommended Labour party responses to be agreed upon within the LWG. As was the case with the reports of the Commission and the Reflection Group before it, the UK White Paper would certainly be placed in this category.

The publication of the White Paper by the UK government, coinciding with the launch of the IGC in March 1996, required careful consideration by the LWG as Labour sought to formulate a public response contrasting the Conservative government's isolation in the EU with its own 'pragmatic engagement' whilst avoiding being portrayed as 'soft on Europe.' Most of the government's positions had already been clear from the UK stance in the Reflection Group. Thus, the White Paper confirmed the government's rejection of any extension of QMV in the Council and even proposed that in those areas where QMV already applied, member states should be able to invoke national interest to block a decision (the so called Luxembourg compromise[29]). The White Paper also confirmed a total rejection of extensions in the powers of the European Parliament and reiterated opposition to any deviation from the pillar structure and from the intergovernmental nature of decision-making in CFSP and JHA. It also underlined UK government opposition to the development of an EU defence role, to the development of treaty provisions on employment, to the social chapter, to any further development of the European citizenship provisions and to the incorporation of a stronger human rights protection component into the treaties. The government also expressed caution in the White Paper about proposals for greater transparency in decision-making and opposed attempts to simplify the treaties, viewing such a simplification as a back-door method of modifying carefully negotiated treaty compromises. The one key institutional reform that the government did support, given the UK national interest as a large state, was the reweighting of Council votes being pushed by France and Germany (FCO 1996).

The Flexibility Issue

Though these government positions had been well sign-posted in advance, Whitty's commentary on the White Paper (LWG IGC10A), circulated to the tenth LWG meeting on 1 April 1996, pointed to a number of additional issues that required an agreed Labour party response. In particular, one 'major strategic issue' was raised, in the form of the Conservative government's apparent endorsement of flexibility or 'variable geometry' within the EU. While rejecting 'the trap of a two-tier Europe' the White Paper suggested that it might be 'perfectly healthy for some member states to integrate more closely or more quickly than others' (FCO 1996: 6). This stance was not altogether surprising given Major's statements in 1994 advocating a 'multi-track, multi-speed, multi-layered' Europe but rejecting the 'hard-core' and 'concentric circles' models proposed by the German CDU and French prime minister respectively (Young, JW 2000: 166, Story 1997: 24, Szukala and Wessels 1997: 91). Though the French and German governments had toned down their earlier indications of support for the latter options, the debate on differentiated integration had continued to develop in 1995. The reports of the EP and the European Commission on the functioning of the TEU submitted in preparation for the work of the Reflection Group in May 1995, and the report of the Reflection Group itself in December 1995 had all referred to the possibility of flexibility provisions being introduced into the new treaty, to allow groups of member states to proceed with closer co-operation in certain policy areas when others were unable or unwilling to proceed, whilst respecting the single institutional framework[30] and *acquis communautaire* (EP 1995, European Commission 1995, Reflection Group 1995). The Commission also stressed that any such differentiation should be temporary. In addition, Kohl and Chirac had appeared to endorse this less divisive approach in their letter of December 1995, calling for such flexibility provisions to enable closer co-operation within the single institutional framework of the EU where one or more of the member states faced temporary difficulties in keeping up with the pace of integration (Dinan 1999: 178). Further formal endorsement for flexibility provisions came in the Commission's opinion on the convening of the IGC in February 1996 and a joint memorandum issued by the Benelux countries in March 1996, though both stressed a rejection of an *à la carte* approach, in which states could pick and choose which policies to take part in (McDonagh 1998: 142-143).[31] Flexibility was cemented in the IGC agenda by the conclusions of the Turin summit of March 1996, at the formal launch of the IGC, which stated that the EU 'must not be forever bound to advance at the speed of its slowest member' and that 'some form of co-operation or integration between those of its members wishing to progress faster and further in the attainment of the treaty's objectives' was required, particularly in the light of enlargement (Duff 1997a: 186-187).

The reference in the White Paper to the acceptability of some member states integrating more closely than others appeared to indicate some convergence of the British Conservative and Franco-German position on flexibility provisions. The British government desire to exclude itself from a further deepening of the integration process and the Franco-German desire to proceed with closer co-operation without the troublesome British holding them back appeared to be leading to this convergence of interests, though differences would remain over how such provisions should operate. Labour's conference document in 1995 had rejected 'permanent opt-outs or variable geometry' though it recognised that some temporary flexibility might at times be required to give 'some states...more time than others to implement common positions and meet agreed standards' (Labour Party 1995: 9). In coming to this tough line against flexibility, the Labour leadership appeared to be consciously seeking to distance itself from the Conservative government's tacit acceptance that Britain should be prepared to stand back and allow other member states to integrate further without British participation. In addition, the Labour party was challenging the Franco-German assumption that continued British government intransigence would make such flexibility necessary in the future. The view of the Labour leadership appeared to be that under a future Labour government, this view of Britain would be reversed: under Labour, the British government would play a full and committed role in the integration process, as symbolised by the Labour commitment to end the one glaring example of variable integration within the existing treaty framework by terminating the British social chapter opt-out. Part of the Labour party strategy to present itself as a responsible party of government in Britain was to contrast its 'mainstream' EU policy with the Conservative government's apparent determination to isolate Britain within the EU.

As the chair's note to the tenth LWG meeting suggested, the Labour leadership needed to decide whether to go along with this Conservative approach or 'continue to attack the government for leaving Britain on the outside track' (LWG10 Chair's Note). According to the minutes of the meeting, in the discussion that ensued, both Blair and Cook spoke on the possible advantages and 'dangerous implications' (LWG10 Minutes). Blair appears to have been quite attracted to the idea of flexibility, much more so than Cook, who argued strongly against Labour endorsing it. In particular, Cook drew attention to the difficulty in identifying the areas of policy in which flexibility provisions might be required and their need justified (Interviews with LWG participants). Further consideration of flexibility was deferred until the eleventh LWG meeting, for which Whitty submitted a discussion paper exploring the issue in greater depth (LWG IGC11D). Although a clear-cut position on flexibility appeared not to have been agreed at the eleventh meeting, Cook's greater scepticism on the issue, rather than Blair's more sympathetic approach, appeared to be reflected in the agreed view that it was in Labour's interests 'to see minimal flexibility proposed before the British general election' (LWG11 Minutes). As Whitty's paper suggested, the Labour leadership would have to exert its influence with its 'potential allies' (i.e. among PES-led governments) to do this (LWG IGC11D). However, given the difficulty in securing the removal of flexibility from the IGC agenda, the Labour leadership would also have to turn its attention to ways of minimising its impact. Debate within the IGC would focus on whether or not an 'enabling' flexibility clause should apply across all three pillars, whether it should be restricted to certain policy areas (or alternatively certain sensitive areas specifically excluded) and whether unanimity or QMV should apply within the Council to any decision to allow a group of member states to pursue flexibility (McDonagh 1998: 144-149). Thus if it failed to prevent flexibility, Labour would need to insist on a unanimity trigger and a restrictive approach to the policy areas in which it applied.

The ECJ and the Legislative Process

Another significant issue that required further consideration by the LWG in the wake of the government White Paper was the role of the ECJ. The role of the ECJ in establishing the supremacy of EC law over British law had increasingly become a focus of resentment within the Conservative party since the late 1980s. Euro-sceptic MPs drew attention to a perceived tendency of the ECJ in its judgements to favour the most 'integrationist' interpretation of various treaty articles (Young, H 1999: 401-403). Indeed, the creation of the intergovernmental pillars within the TEU, outside the scope of ECJ jurisdiction, had been interpreted as a conscious attempt to prevent the ECJ spreading its tentacles into new areas of policy.

However, following Maastricht, a number of high profile ECJ rulings against the UK government had contributed to an increase in support within the Conservative party and government for reforms to reduce the ECJ's authority in its existing areas of jurisdiction (Young, H 1999: 501-502, Duff 1997a: 190, Dinan 1999: 311-312).[32] Indeed a survey in 1994 indicated that 55 per cent of Conservative MPs regarded the practices of the ECJ as a threat to liberty in Britain (Ludlam 1998: 44). Against this backdrop, the White Paper made a number of suggestions designed to limit the role of the ECJ and on the legislative and judicial process in general. These included proposals for a sunset clause for EC legislation, providing for its automatic expiry after a fixed period, a limit on retrospective application of ECJ judgements, and 'streamlined procedures' for the rapid amendment of EC legislation interpreted by the ECJ in a way never intended by the Council (FCO 1996: 10-12, 16-17).

Whitty submitted a commentary on the White Paper (LWG IGC10A) and a separate analysis of the particular proposals on the ECJ, referring to the government's proposals as constituting a 'deliberate misunderstanding' of the role of the ECJ and of the separation of powers between the EU institutions (LWG IGC10D). For example, in relation to the proposal for sunset clauses, he noted that there was no national legislature or legal system that provided for automatic expiry of laws, except in the case of emergency legislation, and that there was no good argument for the EU to do so. Indeed, he suggested that it would seriously undermine the legitimacy of European law if there were an expectation that it would soon expire (LWG IGC10A). Whitty also advocated rejection of the proposal on retrospective application of judgements, arguing that if an act was unlawful when it occurred then the ECJ was not making 'retrospective legislation' in declaring it illegal. Furthermore, he opposed the proposal for streamlined amendment of legislation as in effect giving the Council the right to over-rule an ECJ decision without going through the full process of legislative amendment (LWG IGC10D). Whitty also referred to an apparent contradiction between the government's expressed desire in the White Paper to examine the comitology procedure, whereby delegated legislation was implemented by Commission committees, and the opposition stated later in the same document to the proposal for a hierarchy of norms. Whitty argued that the two issues were linked and that the Conservative government's rejection of the latter proposal, on which it was isolated within the Reflection Group, was incomprehensible. Moreover, he suggested that Labour should be supporting the proposal 'as a central part of the rationalisation of the treaty that the IGC ought to be performing' (LWG IGC10A).

Whitty did acknowledge that some of the government's proposals for procedural improvements to the legislative process and for strengthening enforcement of subsidiarity had merit and could be supported (LWG IGC10A). Following discussion of his analysis of the government proposals, the LWG agreed that Labour should defend the ECJ's overall constitutional role against media and Conservative attacks while recognising that there were some government suggestions that it could support and other improvements that it could advocate itself (LWG10 Minutes). The issue of subsidiarity was considered further at the eleventh LWG meeting, for which both Whitty and Quin produced papers (LWG

IGC11E, LWG IGC11F), following suggestions at the tenth meeting that 'more detailed consideration of the concept' was required (LWG10 Minutes). Nevertheless, the LWG appeared to endorse Whitty's suggestion that Labour support the Conservative government's proposal that the guidelines on subsidiarity agreed by the Edinburgh European Council in 1992 be incorporated into the new treaty (LWG IGC10A). According to these guidelines, the Commission was obliged to justify all legislative proposals in respect to the subsidiarity principle (Dinan 1999: 153-154).[33]

The eleventh LWG meeting also saw deeper consideration of the party's position on transparency, in the light of a Swedish government submission to the IGC for an EU citizens' right of access to EU documents related to decision-making. Though the 1995 policy document had supported the principle of transparency in relation to the Council legislating in public, there appeared to be concern within the Labour leadership that the Swedish proposals were rather wide ranging and could go further than Labour's own domestic freedom of information proposals in forcing the disclosure of sensitive internal government documents relating to EU policy from within the member states. However, following consideration of a paper drafted by Whitty on the issue (LWG IGC11G) and a report of a meeting that Whitty and the then junior home affairs spokesman, Doug Henderson, had had with the Swedish deputy justice minister, in which the latter had provided assurances that the proposal was 'more restrictive than at first sight' and would not cover documents from member states, the LWG agreed that Labour should support the principle of the Swedish proposal 'but be cautious on the detail' (LWG11 Minutes).

The Beef Crisis and the UK Non Co-operation Policy

The eleventh meeting of the LWG was, however, overshadowed by the crisis in the EU caused by the UK government policy of non co-operation, declared on 21 May 1996 in response to the EC ban on beef exports in April (Edwards and Pijpers 1997: 5, Young, H 1998: 460-463, Seldon 1998: 633-656, Westlake 1997). The beef crisis brought into sharp focus the strains placed on Labour's European policy by the domestic political environment. The anxiety of the Labour leadership to avoid being portrayed as somehow 'soft' on Europe led to it providing tacit endorsement of the hostile and damaging strategy being pursued by the government (Duff 1997a: 184).

The Labour position was demonstrated in a press statement issued by Cook on 28 May 1996. Despite blaming the Conservative government for the events that led up to the beef ban and describing the policy of non co-operation as 'an admission of the failure of Conservative diplomacy' because the UK government had not alerted its European partners of the health risk, Cook explained that Labour supported the policy 'in the national interest' as it was vital for UK farmers that the government's tactics succeeded. While criticising government ministers for encouraging a jingoistic and war-like atmosphere, Labour's approach here rather paradoxically appeared to echo the kind of grave bipartisan approach one would normally associate with a war situation. Thus Cook's statement explained:

> Britain is more likely to succeed in negotiation if we can demonstrate a national resolve in support of our objectives. If the government is serious about building a national consensus around their policy of non co-operation, Labour believes that ministers must show it by their actions. *Labour's support for the policy of disruption* [author's emphasis] will depend on ministers demonstrating a commitment to national interest by observing three principles.

These principles were as follows: 1) that the UK government demonstrate that it was 'pursuing confrontation in Europe to further the national interest' not to promote its 'own party political interest' and that in order for Labour to 'better support the government in the national interest' the government 'consult the opposition on the conduct of the policy of non co-operation'; 2) that in view of a number of forthcoming EU measures on the single market, the government 'consult with the CBI and trade organisations before invoking the policy of non co-operation in cases where it would damage British exports and jobs;' 3) that ministers pursue the policy in a dignified and respectful fashion avoiding 'the language of xenophobia or jingoism' and references to 'declarations of war or of war cabinets' which raised 'temperatures and lowers the prospect of a negotiated agreement' (although by promoting the kind of bipartisan consensus and seeking the kind of cross-party consultation present in war situations, Labour was perhaps unconsciously contributing to such a climate). Cook's statement also explained that the foreign secretary, Malcolm Rifkind had been sent a letter setting out these principles and suggested that the government's reply would reveal 'whether they seek a national consensus or party political advantage' (Cook, 28 May 1996). Labour's support for the government appeared to be illustrative both of its terror at the prospect of giving the Conservatives any opportunity to label it as unpatriotic and an extreme timidity and lack of confidence in arguing the pro-European case, almost as if the evolution into a pro-European party under Kinnock and Smith had never happened. Furthermore, in asking Rifkind to demonstrate that the government was acting in the national interest and not for party political advantage, the Labour leadership was itself demonstrating how acutely conscious it was of the way in which the beef issue, and the wider question of the UK's relationship with the EU, could be exploited by the Conservatives for domestic political purposes.

Blair went as far as to make a speech in Germany (in Bonn) on 18 June 1996 supporting the UK government position. Whilst explaining Labour's criticisms of the government's handling of the BSE outbreak and 'unreservedly condemn(ing) the xenophobia...seen in Britain in recent weeks' Blair argued to his German audience that there was a 'depth of feeling' throughout the UK that it was 'being treated unfairly' and that the measures had now been put in place to ensure the safety of British beef. He therefore explained that Labour supported the government's efforts to get the ban lifted, including through non co-operation, arguing that 'our national interest has now been engaged and as a responsible opposition we cannot undermine the national interest. Whilst the government of the day is trying to get the ban lifted we will support that effort' (Blair, 18 June 1996).

Similarly, a press statement from Robin Cook on 19 June had suggested that the UK government policy of non co-operation would be justified if it actually led to a lifting of the ban (though he doubted that this would be the case). In the statement, Cook suggested that Labour had 'always demanded that the test for the policy of non co-operation was whether it forced a lifting of the beef ban within a clear timescale.' Although Cook added that anything less 'would not justify the disruption it has caused and the damage to Britain's standing in Europe', the implication of the statement was that if the desired end result was achieved then the means employed were justified (Cook, 19 June 1996).

Labour's approach caused considerable disquiet among its sister parties in the PES and its representatives in the EPLP, as well as pro-Europeans at Westminster. Not surprisingly, therefore, the minutes of the eleventh LWG meeting on 10 June record that the meeting witnessed a lengthy discussion of the crisis arising from BSE, with Blair explaining the reasoning behind the party's position 'in terms of both the arguments on BSE *and of domestic politics'* [author's emphasis] (LWG11 Minutes). The meeting took place just prior to the Florence European Council which had been intended as a major staging post in the development of the IGC agenda. It was instead dominated by attempts to resolve the crisis. Although the summit was successful in reaching a compromise that allowed the UK government to lift its policy of non co-operation (Young, JW 2000: 172, Seldon 1998: 651-653) the crisis had scuppered any hopes of progress in the IGC being made before the Council presidency passed from the Italians to the Irish at the end of June 1996.

The first signs of life in the IGC came shortly before the LWG met for the twelfth and final time on 8 October 1996. An informal summit in Dublin three days previously had confirmed that the Irish presidency would be undertaking work on a draft treaty text to be submitted in December, though this had already been suggested by the mandate given to the Irish at the Florence summit in June 1996 to provide a 'general outline for a draft revision of the treaties' (Dinan 1999: 177, McDonagh 1998: 69-70). However, the IGC representatives had been meeting weekly since the IGC launch at Turin in March without so far achieving unanimity on any of the major issues discussed. The final LWG meeting considered documents from the Dublin summit and various documents from the Italian presidency as well as documents summarising the IGC positions of the member states (LWG IGC12D) and papers drafted by Whitty which explored various submissions made in the IGC by the presidency, Commission and other member states (LWG IGC12D) and by the UK (LWG IGC12E). With a general election campaign in the UK virtually certain to commence within the next six months, of primary importance to the LWG considerations at this stage were the submissions being made by the UK government to the IGC and the development of a viable response by the Labour party to them. While dismissing most of the UK government submissions in relation to the ECJ, quality of legislation and enforcement of subsidiarity as unworkable and/or political gestures designed mainly for domestic political consumption, Whitty's paper did suggest support for UK submissions on strengthening the CFSP secretariat, enforcement of legislation (which would, contrary to the government's wishes, actually enhance the role of the ECJ), facilitating public/private sector partnerships in TENs, competition in agriculture and animal welfare (LWG IGC12E).[34]

While a few of the UK submissions indicated that the Conservative government was attempting to make some constructive contribution to the reform debate, the general tone of its discourse clearly indicated that it would not agree to any substantive treaty changes in the IGC. Such obstructionism had reached its apotheosis in the beef crisis, and while the non co-operation policy had ended, the behaviour of the UK government continued to be characterised by it, particularly when it came to public statements. The government's IGC stance was clearly being designed for public consumption in the UK. A feeling had hardened across the EU institutions and member states, following the beef crisis, that no real agreement would be achieved at the IGC until after the general election in the UK had taken place (Dinan 1999: 175). While most member governments, not just the PES ones, were clearly exasperated with the UK government following the beef crisis and appeared to be hoping for a Labour victory which would bring a more constructive approach, there was also a view that even a Conservative re-election would improve the situation by at least giving the Major government greater leeway for constructive engagement in the negotiations without having to play to the electoral gallery (McDonagh 1998: 53-54).

Conclusion

Not only had the beef crisis placed the UK government's standing in the EU at a serious low, it also had serious implications for the Labour party. In being forced to give tacit support to the government's non co-operation policy, Labour's stance during the crisis placed in jeopardy its tactic of using the LWG to ensure a coherent party approach on the IGC (in Westminster and in Brussels). Moreover, this also placed at risk the good relations with its PES sister parties (particularly those in government) which were integral to its strategy of minimising undesirable developments within the IGC and allowing it to present itself as in the 'mainstream' of a European agenda which would not threaten UK interests. Labour's response to the beef crisis thus left the leadership torn between maintaining the goodwill of the EPLP, PES group and its PES sister parties and allowing the Conservative government to successfully exploit any political space between government and opposition policy by portraying Labour as betrayers of the national interest. Labour's reaction to the beef crisis appeared to demonstrate the primacy of domestic politics in its IGC policy-making. Nevertheless, in spite of the domestic political climate, the considered approach to policy-making that characterised the workings of the LWG had resulted in the adoption of a set of credible policy positions on the IGC that reflected the Labour party's new pragmatic Europeanism and clearly distinguished it from the destructive isolationism of the Conservative government. The pro-European conversion of the Labour party appeared to be irreversible and was reflected in its engagement with the mainstream IGC agenda developing on the continent. Certain 'Europeanising' influences on policy-making had facilitated this engagement and militated against any major slippage from the social democratic pro-Europeanism that characterised Labour's EU policy statements in the early 1990s. In particular, relations between the Labour leadership and the PES, the EPLP and, to a lesser extent, the trade unions contributed a Europeanising influence on IGC policy. The chapter that follows will explore the impact of these relationships in greater detail.

Notes

[1] Cook had consistently topped the polls (or come close to the top) for the shadow cabinet and the constituency section of the party National Executive Committee (NEC), demonstrating his popularity among both among Labour MPs and the wider party.

[2] Wickham-Jones cites a *New Statesman* article in 1994 which reported that the feeling on the left of the party was that Cook's new posting had removed from a position of influence over economic policy the last remaining senior figure in the shadow cabinet critical of Brown's 'ultra-cautious economic strategy'. Cook had pushed for a more interventionist strategy as shadow trade and industry spokesman, coming into conflict with Brown, and was reportedly upset to be moved from this post. Wickham-Jones cites an official biography of Cook, according to which Cook 'realised it would take him out of the economic policy loop - which was exactly what Gordon Brown wanted' (2000: 105-106).

[3] David Martin had been rapporteur of the Parliament's report on the Maastricht IGC and had produced a number of publications calling for a federal EU constitution (Martin 1992).

[4] The Economic and Social Committee was established by the original EEC treaty in 1957. It comprised representatives of employers, employees (i.e. trade unions) and other interest groups. It was formally consulted in a range of EC policy areas.

[5] This was agreed following discussion of the detailed paper submitted by Whitty on QMV extension (LWG IGC3D), as commissioned by the second LWG meeting (LWG3 Minutes). This went through the existing treaty provisions covered by QMV and unanimity, and made recommendations as regards areas where QMV extension could be supported. Following discussion, it was agreed that the party would support the extension of QMV in all areas of social and environmental policy (but not green taxes, which would come under fiscal policy) and would discuss further the issue of nuclear energy. The party would 'probably' support QMV in the area of culture, most aspects of industrial policy, competition policy and structural policy. However, extension of QMV would be opposed on fiscal policy, own resources and budget, ECB matters, most human rights, JHA and CFSP, and 'probably' also on electoral arrangements and appointments. However, in some of these areas 'more detailed discussion would be needed.'

[6] This was agreed on the basis of a paper on the EP's powers and procedures (LWG IGC4B) drawn up by Whitty. Although Whitty had suggested that one of the EP representatives draft such a paper, the task again fell to him.

[7] This was also agreed on the basis of Whitty's recommendations in his paper on EP powers (LWG IGC4B).

[8] For example on the issue of wide-ranging EU anti-racism provisions, Blair over-ruled Straw, who wanted to restrict anti-racism provisions to the workplace (Interview with Labour MEP).

[9] Strang's paper setting out proposals for CAP reform (LWG IGC7C), submitted to the seventh LWG meeting actually followed on from an initial background paper on CAP (LWG IGC4A) submitted to the fourth LWG meeting by Quin, which drew attention to the enormous potential costs of extending the existing CAP regime to an enlarged EU.

[10] Support for such a strategy by Brown was not entirely inconsistent as he had, as shadow chancellor under the Smith leadership, advocated a European recovery programme, involving counter-cyclical measures, as proposed by Ken Coates and Stuart Holland in 1992 and later included in the Delors white paper on growth, competitiveness and employment in 1993 (Anderson and Mann 1997: 93-97).

[11] Prior to Labour's conversion to pro-Europeanism under Kinnock, Straw had been a founder member of the anti-EC Labour Common Market Safeguards Committee and a political ally of the long-standing anti-EC stalwart Peter Shore (Anderson and Mann 1997: 251-252).

[12] Straw stated on the BBC Radio 4 Today programme on 15 February that 'the issue of border controls and immigration policy must be for the UK government alone to determine and not for European institutions' and declared that Labour MEPs who were expressing support for free movement within the EU and opposition to the Conservative government's insistence on the retention of national border controls were not reflecting party policy (*The Guardian, Daily Mail*, 16 February 1995).

[13] Ford had been rapporteur of the EP's Committee of Inquiry on Racism and Xenophobia in 1990 and had been a member of the Consultative Commission on Racism and Xenophobia established by the EU in 1994. He strongly endorsed the latter's proposal for a first pillar treaty anti-discrimination treaty provision. Straw maintained that such a provision should be placed in the third pillar. Ford would also be rapporteur, in June 1996, for an EP report advocating the elimination of all frontier controls within the EU (Interview with Ford).

[14] The minutes of the seventh LWG meeting (LWG7 Minutes) reported that Straw's working-party had only just met and that the precise draft of its paper on JHA (LWG IGC7E) had not been cleared by Straw or the other participants.

[15] This was based on a recommendations made in a paper submitted by Whitty (LWG IGC5E), endorsing limited EC co-operation in energy and tourism but rejecting any EC role in civil protection. Probably due to the relatively minor nature of the proposals, this was an exception to the general pattern whereby the relevant spokespersons produced position papers on 'vertical' policy issues. Whitty's paper did, however, make it clear that it was drafted following consultations with the relevant front-bench spokespersons.

[16] The minutes of the fifth LWG meeting reported that there was agreement that close contact would be maintained, via Cook and Whitty, with Kinnock's office in the Commission, in order to 'co-ordinate responses to the public release of the Commission's position' (LWG5 Minutes).

[17] The report was submitted to the LWG meeting jointly in the names of both Whitty and Norris.

[18] The system of joint policy committees, composed of representatives of the shadow cabinet and the NEC, was established under Kinnock's leadership, in order to co-ordinate party policy development (Taylor 1999: 15-16).

[19] Following Cook's re-editing, the final version added a new paragraph in the sub-section on the CAP calling for a radical reform of the common fisheries policy as well as the CAP (LWG IGC8A: 7). It also added a new sub-section on the Committee of the Regions and the Economic and Social Committee stating opposition to any attempts to limit or downgrade their involvement, and in relation to the former, stated support for enhancing its independence and authority and ensuring that its membership was determined by the regions themselves rather than central government (LWG IGC8A: 12-13).

[20] The system of nominating Commissioners, and the linked issue of QMV reweighting, had been considered at the fourth LWG meeting on the basis of the discussion paper on the institutional implications of enlargement (LWG IGC4D) submitted by Whitty.

[21] Though there was some resistance to this from John Prescott, partly because Prescott was an intermittent attendee at LWG meetings and was slightly detached from the discussions leading to the adoption of Labour's position on codecision (Interview with LWG participant).

[22] The wording of the reference to the EP role in JHA appeared to have been altered at each stage in the drafting process. Whitty's original draft called for 'greater accountability to the European and national parliaments' but Cook's re-edited draft stated only that the IGC 'should examine ways in which the European Parliament can be more fully consulted' while the final version approved by conference redressed this somewhat by stating that the EP 'should be more fully consulted on justice and home affairs policies.' This indicates that there may have been some haggling within the Labour leadership on this point.

[23] The chair's note for the ninth LWG meeting explained that these events made a meeting necessary (LWG9 Chair's Note).

[24] Corbett's report on the UK positions was annexed to LWG IGC9A.

[25] Although all member states except for the UK indicated support for an extension of QMV, the precise policy areas in which such an extension was supported varied from state to state (McDonagh 1998: 156).

[26] Though the UK was not totally isolated on these issues, for example: Germany shared UK opposition to employment provision, France shared the UK reluctance on Council transparency, and the neutral states shared UK caution on developing the EU-WEU relationship, it was notable that the UK was consistently in the small minority, while the identity of the other member states in this minority differed from issue to issue.

[27] Although there had been some discussion of a general anti-discrimination clause in the context of consideration of anti-racism provisions, a clear line on a general anti-discrimination had not so far emerged.

[28] David Davis had been alone within the Reflection Group in opposing anti-discrimination provisions, and in a minority in opposing ECHR incorporation. Though the Labour leadership broadly endorsed anti-discrimination provisions, the precise scope of their application was a cause of controversy within the LWG because of concerns – similar to those expressed in relation to the more specific anti-racism provisions - about the extension of jurisdiction to the ECJ over sensitive discrimination cases (Interview with LWG participant).

[29] This compromise was agreed in January 1966 after the then French president, Charles de Gaulle had withdrawn French ministers from the Council of Ministers in a dispute over Commission proposals to secure budgetary independence for the EC, increase the role of the EP and move to greater use of majority voting in the Council. The compromise allowed member states to block decisions when vital national interests were at stake (Dinan 1999: 48-49). The consensus view within the EU institutions and member states was that the Luxembourg compromise, which was never a legal principle, had been rendered obsolete by the moves to QMV in the SEA and TEU (Dinan 1999: 262).

[30] Respecting the institutional framework implied that enhanced co-operation under flexibility would have to respect the conventional roles of the Commission, Council and EP in the policy areas in which it was utilised.

[31] McDonagh suggests that the support offered at this stage for flexibility by those IGC players (i.e. the Benelux countries and the Commission) traditionally viewed as staunch defenders of the 'Community method' and the 'integrity of Community institutions' was highly significant (McDonagh 1998: 142).

[32] The Euro-sceptic Conservative home secretary, Michael Howard referred to the need to 'repatriate' the ECJ's powers (Young, H 1999: 501), while his Cabinet colleague, Peter

Lilley, referred to the political nature of its decisions (Young, H 1999: 444). Among the cases that aroused the anger of the Euro-sceptics was the ruling of the ECJ in March 1994 that, in the privatisation of public services the British government had ignored a 1977 EC directive guaranteeing certain employment rights following the transfer of ownership of undertakings (Pilkington 1995: 168-169). Another ECJ ruling that caused controversy in Britain was the Barber judgement of 1990, which ruled that occupational pensions should be paid to men and women at the same age. This and other related judgements obliged the British government to equalise the pensionable ages of men and women in order to comply with art.119 of the Treaty of Rome on equal treatment for men and women. In 1991, Euro-sceptical opinion in Britain was outraged that an ECJ ruling had forced the suspension of a recently adopted act of parliament: the ECJ had ruled that the Merchant Shipping Act in 1988 contravened the EC common fisheries policy, as the provisions of the Act had been used to deny a Spanish-owned but UK-based company (Factortame) access to British fishing quotas (Dinan 1999: 311). Further controversy would ensue later in 1996, when the ECJ rejected a case brought by the British government that the working time directive adopted by the Council in 1993 had gone beyond the scope laid down in the health of safety provisions (art.118a) of the SEA (Young, JW 2000: 173). For discussion of the ECJ's role in furthering European integration see Burley and Mattli (1993) and Wincott (1996).

[33] This would involve the Commission identifying a clear legal base for any proposed legislation or action. It would have to establish that the issue being addressed had a pan-European dimension and that non-action would harm EC interests while action would have clear benefits.

[34] The UK government submission on CFSP provided for a modest strengthening of the Council CFSP secretariat, involving secondment from member states and the Commission and a better interface with the WEU and the external relations function of the Commission. The proposal on enforcement of legislation proposed giving the Commission greater resources to oversee enforcement of EC legislation and encouraging it to make greater use of art. 171 to request the ECJ levy fines for non-compliance with legal decisions. The submission on animal welfare proposed a treaty protocol obliging EC policies in agriculture, transport, the internal market and research to pay full regard to the welfare requirements of animals. The UK government had proposed a protocol to the treaty because it was against its policy of non-extension of treaty competence to propose a stronger wording in the treaty proper. Whitty's paper on the UK submissions proposed that Labour should support a stronger wording on this issue within the treaty proper (LWG IGC12E). The submission on TENs (Trans-European Networks) proposed a treaty provision to provide for public sector-private partnership projects. The submission on competition in agriculture proposed that EU competition rules apply to those agricultural sectors not subject to common organisation.

Chapter 4

The PES, the EPLP
and the Trade Unions:
Europeanising Influences on Policy?

Labour, the PES and the IGC

The downturn in Labour's relations with its sister parties in the PES which was provoked by its response to the beef crisis was unfortunate given that the general view within the Labour leadership at the launch of the IGC was that policy co-ordination between Labour and its PES colleagues on the IGC had been fairly successful. Indeed, on a note of self-congratulation, the chair's note to the ninth LWG meeting in February 1996, just prior to the IGC launch, had declared that the Labour party had managed on most issues to be in the mainstream of the approach of the PES parties (LWG9 Chair's Note). From the outset of the work of the LWG, a key plank of the leadership strategy was to avoid isolation within the PES (though remaining mindful of domestic constraints) while also seeking to indirectly influence the IGC agenda through those PES parties in government in other member states. This necessitated firmly conveying to its PES colleagues the nature of the domestic constraints that Labour was operating under and the extent to which the Conservative government intended to exploit the IGC for domestic electoral advantage. Accordingly, Labour would seek PES co-operation in avoiding the adoption of joint declarations that were likely to cause Labour domestic difficulty while also seeking to cajole those PES colleagues that were in government into minimising developments on the IGC agenda that the Conservatives could exploit for domestic purposes.

The Labour leadership was able to convey its position to its PES colleagues at various levels, including at the regular PES leaders' meetings (usually held to coincide with European Council meetings), PES bureau meetings (comprised of senior representatives from each national party, including Prescott) and meetings of the PES IGC working-group (compromising the leaders' representatives) which had been set up by the PES bureau in September 1994. Reports back from these various meetings would be a regular feature of LWG meetings. One of the initial priorities of the LWG was to influence the work of the PES working-group on the IGC, given its intention to submit a report for consideration at the Valbonne meeting of PES leaders in June 1995, in time to input into the Reflection Group deliberations. Parallel discussions were also being undertaken in order to draft a declaration, which would involve references to the IGC, in time for the PES congress to be held in Barcelona in early March 1995.[1] Quin had initially been appointed as Labour's representative to the IGC working-group. Although Whitty had suggested that he also be made a member, it appears that given the importance attributed to PES developments, Cook became a member of the working-group, and usually led the Labour party delegation at its meetings. Cook would take the lead role in explaining Labour's positions and enhancing its general profile within the PES and seeking the sympathy and understanding of the PES parties for Labour's positions. While Cook was highly successful in this, Blair appeared rather detached from involvement in the PES, generally avoiding attendance at PES leaders' meetings and authorising Cook and/or Prescott to attend on his behalf. This partly reflected his preference for bilateral meetings with other party leaders over the formal set-piece multilateral forums such as PES leaders' meetings towards which he exhibited some impatience (Interviews with LWG participants).

Cook was usually accompanied by Whitty and/or Sigler at the various PES meetings he attended. Sigler was usually in attendance at the PES IGC working-group meeting and drew up reports of their proceedings, which were circulated to the LWG. The overlap in membership between the PES working-group and the LWG was increased by Green and Martin also being members of the PES working-group, due to their respective positions within the PES group and EP. As leader of the PES parliamentary group, Green was also present at PES leaders' meetings, providing the LWG with an additional perspective on these. She was also present at the 'co-ordination meetings' of PES party leaders who were in government (usually held prior to European Council meetings) from which the Labour party had generally been excluded, providing the party with a useful presence and a source of information on proceedings. Green was of particular assistance to the Labour leadership in facilitating its networking with other PES party leaderships and, given her strong personal relationship with Blair, was also active in persuading him to engage more fully in PES activity and talk to other PES leaders (Interview with LWG participant). In addition, Whitty was particularly active in undertaking bilateral meetings with officials from the various PES parties and, in the course of his duties as European co-ordinator, visited most of the PES parties, taking advantages of the contacts he had developed in his nine years as party general-secretary.

Initial developments within the PES did not bode well for the Labour leadership. The chair's note to the second LWG meeting had reported that the Labour party had been in a minority of almost one on the question of QMV extension at the Essen meeting of PES leaders on 7 December 1994, and also described the first draft declaration for Barcelona as a 'disastrous' document that would have to be stopped. This had prompted Blair to make a personal intervention with the PES president, Rudolf Scharping (LWG2 Chair's Note).

However, more detailed discussion of IGC policy within the PES working-group revealed a slightly different story, with divisions existing among the PES parties on a number of issues. In particular, a number of PES parties (predominantly those from the Nordic countries) shared Labour's reservations as regards the federalist tendencies of some of the others, such as the French, Belgians, Spanish and Italians. A report on the positions of the various PES parties, submitted to the third LWG meeting by Sigler (LWG IGC3C) and based on the first exchange of views held within the PES working-group on 12-13 January 1995, revealed that the views of the continental parties were not quite as monolithic as some in the Labour party might have imagined. Following consideration of Sigler's report by the third LWG meeting, there was a feeling within the LWG that PES positions were considerably closer to the likely Labour party position than might have been expected (LWG3 Minutes). Caricatures depicting the Labour party as isolated among a swathe of uniformly federalist PES colleagues were certainly mistaken. There were a number of differing cleavages separating the PES parties, for example, differences between the northern and southern Europeans on some issues, between parties from the smaller and larger states on others, and parties from the original more 'federalist' inclined six EC members and the newer entrants on others. Moreover, a number of parties shared the approach set out in the strategy paper (LWG IGC2A) that Cook had submitted to the LWG, i.e. advocacy of a positive agenda focusing on the concerns of the citizens. For example, the Austrians argued that there would be no point getting into an institutional debate unless the EU dealt more effectively with issues of immediate concerns to the citizens, i.e. unemployment, environmental protection and racism, while the Swedes were similarly arguing that issues such as employment, social affairs and the environment needed to top the agenda, rather than institutional affairs. Indeed, both the Swedes and the Finns were questioning whether further ambitious institutional changes were appropriate at this juncture. The Dutch Labour party (PVDA) and the Spanish PSOE also expressed sympathy with the need for a broader strategic vision incorporating matters of popular concern, though both did favour ambitious institutional reform. But while there were some reservations among certain PES parties about the extent of change, there was a consensus that some institutional reform was required in order to facilitate enlargement (though one or two questioned the pace and extent of enlargement altogether). Cook had placed the Labour party very much in the mainstream of PES thinking during the initial exchange of views in its IGC working-group by indicating support for some QMV extension and for an extension of EP codecision in those areas where QMV applied as part of a wider simplification of decision-making procedures, and for greater transparency in decision-making, while also stressing the need to emphasise a positive agenda based on popular concerns (PES IGC Working-Party, January 1995).

Where differences occurred within the PES, they were generally not differences that isolated Labour and they involved different groupings of national parties. For example, on the changes required to facilitate enlargement, the parties from the smaller states tended to depart from those from the larger states in their opposition to reforms diminishing their voting strength in Council or removing their rights to a Commissioner. Labour was more likely to find itself allied with the French socialists and German SPD on these issues. But Labour was closer to many of the parties from the small states as regards their caution towards the proposals emanating from the French and German centre-right governments for a hard-core or two-speed Europe, although opposition to this also came from the SPD opposition in Germany (the PS in France were closer to their own government).

There were also differences on defence, where Labour allied itself with the Danes and the parties from the neutral states in opposing suggestions from the others that the PES back an EU defence role. In general, the parties from the original six EC member states, together with the Spanish, tended to be the most federalist-minded, while parties from the newer entrants, such as Labour and the Nordic parties tended towards more pragmatic caution (LWG IGC3C, PES IGC Working-Party, January 1995). The parties from the Nordic countries were strongly supportive of attempts by Labour to fend off the federalist advances of some of the other parties. Labour also had support for its positions from other parties on particular issues. For example, on varying issues, Pauline Green suggests that Labour had support from the Dutch (who were the closest ideologically to New Labour), the Greeks, the Portuguese or the Austrians (Interview with Green). This is not to say that Labour was always seeking to form alliances with certain parties in order to stave off the more 'pro-integration' proposals of others. On some issues, Labour was actually closer to the 'pro-integration' camp than some of its PES colleagues. For example, Labour was more sympathetic towards enhancing the EP's power than the French or the Swedes, and more progressive than the Spanish on environment and employment policy (although all the PES parties were generally agreed on the need to strengthen provisions in these two policy areas). Accordingly, the difficulties in reaching agreement between the various PES parties, each with their own national perspective, reduced the likelihood of the Labour party being placed in an awkward position when it came to adopting a final joint PES position on the IGC. Indeed, given the difficulty in agreeing concrete positions among the PES parties, the declaration agreed by the PES leaders for the Barcelona congress of 6-8 March deliberately did not go into great detail on the IGC, thereby avoiding the 'disastrous' position earlier feared by the Labour leadership (LWG IGC5A).

While Sigler's report of the second PES working-group meeting held on 30-31 March (LWG IGC5A) indicated that the Italians, French and Spanish parties 'were still clearly on a much more federalist position'(LWG5 Chair's Note), it was suggested that most PES parties were closer to the pragmatic positioning of Labour. Sigler described Italian proposals presented to the working-group as 'completely detached both from the views of the other parties and of the wider electorate, representing instead a reaction to the peculiar political situation that currently exists in Italy',[2] and those of the Spanish representative as representing an 'extravagant' and rather 'unreal agenda.' As regards the latter, Sigler explained that there had been a general feeling within the PES working-group that the Spanish paper 'was not in touch with the reality of the situation.' The Labour leadership was now displaying confidence that the draft position of the PES working-group would be 'broadly in line with Labour party thinking' (LWG5 Minutes). Indeed, Sigler reported agreement within the PES working-group that the PES position should deal with issues that were critical to the people, setting out a distinct positive socialist agenda. This was a line with strong echoes of Cook's LWG strategy paper (LWG IGC2A).

As intended from the outset, an initial draft report on the IGC from the PES working-group, produced by its rapporteur, the Dutch MEP Jan Marinus Wiersma (and PVDA European secretary) was presented to its third meeting on 11-12 May

(PES IGC Working-Party, May 1995a). As agreed, the report stressed a positive PES agenda on the issues of unemployment, CFSP, enlargement and the creation of a Europe of the citizens, and in exploring institutional change, focused on the themes of transparency, democracy and effective decision-making. At this meeting, Cook had declared himself in broad agreement with the majority of the initial draft report, suggesting that only a few minor changes were needed. Similarly, Sigler suggested that the balance in Wiersma's first draft was right 'with much more emphasis on the issues of concern and less concentration on institutional questions.' Among the changes that Cook sought were removal of a reference to 'extending the resource base' (which he viewed as a veiled suggestion that the EU have tax-raising powers), and a greater emphasis on what the objectives of the CFSP should be, rather than the institutional mechanisms. Additionally, Cook called for a greater emphasis on the need to reform the CAP (an issue that might have been sensitive for the French socialists, among others) and on the benefits of ending the differentiation in social policy, i.e. the UK social protocol opt-out (perhaps reflecting a wish to focus attention on an issue in which Labour was at one with its PES colleagues, markedly in contrast to the British government, and which could be presented positively domestically). Similarly, with half an eye on Labour's domestic constitutional reform agenda, Cook argued within the PES working-group that references to subsidiarity 'should look beyond nations and consider the role of the regions' (LWG IGC6B). Again this was an issue where the Labour leadership hoped to contrast its progressive attitude to the limited and opportunistic interpretation of subsidiarity offered by the Conservative government, i.e. one based solely on concentration of power at nation-state level.

Following consideration of its initial draft report by the PES working-group, Wiersma produced a further amended draft reflecting the discussion in the May meeting (PES IGC Working-Party May 1995b). The second draft actually appeared to employ a more radical discourse than the first draft and one reminiscent of Labour party policy documents in the early 1990s (Labour party 1991a, 1993b) and Cook's earlier LWG strategy papers (IGC2A, IGC3A). It included added references to rejecting the right-wing neo-liberal concept of the EU as merely a free-market zone, to embracing the social democratic rationale for the EU as a means of increasing influence on global economic development, and to employment criteria being a core theme of EMU. However, as desired by Cook, references were added to the need to reform the CAP in the light of enlargement, to the PES parties 'looking forward to a new British government ending the British opt-out of the...social chapter' and to decentralisation below the national level. Wiersma had also responded to the concerns expressed by the Danes among others that there should be more emphasis on environmental objectives. However, references to gradual integration of the second and third pillars into the EC pillar were retained, somewhat contradicting the section on CFSP which explained that it would remain 'largely intergovernmental.' Elsewhere, where the first draft had suggested a reweighting of votes and a reduction to one Commissioner for all member states, the second draft simply referred to the need to examine options for reform, and set out a number of these options. In addition, where the first draft appeared to suggest some form of differentiated integration as inevitable, the second draft downgraded this to a possibility. Dropped completely from the second draft was the suggestion (made in the first draft) to a greater role for the UN security-council members in the CFSP troika, together with the accompanying suggestion that Germany should become a UN security-council member.

This revised text was agreed as a final draft by the PES working-group, with a few additional changes and slight reorganisation in its meeting of 8-9 June, and submitted as a text for discussion for the PES leaders' meeting at Valbonne on 24-25 June (PES IGC Working-Party June 1995, Lightfoot and Wilde 1996: 11). Crucially for Labour, the additional revisions involved rewordings which resulted in the references to the need for the resource base of the EU be broadened and for the second and third pillars to be gradually integrated into the EC pillar becoming options for consideration rather than concrete proposals. The minutes of the sixth LWG meeting recorded a feeling that this revised draft 'was in general consistent with Labour party thinking' (LWG6 Minutes). In potentially awkward areas such as defence, the structure of the Commission and the JHA pillar, the LWG minutes noted appreciatively that the paper simply posed questions or set out options. Avoiding a firm position on JHA and defence was helpful to Labour, as these were the two areas in which its disagreement with the majority of the PES parties was at its greatest (Newman 1996: 24). Restructuring the membership of the Commission provoked wider divisions among the PES parties. But avoiding a firm position here was also helpful to Labour given that official policy within the LWG was to seek to maintain the UK's two Commissioners. Labour would not want this undermined by a contradictory policy in the PES and also would not want to be depicted by its opponents in the UK as ready to negotiate away one of the country's Commissioners. Further reducing the possibility of awkwardness for Labour or the other PES parties, it was agreed that there would no longer be a PES leaders' declaration at Valbonne based on the report, as had originally been suggested. Rather, work would continue within the PES working-group on preparing a position for consideration by the PES leaders' conclave in Madrid in November (originally intended for October), with a final report scheduled for adoption at a second PES leaders' meeting in Madrid, prior to the European Council in December (LWG6 Minutes). Indeed, when the report was presented to the PES leaders at Valbonne, an addition to the introduction stressed that discussion within the PES working-group was continuing and that 'it should be emphasised that the views are not the decided views of the PES and do not bind the PES member parties' (PES IGC Working-Party, June 1995).

It had generally been agreed by the Labour leadership that the positions agreed within the LWG would form the basis of all its interventions in PES discussions (LWG6 Minutes). But in a number of areas, the PES working-group was ahead of the LWG in adopting various policy positions and Cook thus found himself taking positions within the PES in advance of their adoption by the LWG. However, as was the case in all the various PES meetings related to the IGC, these positions were likely to have been taken following consultation between the key figures within the LWG, notably Blair, Cook and Whitty.

Labour's representatives at PES leaders' meetings (usually Prescott and Cook) went equipped with comprehensive briefings on the IGC drawn up by Whitty, setting out the strategy to be pursued by the Labour representatives and providing detailed outlines of the various issues to be discussed, Labour's agreed positions and the positions of the other PES parties. The leaders' meetings were usually held just prior to European Council meetings. However, there were some specially convened meetings, such as the Madrid conclave on 11 November 1995. As the brief for the conclave explained, its aim was to produce a draft declaration for the later Madrid meeting to be held in December (LP PES Brief, November 1995). The paper produced by the PES working-group for Valbonne would provide a focus for discussion, as would papers produced by various members of the working-group on specific issues, such as one by Cook on CFSP. In setting out Labour's general approach to the IGC, the brief for the meeting provided a succinct reflection of Labour's strategy and the pressures upon it:

> Labour uniquely faces an election in the next eighteen months where the main opposition - the government - will run a seriously anti-European campaign. Public opinion in Britain is deeply sceptical about Europe and its institutions. The public position of the party is therefore both pro-European in the British context and cautious in some European eyes...It is important to emphasise that - whilst of course there will be areas of continuity of British interests and British attitudes - a Labour government's role in Europe will be positive and constructive in contrast to the negative and often isolationist position of the Tories. We will be seeking allies in particular amongst the Socialist-led governments.

Labour's representatives would therefore present their views on the IGC to their PES colleagues in terms of a three level approach, which reflected the strategy earlier set out by Cook within the LWG: 1) 'relatively limited' immediate institutional changes 'to improve operational effectiveness and democratic legitimacy' but seen in the context of; 2) the critical requirement that the EU's leaders use the IGC to revitalise the European project by convincing the public that Europe was essential for jobs, for the environment, for social protection and equality and for peace and security. This also required an emphasis on the need for democracy and transparency; 3) thirdly, the feeling that a broader strategic discussion was required on the broader issues facing the EU, i.e. enlargement, EMU, budgetary reform (including financing and reform of the CAP) and the changing role of NATO. It was stressed that decisions on institutional matters needed to be made in the context of the broader European agenda and that any reforms could not be allowed 'to make solutions to these broader problems more difficult' and should ideally 'be designed to make them easier' (LP PES Brief, November 1995).

The Madrid conclave discussed general developments as regards the IGC, including its likely timing, duration and scope. With Spain, then still governed by the socialist PSOE, holding the Council presidency and its representative (Carlos Westendorp) chairing the Reflection Group, the Spanish prime minister, Felipe Gonzales, was particularly well placed to give his PES colleagues an overview of developments. While Labour was seeking to influence IGC developments through contacts with those PES parties that were in government, the latter were in turn eager for Labour's views on developments in the UK, in terms of the likely tactics to be used by the Conservative government, the probable timing of a general election (until when, serious progress in the IGC would be difficult) and the change in approach that Labour would bring. Moreover, the PES parties in government were seeking Labour's view on whether delaying the IGC until the UK general election (and hopefully a Labour victory) would be worthwhile. Cook, Whitty and Sigler had already exploited Labour's PES contacts in visiting Spain on 20 July to discuss the developing IGC agenda and progress in the Reflection Group with PSOE government ministers and party representatives (LWG IGC7B). PSOE ministers had indicated that they expected the IGC to move slowly until the UK general election, after which they presumably hoped that the election of their 'sister' Labour party would bring about a more conciliatory approach on the part of the UK government. Unfortunately for the PSOE it would not be involved in the IGC end game itself, as it would lose office in 1996.

Noting that the PES leaders at Madrid would 'want a steer on Labour's views on the timing of the IGC', the brief for the leaders' conclave suggested that Labour 'should be a bit cautious on this in case it were quoted back in public.' The brief referred to a similar incident earlier in the year, when it was leaked that Chancellor Kohl had indicated that he was waiting for a Labour government (LP PES Brief, November 1995). Such incidents were a double-edged sword for Labour. On the one hand, they could be portrayed positively as illustrating the extent to which the Conservatives had left the UK isolated in Europe so that only with a Labour government could the UK be taken seriously again within the EU. On the other hand, it gave Labour's opponents an opportunity to portray other EU governments as looking forward to a Labour government that would cave in to their demands and 'sell out' British interests.

Accordingly, in discussing IGC timing with their PES colleagues at Madrid, Labour's representatives would point to the uncertainty of the timing of the general election in Britain and therefore suggest that it would be 'imprudent to base the IGC timing on the British electoral timetable.' However, Labour's representatives would stress that the Conservative government would be running an anti-EU campaign in the run-up to the election and would be very reluctant to complete negotiations and sign anything prior to it, 'even a minimalist treaty.' Therefore it was 'marginally better' for Labour 'to give them as short a time as possible with the IGC in the headlines' This pointed towards 'a later rather than early 1996 start.' The brief also pointed to the absence of a coherent agenda for the IGC (when the Reflection Group reported shortly after, surprise was expressed within the LWG at the clear agenda provided) and the poor shape of the Italian government that was about to take over the Council presidency for the first half of 1996 as reasons to delay the launch of the IGC.[3] Though the brief suggested that the best scenario for the Labour party would be to not start the IGC until mid-1997, it was recognised that this was not likely to be acceptable elsewhere. It was therefore suggested that the various considerations outlined made the most feasible option a formal IGC launch under the Italian presidency in June, but with the real work starting in autumn 1996 under the Irish presidency and continuing under the Dutch presidency in 1997. Though 'not necessarily the best scenario for the Labour party in domestic electoral terms', it was suggested that this would at least prevent the Conservatives from running the IGC for a full year (LP PES Brief, November 1995). Although the IGC would actually be launched by the Italians in March 1996, the suggestion that the real work of the IGC would not start until late 1996 proved a fairly accurate estimation.

The brief identified certain 'areas of disagreement' that would be a focus of discussion during the Madrid conclave. These included employment, enlargement, EMU, JHA and CFSP. However, it was only in relation to the latter two issues that Labour was at the centre of the disagreement. In relation to employment, while most PES parties supported the principle of a treaty chapter, one or two were hesitant (with the Spanish particularly negative) and there were differences over how an employment chapter would operate. Similarly, in relation to enlargement, while the rhetoric of all was positive, in practice some parties, notably those from countries that had done well from EC funds, e.g. the Spanish, Portuguese and Irish, were now anxious about losing out to the east, and all parties saw difficulties in terms of the institutional and financial reforms required and the implications for security arrangements. In relation to EMU, while there would be some questioning as regards Labour's attitude to the UK opt-out, the focal point of discussion would be recent negative pronouncements as regards the viability of the EMU project by the German SPD which had 'caused serious problems' for those PES parties in government which had had to pursue unpopular budget austerity in order to achieve convergence. It was the proposals to communitise JHA and (to a lesser extent) CFSP that caused particular difficulty in Labour's relations with some of its PES colleagues. The brief stressed that Labour would continue to make clear its opposition to the merger of the two intergovernmental pillars into the EC pillar in the face of 'pressure from almost all other parties to agree some degree of communitisation of the JHA pillar and from the French, Germans, Italians, Spanish and Belgians for the merger of the CFSP pillar into the first pillar.' While the Labour position on pillar merger bore a close resemblance to that of the Conservative government, Labour's representatives would stress the areas of policy where its positions were in the PES and (unlike the Conservatives) European mainstream, such as the role of the EP, QMV extension, transparency, ECHR incorporation, social policy, environment, subsidiarity and racism (LP PES Brief, November 1995). Indeed, in this and other PES meetings, Labour would seek to allay suspicion among its PES colleagues that a Labour government would not be too different from the Conservatives, by stressing its differing approach on these first pillar issues while also drawing attention to its greater openness towards reaching solutions on the second and third pillars.

The additional discussions on the IGC that took place within the PES both within the IGC working-group and at leader level in Madrid in November, did not result in any major changes either in style or substance from the document submitted to Valbonne. Like the document submitted at Valbonne, the declaration on the IGC finally adopted by the second Madrid meeting of PES leaders in December 1995 employed elements of social democratic discourse, but was rather generalist in its approach and did not put forward a definitive or detailed line in several areas (Lightfoot and Wilde 1996: 11-12). In some respects, the Madrid declaration was less specific than the Valbonne document. For example, it omitted references to Council vote reweighting and Commission reorganisation altogether, given the divisions between the PES parties from small and large states. Conversely, the Madrid declaration was slightly more specific on defence, suggesting that the EU's capacity to promote security through the WEU should be enhanced, while continuing to avoid a firm position on whether the WEU should be integrated into the EU. Similarly, it was more specific in relation to environmental policy, suggesting that QMV extension was required here and stressing that no member state should be forced to lower environmental standards, but it avoided the awkward question (for Labour) of QMV for green taxation. The Madrid declaration was also more fulsome and specific in its treatment of employment, calling for a maximum level of employment to be made a central policy objective of the EU, involving co-ordination of member states' labour market policies, optimal use of EU funds for employment regeneration, reduction of working-time and reorganisation of work and the implementation of trans-European investment programmes. Generally, however, the content of the Madrid declaration echoed the paper submitted at Valbonne both in stressing the need for a positive social democratic agenda which made employment and social and environmental policy goals core elements of EU policy, on a par with EMU, and in the specific reforms proposed, e.g. significant extension of QMV (while recognising that some areas required the maintenance of unanimity), open and transparent decision-making (with legislation adopted by the Council in public), fewer and simplified procedures and an enhanced role for the EP (including codecision where QMV applied and full scrutiny over the whole budget). References to communitisation of the intergovernmental pillars continued to be avoided (PES, December 1995).

Labour's representatives at the second Madrid leaders' meeting, Prescott and Cook, had arrived equipped with a number of proposed amendments to the draft declaration on the IGC (LP PES Brief, December 1995). An examination of the final declaration illustrates that though not entirely successful in getting these amendments agreed, the compromises adopted were compatible with Labour's own positions. The most crucial amendments related to EMU and the JHA pillar. On EMU, Labour had sought deletion of part of a sentence indicating support for the convergence criteria and timetable. Though it did not succeed in this aim, a compromise rewording referred to 'ensuring that those countries proceeding to the single currency meet the agreed EMU convergence criteria and timetable.' This was acceptable as it left open the question of which countries were proceeding to the final stage of EMU. In relation to JHA, though references to communitisation had not been included, mainly because of earlier Labour interventions, the draft declaration had included a sentence calling for strengthened majority decision-making, a stronger role for the European Commission, democratic scrutiny by the EP and the availability of judicial review by the ECJ in JHA. The Labour representatives sought unsuccessfully to have the whole of this sentence deleted. Although references to strengthened decision-making and greater accountability to the EP were acceptable to Labour, its 'bottom line' was to avoid reference to majority voting or to judicial review powers of the ECJ here. The compromise rewording was more imprecise, and therefore acceptable, in referring to a 'strengthening of decision-making in appropriate areas, a stronger role for the European Commission, democratic scrutiny by the European Parliament and the availability of judicial review by the ECJ, in appropriate agreed areas' (this left open to interpretation the appropriate areas of judicial review and strengthened decision-making). Of the other proposed Labour amendments to the declaration, Prescott and Cook were successful in securing the replacement of the reference to 'a flexibilisation and reduction of working time where and when appropriate' with one referring to 'a reduction of working time and re-organisation of work where and when appropriate in agreement with the social partners.' Sensitive to the Labour commitment to the UK's nuclear 'deterrent', the Labour representatives were also successful in replacing the original reference to the EU having 'an active policy aimed at reduction of nuclear threats within Europe and at a global level' with the more modest reference to the EU having 'an active policy aimed at reduction of nuclear accidents and pollution within Europe and at a global level.' Elsewhere, Labour was successful in securing the insertion of a reference to EU citizenship complementing national citizenship rights, deletion of a reference to enlargement requiring 'a full and clear assessment of the possible consequences for citizens in the EU and in the applicant countries' and insertion of a reference to the principle of subsidiarity involving decisions being taken at the appropriate level, including the regional or local one. The Labour representatives were also successful in ensuring that the reference to an EU of about 27 member states not being 'able to pursue policies on the basis of unanimity' (which implied that a blanket extension of QMV was required) was qualified by the addition of the formula: 'across the full range of policies to which unanimity currently applies' (which implied that a move to QMV was desirable in some but not necessarily all policy areas) (PES December 1995, LP PES Brief, December 1995).

Given the resemblance between the positions enunciated by the PES leaders in the Madrid declaration in December 1995 and those in the policy document adopted by the Labour party conference a few months previously, the chair's note for the ninth LWG meeting in February 1996 was able to indicate with broad satisfaction that Labour had managed on most issues to be in the mainstream of the approach of the PES parties (LWG9 Chair's Note). The presentation of a united PES position at Madrid was dependent on glossing over differences concerning the communitisation of the JHA where Labour was isolated from most of the others (except for the Danes), and other areas where there were divisions between different groups of parties, such as CFSP communitisation and EU/WEU merger (which a number of other parties joined Labour in opposing) and reorganisation of the Commission and vote reweighting (where opinion generally divided between parties from the large states and those from the small states).

The end result of deliberations within the PES on the IGC, both at working-group and leader level, was therefore, the adoption of a rather weak document at Madrid in which specific positions on the key areas of institutional reform were largely absent. Indeed, Pauline Green suggests that the working-group rapporteur, Jan Wiersma, had 'lost heart' with the process of trying to get an agreed substantive PES position on the IGC, given that each of its meetings tended to go over the same issues again and again without making a proper decision on many of the key issues (Interview with Green). There were also suggestions within the working-group that the PES 'party' should just use the position adopted by the PES group in the EP. This would most likely have satisfied the PES parliamentary group representatives within the working-group, including Wiersma himself and Green, Martin and Guigou, who were particularly frustrated at the inability of their national leaders to agree on substantive issues. The outcome was a series of weak 'lowest common denominator' positions, the blame for which could be apportioned among a number of the PES parties who were reluctant to depart from their nationally derived positions in order to reach a compromise.

Although not directly or solely culpable for the weak positions adopted, the Labour leadership was within its rights to feel fairly pleased with itself for avoiding isolation within the PES as the IGC was launched in early 1996. However, the good work in cultivating relationships within the PES risked being undone by Labour's response to the UK government's policy of non co-operation within the EU in the spring of 1996. Labour's tacit support for the government's position was met with dismay by many of its PES colleagues, representing a low point in Labour's relationship with its sister parties. This was illustrated by a note sent from Whitty to Blair, Prescott and Cook on 30 May 1996, in which Whitty himself displayed anxiety about the approach Labour was taking. He wrote:

> I have to report the extreme concern verging on serious antagonism amongst our friends and colleagues in Europe on the government's position and our conditional broad support. I am not necessarily advocating a change of stance but you need to be aware of the strength of feeling. It is quite probable that the government tactics will not work in terms of the escalating objectives they have set themselves and the press and Euro-sceptics are setting for them. They do not have a clear escape route; we ought to make sure we do.

Whitty's note suggested that the Labour leadership take a number of steps to alleviate the situation. These involved: 1) a review of Labour's position and a move to 'a more selective form of pressure'; 2) making contact with 'friendly governments' to explain Labour's stance before the Florence PES leaders meeting of 20 June and the PES bureau meeting of 12 June; 3) briefing the EPLP in order to 'counteract...their own inclinations and Socialist (PES) group politics to condemn the UK outright'; 4) discussions with Kinnock on the European Commission role; 5) making plans 'for a renewed charm offensive with other governments in the autumn to repair damage.'

Whitty's note explained that both he and Sigler had 'had contacts at close to leader level from not only Netherlands, German and Austria (direct to the Austrian chancellor, Vranitzky) who are deeply hostile to our substantive position and cannot understand Labour support but also from Sweden and Denmark who are sympathetic on beef but appalled at the non co-operation policy and seriously unsympathetic to Labour's stance; and Ireland and Portugal who see the position as disastrous.' Whitty explained that this would make Labour's position at the Florence leaders' meeting and at the PES bureau 'very difficult unless some earlier direct explanations are made to the leaders.' Blair would be absent from Florence, a situation that would be 'taken as a further slight' unless such direct explanations were made. Planning for the PES leaders' meeting in Florence would therefore be dominated by the need to explain Labour's position and win back some goodwill from the other PES parties. More importantly, Whitty's note suggested that Labour's stance 'could sour relations in government' (if and when Labour won power) and that the broad message was now 'no favours for any British government.' Critically, Labour's apparent endorsement of this stance had made 'people now argue that there is no point in taking Britain's position into account in the expectation of a more constructive stance' (LP Whitty, 30 May 1996).

A briefing provided by Whitty for Prescott ahead of the PES leaders' meeting in Florence included the text of a statement to be used by Labour's representatives (Prescott would be leading the Labour delegation). Although Blair had already explained the Labour position privately to some of his fellow PES party leaders, the statement was presented as an opportunity to explain directly to the PES leaders the party position in this area 'and some of the domestic politics behind the issue.' Though acknowledging the concern felt within the PES at the Labour party position, it was suggested that Labour's PES colleagues needed to understand that there was a 'strong and rational view' within the UK, which had 'nothing to do with xenophobia and anti-Europeanism', that the other member states were 'not dealing with this issue on the basis of facts.' Furthermore, Labour sought particular understanding from its PES colleagues of the difficult domestic factors that overshadowed its European policy and of the electoral calculations that dominated UK government thinking. In a revealing passage, the statement suggested that Labour's PES colleagues needed to recognise that the issue had 'become part of the tactics of the UK government to characterise the (UK) opposition parties as lackeys of Brussels and to play the nationalist card against us (Labour).' It went on:

> The announcement of non co-operation was a trap set in part for the Labour party and in part to ensnare the Tory Euro-sceptics into supporting John Major. If the Labour party had directly attacked the government's non co-operation tactics, we would have seen the spotlight and the blame shift to Labour. We would have been accused of undermining the government and UK farmers and Labour would have been blamed by the British media if no deal had been achieved.

Accordingly, the statement reaffirmed that Labour agreed with the UK government that 'some pressure (had) to be exerted on the other member states' in order to get the ban lifted and therefore that it 'did not oppose the non co-operation tactic in total provided that it (was) in pursuit of the national interest.' Nevertheless, the statement was illustrative of the somewhat contradictory positions that Labour was adopting in supporting non co-operation while also deriding it as emblematic of the failure of Conservative diplomacy. Thus while professing support for non co-operation, the statement explained that Labour had 'queried and opposed many of the instances where the veto has been used' and had 'not supported the use of the veto where it harms British interests or where it harms innocent third parties.' It gave as an example of this, Labour's opposition to 'the use of the veto on development aid issues.' Furthermore, the statement suggested that Labour had been gradually 'creating a distance' between it and the government 'as they take more and more ludicrous decisions to veto and alienate more and more of our European partners.' In further contradiction of its position, the statement suggested that while Labour 'supported the government in its objective of getting the ban lifted' it recognised that 'the way they have chosen to exert pressure has caused serious and damaging irritation amongst our partners' and that the framework agreed with the Commission for a partial lifting of the ban was 'almost certainly attainable without the policy of non co-operation' and would have been achieved weeks before if the UK Government 'had got down to serious negotiation instead of political posturing' (LP PES Brief, June 1996).

Given the difficulties that it was getting itself into in both defining an internally coherent line and in justifying its stance to its PES colleagues, the ending of the UK non co-operation policy, following the Florence European Council compromise on the gradual lifting of the beef ban, came as a tremendous relief to the Labour leadership. It certainly seemed to take the heat out of the situation for the Labour party and appeared to prevent the deterioration in relations with its PES sister partners from reaching a critical stage. With the first signs of progress in the IGC beginning to be displayed under the Irish presidency in the autumn of 1996, attention within the PES switched to focusing more singularly on the reform agenda, as it did throughout the member states. The PES IGC working-group continued to meet, considering papers produced by the various party representatives on particular issues and, along with meetings of the PES bureau and of the PES leaders, sought to formulate coherent and co-ordinated responses to the developments in the IGC agenda as they arose. However, the PES enjoyed rather limited success in achieving this objective.

As had been seen at Madrid, while agreement could be reached on broad themes, division tended to occur over the specific details of institutional reform, particularly over pillar communitisation, defence, organisation of the Commission and Council vote reweighting. On some institutional issues such as transparency in decision-making and the extension of EP codecision there was a more cohesive line. But the PES appeared to achieve a greater unity of purpose in relation to policy issues such as environmental policy, the social chapter and employment. Indeed it appeared to be the combined efforts of the PES governments that were ensuring the continued presence of the proposal for an employment chapter on the IGC negotiating table, in the face of the reticence of the centre-right governments of France and Germany (Ladrech 2000: 110-115). This was illustrated by a note sent by Dick Spring, the then Irish foreign minister (while Ireland was chairing the IGC negotiations) and leader of the Irish Labour party, to all PES leaders on 10 October 1996. Spring was reporting on the conclusions of a PES 'co-ordination meeting' of participants at the special European Council (i.e. all PES parties that were in government) held in Dublin on 5 October. The meeting was attended by the seven PES prime ministers, as well as three foreign ministers (including Spring, who chaired the meeting). Pauline Green was also in attendance as leader of the PES group. The conclusions of the meeting indicated agreement that the governments with PES party participation would 'strive for a broad agenda including themes such as employment, the environment and openness' and that while 'institutional matters were of importance' they 'should not be at the centre of the deliberations before the "substance" had been discussed.' This was a familiar PES formulation that strongly echoed Labour's own agenda for Europe. However, more specifically in relation to employment, the meeting endorsed the Irish presidency proposals concerning the inclusion of an employment chapter in the EU treaty, a principle which had won the support of a large majority of member states, and it was agreed that attempts should be made by the PES governments 'to influence the more hesitant governments in particular those of Germany and France.' Thus, governments with PES participation would use their bilateral contacts with Germany and France to press the case for an employment chapter. It was also suggested that PES parties and representatives on all levels lobby their Christian-democrat counterparts (i.e. the parties that comprised the EPP) with a view to seeking to develop a common approach on employment policy (PES Spring, 10 October 1996).

The focus by the PES on policy issues such as employment suited the Labour party as it was on this kind of issue that it found itself very much in the PES mainstream. But by the end of 1996 it had become fairly clear that Labour was not going to be isolated on the majority of key IGC issues within the PES, and would neither be bounced into adopting undesirable positions nor embarrassed by official PES statements that were not compatible with the official party line in the UK. In this respect, Labour's engagement with its PES colleagues had proved a success. Once the IGC began to progress at the end of 1996, the focus of Labour's activity in relation to its PES colleagues thus switched to ensuring it received maximum information on what was going on in the IGC from those PES colleagues who were in government. This would allow Labour to fully prepare itself to replace the Conservatives in the negotiations should it win the general election. In addition, it would seek to influence developments within the IGC through its contact with these PES governments with a view to ensuring that the negotiations remained open until after the general election in the UK, thus minimising the appearance on the negotiation table of proposals that were likely to cause domestic political difficulty for Labour. In particular, contacts with PES parties in both the Irish and Dutch governments that held the Council presidency during the IGC negotiations would prove extremely valuable to the Labour leadership as it prepared its negotiating strategy for the IGC (see chapter 5). Its involvement in the PES would therefore continue to be of central importance to the Labour party's IGC preparations as the general election neared.

The EPLP and the PES Group

An assessment of the impact that Labour's involvement in the PES had on its IGC preparation also needs to take into account the role played by Labour's representatives in the EP both within the LWG and as a leading force within the European parliamentary group of the PES. The advantages and disadvantages brought by the EPLP's role within the PES group in many ways mirrored those brought through Labour's wider relationship with the PES party confederation. There were however some important differences. Due mainly to the vagaries of the UK first-past-the-post electoral system, the EPLP was the biggest and the most influential national grouping within the PES group, as reflected in Pauline Green's position as leader. But the EPLP could not be regarded as a monolithic structure. Divisions within it were at their most common on questions relating to the direction of European integration. A sizeable minority within the EPLP were prone to ignore instructions from Westminster to abstain from supporting positions deemed as too federalist in the UK. Moreover, unlike PES 'party' declarations, which were based on a consensus among the party leaders, thus giving the national parties an effective veto, the EPLP could not simply veto awkward proposals within the PES parliamentary group. Decisions were taken following votes within the group, which meant that there was always the possibility of the EPLP simply being outvoted on certain issues. The EPLP therefore needed to be quite assiduous in dissuading its PES colleagues from pursuing awkward positions.

A further complication was that the representatives of PES parties in the EP tended to be more federalist minded than their party leaderships, a trait that also characterised the EPLP itself. It was thus more difficult for the Labour leadership in London to prevent the PES group from adopting 'awkward' positions, both because the various national PES party delegations tended to be more federalist than their national leaderships and because a sizeable minority within Labour's own EP delegation sympathised with federalist positions and could not always be controlled either by the London leadership in London or by the EPLP leadership in Brussels. Indeed, while the LWG ensured that the EPLP leadership generally transmitted the line coming from London, some of its MEPs appeared to view their primary allegiance as being to the positions of the PES group rather than the EPLP/leadership line and when the two differed, preferred to vote with the former rather than the latter. Amongst others, this was obviously the case with Pauline Green as leader of the PES group. Her special position was acknowledged by the Labour leadership. Where the EPLP diverged from the rest of the PES group, it was recognised by the leadership that her position obliged her to take the group line and not do the bidding of the Labour leadership. Green's status as PES parliamentary group leader gave her a special role within the wider PES party confederation. She was present at PES leaders' and bureau meetings and was also a member of the PES IGC working-group. Green was therefore not only the key interlocutor between the positions of the Labour party, as developed within the LWG, and the PES group, but also acted as an additional interlocutor between the LWG and the wider PES party confederation. She was also present at 'co-ordination' meetings of the PES leaders that were in government, and was therefore able to pass messages and information on to the Labour leadership and vice-versa. Most importantly, in this respect, she was in regular contact with the PES members of the Irish and Dutch governments when they held the Council presidency and chaired the IGC and was thus able to act as a discreet interlocutor between them and the Labour leadership (Interview with Green).

The other EPLP members of the LWG also had crucial roles to play. Wayne David, as leader of the EPLP, and his deputy, Christine Crawley, had the primary responsibility for ensuring that the party leadership position was understood and complied with by the EPLP and conveyed to the rest of the PES group, and they also conveyed the views of the EPLP members to the London leadership. Indeed, Crawley's responsibilities as EPLP deputy-leader involved overseeing liaison between the EPLP and the Labour frontbench. As EPLP leader, David also had a prominent role within the wider PES group. As leader of a national delegation, he was automatically a vice-president of the group and a member of the group bureau, and was able to use this position to argue the Labour positions within the group. David Martin, as vice-president of the EP and co-rapporteur of its report on the functioning of the TEU in 1995, was a prominent and respected figure within both the EPLP and the PES group. Because of his status, Martin was also a member of the PES IGC working-group, and therefore able to provide an additional perspective on developments within this to the LWG. However, his main role within the LWG appeared to be to explain the general EP position. He was also the most likely to have put the political arguments for the more 'federalist' positions within the LWG, given that he was its most federalist minded member. The meetings of the LWG therefore involved regular reports and updates on developments within the EPLP from David (or Crawley), on developments within the PES group from Green, and on developments relating to the EP's IGC position from Martin. However, there was an obvious overlap in the perspectives the various MEPs could offer in relation to the PES group, the PES as a whole and its individual member parties.

The need to define a line in respect of the development of the PES group position on the IGC was one of the most urgent tasks facing the LWG following its establishment. The PES group needed to agree a position in advance of that adopted by the EP as a whole. The latter would have to be agreed by May 1995 in order to input into the work of the Reflection Group, which would commence its deliberations a month later. An agreed PES position was therefore necessary in advance in order for it to bring its dominant influence to bear over the general EP position. Work was undertaken by the PES group's own IGC working-group chaired by Elisabeth Guigou to develop this position. An early draft position paper produced by Guigou had been described by Whitty's chair's note to the second LWG meeting as 'distinctively unhelpful' (LWG2 Chair's Note). It therefore probably came of some relief to the Labour leadership when Pauline Green reported at the same meeting that Guigou's paper had not been agreed by the PES group and was likely to remain only as a discussion paper.

Guigou's paper was considered in more detail at the third LWG meeting. Among the more 'unhelpful' proposals it contained were those for JHA communitisation, generalised QMV and codecision for all legislation, for 'reinforced QMV' for treaty revisions, international agreements, enlargements and own resources (all with EP assent) and CFSP (with EP consultation), for possible EP election of the Commission president and for the possible development of a European defence system (LWG IGC3B). While the chair's note to the third LWG meeting described this paper as very federalist, some PES members from other countries had actually criticised it for not being federalist enough (LWG3 Chair's Note). The existence of such views amongst the PES parties appeared to encapsulate the difficulties facing the Labour leadership as it sought to ensure that neither the PES group, nor the PES party as a whole, adopted undesirable positions. Nevertheless, this also reflected the tendency of MEPs to be more 'federalist' than their national party leaderships. In any case, by the third LWG meeting in February 1995, it had, as foreseen by Green, been agreed within the PES group that Guigou's paper would be endorsed solely as a 'reflection paper.' It was reported to the LWG that Guigou's paper had provoked a useful discussion in the PES group but that it had represented her personal view and had not been endorsed by the group as a whole (LWG3 Minutes). Indeed, following discussion of Guigou's paper in an extraordinary meeting of the PES group on 6-7 February 1995, Green took the initiative as leader in producing a draft paper setting out the areas of consensus within the group (Lightfoot and Wilde 1996: 10). It was this paper that would form the basis of the official group position in the IGC. Whitty's chair's note described this paper as 'blander' than Guigou's but more detailed than expected (LWG3 Chair's Note).

Green's paper was similar to Guigou's in a number of the proposals made. For example, it called for a single simplified consolidated treaty, spelling out clearly 'the competencies and powers of the European institutions and their limits' and setting out a 'limited number of easily comprehensible decision-taking procedures.' It also called for more explicit protection of citizens' rights, for EP codecision in all legislation, and for the legislative proceedings of the Council to be in public. As with the Guigou paper it also advocated that the EP assent procedure should apply in relation to treaty revisions, international agreements and own resources, that there should be consultation on CSFP, and that there should be a simplified budgetary procedure. In addition, it echoed the Guigou paper in calling for a more explicit link between the EMU provisions and the objectives of article 2 (high employment). More controversially for the Labour party, the Green paper also suggested election of the Commission president by the EP. However, it did not refer to third pillar communitisation and was less forthcoming on QMV, simply suggesting that it would need to be applied far more broadly in an enlarged EU while accepting that the national veto would have to be maintained in some fundamental areas. Elsewhere, Green's paper departed from the rather sympathetic tone towards differentiated integration shown by the Guigou paper. While recognising that some variable geometry might be necessary due to the unwillingness of certain states to deepen co-operation in particular areas, the paper totally rejected the proposition of institutionalising a two-speed hard core Europe (LWG IGC3E).

Despite it being more detailed than expected, Whitty's chair's note to the third LWG meeting suggested that the Labour party could 'live with' the formulations in the Green paper, provided the PES group did 'not seriously amend it' in subsequent discussions. Similarly, following discussion of it by the LWG, the Green paper was described in the minutes of the third meeting as welcome. However, some reservations were expressed within the LWG 'particularly in relation to the EP's powers of appointment of the European Commission.'[4] Cook gave Green further comments on the paper after the LWG meeting, but in general was comfortable with the formulations it contained (LWG3 Chair's Note, LWG3 Minutes, Interview with Green).

By the time the LWG had met for the fourth time in March 1995, and following further discussions within the PES group, a revised version of Green's paper had been produced (LWG IGC4C). Whitty's chair's note highlighted a number of particular revisions that could be problematic for the Labour party. These included: an explicit call for codecision on all internal legislation (whether or not QMV applied) which Whitty suggested might be problematic because it would presumably include the JHA pillar (this was not actually clear, as the paper made no mention of merging JHA into the EC legal framework); a call for QMV in the greatest possible number of appropriate areas, although this was 'deliberately ambiguous' and partly qualified by a reference to preserving unanimity for certain fundamental areas; and a reference to a reduction of the threshold for QMV (although this would be linked to a reweighting of votes) (LWG4 Chair's Note). Despite these reservations, the LWG gave the revised paper its broad support at its fourth meeting, though it was feared that further revisions of the paper would be made at the PES group meeting the following week. However, the chair's note to the fifth LWG meeting was able to report that following some serious manoeuvres by Green, this version of the paper had 'somewhat amazingly been overwhelmingly accepted without amendment' by the PES group meeting of 29 March 1995. This was described as a 'major triumph for Pauline (Green).' While acknowledging that the paper did pose 'a few problems', Whitty suggested that Labour could broadly go along with it and that indeed 'with minor reservations' the adoption of the paper meant that the official position of the PES group 'was pretty much in line with the position we have taken in the working-group so far.' Furthermore, he suggested that 'politically for the first time it means that the ultra-federalists are in the minority whereas hitherto it has been the (EPLP) who were the minority.' This was seen as a major 'positive development' for the Labour leadership (LWG5 Chair's Note). The 'ultrafederalists', as Whitty described them, were in a small minority in voting against the paper as they regarded it as too weak (LWG5 Minutes, Lightfoot and Wilde 1996: 10). The EPLP leadership had been assisted in preventing the adoption of proposals deemed as 'too federalist' by a number of the more pragmatic parties, particularly those from the Nordic countries, who shared Labour's caution over the pace of European integration. While the more federalist inclined parties could have attempted to outvote the EPLP and its more cautious allies, most of the PES group members were aware that adopting a joint PES group position which did not have the support of a number of the national delegations would be a rather empty exercise.[5] A large majority within the group were therefore persuaded of the merits of compromise and voted for Green's paper as a fair representation of the areas of consensus within the group (Interview with Green).

The Labour leadership was less successful in influencing the outcome of the EP's general position on the IGC, despite the fact that it was co-authored by a member of the LWG, David Martin. Given Martin's political independence and federalist views, it was clear from the start that his input into the development of the EP position would not reflect the Labour leadership line. Moreover, the EPLP, while the biggest national party delegation within the EP, would not be able to exert the same level of influence over the EP as a whole as it did within the PES group and would not be able to rely on 'socialist solidarity' in order to persuade other party groupings to agree to acceptable compromises. A draft report from the EP's institutional committee on the development of the EU, which would form the basis of the EP position, was presented for consideration at the fourth meeting of the LWG. While acknowledging with some relief that the draft was 'nowhere near as federalist as the pre-Maastricht reports' and concentrated on improving efficiency and accountability within the existing competences rather than extension of them, Whitty's chair's note to the fourth LWG meeting pinpointed a number of difficulties for the Labour party (LWG4 Chair's Note). Martin's draft called for the eventual complete abolition of unanimity in the Council (though with a reinforced 'super-QMV' on delicate issues) and communitisation of both the JHA and CFSP pillars. Although less preoccupied with matters relating to social and economic cohesion, Martin's draft was in most respects similar to the papers produced by Guigou and Green for the PES group. Indeed, Green suggested that about 85 per cent of the final draft report submitted to the EP plenary was in line with the paper adopted in her name by the PES group (LWG IGC6B),[6] though it was even closer in content to Guigou's earlier paper. However, Martin actually went further than Guigou in calling for CFSP communitisation and for the Council and EP to be 'equals in all fields of EU legislative and budgetary competence' and also called for the right of larger member states to appoint a second Commissioner to be removed. In addition, the draft suggested that consideration be given to an EU-wide referendum on the outcome of the IGC and suggested that the EP be put on an equal footing with the member states insofar as being able to propose treaty amendments and approve the final text for future IGCs. It also suggested that the requirement for unanimity for treaty changes be replaced with a vote based on a high double majority of member states and population (LWG IGC4E).

The broad thrust of the Martin draft would remain intact despite undergoing a number of amendment processes as it went through its various parliamentary stages. It would thus remain far too 'federalist' for the Labour party to support (LWG5 Minutes). The draft would firstly be altered by amendments from Martin's co-rapporteur, the French Christian democrat Jean-Louis Bourlanges. A further 600 amendments would be considered in the institutional committee when it met on 3 May, and a final text would be decided upon by the plenary session of the EP on 17 May, when it would be subject to further votes on amendments from the various political groups, other committees and individual MEPs. This would then form the EP's submission to the Reflection Group. The chair's note to the fifth LWG meeting suggested that it was likely that Martin's position would largely prevail, and that this would be 'a more federalist agenda than we (Labour) could support.' The question of whether Labour MEPs voted for it was therefore described by Whitty as a 'vital and tricky one.' He warned that 'if we definitely want the EPLP to oppose or abstain there will be a row, but we should make clear that we might ask them to do so when we see the final draft' (LWG5 Chair's Note). It was acknowledged within the LWG at its fifth meeting that the final EP report would 'obviously...reflect cross party views and would be more ambitious than the Labour Party or (PES) group positions even if David Martin's draft largely survived amendment.' Accordingly, the LWG recognised that 'voting by the EPLP and the media reaction to the publication of the report would need to be handled carefully'(LWG5 Minutes). There would therefore be close contact between the national leadership and the EPLP on how to deal with this vote, which was perhaps the biggest test so far of the LWG's ability to ensure that the EPLP did not deviate from the agreed party line adopted in London.

When the final vote came on the Bourlanges/Martin report on 17 May following the various amendments in committee and plenary, the Labour leadership instructed the EPLP to abstain given the various difficulties it had with the final resolution. As a note by Whitty explained, among the difficulties that the Labour leadership had with the resolution were the references it contained to communitisation of CFSP and JHA, to extension of QMV to all areas (including JHA and CFSP but with the exception of treaty amendments and constitutional issues), to election of the Commission president by the EP (though this proposal was also contained in Green's paper which Labour had supported) and an EP power to force the retirement of Commissioners, to a possible Euro-tax and to a possible EU-wide referendum to ratify the treaty (LWG IGC 6A). Despite the clear instruction to abstain, a significant minority of EPLP members joined Martin in voting against the nationally imposed line and voting for the resolution (including Green, reflecting the general PES group position), while one member of the EPLP voted against the resolution.

The instruction to abstain was itself a compromise, as the leadership had originally attempted to get the EPLP to vote against the resolution. A note from Whitty to Prescott, Cook, Quin and Powell on 16 May explained that, at the meeting of the EPLP on the previous Monday, both Whitty and David had made 'heavy interventions' in order to persuade the EPLP to vote against, and that the EPLP had voted twenty-seven to ten in favour of the leadership line. However, this line did not hold when a vote was taken within the PES group, with the EPLP splitting three ways, though a majority had voted against the report (and with the leadership line). Whitty's note explained that many of those voting with the EPLP line 'did so with reluctance and several normally "loyalist" elements abstained or voted for the report.' Whitty therefore suggested that in these circumstances 'there was no way a vote would hold.' After consultation with Whitty and Cook, David recommended abstention on the final vote following recorded opposition on the key points. Whitty reported that in the course of a meeting on 15 May and 'after some acrimony' the EPLP voted by twenty-seven to six to abstain (LP Whitty, 16 May 1995). Despite a disciplinary code that obliged the EPLP members to follow the party line in plenary sessions, this division was also reflected in the final vote on the resolution. Whitty's commentary on the resolution (LWG IGC6A), submitted to the sixth LWG meeting, noted that this had left the party leadership in a difficult position in relation to sections of the EPLP and also created a difficult situation for the EPLP within the PES group. Nevertheless, as Whitty pointed out, there had been a greater division among the Tory MEPs.

Although the Conservatives' ability to make political capital out of Labour's divisions had been somewhat neutralised by their own divisions, the vote still caused Labour public embarrassment and the instruction to abstain had rankled among sections of the EPLP as well as their colleagues in the PES group. Furthermore, this was also a blow to the strategy of ensuring a common line on the IGC was pursued by the Labour party in both London and Brussels, and of preventing Labour from becoming detached from its PES colleagues. But in such situations the greater pressures and immediate necessities implied by the domestic political climate in which the Labour leadership had to operate won the day. In this context, stories of splits in Brussels amongst the EPLP and with its PES colleagues were preferable to the Conservative and hostile media caricatures of a Labour party in thrall to European federalism that would have ensued had the Labour leadership in London and Brussels endorsed the EP position.

This whole scenario was repeated again in early 1996, when the EP adopted a new resolution on the IGC, in the light of the report of the Reflection Group. This resolution was based on the Dury/Maij-Weggen report of the institutional affairs committee, and generally reiterated the positions set out in the May 1995 resolution, with additional references to employment and public services. The EPLP was again obliged to abstain, and again a sizeable minority caused embarrassment for the party leadership by rebelling against the party line and voting for the resolution.[7] As the chair's note to the tenth LWG meeting explained, Pauline Green had to speak for the PES group and voted with it for the resolution while David 'dragooned the EPLP into abstaining' (LWG10 Chair's Note). In the EP debate on the resolution on 13 March 1996, David replicated the leadership line as directed by London, just as he had in the May 1995 debate. Thus, on behalf of the EPLP, David welcomed aspects of the resolution, such as the proposals for an employment chapter, anti-discrimination provisions, greater environmental protection, and simplification of legislative procedures including the extension of codecision wherever QMV applied. However, he explained that the EPLP would be abstaining because of its proposals to communitise the intergovernmental pillars, to merge the WEU into the EU and because Labour did not wish to depart from unanimity with regards to treaty changes, budgetary policy, taxation, external border controls and CFSP (European Parliament, 13 March 1996).

The two votes on the EP position caused obvious public discomfort for the Labour party, and difficulties in its relationships with the EPLP. Disquiet extended beyond those who disobeyed the party line and voted for the resolution to those who acquiesced with the order to abstain for the sake of party unity rather than because of a conviction that the leadership's caution was correct. This disquiet also surfaced on a number of other occasions on particular areas of IGC policy, most notably over the party's position on JHA policy. Jack Straw's hardline stance in this area of policy severely antagonised sections of the EPLP, and the situation was compounded by him not being a member of the LWG and appearing to be less than fully informed about the nature of the JHA pillar, at least in his first few months in the home affairs post. The situation was further inflamed by the attitude taken by the EPLP spokesman on JHA matters, Glyn Ford. He generally took the opposite view of Straw and often in a rather outspoken manner. In making clear his antagonism towards an EU role in immigration policy and in relation to the enforcement of freedom of movement within the EU, Straw suggested that there 'wasn't a cigarette paper' between him and the right-wing Conservative home secretary, Michael Howard, in this area (Interview with Labour MEP). Following the dispute between Straw and the EPLP on this matter in February 1996, the chair's note to the third LWG meeting explained that a number of MEPs, including Pauline Green, were upset with Straw, who, in turn, was upset with them (although some of the MEPs, including Green, were none too happy about the antagonistic manner in which Ford was pushing his arguments either, despite agreeing with his general line) (LWG3 Chair's Note, Interviews with LWG participants). Thus what was described by the minutes as a lengthy discussion of statements by members of the frontbench and EPLP regarding free movement within the EU took place at the beginning of the third LWG meeting. In the course of the discussion, Blair had stressed that it was essential that communications between the frontbench and EPLP were improved and the policy line adhered to. This was agreed. To this end, it was agreed that minutes should be circulated promptly after LWG meetings, outlining agreed positions and that LWG members should convey the outline of positions reached to the shadow cabinet and the EPLP. Prescott had already discussed these issues with the EPLP a few days previously. Both he and Whitty would make recommendations to the EPLP meeting in Barcelona (coinciding with the PES congress) on improving liaison (LWG3 Minutes).[8] The chair's note for the meeting had also emphasised that these points would require discussion in the shadow cabinet. Straw also met with the EPLP on 1 March for a frank discussion of the issues. The decision to transfer consideration of the JHA issue to the parallel working-party on immigration chaired by Straw, following the discussion in the third LWG meeting, provided the EPLP with another forum in which to influence IGC policy, with Ford and Michael Elliot joining David and Crawley as the EPLP's representatives in this policy-making forum. In making Straw chair of this working-party, the Labour leadership were putting him in pole position in terms of policy-making. Indeed, Straw appeared to win the day as regards the general stance on JHA adopted by it. However, on related issues, such as the EU's role in combating racism and other forms of discrimination, the positions supported by the EPLP did appear to win out over Straw's negative approach. Crawley suggested that the LWG needed to address the issue of an EU anti-racism competence at its fifth meeting and the EPLP argued strongly for a firm EU mandate on combating all forms of discrimination (LWG5 Chair's Note). The issue of EU anti-racist policy was a rare one on which the whole EPLP (i.e. left and right, Euro-phile and Euro-sceptic) could unite in favour.

The row over JHA issues had followed shortly after an incident that had caused serious damage to the relations between Blair's office and much of the EPLP, overshadowing early attempts to develop a coherent line between the London leadership and the EPLP on IGC issues. In January 1995, a furore ensued when thirty-two Labour MEPs signed an advertisement in *The Guardian* opposing the abandonment of clause IV of the party constitution, a change that was in the process of being engineered by Blair as a key plank in his party modernisation strategy. The timing of the advertisement had been viewed as particularly offensive by Blair's office as it came as Blair was preparing to address a business seminar in Brussels. Blair denounced the MEPs for 'infantile incompetence' while one spokesman from his office dismissed all Labour MEPs as 'non-entities.' Though thirty-six Labour MEPs, including some of the original signatories to the *Guardian* advert signed a letter distancing themselves from the statement, the damage to relations between the Blair office and much of the EPLP had already been done (Anderson and Mann 1997: 140-141).

While many Labour MEPs were now *persona non grata* among the Blairites, the row over clause IV did not appear to do too much damage to the relationship between the Labour leadership and the EPLP representatives within the LWG. Aside from JHA, most differences between the EPLP and the London leadership were kept within the confines of the LWG. Furthermore, while differences did emerge on a number of issues, there was not the clear division between the London and Brussels based members of the LWG that one might have expected. In addition to the disagreement over JHA, the early meetings of the LWG did reveal a few differences between the EPLP and the leadership. For example, the minutes of the second LWG meeting report that the EPLP members had conveyed the general EP view that a simplified codecision procedure should apply wherever there was QMV, but that 'others felt that this...should be examined issue by issue' (LWG2 Minutes) and the chair's note to the third meeting reported that the hard line on CFSP and defence that Cook had taken in his speech to the European Policy Institute on 30 January 1995 (rejecting an EU defence policy and any involvement of the EC institutions in CFSP and stressing the pre-eminence of the nation-states) had slightly taken aback the MEPs in the LWG (LWG IGC3A, LWG3 Chair's Note). However, there were some in the leadership who were more sympathetic to the positions being argued by the MEPs within the LWG on these and other issues. In many cases, the differences within the LWG were quite subtle and often simply reflected differing perceptions over what was acceptable in the domestic circumstances and the differing environments within which the Westminster and Brussels based members operated. Thus it was the tone of Cook's comments on CFSP that appeared to be particularly disconcerting for the MEPs while differences on codecision stemmed more from disagreement on whether or not it should be based on a tidy formula rather than the principle of extension itself. As regards the latter, the principle of codecision extension seemed to be embraced by all in the LWG and the position eventually adopted appeared to reflect that initially advocated by the MEPs. In relation to CFSP, the essence of Cook's earlier position was adopted by the LWG, but this was couched in a much more sympathetic discourse and involved flexibility on some secondary aspects of policy.

In general, there was not really a clear fault-line within the LWG between the EPLP and the London leadership. Positions within the EPLP itself were quite varied. David and Crawley were more pragmatic than Martin, while Green's position was particularly nuanced due to her leadership of the PES group and her involvement with the wider PES party confederation (Interviews with LWG participants). Where there were differences within the LWG, some within the leadership were more sympathetic to the positions supported by the EPLP than others. In particular, through his post as European co-ordinator, Whitty had close and regular contacts with the EPLP, becoming quite sympathetic to its positions, while Quin was a former MEP and accordingly very sympathetic to the EPLP position. Furthermore, while viewed as the leading Euro-sceptic in the shadow cabinet before becoming shadow foreign secretary, Cook increasingly began to embrace pro-European arguments once he immersed himself in the subject. Moreover, while Blair's thinking was dominated by the domestic political climate and the constraints it placed on policy-making, he too retained strong pro-European instincts (Interviews with LWG participants).

The differences that did emerge between the Labour leadership and the EPLP were probably more to do with the more positive attitude held by the latter towards the benefits of European co-operation as a means of resolving certain policy dilemmas and a greater preoccupation by the former with the constraints placed on policy-making by the domestic political climate in the UK. There were some differences between the EPLP and some individuals within the leadership over the extent to which QMV should be extended, though some in the leadership, including Cook, were actually closer to the EPLP position. But on most major issues, there was general agreement, particularly on policy issues such as the social chapter and the CAP. Differences did however occur on peripheral issues such as the abolition of duty-free and various taxation issues (Interview with LWG participant).

One other major issue that caused some differences between the EPLP and frontbench was EMU. However, differences were also apparent within the EPLP on this. This was illustrated by the chair's note to the ninth LWG meeting in February 1996 which warned that there were a number of EP reports in the pipeline related to EMU which had the potential to expose differences between the EPLP and the frontbench and also within the EPLP (LWG9 Chair's Note). Within the EPLP, Wayne David was arguing that EMU should be delayed, while Alan Donnelly (PES group EMU spokesman)[9] was arguing for commitment to the EMU timetable. The Labour leadership brought pressure to bear on the EPLP to prevent awkward public divisions on this issue, as indicated in the minutes of the tenth LWG meeting on 1 April 1996 (LWG10 Minutes). These reported that a meeting had taken place between the Labour members of the EP's economic and monetary affairs committee (EMAC) and the front-bench treasury spokesman Andrew Smith as a result of which Donnelly's report on EMU for EMAC had 'probably (become) more cautious.' It was added that, following these discussions, there was now 'generally more caution around on EMU in the EPLP and the (PES) group.'

As with relations with the PES, the one development that caused particular strains in relations between the party and the EPLP was the beef crisis of spring 1996 and Labour's response to the government's non co-operation policy. Whitty's note to Blair, Prescott and Cook on 30 May 1996 explained that there was 'privately almost universal disagreement with our conditional support for the government within the EPLP' and unhappiness about statements made by both Blair and Cook, although the EPLP leadership was managing to keep a lid on public dissent. Whitty warned that there was 'both press pressure on individual MEPs to give their views and intense pressure amongst the "loyalist" element to write a "private" letter to Tony opposing our stance.' Whitty predicted that the forthcoming mini-plenary session of the EP in Brussels would be 'a fraught time' with 'some split stories...bound to emerge.' The mini-plenary saw the adoption by the PES group of a resolution condemning the UK government, in contradiction of Labour's policy of tacit support for the government. Whitty's note expressed concern about the resolution but explained that the EPLP leadership had been unable to prevent the PES group from tabling the resolution, for which Pauline Green as leader, inevitably gave public support, as did other members of the EPLP (LP Whitty, 30 May 1996).

When the EP plenary convened again just prior to the Florence European Council, a further resolution was adopted, again with PES group support, this time attacking UK government blackmail and obstructionism and accusing the UK of acting illegally. In a similar vein to his note of 30 May, Whitty's note to Prescott, Cook and Powell on 18 June, warned of the embarrassment that this would cause and the apparent contradiction should EPLP members vote with a resolution attacking the Conservative government in this manner when the Labour leadership in London was giving tacit support to it. However, the note also indicated that the EPLP leadership's tendency to do the bidding of the London leadership was backfiring, with a number of EPLP members expressing increasing disgruntlement with the EPLP leadership. Whitty warned that heavy handed attempts to get the EPLP to support the London line would increase the likelihood of very public splits being aired within the EPLP and between the EPLP and the London leadership. Indeed, Whitty warned that the situation was particularly sensitive given that the EPLP annual general meeting (AGM) would also be taking place during the EP plenary. Accordingly, there was a risk that left-wingers and the more 'federalist' inclined MEPs would combine to rebel against David's leadership at the AGM, on the grounds of David's lack of independence from the London leadership. The London leadership therefore sought to keep the issue 'low-key' (LP Whitty, 18 June 1996).

The difficulties that the party leadership encountered in maintaining a united party line in London and Brussels during the beef crisis should not detract from the general success enjoyed by the LWG in ensuring a coherent line on the IGC itself. This appeared not to be affected by the discontent felt by many in the EPLP at the leadership stance on the non co-operation policy. In this respect, the imminence of a general election in the UK, now certain within the next year, helped to concentrate the minds of all concerned on the need to maintain unity and not give any hostages to fortune in the crucial pre-election period. While not being altogether happy with some of the statements made by various frontbench spokesmen on European issues in this period, it was generally understood within the EPLP that such statements were designed for electoral purposes, even if Labour MEPs were not always convinced of the necessity of certain statements. Furthermore, most of the key figures within the EPLP appeared content with the positions on the IGC contained in the policy document adopted by the Labour party conference in September 1995. While some in the EPLP might have privately preferred more progressive positions, there was a recognition that it was a fairly progressive document in the light of the domestic political context in which the party was operating (Interview with Green). The various proposals to strengthen the EP's powers that it contained were particularly welcome within the EPLP.

The positions that Labour had adopted on the EP were illustrative of the influence that the EPLP representatives had within the LWG. Many of the formulations adopted, particularly in relation to the simplification of the codecision procedure, general rationalisation of procedures and extension of codecision where QMV applied, were very close to the position of the PES group and the EP itself. This was not pure coincidence and must have had some connection to the influence that the EPLP had within the LWG, although on many aspects of the EP powers, the EPLP representatives did not have too much difficulty in winning support for their line given the generally positive perception of the EP that had developed within the Labour leadership since the late 1980s. One could also argue that the influence was also felt strongly in the opposite direction, with the Labour leadership directing the EPLP, which as the largest national grouping within the EP, holding a number of key parliamentary positions, was in a very good position to shape the positions of the EP.

The influence of the EPLP within the LWG extended beyond the discussions on the EP's powers. In relation to various items on the IGC agenda, the EPLP, at the very least, played a useful function in keeping the Labour leadership informed of the debates taking place on the reform issues and of the various options that were being discussed and in making the leadership aware of the various proposals being made, so that discussion could then take place within the LWG on the feasibility of adopting such proposals. There was a great deal of contact between the leadership and the EPLP both through the LWG and other forums such as party conferences and the NEC (on which David sat). Channels of communication between Green (especially) and David and the leadership were particularly strong. This informal and formal contact with MEPs obviously had some effect on the approach that the Labour leadership took on the IGC. While it would be difficult to quantify this influence, it was clear that the Labour MEPs had a critical 'explaining role', making the party aware of the agenda and options on the table. In many cases, the MEPs had the advantage in terms of technical expertise on certain issues, which they could exploit both in making the argument for a particular reform and in obliging the Labour leadership to take notice of their opinions when an issue needed explaining.

Cook and Whitty, in particular, would have regular contact with the EPLP because of their respective roles, and this appeared to affect the way in which they approached European and IGC policy-making. Indeed, in his role as European co-ordinator, Whitty visited the EP nearly every week, and discussed the IGC and other European issues with various MEPs who had expertise in the relevant areas as well as with the EPLP and PES group leadership. He also developed an important working relationship with the leading authority on institutional reform within the PES group, Richard Corbett,[10] who until December 1996 was deputy general-secretary of the PES group and special adviser to Elisabeth Guigou, the EP and PES group representative in the Reflection Group and then in the IGC. As adviser to Guigou, Corbett was present at all Reflection Group meetings and also at those IGC meetings at which the EP representatives were allowed to take part. He was therefore the only member of the Labour party to have set foot in either the Reflection Group or the IGC (until May 1997), and was able to provide Whitty with a number of progress reports and detailed information on the positions being taken by the various member states within these forums. This included detailed briefings on the positions taken by the various member states in the Reflection Group, highlighting the UK's isolation, which Whitty circulated to the LWG.[11]

Corbett also played a discreet role, within the Reflection Group and in the early stages of the IGC, in seeking to ensure that the various representatives of the member states were kept informed of Labour party positions. For example, he distributed copies of Labour's 1995 party conference document to the various member states' representatives and was taken aside by some of them and questioned on what the position of a Labour government might be.[12] Many of the Reflection Group/IGC representatives (including those from centre-right governments) were clearly exasperated with the positions being adopted by the Conservative government representative, David Davis, and Corbett was able to provide them with informal advice on the difference between Conservative and Labour policy (Interview with Corbett).

Corbett and Whitty would usually meet to discuss IGC developments on Whitty's regular visits to Brussels. Corbett therefore had a key role in furnishing Whitty with advice and information. Most of the official documents from within the EU institutions that Whitty circulated to the LWG were passed to him by Corbett. Moreover, the drafts of most of the position papers that he produced for the LWG were passed by Whitty to Corbett in advance, for comment.[13] Corbett's advice would be particularly useful for Whitty in relation to some of the more technical issues being discussed at the IGC.[14] As the PES group official with chief responsibility for the IGC, Corbett was also instrumental in developing the general PES group position (which itself influenced the Labour party and general PES positions) and drafting its statements on the IGC, and he drafted speeches and statements made on the IGC by Green. He initially wrote a reflection paper on the IGC for the PES group in the summer of 1994 (PES Group 1994) and many of the suggestions contained therein found their way into the Guigou and Green papers (both of which Corbett actually drafted), and eventually into the general position adopted by the EP. These included his proposals for a rationalisation of EP procedures and simplification and consolidation of the treaties. Indeed, Corbett suggests that he devised the formula for simplifying the codecision procedure, as contained in his PES group reflection paper, which was then adopted by the PES group as a whole as well as the Labour party, and then by the EP as a whole, and was eventually agreed in the final treaty revision at Amsterdam (Interview with Corbett). Corbett also played a role in advising the wider PES party confederation on IGC developments.[15]

Corbett's role in the IGC and within the Labour party altered somewhat in December 1996 when he was elected to the EP, following a by-election in the vacant seat of Merseyside West, and thus stepped down as PES group deputy secretary-general and adviser to Guigou. While no longer occupying these official positions, he became an influential and informed advocate of institutional reform within the EPLP and continued to provide advice to the Labour leadership in opposition and government until the closing stages of the IGC.[16]

Another useful point of contact within the EU institutions was the former Labour leader Neil Kinnock. Kinnock had informal contact with the Labour leadership at various party conferences and private meetings as well as PES meetings, at which the PES Commissioners had a formal presence. Whilst a high proportion of documents on the IGC he obtained came from Corbett, Whitty also received some assistance in obtaining documents and general information on developments in the IGC from Kinnock and his office in the Commission. Having been general-secretary of the party for most of Kinnock's leadership, in which time he was a close ally of Kinnock in implementing party reforms and defeating the hard left (Anderson and Mann 1997: 15-16), Whitty continued to enjoy a good working relationship with him, as did Blair and Cook, both of whom served in Kinnock's shadow cabinets. Contact between the LWG and Kinnock's office was evident prior to the launch of the Commission's paper on the functioning of the TEU in May 1995. The minutes of the fifth LWG meeting recorded agreement that Whitty and Cook would keep in close contact with Kinnock's office in order to 'co-ordinate responses to the public release of the Commission's position' (LWG5 Minutes). Among the documents passed to Whitty by Kinnock's office were reports on the Reflection Group and the positions taken within it by the UK, which complemented the reports provided by Corbett.[17]

The roles played by both Kinnock and Corbett were illustrative of the wider engagement with the European agenda that Labour's involvement in a transnational party confederation facilitated, particularly as the PES was the largest and most cohesive of the EU party federations. Although Kinnock would have been a valuable contact, whether or not the PES existed, his special status within the PES as one of its Commissioners added to this. However, the value of individuals such as Corbett, and to an even greater extent, Pauline Green, really stemmed from their involvement in the PES group, and their ability to shape its agenda, while also acting as interlocutors between the Labour leadership and the PES group and individual PES parties, and providing the Labour leadership with highly informed accounts of developments within the EU institutions, the member states and the PES parties. Moreover, the leading role that the Labour party played within the PES proved a stark contrast to the isolation experienced by the Conservative government amongst its colleagues in the European Peoples' Party (EPP) confederation and in relation to its fellow centre-right governments in the EU. This isolation was further illustrated by the distance which opened between the government and the Conservative member of the Commission, Sir Leon Brittan - again a distance that contrasted with the warm and close relations enjoyed between Labour and its Commissioner (Seldon 1997: 669-670, Brown Pappamikail 1998: 212-218).

A Role for the Trade Unions?

A relationship that distinguished the Labour party from both the Conservatives and most of its PES colleagues was its historic organic link with the trade union movement (Minkin 1991). While the PES party and parliamentary group were involved in close discussions with the European trade union federation, the ETUC, most PES parties did not have the same kind of organisational relationship with their national trade union groupings as Labour had in the UK (Sassoon 1997: 10). The Labour party was accordingly identified by the public in the UK with positions adopted by the trade union movement. An awareness of this was reflected in the concern expressed in Whitty's initial memo of November 1994 at the development of positions on the IGC within the trade unions which might conflict with the approach Labour wished to take. While these concerns were similar to those expressed over the development of the EPLP and PES group positions, the trade unions were not given the same input into policy-making as the EPLP and were not represented on the LWG. The positions of the trade unions were viewed in a more overtly negative fashion as potentially damaging to the Labour party, and efforts were accordingly concentrated on ensuring that their positions were compatible with Labour's, rather than, as had been the case with the EPLP and PES 'party' and group, encouraging a formal input into policy-making. As a creature of the trade unions himself, Whitty had suggested in his initial memo that the TUC have some representation in the LWG (LP Whitty, 1 November 1994). However, the membership list agreed at the first LWG meeting did not include a trade union representative, though it was agreed that David Lea, the assistant general-secretary of the TUC (and also a member of the ETUC executive), would be kept informed (LWG IGC1B). Trade unions were thus denied the formal input into policy-making accorded to the EPLP and PES group. The lack of trade union input in policy-making reflected the general trend in all areas of policy under the Blair leadership, given the conscious and concerted strategy pursued by the architects of 'New Labour' to distance the party from its trade union roots and proletarian image (Anderson and Mann 1997: 323-326).

The prime concern for the Labour leadership in managing its relationship with the trade unions was to ensure that the latter did not cause it any public embarrassment. In relation to IGC policy-making, the initial concern of the Labour leadership, as expressed in Whitty's initial memo, was that the ETUC intended to produce a statement to input into the Reflection Group, aiming to produce a draft of this by March 1995, in time for it to be debated upon and then adopted at the ETUC congress in May 1995. In order to influence the ETUC position, the TUC would be adopting its own position in advance of these dates, and had set up its own working-group, the 1996 group, to develop this position. Although Whitty's initial memo had included Prescott, Green, David and Sigler in the membership of this group, the Labour party representatives who were regular attendees of the meetings of the 1996 group were Whitty, Quin and David (TUC 1996 Group, October 1994). This still represented a significant presence for the Labour leadership, overlapping with the membership of the LWG and contrasting with the absence of trade union involvement in the LWG. This seemed to confirm the fairly one-directional nature of influence between Labour and the unions in this area of policy-making. However, there were a number of other formal and informal forums through which the Labour party could influence the unions, and the unions attempt to influence Labour, including the Labour party NEC, within which the unions were strongly represented, and the Labour party-TUC contact group in which the party and trade union leaderships met to discuss various issues.

In its annual report to congress in September 1995, the TUC general council explained that the TUC had engaged in discussions with representatives of the Labour party, the EPLP, the PES group and the ETUC 'with the aim of aligning policies from an early stage' (TUC, September 1995).[18] Indeed it appears that the alignment of the TUC's position with the Labour party's approach had taken place with the production of a paper at the end of November 1994, subsequently adopted by the TUC general council, which had strong echoes of the broad approach the Labour leadership was taking (TUC, November 1994). The paper (also summarised in the general council report) referred to the need to place an emphasis on the social dimension, to rebalance economic and industrial policy away from monetarism and democratise the EMU project, to prohibit all forms of discrimination, and to strengthen subsidiarity and democratise the EU institutions.

Although bringing the TUC into line with the approach Labour was taking was an initial objective for the Labour leadership, this was viewed as a first stage towards getting the TUC to influence the ETUC's position and thus bring it into line with the Labour approach as well. An early draft of the ETUC position passed on to Whitty by Tom Jenkins, international secretary of the TUC (also chairman of the workers group in the EU Economic and Social Committee) illustrated the task facing the TUC in achieving this. The draft referred to the maintenance of the trade union movement's unremitting support for European integration, the need to press for an ever-closer union, supranational responsibility over economic, political and social issues, a federal scheme of European integration and, more specifically, communitisation of the second and third pillars and the generalisation of QMV (ETUC, January 1995). A note from Jenkins to Whitty explained that the TUC was seeking to 'tone it down' but that this was no easy task. However, a draft of the ETUC position agreed by its executive committee in early April 1995 provided an indication that the TUC did have some success in performing this task. A note from Jenkins to Whitty enclosing the document on 10 April explained that the TUC had managed to maintain its position within the ETUC and that the TUC's own executive would be endorsing it, and would be resisting attempts by federalist unions, such as the Italians and Belgians, to strengthen references to CFSP communitisation, QMV and taxation (TUC Jenkins, 10 April 1995). Whitty sent the draft to Cook and Prescott on 11 April, with a note attached explaining that the TUC would be backing the draft, while resisting federalist amendments. Whitty reminded Cook and Prescott that, if adopted, the document would form the TUC position at is own congress 'and to some extent "lock in" (Labour) affiliated unions.' Whitty suggested that from Labour's point of view the draft was 'much improved from the earlier ultra-federalist draft' and that the TUC had 'obviously done a job on it.' Even so, he suggested that there were still some remaining problems of language, with references to 'deepening' and to 'more rather than less integration' and 'political union.' Furthermore, a reference to making free movement of persons a reality remained, which Whitty suggested could be 'used against the line we have taken.'[19] More positively, he suggested that the line on QMV was one that Labour could 'live with' and 'much more acceptable than might have been expected' while the general tone on transparency and emphasis on the social dimension were 'also well in line with our position' (LP Whitty, 11 April 1995). The new draft had dropped the call for generalised QMV, replacing it with a less precise call for QMV extension, and more specifically for its extension to all social and environmental questions. The references in the earlier draft to communitisation of the second and third pillars had also been removed. But references to a 'federally balanced scheme of European integration' and 'the exercise of supranational responsibility' did remain. Other elements of the document that might have been problematic for Labour were the suggestion that the Commission evolve into a genuine European 'executive' and the call for an EU economic and fiscal policy (ETUC, April 1995).

Despite the inclusion of these statements and while continuing to express some reservations, the chair's note to the fifth LWG meeting was more upbeat about the whole document suggesting that it was 'sufficiently generalised not to be too easily quotable as the British union's position and therefore the Labour party's' (LWG5 Chair's Note). The minutes of the LWG meeting recorded that in discussion of the ETUC document it was recognised 'that whilst there was still some federalist language the document was close to the Labour party position and the TUC had clearly had a positive influence on the draft.' The LWG had therefore agreed to express appreciation to the TUC for this positive influence, and to keep in close contact with it in relation to developments in the ETUC (LWG5 Minutes). The TUC was later able to report that it had further improved the ETUC statement at its May congress by successfully preventing the adoption of the reference to 'a federally balanced scheme of European integration' (TUC September 1995, LWG IGC8B). Similarly, a further statement on the IGC issued by the ETUC following the Madrid summit in December 1995 echoed the TUC influenced positions set out in the earlier May 1995 statement, emphasising the three themes of employment, social solidarity and democracy and avoiding overtly federalist language and policy proposals (ETUC January 1996).[20]

Though influence generally flowed in one direction between the Labour leadership and the TUC in terms of IGC policy-making, there was some variation depending on the particular area of policy concerned. Labour's influence was likely to be stronger in relation to institutional issues such as the pillar structure and Council decision-making, where the unions did not have a direct interest and were therefore more pliant, than in those policy areas directly related to the day-to-day interests of the trade union movement, most notably the issues of social policy and employment. The very nature of the Labour party's organic links with the wider labour movement conditioned its thinking in matters relating to social and employment policy. Accordingly, Labour's consultations with the unions on these areas were more significant and the party was more prone to the unions' influence. This was evident in the inclusion in the 1995 party conference document of an approving reference to the Swedish government's proposals for an employment chapter. This reference was not present in Whitty's initial draft (LWG IGC7D) presented to the LWG in July 1995, but was included following an intervention by the TUC. In a fax sent to Whitty on 20 September and just prior to the Labour party conference, David Lea noted that there was no mention of the employment proposal in the draft document and suggested 'that it would be useful to make some reference' to it (TUC Lea, 20 September 1995). A few days later, Whitty sent a note to Cook and Prescott explaining that the TUC had strongly suggested that a positive reference to the proposal be made in the conference document. Furthermore, Whitty explained that following a meeting with Danish government ministers the previous day, it was clear to him that reference to the employment proposal would 'help to cement our growing alliance with the Nordic countries on the IGC as a whole' (LP Whitty, 26 September 1995).

Within the LWG, it was those members with a personal grounding in the trade unions who were most likely to be most sympathetic to their positions on social policy and employment, notably Whitty and Prescott. Prescott's trade union background was also useful to the PES. Prescott was given the role of PES vice-president with special responsibility for liaison with the trade unions. In a similar vein to the Labour party, the PES as a whole appeared to pay more attention to the views of the trade unions confederations when it came to social and employment policy. Prescott was therefore mandated to represent the PES in an exchange of views on the IGC and employment with the ETUC executive steering group on 1 February 1996. This resulted in a joint PES-ETUC statement that called for the IGC to focus on the issues of employment, social development, non-discrimination, environmental protection and effective, transparent and democratic decision-making. More specifically, the statement also referred to the need for effective European economic co-ordination and a rebalancing of the European integration process away from its monetary emphasis, EU accession to the ECHR, prohibition of all discrimination, QMV in social and environmental matters and a central role for the EP in decision-making (with full EP scrutiny over the budget and a right to nominate candidates for the Commission presidency) (ETUC February 1996, LWG IGCM). Prescott's visible association with this statement was a clear demonstration of Labour's engagement with the agenda of both its sister PES parties and that of the European trade unions, which had led to the dilution of federalist discourse and a greater concentration on 'popular' policy issues in the public stances of both.

Conclusion

The interconnected relationships between the Labour leadership and the EPLP, PES, TUC and ETUC allowed Labour to exercise a strong influence over the respective IGC positioning of these related policy actors, whilst simultaneously allowing these actors to exercise a subtle Europeanising influence on the direction of official Labour party policy. In terms of influencing the positioning on the IGC of these related policy actors, the structure of policy-making devised by the Blair leadership in late 1994 appeared to have served its purpose by late 1996. The position of the TUC had been 'neutralised' as regards its potential to harm Labour's policy formulation process (though any harmful positions that the TUC might have adopted would, in any case, certainly have been ignored by the Blair leadership). Furthermore, the LWG had served to ensure that there was no public discrepancy between the positions being formed in London and the official line of the EPLP. Although the strong direction exercised by the LWG was not sufficient to prevent certain elements within the EPLP from contradicting the official line, the embarrassment caused to the Labour leadership by the evident division in EPLP ranks in relation to the adoption of EP resolutions on the IGC was limited. Moreover, partly as a result of Labour's active engagement with the PES, the adoption of potentially embarrassing joint positions by it had been avoided. But Labour's caution was not reflected in a purely negative approach to the IGC issues. Particularly in relation to first pillar issues, its policy-making process had resulted in the adoption of a number of positions that were in the mainstream of those being pursued by other PES parties and other member governments. These positions reflected Labour's recent conversion into a European social democratic party, and its willingness to engage constructively and pragmatically with the reform agenda. The role played by the EPLP and the PES in facilitating this engagement was vital. However, as the general election drew closer, the shadow cast by domestic political factors would become more pronounced and the Europeanising influences of the EPLP and the PES would diminish. The effect this would have on Labour's IGC policy-making process will be explored in the next chapter.

Notes

[1] The Labour leadership had, in some documents, displayed a misplaced anxiety that the PES IGC working-group would be submitting a draft position for Barcelona (LP Whitty, 1 November 1994, LWG2 Chair's Note).

[2] This was a reference to the *tangentopoli* scandal and consequent collapse of the established ruling parties (including the Socialists) that had engulfed Italian politics in the early 1990s. It is not clear here whether Sigler was referring to the Italian Socialist Party (PSI), which had by then practically collapsed, or the larger ex-Communist Democratic Left Party (PDS). Both were members of the PES.

[3] The Italian government was liable to collapse at any time given the instability in Italian politics following the *tangentopoli* scandal in the early 1990s and the subsequent collapse of the ruling parties. A caretaker administration of 'non-party' figures led by Lamberto Dini had been in power since the collapse of the right-wing Berlusconi government in late 1994, but pressure was growing in Italy for early elections. Elections were finally held in April 1996, resulting in a surprise victory for the PDS-led centre-left *Ulivo* coalition.

[4] A paper submitted by Whitty to the first LWG meeting had described the proposal for the EP to elect the Commission president as an 'extraordinary suggestion, way beyond anything…(the party) could support' (LWG IGC1D).

[5] The Italians appeared to be the most disgruntled amongst the PES parties at the lack of 'federalist' content in Green's paper. Sigler reported that the Italian delegation at the PES working-group meeting of 30-31 March 1995 had argued that Green's paper was 'too minimalist' and risked 'jeopardising both the success of the IGC and the future development

of the Union.' Sigler noted that in arguing this the Italians were completely detached from the views of the other PES parties (LWG IGC5A).

[6] She stated this at the PES IGC working-group meeting of 11-12 May 1995. A summary of this was submitted to the LWG by Sigler as IGC6B.

[7] Six members of the EPLP, including Green, voted with the PES group in favour of the resolution.

[8] Relations between the Labour frontbench and the EPLP continued to cause sporadic problems. For example, the minutes of the seventh LWG meeting in July 1995 recorded that 'after discussion of a recent incident it was agreed that meetings between the EPLP and visiting frontbench spokespeople should be treated as confidential meetings' (LWG7 Minutes).

[9] Donnelly would later succeed David as EPLP leader.

[10] Corbett has written a number of books and journal articles on the EU, treaty reform and the role of the EP in particular.

[11] Corbett provided an analysis of the positions taken by the UK representative in the Reflection Group, which Whitty circulated as an annex to his own paper analysing the Reflection Group outcome (LWG IGC9A) submitted to the ninth LWG meeting on 5 February 1996. Whitty had also drafted a progress report on Reflection Group developments for the eight LWG meeting on 14 September 1995 (LWG IGC8C), which was based on a report by the Reflection Group chair, most likely passed on by Corbett.

[12] This included representatives of centre-right governments, such as the French Europe minister, Michel Barnier, who took Corbett aside on a number of occasions and questioned him about Labour's position in particular areas (Interview with Corbett).

[13] If required Corbett would comment on the factual accuracy of Whitty's papers, and he would also sometimes, if he felt it necessary, make suggestions to Whitty as regards the feasibility and the desirability of the line of argument he was taking in the position papers (Interview with Corbett).

[14] On such technical issues in particular, there was sometimes a resemblance between the commentaries provided by Whitty for the LWG, and those that Corbett had provided for the PES group and copied to Whitty.

[15] For example, Corbett presented a progress report on IGC developments to a meeting of the PES IGC working-group on 16 September 1996. A summary of the meeting, drawn up by Sigler, was included as an annex to LWG IGC12A, which provided a general update of developments in the IGC. Corbett's report involved a comparison of the goals set by the PES Madrid declaration. Accordingly, Corbett suggested that most of the issues identified in Madrid had majority (but not unanimous) support in the IGC.

[16] For example, in March 1997, Corbett sent a detailed brief on the various IGC issues, complete with suggestions on how an incoming Labour government should approach them, to Blair, Cook and Whitty, reminding them of the insights he had to offer as the only member of the Labour party to have thus far set foot in the IGC (LP Corbett, 21 March 1997).

[17] For example, a briefing compiled by Kinnock's office for a meeting Kinnock had with the UK representative, David Davis, on developments within the Reflection Group and the UK positions being taken, was passed on to Whitty, and enclosed with a note that Whitty sent to Cook on 25 October 1995. The briefing provided an analysis of the positions taken by Davis, exploring the specific proposals made by him on behalf of the UK government, such as those on the ECJ and the legislative process (LP Whitty, 25 October 1995).

[18] The relevant excerpt from this report was also circulated to the LWG as IGC8B.

[19] This was a clear reference to the Labour leadership stance that Britain should retain its frontier controls with the rest of the EU and resist pressure to incorporate the Schengen agreement on free movement into the EU treaties.

[20] The ETUC Statement, *The three challenges for the IGC: Employment, solidarity and democracy*, was also submitted to the ninth meeting of the LWG as IGC9F.

Chapter 5

The Countdown to Government

The Nature of Policy-Making

The process of policy-making on the IGC undertaken by the Labour leadership through the LWG could be characterised as rather elitist, with a few individuals within the leadership formulating and agreeing policy (i.e. Blair, Cook and Whitty) following consultation with others in the leadership (e.g. Brown, Prescott and Straw). Nevertheless, the involvement of representatives of the EPLP and the PES group, as well as the limited consultation with the trade unions, provided a degree of pluralism to this policy-making framework, while the consultation with its PES party colleagues undertaken by the Labour leadership, and its attempts to ensure some co-ordination of positions with them, indicated a refreshing willingness to engage with the agenda being developed on the continent. However, those representatives of the EPLP and the PES group who were actually influential in policy-making themselves constituted a rather tiny elite of one or two elected politicians (Green and David) together with a well-placed official (Corbett), while discussion with the other PES parties itself constituted an interplay with the party elites from the other member states. Moreover, discussion with the trade unions was designed primarily to ensure that they were in accordance with the line agreed by the party leadership. There appeared to be no evidence of wider consultation of the Labour party membership as a whole on the positions that the LWG was taking. The party conference, previously the sovereign policy-making organ of the Labour party, served simply to rubber stamp the policy document on the IGC once it was agreed within the LWG. Furthermore, apart from the discussion that took place with key spokespersons on relevant issues, there did not seem to be a great deal of involvement of the parliamentary party in shaping Labour party policy. This appeared to reflect a wider pattern. Conventional party policy-making procedures were totally bypassed in the formulation of the Labour party manifesto for the general election in 1997. A pre-manifesto document: *New Labour, New Life for Britain* was drawn up by the leader's office as a basis for Labour's electoral programme and then put to the party membership for approval as a *fait accompli*, with no opportunity for amendment, in a party plebiscite held in November 1996 (Labour Party 1996, Anderson and Mann 1997: 46-47).[1]

This elitist form of policy-making was illustrative of the centralisation of policy-making within the Labour party that had accelerated under the Blair leadership (Davies 1996: 445-448). Nevertheless, IGC policy-making represented something of an anomaly in relation to the general style of policy development under Blair. While policy-making on the IGC evolved through a formally co-ordinated and fairly open structure of formulation, involving the input of the key Westminster spokesmen and representatives from the EP, in other areas of policy key policy decisions were increasingly taken on the basis of discussions between Blair and his 'inner circle' of selected appointed advisers and the other key architects of the 'New Labour' project within the parliamentary party (notably Gordon Brown and Peter Mandelson). It was often the case that the relevant shadow cabinet spokesperson would be bypassed in this process, and if policy decisions contradicted party conference resolutions, it was presumed that the latter could safely be ignored (Leys 1997: 20-21). Given his stature within the party, it was difficult for Blair and his advisers to bypass the relevant spokesman for foreign affairs, Robin Cook, and Cook was therefore able to carve out a leading role for himself in formulating EU policy. Furthermore, the complexity of the IGC, together with a recognition within the Labour leadership that, for reasons of party management and broader European strategy, connected policy actors such as the EPLP and the PES could not be totally ignored and could actually be utilised positively, led to an acceptance that policy-making in this sensitive area required a more formal and open approach.

However, once the LWG stopped meeting in October 1996, policy-making on the IGC began to bear a stronger resemblance to the general policy-making style of Blair's leadership, with decisions being taken by a few key individuals on the basis of confidential discussions, often resulting in subtle shifts from previously agreed policies. Thus the nature of policy-making became even more centralised and elitist from the end of 1996 as the Labour leadership became more singularly focused on the need to ensure an election victory (with a 'phoney' election campaign already in full swing). This resulted in policy being even more tightly controlled by the Labour leadership, for fear of giving its opponents in the Conservative party and media any opportunity to cast aspersions on Labour's patriotism and commitment to the national interest. The neurosis of the Labour leadership in this respect had already been evident in its positions during the beef crisis, causing difficulties in its relations with the EPLP and PES. But this anxiety became an enduring theme in the run-up to the election, resulting in an increasing caution on the part of the party leadership and an apparent diminution in the role of the Labour party EP representatives in ameliorating these tendencies and encouraging a more positive pro-European message. Labour's more hardline Euro-sceptical statements leading up to the May 1997 election, on issues such as QMV and the social chapter, would cause some consternation in the EPLP (and the TUC in respect of the latter).

The discontinuation of LWG meetings after October 1996 meant that there was no longer a formal forum in which Labour's EP representatives could influence the direction of policy on the IGC, and their influence consequently became more marginal. Although it was agreed at this final meeting that Whitty should keep LWG members informed of further significant developments within the IGC, the focus appeared to switch to bilateral and multilateral contacts between a smaller group of individuals. Whitty did, nevertheless, continue to receive assistance in his close monitoring of IGC progress through close and regular contact with the key figures in the EPLP, the PES group, the leadership of other

PES parties and Kinnock's office in the European Commission. Though, by this time, the post of European co-ordinator had been shifted from the leader's office to the office of the deputy-leader (perhaps reflecting his closer political relationship to Prescott), Whitty remained in the post and continued to hold the central role in the policy-making process. He remained the focal point of the network of contacts within the Labour leadership as it sought to maintain a common line in its approach to the IGC, both in keeping the key figures informed of developments (particularly Blair, Prescott and Cook) and in conducting exchanges of views on developments with these key figures and other relevant Labour party spokespersons and officials.[2]

With the IGC beginning to develop momentum in the second half of 1996 and a steady stream of proposals being tabled by the Council presidency, Commission, UK government and other member governments, the focus of policy activity on the IGC within the Labour leadership became more concentrated on ensuring a coherent and agreed reaction to these proposals. The discontinuation of LWG meetings could be partly attributed to a feeling that its work in agreeing a common party line in London and Brussels on the IGC had been completed. However, the stream of proposals from the IGC often raised new questions that needed to be addressed by the leadership. In response to these proposals, Whitty developed the practice of sending all IGC documents he obtained to Cook and copying them to Quin and Cook's adviser, David Clark, and to other relevant frontbench spokespersons in particular policy areas. These documents usually came with explanatory notes and commentaries produced by Whitty, containing tentative assessments and a suggested party line. However, in relation to some horizontal questions of institutional reform, Whitty continued to circulate documents to all members of the LWG, again with his own explanatory notes and suggested responses.

The end of October 1996 saw the release of the first proposal of major significance submitted to the IGC: the joint Franco-German submission on flexibility (McDonagh 1998: 142-146). The submission proposed a framework in which member states who wished to do so could pursue closer co-operation in certain policy areas, while excluding those that chose not to take part from decision-making in the Council. Perhaps provoked by the UK policy of non co-operation, the submission departed from the previous affirmation in the Chirac-Kohl letter of December 1995 that any such differentiation should only be temporary (Duff 1997a: 189). Whitty circulated a commentary on the submission to key figures within the leadership, counselling against the proposal and suggesting that an early discussion should take place on how to deal with it (LP Whitty, 30 October 1996).[3] Whitty warned that the proposal could lead to the exclusion of the UK from major areas of policy co-operation, with its veto meaning only that it ruled itself out, and not that it stopped things happening. He thus argued that closer co-operation by a group of states should only be allowed to proceed on a case-by-case basis and following the granting of permission by unanimity among all member states. The issue of flexibility would prove to be a particularly difficult one for the Labour leadership. Although the LWG had agreed to seek to minimise the likelihood of any such arrangements being agreed, this had been before specific proposals had been tabled. A more considered response was now needed to more specific proposals on an issue that would be central to the continuing IGC discussions.

In a similar vein, it was also becoming apparent that the leadership needed to undertake further consideration of the issue of JHA communitisation. While agreeing that this should be opposed, the LWG had not given consideration to the details of any compromise that might need to be negotiated if it could not prevent this from happening. The necessity of reaching such a compromise was becoming increasingly apparent towards the end of the 1996 given the determination of a number of member states to ensure that JHA communitisation remained central to the IGC agenda and the widespread support for the option across the member states. The need to further develop party policy and respond to various IGC proposals on the issues of JHA communitisation and flexibility would therefore dominate consideration of IGC policy within the Labour leadership in the run-up to the election. Indeed, proposals relating to reform of the JHA pillar were a key feature of the draft treaty text produced by the Irish presidency for the Dublin summit in December (McDonagh 1998: 165-172).

The submission of the Irish treaty draft was the most significant development of the IGC thus far, providing a basis for all further IGC discussion (McDonagh 1998: 125-132). The text caused difficulties for the Labour party in a number of areas. The brief on the treaty drafted by Whitty and circulated to LWG members on 8 December categorised these difficulties into two types of overall 'serious problem' for Labour. First, those areas where Labour 'would have real difficulty on agreeing the draft as a government' and secondly, those areas where Labour did not want 'too much difference opening up now with the government position thereby giving them a target.' The Irish draft set out a proposed treaty text for many of the areas under discussion, but in some of the most contentious areas it merely set out a number of options, returning to the ground covered by the Reflection Group (McDonagh 1998: 105-108).[4] In terms of the first type of problem, the main area of difficulty for Labour as a government, and one where, particularly on border controls, it would generally agree with the Conservatives, was the proposal for a new treaty title establishing an area of freedom, security and justice. This involved setting a timetable for the establishment of common policies on immigration, asylum, visas, the crossing of the EU's external frontiers and the rights of third country nationals resident within the EU. However, given its sensitivity, the question of whether this new title should be in the first pillar, the third pillar or a new pillar was left open by the Irish, though they indicated a preference for the first pillar (McDonagh 1998: 171-172). Whitty suggested that Labour might want to be more constructive than the Conservatives on this proposal, for example by supporting some improved decision-making, but expressed doubts over whether this would be possible given Jack Straw's intransigent line.

Whitty's commentary on the second type of problematical issue, i.e. those areas where Labour differed from the government, and where the Conservatives could use its support for the proposals against it, again revealed the anxiety of the party about being depicted as soft on Europe. Whitty noted with relief that, fortunately for Labour, consideration of most of these issues had been postponed in the Irish draft, e.g. flexibility and QMV in the first pillar (though options were explored), and the UK's own submissions on the ECJ and other issues. However, he did refer to 'serious problems on voting and on flexibility in both the CFSP and JHA pillars' on which Labour needed to take a position, i.e. proposals for QMV in CFSP for all areas bar joint actions and defence, though with a facility for 'constructive abstention' and for flexibility in the adoption of JHA conventions. Whitty suggested a positive stance on the latter, allowing conventions to be implemented by two-thirds of member states once they had ratified them. However, he was more dismissive towards the proposal for 'constructive abstention.' This entailed allowing individual member states to indicate their abstention from a CFSP decision without preventing the rest of the EU from proceeding with its implementation (McDonagh 1998: 115). Labour's IGC policy document of 1995 had indicated that it would not support such a mechanism, emphasising that 'actions taken in the name of the European Union must be supported by all its member states' and therefore stating that 'Labour does not support proposals to allow some member states to opt out of some joint actions' (Labour Party 1995: 14). The developing consensus behind this proposal, as reflected in its inclusion in the Irish draft, would oblige the Labour party to reconsider its position. Nevertheless, the attitude towards it continued to be negative. Whitty commented: 'Being crudely realistic, a European policy cannot be regarded as "common" in the international arena, unless it is supported by all of the larger countries. Even constructive abstention does not meet that if the abstainer is a large country. Any dilution of the voting that does not recognise that for the principled decisions should not be supported.'

Whitty also pinpointed defence and the proposals for a non-discrimination clause in the Irish draft as potentially difficult areas for Labour. On defence, there were mild proposals for closer links between the EU and the WEU in relation to the so-called Petersberg tasks (relating mainly to peace-keeping and humanitarian missions).[5] Whitty predicted that the Conservative government would go along with this and that Labour should do the same, though he noted that the French and Germans regarded this as a weak proposal and wanted full WEU/EU merger.[6] On the proposal for a general anti-discrimination clause, Whitty expressed concern that while the party was generally in favour and would be under 'immense pressure from other governments and within the party and lobby groups to agree' Labour could be subject to political ridicule in the UK about it. Though the 1995 policy document had indicated Labour's support for anti-discrimination provisions, some within the Labour leadership had expressed concern at the scope such provisions might give to the ECJ to make judgements on anti-discrimination cases in the UK (Labour Party 1995: 16, Interview with LWG participant). Indeed, Whitty's commentary also expressed doubts about Jack Straw's willingness to support the proposal even if unanimous decision-making was guaranteed. However, some form of anti-discrimination clause was supported by all of the PES governments, apart from the Danes, and Whitty advocated continuing support, whilst insisting on unanimity and 'watching the wording carefully.' Elsewhere, Whitty pointed to a number of other significant areas in the draft where Labour differed from the government, but where he viewed Labour as having a defensible political position. These were the proposals for a new employment chapter, strengthened provisions on environmental and consumer protection[7] and a strengthening of the EP powers. While generally pressed by the PES governments, the employment chapter proposal continued to meet with opposition from the centre-right governments of France and Germany, though Whitty suggested that the French would come round to supporting it eventually. However, he noted cautiously that some of the PES governments might push for something stronger. The proposal on environmental protection involved integrating environmental and sustainable development criteria into all EC policies (McDonagh 1998: 87-88). Whitty warned that Labour might need to react to future suggestions likely to come from the Nordic countries to strengthen provisions allowing member states to maintain higher environmental standards that might conflict with single market provisions. The proposals on the EP were generally in line with Labour's agreed position on reducing the number of procedures to three (codecision, assent, and consultation), reform of the codecision procedure itself and EP approval of the Commission president (McDonagh 1998: 155). Whitty described these proposals as defensible 'in terms of democratic principle' (LP Whitty, 8 December 1996).

The Role of Sir Michael Butler

The need for the Labour party to react to these significant IGC documents coincided with the intensification of its general strategy to present itself as a respectable alternative government in the run-up to an almost certain spring 1997 general election. Against this background, the party leadership gave a clear public signal of its determination to present itself as a party of government fully prepared to represent the UK in the European arena with the appointment of Sir Michael Butler as the party's envoy on EU enlargement (Tonra 1997: 19). Butler's credentials in representing the UK in the EU were impeccable having served as the UK's permanent representative to the EC between 1979 and 1985 and having held a number of senior positions within the foreign office (FCO) prior to 1979 (Young, H 1999: 177).[8] Although Butler left the diplomatic service in 1985 to work in the City, he continued to be active in terms of writing, public speaking and consultancy on EU policy. Though not a 'natural' Labour party supporter, Butler had, in his own words, become increasingly disgusted at the Major government's antics as regards the EU, particularly in relation to the beef crisis, and had written a number of articles in 1996 criticising the government (it may have been these articles that alerted the Labour leadership to the possibility of Butler being brought on board) (Interview with Butler). Butler was first approached by Blair's chief of staff, Jonathan Powell, to act as Labour's envoy, towards the end of September 1996. He met with Cook shortly after to discuss the role, and his appointment was made public at the Labour party conference at the beginning of October. Butler's appointment was beneficial to the Labour party on a number of levels. In terms of public perception of the Labour party, that such a well-respected former senior foreign office apparatchik was prepared to publicly associate himself with

Labour's EU policy would serve as a signal that it was Labour, rather than the Conservatives (as had traditionally been the case) that now represented the mainstream pragmatic establishment view on Europe. On a more practical level, in terms of indirectly influencing the IGC, further developing a network of contacts with the key IGC players in the UK, other member states and the EU institutions, and formulating a more detailed potential negotiating strategy ready for the entrance to government, Butler's appointment added a new dimension to the party given his contacts, wealth of diplomatic experience and inside knowledge of European negotiations. Although Butler's role officially related to enlargement, it soon became apparent that in practice his role would be focused on IGC preparation. The two roles were obviously intertwined. By giving Butler the official assignation of enlargement envoy, the Labour leadership may have been deliberately attempting to link the issues of enlargement and the need for IGC reform in the public mind. Given the much greater degree of public consensus on the desirability of enlargement, a portrayal of the IGC as essential for enlargement would be a means of increasing public consent for it.

At Butler's first meeting with Cook, it was clear that the latter was more interested in receiving assistance and advice on the IGC, than on enlargement. Indeed, Cook emphasised the critical importance he attached to the IGC given its proximity to the general election, and acknowledged that the IGC was perhaps the most difficult immediate political issue that Labour would face should it win. Thus, while Butler would 'do the round' in terms of meeting the ambassadors of the CEE applicant countries to talk about enlargement, and visited a number of these countries, this was not central to his role. Rather, in practice, Butler's role would focus on the IGC as this was seen as the most pressing issue (Interview with Butler).

Butler's appointment opened up a new and more politically neutral line of communication with the governments of the other member states. As well as numerous meetings with representatives of the other member states, Butler also held meetings with European Commission officials and UK government officials (from the FCO and cabinet office) on behalf of the Labour party. The willingness of both UK government officials and those of other member states to meet with Butler was illustrative of the degree to which the Labour party was being viewed as the likely party of government for the final stages of the IGC, and of their eagerness to prepare for such an outcome by acquainting themselves with the positions that a future Labour government would take in the final negotiations. It was also illustrative of the exasperation felt among the governments of the UK's European partners at the increasingly hostile Conservative government and of a recognition among the governments that an acceptable treaty agreement was only likely to occur following the British general election and the replacement of the Conservative government by a more constructive Labour government (McDonagh 1998: 53-54, Dinan 1999: 177).

Although both Whitty and Quin were in close contact with people in the other EU member states, these were, in the main, representatives of PES parties who were generally not closely involved in the IGC negotiations. Butler's advantage was that he had contacts with the officials in the member states that were actually involved in the details of the negotiations. It was also less politically sensitive for him to meet with them, and they were able to be more frank with him than they would with Labour party representatives. They knew that Butler 'knew the rules' as regards being discrete in these matters. Similarly, Butler was able to use, to his and the Labour party's advantage, the extensive range of contacts he had within Whitehall and the FCO. He was well acquainted with the key officials involved in EU policy within the cabinet office and FCO, and they utilised to the full the discretion afforded them by civil service rules to keep the opposition informed in the run-up to the election (Interview with Butler).

The employment of Butler provided the clearest illustration of attempts by New Labour to display its new found credibility with the business, financial and Whitehall establishment more traditionally associated with support for the Conservative party. While this applied generally across New Labour's political strategy, it was especially valuable in European policy as it afforded Labour the opportunity to portray itself as more in tune with the interests of this 'conservative' but pragmatic and internationally orientated establishment than the increasingly nationalistic Conservative party (Marquand 1998: 24). In a similar vein, the Labour leadership also courted other former senior diplomats, notably Sir Robin Renwick and Sir David Hannay. Blair held a number of private seminars on Europe with Renwick, Hannay and Butler, focusing on the broader approach Britain should be taking towards the rest of Europe (Interview with Butler).[9]

The Secret Channel to the Dutch Presidency

The willingness of the Labour leadership to court the involvement of these establishment figures was illustrative of its strategy of presenting itself as a potential government capable of securing UK interests within the EU. The role that Butler would play in particular would prove critical to this strategy. He was able to bring to the Labour party an insider's appreciation of exactly how intergovernmental negotiations at the EU level would work. This was especially useful in developing negotiating positions and strategies (where Butler played a particular role). Increasingly, in the first half of 1997, Butler would also take a lead role in producing draft position papers/strategy papers and briefings on the IGC. Leading up to the May general election, Butler would meet with officials from all the important EU member states to discuss IGC developments and their positions. According to Butler, most of his old friends in the other EU embassies and EU institutions were very keen for Labour to win the general election and were therefore 'immensely co-operative' in providing him with details of positions and exchanging information. Indeed, Butler suggests that EU government representatives, and all the EU ambassadors in particular, were 'pursuing me like mad' once they found out that he was advising the Labour leadership (Interview with Butler). In particular, the Dutch, under whose Council presidency the crucial final negotiations would take place, were especially keen to set up a detailed exchange of information and would provide Butler with a fairly comprehensive flow of information and documents from the IGC.

To this end Butler established a private channel to the Dutch government several weeks prior to their assumption of the presidency, in anticipation of the intensification of the IGC negotiations and their likely conclusion by a Labour government. A confidential fax sent by Butler to David Clark on 12 November 1996 confirmed the establishment of this arrangement by Butler on the previous day, on the understanding that he (Butler) was acting on behalf of the Labour leadership and that the channel should be kept secret in order to avert embarrassment on all sides. The fax also illustrated the extent to which the Labour leadership was attempting to indirectly influence the negotiations and to ensure that sensitive issues were left open until after the general election. Thus Butler wrote:

> As agreed yesterday afternoon, I proposed to the Dutch Ambassador (when he came to see me this morning) that we should establish a private channel of communication so that Robin Cook and his colleagues could be fully informed of the issues likely to form part of the endgame in the IGC. I said that we would aim to keep the channel and what passed over it from public view and assumed that the Dutch would wish to do the same. The Ambassador said that he thought it was an excellent idea and would deal with it on a 'need to know' basis. But he did not dissent when I said that if by any chance there was a leak I believed that it could be handled without embarrassment on either side. That being said, we should aim not to have to talk about it in public. I also made the point that, if a Labour Government was to be able to negotiate rapidly after the Election, it would be very important that the situation should be kept reasonably fluid in the period leading up to it. The more brackets in the text the better,[10] even if some of them could reasonably easily be removed. We would need to be seen to have a real negotiation and to bring home some successes, for example, on the Employment Charter (sic). The Ambassador seemed sympathetic to this approach (LP Butler, 12 November 1996).

Later evidence suggests that the Dutch ambassador did, throughout the period of the Dutch presidency leading up to the May election in the UK, provide the Labour leadership with most (though perhaps not all) of the papers being submitted to the IGC, and that both he and senior officials and ministers from the Dutch foreign ministry would be in regular contact with Labour's representatives, particularly Butler, Whitty and Clark. For its part, the development of a channel of contact with what it viewed as a UK 'government in waiting' was integral to the Dutch government's strategy for handling the final and critical phase of the IGC. In particular, the Dutch wished to prevent the IGC agenda from developing in a manner that would allow it to be exploited for domestic political purposes in the UK, and which would consequently make a final agreement with a British government more difficult. As Moravcsik and Nicolaidis note, the presidency would hesitate to publicise positions before the election 'for fear of aiding the Tories' (1999: 67). Contact with the Labour opposition in Britain was therefore useful for the Dutch government as it sought to steer the IGC in a politically sensitive fashion. As Bobby McDonagh, a member of the Irish IGC negotiating team, writes: 'it was clearly in nobody's interest that the (IGC) be handled in a way which would allow it to become a divisive issue in the British election. The more controversial it became from a domestic UK point of view, the more the hands of a new British government of either complexion would be tied' (1998: 138). Labour's representatives were clearly in a prime position to advise the Dutch as to which issues should not be pushed until after the election.

From the end of 1996 until the May 1997 election, there was close informal co-ordination between Whitty, Butler and Cook's office (usually through his adviser, Clark) and to a lesser extent Quin, in order to continue the maintenance of a cohesive party response to IGC developments and formulate a negotiating strategy ready for implementation upon entrance to government. Crucial to this was the intensification of contacts with Dutch ministers, government and party officials prior to and during the Dutch presidency (Tonra 1997: 19). While the bulk of this networking burden appeared to fall upon Butler and Whitty, it was a task also shared by Cook and Quin, with Clark generally acting on Cook's behalf. For example, Clark and Quin met with the Dutch minister for Europe, Michiel Patijn on 9 December 1996. Patijn would go on to chair the IGC representatives group under the Dutch presidency. Although he served in a Dutch government led by the PVDA, which was perhaps the Labour party's closest ideological ally among the PES parties (Marliere 1999: 13-15), Patijn himself was actually a representative of the Dutch Liberal party, the PVDA's centre-right coalition partner. Yet he appeared just as eager as his government colleagues to furnish the Labour party with information and assist it in preparing for government. The report of the meeting provided by Clark and Quin explained that Patijn had acknowledged the domestic difficulties involved for the Labour party and indicated his wish to assist Labour in the preparation of negotiations. Despite Patijn's political affiliations, Clark and Quin reported that he was 'keen to establish a discreet channel of communication to keep us informed about developments at the IGC.' Clark and Quin had accepted this offer, although there would be consultations within the Labour leadership on the best way to take communications forward.

On the substance of policy itself, while understanding its problems over immigration and asylum, Patijn expressed concern that the UK should not block progress on third pillar issues, even if this meant some kind of opt-out or flexibility arrangement, and sought Labour's approval for stronger co-operation on tackling crime and drugs. On CFSP and defence, he sought to reassure the Labour representatives that it was unlikely that anything ambitious would be attempted in this area, though he suggested that the UK position was still too restrictive because an outcome that did not 'allow the EU to discuss issues with a military dimension' would not be accepted (LP Quin and Clark, 9 December 1996). Clark and Quin noted that there were was a 'clear impression' that there were differences within the Dutch coalition government between the parties of the left and right, with Patijn for example expressing strong scepticism about the proposed anti-discrimination provisions and employment chapter and any costly measures under the social chapter, all of which one would have expected the PVDA to support (although given that the PVDA were the most Blairite of Labour's sister parties, its ministers may have shared some of Patijn's caution). Knowledge of divisions on IGC issues within the governments of other member states would also prove useful to the Labour party in formulating a negotiating strategy, with ministers more sympathetic to Labour's positions, whether from PES parties or not, being singled out for special attention. The Dutch Liberal party had taken on a more questioning tone towards the traditional 'federalist' inclined Dutch view of EU policy (Pijpers and Vanhoonacker 1997: 126-127). Thus, although the PVDA was perhaps closer ideologically to the Labour party on social and economic matters, the Dutch Liberals may have been closer to the Labour party in their more pragmatic view of European integration.

By early February, contacts with the Dutch presidency were intensifying, with Butler, Cook, Whitty and Clark working closely together both to ensure that the Labour leadership had a coherent picture of the state of play at the IGC and to discreetly influence the proceedings at the IGC in order to minimise domestic difficulties for the party and leave the negotiations loose until after the general election. This rested on encouraging the assumption among the Dutch and other member states that they would then be dealing with a newly elected and far more constructive Labour government. A note from Butler, dated 13 February, indicated that Labour's strategy appeared to be bearing some fruit. Recalling that it had been requested of the Dutch that they 'should try to keep the formal position as open as possible to avoid Tory exploitation of the IGC situation, either in the election campaign or afterwards' Butler noted that the Dutch had 'taken this message to heart' and would not 'be trying to create a 14-1 situation on issues that are difficult for us.' Butler's note was based on conversations that Butler had had with Tom de Bruijn, EU director of the Dutch foreign ministry (and deputy to Patijn in the Dutch IGC team), and Cook with Patijn. The note explained that the Dutch were working towards tabling a complete draft treaty immediately after the UK general election 'though still with lots of square brackets.' Nevertheless, Butler warned that the Dutch still intended to table draft treaty texts on JHA in February, and flexibility in March.[11] A Labour election victory now appeared to be being taken for granted on the continent. Butler's note explained that the Dutch were hoping that a Labour government would be 'in a position to participate actively in the IGC group at least on some of the issues within a few days of the election.' The Dutch had also pencilled in dates for at least one, possibly two, informal meetings of foreign ministers between then and the Amsterdam summit. Wim Kok was also planning an informal dinner soon after the election to allow Blair to 'set the scene' (LP Butler, 13 February 1997).

Butler's note suggested that for both Patijn and de Bruijn 'though from slightly different angles' flexibility appeared to be the main issue. This was linked to JHA communitisation where pressure was growing for the option of moving ahead without the UK and bringing parts of it into the first pillar. The Dutch were also intent on including measures to incorporate the Schengen arrangements in the proposed text on the communitised area of freedom, security, and justice (McDonagh 1998: 173-176).[12] This would involve giving the UK an opt-out as regards control of frontiers. According to Butler, Patijn had indicated that among the member states 'the score so far was 11:4 (in favour of this) soon likely to rise to 13:2' (with the Danes probably also opposing). Butler's note indicated the extent to which the Dutch were willing to smooth the path for agreement with a future Labour government while minimising political difficulties for it in the meantime. It explained that Patijn had stressed that assuming the election of a Labour government 'his aim was to move from total non co-operation by the British to as much co-operation as we might find useful or possible' and that he 'had already made it clear publicly that the Dutch would not be pressing us to give in on border controls' (LP Butler, 13 February 1997).

Butler's note explained that de Bruijn had stated the Dutch intention to table a text on a general flexibility clause. In light of this the Labour strategy appeared to be to seek to minimise the likelihood of such a clause being agreed by exposing the motives behind the proposals, i.e. UK intransigence, and accordingly stress that a change to constructive engagement under a Labour government would make this unnecessary (particularly as regards first pillar issues). In addition, Labour representatives would also seek to cultivate reservations about the practical implications of the clause, particularly by drawing attention to the undesirable prospect of departure from the principle of legal uniformity. Thus while Patijn had stated to Cook that Franco-German motives on flexibility were not clear, de Bruijn had been more frank in explaining that it was a response to the UK policy of non co-operation. When de Bruijn had also suggested that it was now too late to take the proposal for flexibility in the first pillar off the table because it was also necessary for enlargement, Butler had referred him to the public statement of the Commission official in charge of enlargement the previous day that first pillar flexibility was not important for enlargement as temporary derogations or transitional periods would meet this need. Butler explained that when he put this point to de Bruijn 'he admitted it was probably true' (LP Butler, 13 February 1997).

The discussions with Patijn and de Bruijn had also covered a number of institutional questions, notably the extension of QMV. On QMV, there was a strong indication that a Labour government, with its support for limited extensions, would be very much in the mainstream, with Patijn reassuring Cook that 'a massive extension...was not on the cards.' However, the Dutch were thinking of setting out a list of subjects such as treaty change, own resources etc. where QMV would definitely be excluded and then reversing the argument in other areas by inviting member states to provide arguments as to why unanimity should be maintained.

Recognising that these meetings had not allowed for a fully comprehensive coverage of all the issues on the agenda, Butler's note explained that shortage of time had prevented such discussion and that de Bruijn would be returning to the UK in March and would be setting aside a whole half-day to cover all the subjects. De Bruijn had also agreed to convey to Butler 'in strict confidence' all the presidency papers, while also signalling willingness 'to answer questions or receive comments on the telephone at any time' (LP Butler, 13 February 1997).

Contacts with Other EU Governments and the EU Institutions

Although the cultivation of contacts with the Dutch presidency appeared to be the focal point of the Labour leadership's networking strategy, particular attention was also paid to developing relationships with the key member states. This was illustrated by the private visit made by Blair to the French president Jacques Chirac, in early November 1996. The willingness of the French president to meet Blair to discuss the IGC was another indication of the extent to which the other member states had lost patience with the Major government and were viewing Labour as the party likely to be governing the UK for the crucial final negotiations (Laffan 1997b: 30). The brief provided for Blair for his meeting with Chirac also served as an illustration of the extent to which the Labour leadership was now allowing Butler to take the lead in drafting such documents, thus utilising his vast diplomatic experience. Butler sent a draft brief for the Blair-Chirac meeting to Whitty on 6 November, though this may have been slightly amended in a number of areas (following Whitty's suggestions) before the final draft went to Blair. Butler indicated an awareness of the sensitivity of a meeting between the French head of state and the UK leader of the opposition, particularly given that Chirac was a centre-right politician more normally expected to be politically closer to John Major than Tony Blair. Given that Chirac was meeting Major the following week, Butler speculated over whether Chirac was likely to give away Blair's private thoughts to Major (though this seemed unlikely). Butler wrote: 'Chirac is seeing Major in Bordeaux on Friday next week. I have given thought to whether any of the recommended "lines to take" would be embarrassing if recounted to Major. I hope not.'

While pointing out that Chirac would be briefed 'to find out what he can expect of a Labour government', Butler suggested that Blair himself take 'an interrogatory line' with Chirac and make clear that he wished to understand which IGC issues were important to Chirac and what the substance of his position would be. It was recommended that Blair should aim to get across a number of points emphasising Labour's good intentions but stressing the domestic constraints it was under and seeking assistance in preventing developments that would allow the UK government to exploit the situation. Thus Blair would stress: 1) that a Labour government would bring a fresh start to the UK's relations with its European partners; 2) that the Conservatives would attempt to misrepresent the Labour party as betraying important national interests at the forthcoming general election, for example over border controls and immigration, and that Labour obviously could not allow this (implying that Labour would take a similar line to the Tories on these issues); 3) that Labour would like to conclude the IGC in June, if it could, and that 'the French, the Presidency and others can in turn help us to make this possible by thoughtful presentation'; 4) that in terms of public presentation of the negotiations, a '14 to 1 line-up against the UK on election day would not be helpful' to Labour and that therefore 'the more square brackets remain in the draft treaty the better' as a Labour government would 'need to be seen to have a real negotiation and to bring home some successes.' Butler also suggested that, as with the Dutch, if his conversations with Chirac went well 'Blair might open up the possibility of a private channel of communication between his office and the Elysee between then and the election designed to help Labour to prepare to negotiate constructively very soon after it' (LP Butler, 6 November 1996). Informal contacts between French officials and the Labour party did appear to continue after this meeting, although they did not appear to be anywhere near the level of intensity of Labour's contacts with Dutch officials.

As indicated by the initial contacts with the Dutch, it was becoming increasingly clear to the Labour leadership that the issues where it would have the greatest difficulty in finding common ground with the other member states were the (possibly related) issues of flexibility and the third pillar. It was on these issues in particular that Butler would lend his diplomatic expertise and inside knowledge of European negotiations to assist in the formulation of Labour's negotiating strategy. Indeed, a briefing note drafted by Butler on 13 January 1997 on these issues affirmed that the 'closely related' issues of flexibility and the third pillar were 'the two most difficult subjects for us at the IGC.' Nevertheless, Butler suggested that in considering its strategy for the IGC, Labour could bear in mind the following:

1) that there was a consensus among the member states that these difficult issues should not be pushed too far with the existing UK government and that these issues would be settled as part of the endgame of the IGC, taking place after the UK general election possibly with a new Labour government;

2) that if a Labour government generated some goodwill in the endgame, other member states might be 'prepared to settle for quite a modest outcome to the IGC as a whole';

3) that other member governments were 'completely fed up with John Major' and most UK ministers were 'regarded with contempt by their colleagues in the Council' with UK influence in the EU 'at an all time low.' Thus Butler suggested: 'Provided we can avoid saying things in the election campaign which grate on their ears, our European partners will be disposed to go some way to meet us, especially if the manifesto itself repeats the line taken in the road to the manifesto.'[13]

In examining the various possibilities as regards the third pillar and flexibility, Butler noted that a Labour government might not necessarily be so isolated, for example, the Danes were also reticent over third pillar communitisation. In addition, the detailed position of a number of member states, including the French, on both this issue and flexibility remained obscure. Thus Butler suggested that before Labour could see how to play the endgame in detail on these issues, it would need far more information on what other governments wanted in practice. Among his other recommendations, Butler suggested that where Labour did not agree with other member governments on these issues, it should 'rely as far as possible on practical rather than ideological arguments' and that it should 'aim to reach a position in the endgame where, thanks to the tone of ministers' speeches and to constructive compromise on issues such as the organisation of the European Commission, majority voting, weighting of votes etc' other member governments would be 'prepared to settle for improving their co-operation under the third pillar and to put off for, say, five years' time the consideration of third pillar issues.'

Butler concluded by rather optimistically suggesting that, at the very last, Blair might be 'able to appeal privately to Kohl and Chirac to drop flexibility as far as pillar one is concerned in return for constructive engagement in the EU and positive efforts to educate UK opinion about the myth and lies propagated by the Euro-sceptics' (LP Butler, 13 January 1997).

While Butler appeared to be taking the lead in terms of maintaining close contact with the Dutch presidency, Whitty continued to take a lead in cultivating contacts among other governments led by PES parties. As with those with the Dutch presidency, these contacts were useful to the Labour party both as a means of obtaining information on what was going on at the IGC and on the attitude of the other member states, and in providing it with an opportunity to influence the negotiations by conveying how a future Labour government would act. Particularly useful were contacts with the Nordic parties who shared the more pragmatic approach of the Labour party. This was illustrated by the meeting between Whitty and the Swedish IGC representative, Gunnar Lund, minister for European affairs in the Swedish socialist government (he was accompanied by his deputy at the IGC, Sweden's permanent representative, Sven-Olof Petersson). A note on the meeting sent by Whitty to Cook, Quin and Powell, dated 14 February, explained that the Swedes had conveyed their wish 'to be as helpful as possible for an incoming Labour government.' Thus the Swedes had provided Whitty with a comprehensive set of papers from the most recent IGC representatives meeting of that week, together with cover notes providing a summary and Swedish analysis of the outcome of the discussions. The papers discussed covered flexibility, extension of QMV, reweighting of votes (where there was still opposition from smaller states) and legislative procedures, i.e. codecision extension. A timetable for the IGC meetings and key general affairs councils under the Dutch presidency leading up to the Amsterdam summit in June was also provided. Whitty's note explained that the general impression was that some degree of consensus on these issues could emerge by the time of the general affairs council of 24-25 March, with the UK 'plus one or two on different issues' dissenting. However, he emphasised that all involved were 'intent on avoiding a breakdown prior to the British election.'

The discussions with the Swedes had also covered developments as regards the third pillar. After Denmark, Sweden was the member state most sympathetic to the UK's position as regards the retention of intergovernmentalism in the third pillar. However, Whitty explained that the Danes were 'now wavering' whilst the Swedes did not want to be 'on their own.' There was therefore a 'growing consensus outside the UK that migration and asylum and border controls plus most of Schengen should be communautised (sic)' with some kind of opt-out for the UK. Warning that this would lead to a greater acceptance of flexibility in the first pillar, Whitty commented that it seemed 'more than a little illogical to transfer items into the First Pillar and then give the UK (and a reluctant Ireland) a permanent and drastic opt-out' but this now seemed to be 'the way things are going.' He also noted that David Davis was now referring to this as 'a triumph of negotiation.' On flexibility itself, the Swedes had passed on to Whitty an IGC presidency paper, which included drafts for a general flexibility clause plus specific versions for the EC, JHA and CFSP pillars. Consideration of this inevitably overlapped with perceptions of the future of the JHA pillar. As on JHA communitisation, Whitty reported that there was a broad consensus in support for a general flexibility clause, with the Swedes among the most reluctant and the UK opposed. There was, however, a general view that the application of flexibility needed to be very restricted indeed in the first pillar. The implication of Whitty's note was that the Swedes, in their reluctance here, would be a likely ally of a future Labour government on this issue.

The Swedes had provided Whitty with the Dutch presidency paper on the extension of QMV, flagged up by Butler's note the previous day, in which it sought to identify those areas where unanimity should remain and then listed those articles 'which could form a working basis for examining a possible extension of QMV.' Those areas where unanimity should remain the rule were identified as: 1) constitutional issues and treaty changes; 2) derogations on the internal market; 3) provisions with a direct impact on members states' budgets, including tax, social security and the definition of the structural funds. Whitty referred to the list of areas where QMV could be extended as 'relatively short' and not 'in general...a difficult list for us to accept.' A similar exercise had been undertaken by the Dutch on the extension of codecision, with the list of areas for extension roughly corresponding to that on QMV (McDonagh 1998: 161-162). Whitty described this as relatively straightforward for Labour to support.

The Swedes had submitted further papers to the IGC calling for stronger measures on employment, environment and transparency. Whitty reported that although these proposals were mainly a tactical ploy to ensure that there was no dilution of the Irish draft treaty text, the Swedes were seeking some strengthening in these areas, and would be looking for a Labour government's support on them. As Whitty explained, the Swedes had made clear to Whitty their expectation of and preference for a Labour election victory, and their hopes that this could lead to a tactical alliance at the IGC. In order to explore this possibility, it was suggested that Blair 'talk to (Swedish) Prime Minister Persson at some point before 25 March' (LP Whitty, 14 February 1997).

Whitty's relaxed view of the Dutch presidency proposals on QMV extension was contradicted somewhat in a later note sent by Butler to Whitty, Clark and Quin on 19 February. In the note, Butler explained that following careful reading of this list, it was his view that some of the items might be 'more difficult for us than appears at first sight', e.g. right of movement and residence (which the Danes would also oppose), professions, industry (which was very broad) and financial regulation. He therefore suggested that the party 'set in hand a study of all these items.' In suggesting this Butler may not have been aware of the earlier, article by article examination carried out by the LWG of the areas in which QMV extension could be countenanced on the basis of Whitty's discussion paper (IGC3D). In this note, Butler also appeared to be suggesting that, for the time being, Labour keep its own counsel on its preferences as regards possible extensions of QMV, to be used as bargaining chips in the final negotiations. He explained: 'We will need some concessions for Robin in the Council and for Tony Blair at Amsterdam. So I suggest that all of us should take the line up to the elections and probably throughout May that it would be very hard for us to go beyond our long-standing positions on QMV. We will study the list when we are in office but cannot do so effectively before' (LP Butler, 19 February 1997).

This strategy was also reflected in the brief provided for a meeting that Cook had with the Commission president, Jacques Santer in early March. Labour's networking in this period also involved contacts with the Commission, with Kinnock being the obvious point of contact. The exasperation felt by the Commission at the antics of the British government matched, if not outstripped, that felt by many of the member governments (Dinan 1999: 173). Santer therefore shared the strong interest being taken in Labour's IGC positions, as illustrated by the meeting with Cook. A note from Butler to Clark (copied to Whitty and Quin) stressed the interest that Santer would take in Cook's views. However, Butler suggested that Cook should not give too much away to Santer, as regards how much Labour actually knew about the IGC, and the extent to which it was preparing detailed negotiating positions. He suggested that Cook should not go further than restating Labour's already enunciated public positions. On subjects such as QMV, Butler advised Cook to take the line that Labour had 'taken some positions publicly' and would stand by them. In general, Butler advised Cook to take the following line with Santer: 'The negotiations are moving forward and, though we are doing our best to keep ourselves briefed, we naturally cannot have a complete picture of what is going on before we are in government. So it seems best to listen and learn and get ready to negotiate as soon as possible after 1 May' (LP Butler, 4 March 1997).

In short, Labour was playing a 'double game' of pretending not to know what was going on at the IGC so that it did not have to commit itself publicly in the sensitive general election atmosphere. Even in private conversations with representatives of other member governments or the Commission, Labour was keeping its cards close to its chest, lest it weaken its negotiating position once in office, or worse still, risk having the concessions it was willing to make leak into the public domain in the fevered UK pre-election atmosphere. Butler stressed that Labour should keep back any concessions that it wanted to make until the general affairs Council on 2-3 June or the Amsterdam summit itself (LP Butler, 4 March 1997).

In terms of discussing specific issues with Santer, Butler suggested that Cook maintain the focus on flexibility and third pillar issues, as Labour was doing in its contacts with the various member governments. Butler recommended that Cook once again stress the difficulty that Labour had with first pillar flexibility and emphasise the need to maintain legal uniformity in EC law, particularly as Labour was committed to closing the unfortunate gap in legal uniformity created by the social protocol opt-out. On the third pillar, Cook would stress that some aspects, i.e. border controls and immigration, would be very difficult for Labour, but that a Labour government would 'like to look at each subject on its merits and (would) have no objection in principle to a role for the European Commission.' This would be part of a strategy of stressing that Labour's approach would be 'pragmatic, not ideological' (LP Butler, 4 March 1997). However, Cook would employ the same reasoning as on flexibility in stating Labour's opposition to combining the communitisation of elements of the third pillar with the creation of opt-outs for the UK.

Labour's representatives also continued to press these arguments on flexibility and the third pillar in discussions with representatives of other member governments. While viewing PES-led governments in the smaller member states such as those in the Netherlands and Sweden as its closest potential allies in the negotiations and perhaps as the best conduits for indirectly influencing the negotiations, the Labour leadership was acutely aware of the need to maintain dialogue and press its case on these and other issues with the governments of the two member states historically associated with driving the process of European integration, France and Germany. Thus Butler, Quin and Whitty together spent about an hour and a half each with the French ambassador and the German deputy-ambassador in London on 5 March 1997. These meetings took the form of the French and German representatives giving an outline of their respective countries' IGC priorities, but also gave Labour's representatives a further opportunity to attempt to undermine the proposal for flexibility in the first pillar by questioning its necessity. Butler's report recorded that when the French ambassador had restated his country's support for a general flexibility clause (to be triggered by QMV) applying in the first pillar, the Labour representatives had made clear their opposition and questioned him as to what subjects in the first pillar it might apply, at which he stated 'that it was not especially the first pillar they had in mind.' Similarly, Butler reported that the German deputy-ambassador had 'plunged' straight into the question of flexibility, which 'he clearly regarded as the most difficult' but that in response to the arguments of the Labour team the deputy-ambassador had 'concluded that the Germans were quite reticent about flexibility in the first pillar' and suggested that this 'was not a breaking point.'

In a similar vein, Butler recorded some helpful signs as regards the French and German attitudes to the third pillar. According to Butler, the French position appeared confused, with the ambassador denying that the French wanted to bring Schengen into the first pillar, rather wanting it in the third pillar, and suggesting that 'as far as most third pillar issues were concerned it might be possible to achieve greater efficiency by "borrowing" the methods and institutions of the treaty.' This was a position likely to be more acceptable to Labour. Furthermore, the German deputy-ambassador had indicated German opposition to QMV in the third pillar and suggested that the Germans would be content with simply bringing Schengen into the treaty, and that while 'ideally' it wanted this in the first pillar, the third pillar 'would be sufficient for now.'

Elsewhere, Butler's report of the meeting recorded French and German support for the Dutch presidency proposal on QMV (linking this to vote reweighting) and for a streamlined Commission (in response to which Quin stated a Labour preference for the retention of two UK Commissioners). Both countries also sought reforms of decision-making in CFSP, with the French supporting enhanced co-operation and constructive abstention and the Germans wanting QMV with 'protection for national interests' and being prepared to consider constructive abstention. Both also sought the creation of a new CFSP figurehead, though the Germans preferred a lower profile figure to the French. The French also combined a desire to enhance the role of national parliaments (including in relation to supervision of the correct application of subsidiarity), which was in tune with Labour thinking, with a reticence over granting the EP more powers (where Labour appeared more progressive than the French). Perhaps surprisingly, the French ambassador also indicated that, while not sharing the Tory distaste for the ECJ, the French quite liked some of the UK government proposals for improving it. At this, Butler suggested that Labour take another look at the UK government paper on the ECJ. Butler's report also demonstrated that Labour was actually more progressive than both the centre-right French and German governments in respect of the proposal for an employment chapter. Both the French and German representatives stated their governments' view that employment policy should remain a national concern. But Butler recorded that when it was put to the French ambassador that 'public opinion would favour the EU discussing measures against unemployment, that a common analysis could prove useful and occasionally lead to common measures...(he) indicated that they might agree as long as there was no expenditure.' However, the Germans appeared to be more adamant that there should be no new funds or common policies in this area (LP Butler, 6 March 1997).

The Final Days of Opposition

By the time John Major had, on 17 March, confirmed the widespread expectations of a 1 May election date, the eagerness of the other European governments to commence serious IGC negotiations with a Labour government was becoming increasingly clear, as was the nervousness of the Labour leadership of being portrayed as ready to 'sell out' to Europe. This was illustrated by a note sent from Whitty to Cook and Powell on 18 March. The note explained that the French government, apparently backed by a meeting of Christian-democrat leaders a fortnight previously, had been trying to persuade the Dutch that there should be an additional heads of government meeting shortly after the UK general election, with 9 May the preferred date. Whitty expressed some caution about the French motives in his response to this:

> We need to convey Tony's view on that proposition to the Dutch. The French undoubtedly see it as a chance to bounce a Labour government and other governments are warning us of that. On the one hand there are some domestic advantages of going to an early meeting and not immediately agreeing but putting down clear markers. On the other hand we do not want to get off to a conflictual start with our partners. My own feeling is that we could agree to a somewhat later extra summit towards the end of May but that May 9 is too early and does not allow Tony time to meet on a bilateral basis with Kok, Kohl and Chirac to establish relationships and assess strategy.

In addition to this, Whitty expressed concern about a planned PES Leaders meeting on 26 April. Whitty explained that though the meeting was a 'conclave' and hence there would be no statement, the press would be aware that it was happening. Moreover, Whitty had the impression that Kok still hoped that Blair would attend the meeting. Whitty stressed the perils of this (although it is unlikely that Blair would have countenanced going, given the proximity to 1 May):

> There is no way I would advise Tony - or John Prescott - to go and I do think it is difficult for Robin to do so without the *Daily Mail* portraying it as 'preparing to sellout.' It is probably best left at office level because we don't need to be there. However, whatever the decision it would be diplomatic for Tony to speak to Wim Kok soon about his non-attendance and if at all possible about the agenda nearer the time. Robin could do the latter, but Tony himself should do the former' (LP Whitty, 18 March 1997).

Whitty himself would actually represent the Labour leadership at this PES conclave.

The eagerness of the Dutch presidency to step up negotiations with a Labour government after 1 May was also demonstrated by a note sent from Butler to Whitty, Clark and Quin the next day, based on a conversation he had just had with de Bruijn. Butler reported that the Dutch were expressing hope that a new Labour government would be able to start stating its clear views on the various proposals on the table very soon after the election. Furthermore, as indicated in Whitty's note the previous day, the presidency were hoping that it would be possible to stage a heads of government meeting over dinner on 9 or 12 May 'to enable Tony Blair to get to know his colleagues and vice-versa.' Butler explained that the presidency would be producing new draft treaty submissions the next day for the conclave of foreign ministers the following week. These would take the form of addendums to the Dublin draft. Among the key issues covered would be the proposed area of freedom, security and justice, other third pillar issues, CFSP, flexibility and fundamental rights. Butler's note illustrated the extent to which the Dutch were helping to prepare the Labour leadership for entrance into the IGC negotiations proper, explaining that 'de Bruijn is keen to give us his latest papers and his own assessment of the situation just before we finalise our own paper for the incoming government.' Plans were being laid for both Butler and Whitty to meet with de Bruijn in the week before the election, with de Bruijn willing to go out of his way to make sure that they were fully prepared by coming to London if a mutually convenient date for a meeting in The Hague could not be found (LP Butler, 19 March 1997).

By 25 March 1997, Whitty had produced an analysis of the Dutch draft treaty texts published on 19 March. These were the result of a three month thorough examination by the presidency of the areas which appeared, in the light of the Dublin draft, to require the most work. This generally involved a focus on flexibility, sensitive institutional reform questions and JHA, while refining texts on which the Irish had already made good progress such as on CFSP and fundamental rights[14] (McDonagh 1998: 138-139, 166-167). Whitty's commentary revealed anxiety about IGC developments in a number of areas, indicating that tough negotiations would be required once Labour entered government despite the new constructive approach it would bring. The Dutch had produced a virtually fully redrafted text on the following: freedom, security and justice; enhanced co-operation (flexibility); CFSP and fundamental rights. However, the Dutch texts had not dealt with the social protocol, the employment chapter, environment, consumer policy, transparency, subsidiarity and external economic relations. On most of these, Whitty suggested, the Dublin draft still stood. An IGC representatives meeting on the 25 March considered the Dutch texts, which also included an additional paper on treaty simplification. Predictably, it was the presidency text on 'freedom, security and justice' that appeared to be the most contentious for the Labour party given that it proposed that this title be in the first pillar, involving a phased communitisation of border controls and immigration and asylum matters together with the incorporation of Schengen into the first pillar (McDonagh 1998: 173-177). Whitty commented that 'virtually all of this' was contrary to the Labour position. He also suggested that the presidency optimism that this would be achieved (as it indicated in its cover note) was at odds with much that other governments had indicated privately, though he conceded that there did seem to be some increased acceptance by the most reluctant states such as the Danes and the Swedes. Whitty expressed particular concern that while the presidency appeared to recognise the need for flexibility in the position of the non-Schengen states (i.e. the UK and Ireland), the implication in the presidency commentary was that any opt-out would be on a 'case by case' basis. Whitty stressed that if the UK's protection was to be on this basis, then 'a Labour government would not agree to signing up to this area at all…(and)…would veto it going ahead.' Moreover, Whitty argued that this proposal had implications for the general issue of flexibility as the transfer of these policies into the first pillar would inevitably require 'a substantial degree of flexibility' to accommodate the UK and Ireland, thus running 'counter to the aim of as far as possible maintaining the first pillar as the area where EU law applies to all member states' and acting as a 'potential Trojan Horse for other areas of flexibility in the first pillar and hence a two-tier Europe.' To compound Labour's difficulties, the presidency text on enhanced co-operation in any case provided for a general flexibility clause that would apply in the first pillar. Indeed, Whitty warned that the presidency text went 'substantially beyond what Labour could accept and (was) very close to the Franco-German position' in providing for 'a general flexibility clause allowing a majority of member states to go ahead in any part of the treaty' provided a number of conditions were satisfied. Elsewhere, Whitty also expressed anxiety about the proposals - all going further than the agreed Labour positions - to enhance ECJ involvement in issues remaining under the third pillar and, in the CFSP, for QMV to be the rule in implementing decisions and for strengthened defence objectives and the gradual integration of the WEU into the EU (LP Whitty, 25 March 1997). The Dutch text also included a proposal to bestow legal personality on the EU as a whole (seen as necessary to allow the EU to conduct international agreements).[15] This was a technical issue on which Labour's position was not yet fully clear.

Although in private the Labour leadership was mulling over the implications of these presidency proposals, a note sent by Whitty dated 23 March confirmed that in public, Labour's strategy was to deny all knowledge of the IGC negotiations. The note, sent to a number of key party officials: Labour party head of policy Matthew Taylor, international officer, Nick Sigler and Liz Lloyd from the leader's office, indicated that while in reality the party was receiving intimate information on the IGC negotiations, particularly through its close relationship with Dutch ministers and officials, in public forums it would plead ignorance of the details of the negotiations. This would allow Labour to appear non-committal as regards detailed positioning on awkward issues, providing another safety mechanism against appearing too willing to cede to the more pro-integration urges of the other member states. Explaining that the Conservative foreign secretary Malcolm Rifkind would be attending a meeting of EU foreign ministers to discuss the Dutch draft proposals, Whitty emphasised that the public line needed to remain as indicated: 'that we have not received these proposals nor are we party to the negotiations and hence we cannot comment other than repeat our existing public position.' This public position was defined as follows: 1) a clear rejection of the moves on communitising border controls and related matters; 2) a clear commitment to maintaining unanimity on all key intergovernmental matters; 3) an objection to flexibility without consent particularly in the first pillar (meaning that Labour wanted to ensure that any moves to enhanced co-operation by a group of states had to have the unanimous consent of all member states) (LP Whitty, 23 March 1997).

The Dutch addendums to the draft treaty were discussed at a special meeting of foreign ministers in Rome on 25 March (held to commemorate the fortieth anniversary of the Treaty of Rome) though the presidency did not seek to have them formally endorsed and the meeting adopted no formal conclusions (McDonagh 1998: 140). The following day, Whitty and Powell had a timely meeting with two senior French officials, Pierre Menet from Chirac's office and Jerome Grivet from Prime Minister Alain Juppe's office. Indeed, while not comparable with the level of contact enjoyed with the Dutch, the French seemed to be taking a particular interest in Labour's positioning, perhaps, as Whitty had previously suggested in his note of 18 March, because they perceived a possibility of 'bouncing' an inexperienced Labour government into an agreement. The meeting appeared to be indicative of French diplomatic manoeuvring, whilst also demonstrating both the Labour leadership's confidence in arguing its case and its eagerness to seize every opportunity to cultivate contacts in key member states and receive as wide as possible a spectrum of informed inside views of the negotiations. A note on the meeting by Whitty sent to Cook, Quin, Butler and Clark, explained that the French had reported that nothing of any substance had been even tentatively agreed in Rome. In general, the meeting between the French and the Labour representatives provided another opportunity to discuss their respective positions. The French offered some succour to Whitty's previous suggestion that the presidency was possibly being over-confident in assuming support for its proposals on third pillar communitisation. They again suggested that they did not really want communitisation of border controls and asylum and immigration. However, they did want majority voting in some of these issues (for example, to force the Dutch to tighten up their drugs laws). They were not keen on enhanced co-operation in JHA either, as those not involved would undermine security, but they did accept that the UK would have to have some kind of opt-out on any agreed border controls regime. Furthermore, while stressing their support for a general flexibility clause, the French offered sympathy to Labour's *'communautaire* argument for keeping border controls out of the first pillar' accepting that flexibility needed to be very limited in the first pillar. The French also reiterated their position on CFSP (involving unanimity on strategic decisions, and QMV for implementing decisions) and defence. France and Germany had made a joint submission in relation to the latter, backed by Spain, Italy and the Benelux countries (Moravcsik and Nicolaidis 1998: 27) which involved a phased integration of the WEU into the EU, culminating in the EU taking over the WEU's 'article five' territorial defence functions. Whitty reported that he had indicated to the French that any military role for the EU was problematic for Labour and that 'there was no chance of us agreeing even for the very long term anything that went into article five areas.' Whitty also reported that the French had spent a lot of time canvassing their proposition to streamline the Commission to 10 or 12 members and that he had indicated that a Labour government would not support this (LP Whitty, 26 March 1997).

The coolness displayed by the French on third pillar communitisation may have prompted Butler to go on the offensive towards the Dutch ambassador, on this and the related issue of flexibility, in a telephone discussion on 7 April. In a note on the discussion, sent to Whitty, Quin, Powell and Clark, Butler reported that he had 'had a go at him (the ambassador) about flexibility in pillar one' and also on JHA communitisation: 'I told him that I personally thought the Dutch were ahead of the pack in proposing to put Schengen and other JHA issues into pillar one and that this might ruin the whole negotiation.' Butler reported that he felt that the ambassador had some sympathy with his views and that these views would be passed on to the Dutch government (LP Butler, 7 April 1997).

The presidency produced further IGC submissions for the foreign ministers meeting on 6-7 April. An analysis of these was produced by Whitty and sent to Cook, Quin, Powell, Butler and Clark. A submission on CFSP and defence echoed the Franco-German proposal for a phased integration of the WEU into the EU, on which Whitty commented: 'Although the text provides that triggering of the phases is by unanimity, this goes substantially beyond our position.' Nevertheless, a Labour government would be able to rely on the support of the Danes and the neutral states in resisting this proposal. In addition, the Dutch had put forward papers setting out options for the reform of the Commission structure and for reweighting of Council voting, without making clear proposals. Further proposals were put forward on employment and the social chapter. Whitty reported that on the former, the Dutch had simply re-circulated the Dublin text and that the Germans 'were softening their opposition to this relatively minimal formulation' (LP Whitty, 6 April 1997).

In relation to the social protocol, the presidency proposal dealt for the first time with how to deal with its incorporation into the treaty proper, while also raising the question of incorporating social and economic rights and measures to combat social exclusion into the treaty and strengthening the social dialogue.[16] Whitty's analysis of this proposal demonstrated the lack of confidence the Labour leadership was displaying in the run-up to the election as regards its own long held positions on the social chapter. Whitty warned that the raising by the presidency of these issues and their link with trade union issues, workers' rights and corporatism 'could cause frisson in our campaign' (LP Whitty, 6 April 1997). This appeared to be an area that was causing particular concerns for the Labour leadership in the run-up to the general election and there appeared to be a collective loss of self-confidence in its previous position of supporting the incorporation of the social chapter into the treaty proper and the extension of QMV in social matters as espoused in both the 1995 policy document and the 1994 EP manifesto (Labour Party 1995: 11, Labour Party 1994: 22). This could partly be attributed to the proximity to the general election and the leadership fear that the Conservative party and its allies in the press would successfully convince the British public that such a position would create massive new costs to business and therefore lead to a surge in unemployment. However, there also appeared to be a real policy shift on the issue of EU level employment rights, as 'New Labour' sought to court its new friends in big business and distance itself from the unions, replacing its previously strong commitment to the high levels of employment protection advocated by the latter with a new emphasis on the labour market flexibility favoured by the former (Anderson and Mann 1997: 323-326, Taylor 2001). This shift in policy more or less coincided with the appointment of the Blairite moderniser, Stephen Byers, as the party employment spokesman on the social chapter and industrial relations in July 1996.[17] Byers would instinctively take a line against social chapter measures that were in the pipeline (Interview with LWG participant). Indeed, the positions taken by Byers on the need for flexible labour markets in the EU may have caused some consternation among those developing the party's IGC policy. Whitty wrote to Byers in February 1997, expressing his bafflement at a document produced by Byers in which it was stated that Labour's proposals would 'not import the over-rigidity of some areas of the European labour market' and would instead 'result in a labour market less regulated than that of the USA' (LP Whitty, 3 February 1997).

Nevertheless, the shift in policy had already been demonstrated in a speech by Blair on 3 July 1996 to the Chambers of Commerce in London, in which he stated: 'As we have constantly made clear, we are not proposing any move to weaken the national veto in the Social Chapter.' In a note sent to Cook on the same day, Whitty suggested that though it could be argued that this statement was still compatible with the formulation in the 1995 policy document 'in that not "proposing" any change does not mean we would not in certain circumstances accept it', he conceded that this was a tenuous argument and 'that clearly the whole tone is very different from what we have said elsewhere' (LP Whitty, 3 July 1996). Not surprisingly, as Whitty noted, the speech had not gone down too well with the TUC. The shifts in policy were also causing consternation within the EPLP. Though ambiguity remained as to whether Labour would support QMV extension in some of the other areas of the social chapter, Blair had made it clear that Labour would not support the extension of QMV within the social protocol to the areas of representation/codetermination of workers[18] and social security (*Financial Times*, 5 August 1996). This was confirmed by Gordon Brown in a speech to the Confederation of British Industry (CBI) in November 1996 (LP Brown, 11 November 1996). Whitty had warned Cook and Byers, prior to the Dutch proposals, that QMV extension in the social protocol 'could get swept up in a generalised approach to QMV' and that this approach was supported by Labour's allies in the ETUC and the TUC (LP Whitty, 18 February 1997). Furthermore, in a memo to Prescott, Whitty had noted that the TUC was beginning to express anxiety at Labour's backtracking on the social chapter, though he had suggested that Labour did 'not need to take a position and we need scope for negotiation' (LP Whitty, 19 February 1997). The intention appeared to be to prevent discussion of these issues until a more politically convenient time for the Labour party, i.e. after the general election. Yet it was becoming increasingly unclear whether Labour would even support a broadening of the social chapter once in power. In a note to Cook and employment spokesman David Blunkett (copied to Byers) on 1 March, Whitty had commented: 'An incoming Labour government could be faced with the choice of vetoing a strengthening of equality provisions and positive rights - and at the cost of alienating some of our closest potential allies by doing so' (LP Whitty, 1 March 1997).

Post-Election Strategy

As the election drew nearer, attention within the Labour leadership began to focus on the precise negotiating tactics it would have to pursue once it entered government and its representatives were propelled into the IGC negotiations. Butler appeared to be taking the lead in developing a comprehensive strategy to be pursued in the immediate post-election period. For this, he required a complete set of texts being discussed within the IGC. Though most of the key texts appeared to have been passed on by the Dutch, Butler had informed the Dutch ambassador on 7 April that the party knew 'from other sources' that it had not received a complete set, and that both he and Whitty needed to be sure by the 14 April that they had 'a complete summary for shadow ministers of all the issues which would face the new government.' Butler and the ambassador would meet again on the 14 April and the ambassador agreed to do his best to meet this request by then. Nobody, at this point, appeared to be in any doubt that Labour would be forming the new government in the UK at the beginning of May (LP Butler, 7 April 1997).

Butler would be working practically full-time for the Labour party in the final month of opposition, taking the lead both in finalising its strategy and continuing discussions with senior Dutch, EU and UK officials to ensure that the transition to government and entry into the negotiations was as smooth as possible (Interview with Butler). Indeed, the finalising of preparations for the negotiations also required acquainting the Labour leadership with how the machinery of government worked, especially in relation to European policy formulation and co-ordination. This was an area of expertise in which the Labour party was clearly lacking, and in which Butler was extremely well placed to advise. He produced a paper sent to Cook on 27 March which gave an outline of the structure of ministerial, cabinet and other committees in government, illustrating the framework in which Labour's European policy-making would be obliged to operate once in government. The paper stressed the importance of good government planning and co-ordination to success in EU negotiations. Although UK governments had, until recent years, benefited from such strengths, UK performance in the EU had fallen 'to a dismally low level' because of the internal divisions and the lurch to Euro-scepticism within the Conservative party. Butler stressed that Labour would have an opportunity to rectify this and that 'how well and how fast' this was done would play a vital role in the success or failure of the government in the IGC (LP Butler and Whitty, 27 March 1997).

To aid in this process of transition to government, Butler met with a number of senior Whitehall officials dealing with the IGC in April 1997. Taking full advantage of Whitehall rules that allow senior officials to make themselves available to brief the official opposition parties during general election campaigns, he met with Paul Lever, deputy secretary with lead responsibility for the IGC at the FCO, on 8 April, Brian Bender, head of the European secretariat of the cabinet office, on 16 April, Paul Lever and Simon Gass (EU department) of the FCO on 17 April (where Whitty was also present), and Simon Gass and other FCO officials two days before the election on 29 April. Clark and Whitty were also involved in a number of separate meetings with FCO officials in the run-up to the election. All this was likely to have been of great assistance to the task of ensuring both that the Labour leadership was fully acclimatised to how the machinery of government would work in the deployment of its IGC strategy and that Whitehall officials had a clear understanding of the new approach to the EU that the Labour government would be pursuing. To similar ends, both Butler and Whitty met with the UK's permanent representative to the EU, Sir Stephen Wall in Brussels on 22 April (the UK lead negotiating team comprised Wall, Bender and Lever). Butler and Whitty also had a number of meetings with senior EU and Dutch presidency officials in the final few days of opposition. On 22 April, before meeting with Wall, they met with David Williamson, secretary-general of the European Commission. On 26 April, as previously indicated, they met with de Bruijn as well as Patijn in The Hague. In the last week before the election, Butler, Clark and Whitty also met with a number of IGC representatives from the other member states (LP Butler, Undated 1997). All this was designed to ensure a smooth transition after 1 May, when it was expected that Labour's representatives would take their place in the IGC negotiations proper.

These discussions were undoubtedly indispensable to the drafting of the comprehensive post-election strategy paper that was sent to Cook (and most likely to other senior party figures) on the eve of Labour's election victory. Though the paper was submitted in the names of Butler, Clark and Whitty, it was based on a provisional draft produced by Butler. An introductory note to the paper, drawing on the final week or so of intensive discussion, referred to the extensive contacts that Whitty and Butler had had over the previous ten days with the Dutch presidency, the European Commission, UK officials and with several ambassadors in London and stressed that there were a number of issues on which a 'government line will be required quickly and where other ministers will need to be consulted.'

The paper emphasised that agreement at the IGC would not be easy for the following reasons:

1) the IGC had been going on for over a year and therefore, amongst other member states 'a fair measure of implicit if not formal agreement has been achieved on complicated draft treaty articles' some of which would not be acceptable to a Labour government. This included 'a bandwagon of support' for some of the proposals that were 'least palatable' such as communitisation of asylum and immigration controls;

2) despite the isolation of the Conservative government within the IGC, it would 'not be simple' to demonstrate how different the Labour government would be because on a number of questions which had become essential to the strategy 'implicitly agreed by the others' (presumably the various election campaign strategists around Blair), Labour's position would 'appear much the same as the Tories.' This impression would have been 'enhanced as a result of positions adopted in the election campaign';

3) time was short 'to change the overall mood in the conference and to persuade the others to go along with solutions which are less integrationalist than some of them, including particularly the Dutch presidency and the Germans, appear to want.' Labour therefore needed to stress that its positions were 'not motivated by ideological Euro-scepticism but by what will work and what will be politically acceptable.'

The introductory note had included a provisional timetable of IGC and related meetings that the new government would be plunged into. These included IGC representatives meetings on 5 May and 15-16 May, a foreign ministers' meeting on 20 May, and a possible informal heads of government summit on 23 May. There would also be a PES leaders' meeting on the eve of the PES congress in Malmo on 5 June. The presidency had intended to produce a comprehensive draft treaty by 14 or 15 May. However, things had now been complicated by Chirac's decision to call national assembly elections in France. Thus it was now unlikely that a full draft would be produced, though a number of partial drafts would be.

In the light of the tight timetable, decisions would be needed on a number of questions relating to internal government co-ordination and external diplomacy. A full bilateral discussion would have to take place between Blair and Cook to ensure that they were 'agreed on strategy and tactics' and conveyed 'the same message to other member states.' Furthermore, Blair would need to respond to a request from the Dutch prime minister, Wim Kok, for a bilateral meeting in London as soon as possible, probably on May 8-9. Decisions would also be required on whether to organise bilateral meetings between Blair and Cook and their French and German counterparts before the proposed informal summit at the end of May, and whether Blair (as expected by Labour's PES allies) should attend the PES meeting at the Malmo congress.

In terms of handling the negotiations, a stress was placed on the need for a 'carefully thought out strategy in advance, obviously adaptable to negotiating positions taken by others.' The aim would be 'to change the mood within the IGC in terms of their attitude to the British Government as soon as possible in early

May, but thereafter to keep important concessions in reserve for foreign ministers or heads of government in the final stages.' More specifically, the strategy paper made the following recommendations:

1) that at the very first representatives meeting on 5 May, the UK representative should indicate a positive change of mood by setting out in broad terms to the other members the positions that Labour had taken publicly, i.e: more majority voting in certain fields; codecision for the EP; UK accession to the social chapter; support for the employment chapter; support for transparency provisions; an end to attacks on the role of the ECJ (leaving room to make further positive moves later on other areas such as non-discrimination measures and stronger environmental provisions).

2) this should then be combined with 'rigorous intellectual debate on some of the least attractive proposals on the table' namely flexibility/enhanced co-operation in pillar one, incorporation of large parts of JHA plus Schengen into pillar one and WEU/EU merger. The paper suggested that in arguing against these, the new government would use '*communautaire* arguments as far as possible' deploying its 'publicly known positions where they have changed from those of the previous government.' Setting out these limited versions of the new government positions would enable the Dutch to present 'some tentatively agreed text' by around the time of the proposed informal heads of government summit on 23 May.

3) at this proposed heads of government meeting, while indicating that the UK government was making a fresh start and regarded many of the IGC proposals positively, particularly in anticipation of enlargement, Blair would 'refuse to negotiate definitively on anything on the ground that he had not had time to study the total draft' but would reiterate 'the areas on which our changed position should allow an agreement to be reached relatively early.' Furthermore, the paper recommended that Blair 'launch a broadside at flexibility/enhanced co-operation in the first pillar on the ground that it was originally invented to get around an uncooperative British Government - which this will not be; that it would undermine the principle that EU law should as far as possible apply in all EU countries (a concept which is aided by the UK abandoning the opt-out for the social chapter); and that Commission officials admit that flexibility is not necessary for purposes of enlargement.' However, Blair would indicate a UK preparedness to accept some degree of flexibility for the other two pillars. He would also indicate that Labour was reviewing the areas on which the UK government had previously submitted proposals, some of which it would not wish to pursue. He would however indicate that some difficult issues, such as quota-hopping would be kept 'on the table unless progress can be made elsewhere.'[19]

Given his vast diplomatic experience, Butler's hand in devising this sophisticated negotiating strategy was clearly apparent. The strategy appeared to be a cagey one, sending out positive signals but avoiding getting into detailed negotiations. The new government would emphasise the areas in which it was willing to make progress where its positions were already in the public domain. However, it would hold back its positions on the other areas in which it was willing to make progress, for use as possible bargaining chips to be offered in exchange for concessions on some of the more 'unpalatable' proposals. While the general principles of its positions would be outlined, the new government would be cautious about getting into the 'below the line' details of these positions, particularly as regards areas where it was prepared to make concessions in the final 'endgame' as part of an overall package. As the strategy paper explained, the new government would not make any new concessions in the IGC representative group, leaving detailed negotiations to the later foreign ministers' and heads of governments' meetings. It explained that Labour's representatives would 'need to have in mind the points on which we will not be prepared to negotiate through to the "endgame" in June, and which points there are where some compromise solution may be possible at foreign minister level.'

The paper suggested that either the foreign ministers meeting on 20 May or the informal summit on 23 May could be the opportunity to set out the principles of Labour's approach to each of the three pillars. In an indication of how the new government would seek to take public credit for certain 'deals' which were already on the table for the Conservative government, Butler suggested that this would also include expressing support 'for those things with which we agree and which are going to happen anyway so that we can claim afterwards some of the credit at Amsterdam.' In addition, the paper stressed that a co-operative approach in some areas, building up goodwill among other member states, would facilitate a favourable resolution of the issues seen as difficult for Labour. For example, it was suggested that other governments would 'privately agree with our thesis on flexibility' but that 'flexibility in pillar one will be kept on the table until the French and the Germans can assess how co-operative we are on other matters' (in hindsight, a miscalculation). Thus Butler advocated that the new government 'endeavour to develop arguments which steer discussion away from a 14 to one confrontation, toward grounds on which we can compromise at foreign minister or prime minister level given that we can reasonably hope to persuade other members to drop or to postpone more ambitious proposals.'

The strategy paper also provided a more detailed re-examination of some of the more contentious areas to be resolved at the IGC. In relation to what was described as the most difficult area, the JHA pillar, it was conceded that there was 'a strong bandwagon for changing the third pillar's decision making and instruments' with most presuming that this involved 'at least a partial communitisation of the pillar' as well as Schengen incorporation. However, Butler used as evidence the previous indications from the French that they were concerned with 'outcome rather than institutional forms', together with the reservations displayed by certain other member states on bringing these issues into the first pillar, to make the optimistic prediction that it was likely that border controls would not be fully transferred into the first pillar. It was thus suggested that Labour 'make clear and public our opposition to that happening and again gain some domestic credit at Amsterdam.' The paper did however suggest that the new government break from the Conservative government's opposition to any method of Schengen incorporation and 'be prepared to consider bringing Schengen into the treaty under intergovernmental arrangements but not into pillar one, and with Britain not participating in most of the border control, immigration and asylum matters.' It was recommended that Labour 'think carefully' about possible compromises it could propose to avoid isolation in an issue seen by other member states as central to the IGC. A number of compromise options were canvassed. These would involve closer co-operation in relation to border controls, immigration and asylum while retaining an intergovernmental structure, but with more effective forms of decision-making, possibly through flexibility arrangements to allow groups of states to adopt conventions, and/or enhanced roles for the EP, Commission and even the ECJ (albeit limited to conventions and disputes between member states and the institutions). Such compromises would avoid bringing decision-making into the first pillar and 'thereby creating a system where EU law applied in some states but not others.' Because this was likely to be the most difficult final negotiation, it was suggested that Labour 'should try to defer any definitive discussion of these subjects until the end of May and into June.'

The strategy paper was more upbeat about the prospects of a satisfactory agreement on CFSP, describing most of the proposals being discussed as sensible. These were as generally put forward in the Irish draft in December 1996 (McDonagh 1998: 115-117). Accordingly, support was recommended both for the 'high representative' proposal, provided the Council retained control 'of those who speak for the EU' and (unlike Whitty's earlier commentary) for a positive line on 'constructive abstention.' It was suggested that the latter proposal would 'probably deal adequately with most foreign policy differences.' But Butler warned that the proposal to differentiate between general principles and common strategies (to be decided by unanimity) and implementing measures within these agreed frameworks (to be decided by QMV) 'could give rise to formidable problems of definition.' Concerns about this had been ameliorated by the latest proposal that a dissenting member state be able to block a QMV decision by pleading national interest. However, Butler suggested that Labour 'think hard (about) whether we could devise a better formula.' On defence, it was noted that the UK would not be isolated, as there would be opposition from others to the proposal on EU-WEU merger. Nonetheless, it was stressed that a Labour government 'should vehemently oppose the final stage of merger proposed in the Franco-German paper, i.e. the EU taking on territorial defence commitments.'

Turning to pillar one issues, the strategy paper noted that while there were, in reality, a lot of outstanding issues, the UK position under a Labour government was 'more likely to be in line with the centre of gravity of the other countries.' But the paper rather accurately suggested that difficulties would still arise because 'the removal of the Tory Government's objection to change of any sort will probably lead to certain other countries being forced into explicitly making their own objections.' This would make it difficult to predict the final outcome. Among the institutional issues, Butler explained that the new government would need to decide how far QMV should be extended and by what formula a vote reweighting should take place. Similarly, the new government would need to decide how far codecision should be extended and whether it should support a uniform electoral system for the EP. On reform of the Commission, it was noted that one Commissioner per country was now being proposed and that 'this could give us political problems of both giving away a Commissioner and abandoning the bipartisan arrangements.' In addition to these issues, there would be pressure to give legal personality to the EU. But the paper suggested that Labour should oppose this. Among the substantive issues, Labour would need to decide whether the Dublin texts on fundamental rights and non-discrimination should be adopted or changed. In addition, decisions were needed on the form that the incorporation of the social chapter should take, the exact terms of the employment chapter and the strength of environment provisions. On external trade, the Dublin text had included proposals to extend the Commission powers to negotiate on behalf of the EU to services as well as visible trade, recognising the increasing importance of the former to international trading patters (McDonagh 1998: 120-122). Butler explained that these proposals were still on the agenda, though they would probably be limited to a negotiating mandate within the WTO, and that there were 'pros as well as cons.' A Labour government would therefore 'need an interdepartmental view.'

The paper stressed that once in office (again this view appeared to be based on information Butler had received in his meetings with senior Whitehall officials), Labour ministers would receive and would 'need to consider urgently' a comprehensive paper on all of the IGC issues. In terms of the task ahead, it was suggested that, on the whole, pillar one issues looked rather less difficult than the others and that one option was to try to make progress on them at the foreign ministers meeting at the end of May. But the paper also again stressed the undesirability of the new government revealing all of its cards, suggesting that some issues needed to be kept for the Amsterdam European Council. These would be 'issues which would not cause us real political pain to concede.' In addition, it was suggested that the new government make an effort to 'think up new and ingenious proposals which could carry the day (at Amsterdam) and provide the basis of a settlement of difficult issues.'

A list of outstanding issues was enclosed with the strategy paper. It was explained that this was 'so that Robin Cook and Tony Blair can have some idea of the scope of the problem' as regards the range of issues on which the new government would 'need to take a position…quite fast.' It was therefore requested that they indicate any specific issues on which they wished to receive more details. It was also explained that Butler and Whitty were talking to the government officials who would be providing a comprehensive paper on all the issues. These officials had developed a clear understanding of the approach Labour ministers would want to take both from the party's public statements and their private discussions with Labour's representatives. Butler and Whitty had already made arrangements for initial ministerial meetings with the relevant officials. Both within the Labour party and Whitehall, it was clearly being assumed that Cook would be foreign secretary in a Labour government by the first weekend in May and would be immersing himself immediately in the IGC. Indeed, the paper suggested a meeting involving Butler, Whitty, Cook, Wall, Lever and Bender over this first weekend.

The strategy paper also addressed the immediate tactical needs of the IGC representatives meeting scheduled for 5 May, just four days after election day. Butler and Whitty had arranged for Wall to attend alongside the newly appointed minister for Europe should he/she be appointed as the representative. At this stage, the assumption appeared to be that Joyce Quin, who had held the shadow post for four years, would be appointed as Europe minister. But it was not clear whether the new Europe minister would be appointed as the IGC representative. Wall's presence at the dinner, whether or not he continued as representative, would serve to provide some continuity. However, one disadvantage of continuing to have Wall around was (irrespective of his own private views) his association with the hostile positioning of the Conservative government. Appointing a new representative, in the shape of a new government minister, would be a positive signal of the Labour government's intention to provide a fresh start (LP Butler, Clark and Whitty, 30 April 1997).

Although the Labour leadership was in private confidently putting the finishing touches to its strategy for the transition to government, in public it was still taking no chances. While the strategy paper illustrated its private willingness to countenance a number of concessions, a note sent by Whitty to Cook on 30 April, demonstrated its determination to maintain a 'tough' position on Europe, not dissimilar to that of the Conservative government, right up to election day, despite all opinion polls pointing to the likelihood of a massive election victory on the following day. The note, also copied to Labour's campaign headquarters, provided a short briefing on an EU foreign ministers meeting taking place that day. It explained that David Davis would be representing the UK government and would try to make capital out of the IGC issues being discussed, i.e. CFSP and size of the Commission. The note therefore stressed that on foreign policy and defence, Labour policy was 'not very different from the Tories.' On the number of Commissioners, the note explained that the fourteen other member states were likely 'to agree to cut larger states to one Commissioner each from about the year 2000' but that neither Labour, nor the government, had taken a public position on this. The note went on: 'David Davis will oppose and represent this proposal as reducing the UK's influence in the EU. We should say we have not accepted, and would not accept this reduction, unless there was substantial compensation in terms of the UK weight of voting in the Council of Ministers' (LP Whitty, 30 April 1997).

Evaluating Policy-Making in Opposition: The Shadow of Domestic Politics

As this final note on the day before the election illustrated, the shadow cast by domestic political factors over Labour's policy-making on the IGC was apparent right up to its entrance into government. Until the party's crushing victory on 1 May, Labour remained deeply anxious to avoid giving the Conservative government any opportunity to portray it as soft on Europe. In its determination to present itself as staunch a defender of national sovereignty as the Conservative government claimed to be, the Labour leadership increasingly appeared to mimic the positions and indeed, to some extent, the discourse employed by the Conservatives. This led some observers to predict that a Labour government would not make much difference to the UK's position in the EU to that under the Conservatives (George 1997: 115-116, Ludlam 1998: 53). Andrew Rawnsley describes the Labour leadership as having 'surrendered conviction to expediency during the election campaign' in which it 'deployed slogans and symbols which pandered to anti-European prejudice' (2000: 73).[20] Labour's feverish donning of the Conservatives' nationalist clothes reached its apotheosis with the article published in *The Sun* in Tony Blair's name on 22 April 1997, the day before St. George's day (perhaps the closest England comes to a national day). Occasional articles under Blair's name published in *The Sun* (usually drafted by his press secretary, Alastair Campbell) had become a feature of Blair's leadership as he sought to win the support of the Murdoch-owned press in the election. In an astonishing piece, Blair wrote: 'Tomorrow is St George's Day, the day when the English celebrate the pride we have in our nation.' Promising that a Labour government would protect national identity he went on: 'St George did not slay a dragon so that England could follow the rest. He did it so that we could be strong and ready to lead.' Adopting such a nationalist, Euro-sceptical stance appeared to be central to Blair winning over *The Sun* to Labour's side in the general election. Indeed, Rawnsley describes this as Blair's side of his Faustian bargain with the populist tabloid (2000: 73). Although the logic of its previously stated view that Europe (and rejection of further integration) was the real issue in the election implied support for the Conservatives, *The Sun* had already declared support for Blair. Blair's adoption of a more Euro-sceptic stance clearly aided this Damascene conversion process. For example, in *The Sun* on 17 March, under the heading: 'I'm a British patriot' Blair declared in Churchillian tones:

> We will fight for Britain's interests and to keep our independence every step of the way…I am a British patriot. Anybody who believes I would sell my country short has not listened to a word I have said in the past three years. I didn't change the Labour party into the party it is today to give it all away to Europe or anybody else.

This was interpreted by *The Sun* as a profound shift by Labour towards a Euro-sceptic stance (allowing it to justify its decision to support Blair). Indeed, *The Sun's* political editor, Trevor Kavanagh wrote that Blair had emerged as 'almost as sceptical on Europe as the most outspoken Tories…His pledges will reassure voters that New Labour still has strong reservations about a totally pro-European policy…Privately, Blair has been constantly questioning New Labour's relationship with Europe' (*The Sun,* 17 March 1997, 22 April 1997, *The Guardian,* 22 April 1999).[21]

   This, and similar statements made by the Labour leadership in the election run-in appeared to indicate that the more Euro-phile elements within the leadership had become marginalised. Indeed, Pauline Green suggests that in 'the final run-up to the election…some policy statements were made which…many of us felt quite uncomfortable with in the context of populist electioneering.' Nevertheless, there was a degree of acceptance that this was 'the nature of the political game' in the UK electoral context. Green explains that European politics was 'seen as a Tory agenda...we never led on it and we tried not to lead on it' (Interview with Green). This meant that when the question of the IGC negotiations did come up in the election campaign, Labour was usually in defensive mode, presenting its approach as a hardline defence of UK interests. On areas where it was particularly vulnerable to Tory and press attacks, such as its long-held support for ending the social protocol opt-out, the shifts in Labour's public line were marked and caused dismay within the trade unions and the EPLP. Indeed, in his memo to Prescott in February 1997, Whitty explained that the TUC were taking the view that Labour had 'moved from a position where we were enthusiastic about the social chapter and European employment creation to one where we are against (and instead) in favour of deregulation in the labour market and against European social partnership.' Although Whitty suggested that the Labour leadership offer the TUC some assurance, he also conceded that 'some of our statements do indeed suggest this' (LP Whitty, 19 February 1997). In a similar vein, the launch of Labour's business manifesto in April 1997 may have caused a few eyebrows to be raised amongst Labour's allies in the unions and within the PES. The launch of an election manifesto aimed explicitly at business was itself an illustration of the degree to which the party's transformation had been accelerated under Blair's leadership. The section of the business manifesto devoted to Britain's role in Europe stressed the need to complete the single market in order to remove distortions created by 'hidden barriers and unfair state aids.' In relation to the social chapter it stressed that, while signing up to the chapter, Labour would not agree to QMV extension in matters relating to social security or to co-determination in the boardroom. It avoided mentioning possible QMV extensions elsewhere within the social chapter. However, it suggested that there was 'no appetite among other EU governments for significant new labour market legislation' but that, should there be, a Labour government would 'make sure the issues of employability and competitiveness are central to the decision-making process' (Labour Party 1997a: 12-13).

Labour's election manifesto proper more or less replicated the line set out in the business manifesto as regards the social chapter and on completing the single market, stressing that the latter was one of its key priorities. The other priorities for EU policy outlined by the manifesto were enlargement, urgent reform of the CAP, greater openness and democracy and 'retention of the national veto over key matters of national interest, such as taxation, defence and security, immigration, decisions over the budget and treaty changes' (Labour Party 1997b: 37). In outlining this agenda for reform but putting a rather negative emphasis on the retention of the veto in areas of national interest the manifesto more or less replicated the line set out in the earlier pre-manifesto document approved in the party plebiscite in November 1996 (Labour Party 1996: 35-36). Unlike the pre-manifesto document, the manifesto proper did also suggest that QMV extension would be considered 'in limited areas where it is in Britain's interests.' But this was hardly a ringing endorsement for institutional reform. Moreover, although the paragraph on institutional reform suggested that Labour would support institutional reforms to ensure an enlarged EU worked more efficiently, it did not specify what these reforms might be. It was only the paragraph on greater openness and democracy that gave any clue of the detailed preparations on institutional reforms that had led the party leadership to privately assert that it was in the European mainstream. However, even here, the formulation was slightly ambiguous, stating Labour's support for 'open voting in the Council of Ministers and more effective scrutiny of the Commission by the European Parliament' (Labour Party 1997b: 37). Although the manifesto presented Labour's EU strategy positively as restoring Britain to a leading role in the EU, it was quite defensive and ambiguous in setting out its priorities and no actual mention of the IGC was made.

The defensive nature of the manifesto and other public statements made by the Labour leadership in the few months leading up to the election seemed to represent a shift from the generally positive tone set out in the 1995 policy document. Although it is impossible to quantify precisely the influence played by Labour's EP representatives in the formation of this policy document, it is clear that their presence in the LWG had some effect on the LWG's deliberations as it agreed the positions that would form the basis of this document. At the least, the EP representatives provided valuable information to the Labour leadership on developments elsewhere in the EU, furnishing it with a fuller understanding of the more technical issues, made the Labour leadership aware of various reform options, and acted as advocates for a more Euro-phile interpretation of and reaction to the various proposals. This undoubtedly influenced the positions adopted. A similar effect was derived from Labour's interaction with its sister parties in the various PES forums, while interaction with the trade unions may also have played some influence on the development of Labour's positions on the issues of particular concern to them. However, once the LWG stopped meeting and the atmosphere of populist electioneering in the UK began to accelerate towards the end of 1996, there did appear to be some slippage towards a more negative positioning on EU matters. This was accentuated by the increasingly closed and elitist nature of policy-making that developed within the leadership in this period, in which the leadership was more inclined to take the advice of an apolitical former diplomat (Butler) than from its own MEPs, sister parties in the PES or affiliated trade unions.

In these final few months of opposition, the exigencies of electioneering became paramount and Labour's public statements on the IGC became totally subservient to electoral needs. As the election date drew nearer, the parameters of policy-making, shaped as they were by domestic factors, became more restrictive. However, while the increasing scepticism on matters relating to the social chapter and employment appeared real, and was later borne out by developments after 1 May, the negative tone of some public statements on the IGC did appear to be designed with electioneering in mind and did contradict what was being said and done in private. Examination of the position papers prepared by Butler, Cook and Whitty, the various commentaries produced on IGC proposals, and the discussions they were having with the Dutch and others indicates that while Labour's public statements were hardline and bordering on the nationalistic, in private they were preparing to negotiate agreements on a number of issues far beyond either what the

Conservative government was willing to undertake or what Labour's own public statements implied. Particularly in the final weeks of the election campaign, a gap developed between what was being said in public and what had been agreed in private. Moreover, as Whitty's note to key party staff on 23 March indicated, Labour was able to justify the ambiguity of some of its statements on the IGC by 'playing dumb' as regards its knowledge of what was going on at the IGC (LP Whitty, 23 March 1997). Although the Dutch government did inform the British government that it was in contact with Labour party representatives, the Conservatives appeared to be unaware of the extent of in-depth information that Labour was receiving.

If the Conservatives were aware of the level of contact between Labour and the Dutch, they did not draw attention to this, perhaps because this would have been an admission that they were no longer being taken seriously by their European partners and that a Labour victory in the election was seen as a foregone conclusion. If the extent of Labour's contact with the Dutch presidency and its possession of detailed information on the negotiations had been publicly discussed, the Labour opposition could have faced accusations of negotiating behind the government's back and thus undermining UK interests and/or preparing to sell out. Moreover, Labour would have been pressed by the Conservatives to make their views clear on many of the complex issues under discussion, bringing the dilemma of whether or not to endorse the government's nationalistic positions or reveal its more progressive privately held positions. Labour's discussions with the Dutch presidency (and other EU governments) did to a certain extent resemble tentative parallel negotiations, even though the Labour representatives were keeping their cards close to their chests. The contacts that Labour enjoyed with the Dutch and others allowed both sides to explore the parameters within which negotiations could take place should Labour enter government, to assess the relative importance attached to particular issues by each side (and other EU governments) and identify issues on which bargains could be struck. These contacts were central to the detailed level of preparation undertaken by the Labour party for the IGC and facilitated an engagement with the developing political agenda of continental Europe that was unprecedented for a party of opposition in the UK. This unique level of preparedness allowed Labour to 'hit the ground running' when the long wilderness years of opposition were finally brought to an end on 1 May 1997.

Notes

[1] The document was approved by 95 per cent to 5 per cent on a 61 per cent turnout of party members.

[2] Whitty's role in relation to the EPLP temporarily became a more formal managerial one at the end of 1996, when he was given the additional post of acting chief executive of the EPLP following the departure of Dianne Hayter from the post. Whitty undertook a caretaker role until a permanent replacement, Peter Coleman, was appointed to replace Hayter. Blair's need to nominate a number of new working peers also led to Whitty being elevated to the House of Lords in late 1996.

[3] Whitty circulated the text with his commentary attached to Cook, Quin, David and Blair's chief of staff, Jonathan Powell (communication with Blair by this stage appeared to be via Powell).

[4] Bobby McDonagh, Ireland's deputy IGC representative and a member of the Irish Presidency team, explains that the draft treaty represented an approximation of the balance of the discussions thus far in the IGC, but that in some contentious areas 'it was self-evidently not opportune to table treaty texts' (1998: 105-108).

[5] The Petersberg declaration of 1992 adopted by the WEU members stated that in addition to its traditional collective defence function, the WEU could be employed for humanitarian and rescue tasks, peacekeeping tasks and tasks of combat forces in crisis management, including peacemaking (van Ham 1997: 310-311).

[6] The Irish text on EU-WEU relations was very much a compromise between those, led by France and Germany, who wanted full merger, and the UK and the neutral states (including Ireland) who wished to maintain the EU and WEU as separate organisations and prevent the EU from taking on a defence identity (McDonagh 1998: 117-120).

[7] This originated from a Finnish proposal late in the Irish Presidency (McDonagh 1998: 91-92).

[8] As head of the European integration department at the FCO from 1972 to 1974 and then assistant under-secretary at the FCO from 1974-76, Butler had played a key role in the UK's accession to the EC (Young, H 1999: 254-255) and in the 1975 renegotiation (Young, H 1999: 278-279). Butler himself claims to have had responsibility for the whole renegotiation process in 1975 (Interview with Butler).

[9] However, Renwick (a former ambassador to the USA who was also working in the City, for the Robert Flemings Consultancy) also provided advice on the detail of policy. For example, in response to a suggestion from Jonathan Powell that Renwick identify for the Labour leadership 'a couple of areas in which it would actually be in Britain's interest to see an extension of majority voting,' Renwick had identified research, where the UK stood to benefit from having a relatively large number of projects allocated to it, and trade, where he suggested that the UK should actually be insisting on QMV for trade negotiating positions on services and intellectual property in order to 'achieve more liberal EU positions in the WTO' (LP Renwick, 31 January 1997).

[10] These brackets would contain options still requiring discussion and agreement.

[11] An initial draft treaty text on a flexibility enabling clause was actually tabled by the Dutch presidency for the IGC representatives meeting of 17-18 February (McDonagh 1998: 148). Proposals on JHA were tabled for the ministerial meeting of 24 February (McDonagh 1998: 176).

[12] The Irish presidency had avoided including Schengen incorporation in its draft treaty text because of its own reluctance to take part in the Schengen arrangements. This related to its unwillingness to jeopardise Ireland's long-standing common travel area with the UK, given the UK refusal to take part in Schengen (McDonagh 1998: 168-170).

[13] Butler was referring to the document *New Labour, New Life for Britain* - the pre-manifesto document approved by party plebiscite in autumn 1996, which stressed Labour's intention to develop a constructive approach to EU relations (Labour Party 1996: 33-37).

[14] The Irish draft text on fundamental rights had proposed a reaffirmation of the principles of human rights, democracy and fundamental freedoms in the EU treaties, and a procedure for identifying whether a member state was in breach of these principles, and for the suspension of the membership rights of the state in question. This procedure would only be used in extreme cases, such as the establishment of an authoritarian dictatorship in a member state.

The text also proposed conferring an explicit jurisdiction on the ECJ to ensure that EC acts respected certain fundamental rights principles (McDonagh 1998: 166).

[15] The existing situation was that the EC had legal personality but not the EU as a whole. This meant that international agreements could only be conducted in relation to the EC pillar and not the two intergovernmental pillars.

[16] This had been formalised by the SEA, and involved the promotion of dialogue between the representatives of employers and employees (the social partners) and their involvement in the development of EC legislation. The social protocol of the TEU provided for framework agreements in relation to employment rights to be negotiated between the social partners and adopted as directives by the Council of Ministers (Dinan 1999: 420-428).

[17] Byers gained notoriety during the TUC annual conference in September 1996 when he suggested to journalists that Blair might seek to end Labour's organic link with the trade unions once Labour was returned to government (Anderson and Mann 1997: 324).

[18] Relating to measures to include employee representation on company boards.

[19] An annex explained the line on the UK government submissions in more detail. It recommended dropping most of the UK proposals on the ECJ and proposals on quality of legislation, the working-time directive and CFSP and pursuing proposals on subsidiarity, allowing public/private partnerships in TENs, competition in agriculture and animal welfare provisions.

[20] This included the adoption of a bulldog - generally viewed as a nationalist right-wing symbol - as a campaign mascot (an idea instigated by Peter Mandelson).

[21] A few months later, *The Sun* was describing Blair as the most dangerous man in Britain because of his alleged plans to take the UK into the single currency (*The Sun*, 24 June 1998). For a discussion of the St. George's day article see also David McKie 'By George! What a con' *The Guardian*, 22 April 1999.

Chapter 6

Labour in Government: The IGC Endgame[1]

The Entry to Government

Although the extent of the Labour party's landslide victory in the general election of 1 May 1997 came as a shock to some, its entrance into government came as a surprise to no-one, not least the team of foreign office officials who awaited Cook. As indicated to the Labour leadership in advance by Butler, the civil servants of the FCO had prepared thoroughly for the change in IGC positioning that the new government would bring, drawing up a thorough briefing on all the IGC issues which landed on the desk of foreign secretary Robin Cook as he assumed his new position. The detailed brief received by Cook reflected both the extent of preparation by the FCO and the interaction that had taken place between FCO officials and Labour's representatives in the days leading up to the change of government. It also illustrated the professional machinery now at the disposal of the Labour party. The brief included a detailed note explaining the forthcoming timetable and agenda of IGC meetings and making suggestions for internal government co-ordination, which involved bilateral and multilateral communication with cabinet colleagues (and briefings on relevant departmental issues) and cabinet committee meetings, and for bilateral contacts with the key European partners. The brief also included a draft of the opening statement to be made by the new IGC personal representative at the representative group meeting of 5-6 May, and a draft letter from Cook to Blair making a series of detailed recommendations on the positions that the new government should take at the IGC. Also attached were a series of detailed briefs (divided into 31 different topics) on each of the areas being discussed at the IGC. The briefs had been designed to identify the key decisions or judgements that ministers would need to address, though they did not contain specific policy recommendations. They ranged from the key high profile issues such as JHA, CFSP and defence, flexibility, QMV scope, Council vote reweighting, Commission size and the role of the EP, policy areas such as employment, environment and consumer policy, and broader horizontal issues such as legal personality, subsidiarity, transparency, fundamental rights and treaty simplification.

Each of these issues was dealt with in the same structured format by the briefs. First of all the nature of the issue under discussion was explained. This involved explanation of the finer points that needed to be resolved. Any draft treaty texts that were on the table would also be explained (these were usually presidency texts which were attached as annexes). The level of agreement and the point to which the discussions had reached would also be indicated. Then each brief would attempt to encapsulate the position of the new government based on the election manifesto and the pre-manifesto document. This would be followed by a summary of the views of the other member states, also indicating the level of importance that other member states attached to the proposal (as well as whether they supported or opposed). The likely future development of discussion on the issue in question, and the extent to which (and on which points) agreement would be likely would then be assessed. This would be followed by a brief encapsulation of the policy of the previous UK government (usually based on the IGC White Paper and/or on memoranda submitted to the IGC). There would then be an assessment of options for consideration by the new government. These would cover possible acceptance of presidency texts or possible compromises, the extent to which bargaining would be possible (and to which alliances could be formed with other member states in the bargaining process) and areas where the UK government would have to 'go to the wire' in preventing texts being agreed, rather than accept any compromise. The briefs would conclude with an explanation of the next steps that would need to be followed, i.e. whether the FCO or another government department would be taking the lead on a particular issue, and the extent to which other government departments would have to be kept informed and to which collective discussion would have to take place, and also possible bilateral representations that could be made to other member states in order to cement alliances on particular issues.

The options for consideration set out in the briefs provided a particularly illuminating illustration of the kind of bargaining (encouraged by the FCO) that was likely to take place in the negotiation process. For example, the brief on QMV asked whether there were issues on which the government would wish to oppose QMV for tactical reasons, i.e. with a view to dropping such opposition in return for the achievement of other negotiating goals. Moreover, in relation to the range of minor issues being touted by particular states, it was suggested that ministers might wish to consider whether the importance attached to any of these proposals by particular member states could offer opportunities for leverage in the endgame by establishing linkages to UK priorities.

As instructed by his officials, Cook would be holding a meeting during his first weekend of office to focus on the handling of the IGC representatives meeting on 5-6 May, the co-ordination of work within Whitehall and initial contacts with the key negotiating partners (it was not surprising that Cook later described his first few days as secretary of state as akin to being taken prisoner by his civil servants). Cook was presented with a tight and demanding timetable of government co-ordination to ensure agreement on its negotiating positions. By the end of his first full week in office (around 10 May) Cook was expected by his officials to have sent a minute to key cabinet colleagues proposing broad objectives, strategy and priorities for the negotiation together with a proposal for the Whitehall handling of IGC issues and guidance on media handling. This minute would then be discussed in cabinet or a cabinet committee on 15 May. On the basis of the outcome of this meeting, officials from 'the lead departments' would produce for submission to Cook, and to the departmental minister concerned, more detailed policy papers on each of the key IGC issues (according to Cook's officials these were JHA, CFSP/defence, main institutional issues, flexibility, social/employment and quota-hopping). These minutes would then be circulated in time for a further collective ministerial discussion probably just before the informal European Council on 23 May.

In addition to these, Cook or the new minister for Europe would aim to circulate three minutes to colleagues, each dealing with a range of the remaining, less central subjects, to be issued at the rate of one a week, beginning with the week beginning 5 May. The first of these would deal with 'complex horizontal issues' such as fundamental rights, legal personality, external economic relations and treaty simplification, the second with first pillar policy subjects and the third with institutional and other miscellaneous questions. It was suggested that such collective discussion as might be needed on these points could be organised either in the cabinet committee on EU matters or by ad hoc matters chaired by Cook or the Europe minister. The FCO sought Cook's approval to drive forward the process of formulating and co-ordinating the new government's positions on the IGC in order to avoid 'a snowstorm of paper as each department launches proposals for the handling of issues which come within its domain.'

It was suggested that this process would need to be supported where possible with bilateral or trilateral meetings between Cook and his cabinet colleagues. Most importantly, this would involve a discussion during the new government's first week of office between Cook and Blair. This would be before Cook issued his first minute setting out the government's IGC objectives. Meetings would also be necessary between Cook and other key cabinet colleagues such as the new chancellor of the exchequer, Gordon Brown, and the new home secretary, Jack Straw. The bilateral meeting with Straw in the week beginning 12 May would be an opportunity to clear the ground on the complex JHA dossier. A short bilateral meeting was also required with the new defence secretary, George Robertson, before the WEU ministerial meeting in Paris on 12-13 May, where the views of the government on European defence issues would undoubtedly be sought. Cook or the minister for Europe would also hold ad hoc meetings with ministers from other government departments to resolve some of the less central issues. This would help prepare or even obviate the need for formal collective ministerial discussion.

Cook was also presented with a detailed schedule of meetings with his own FCO officials. These would involve a programme of meetings to consider the main IGC issues and strategy and to prepare for ministerial discussion and key meetings with other foreign ministers from the EU partners. Similar arrangements would be presented to the new Europe minister. A video conference link with the UK representation in Brussels allowed discussions to include Wall. It was suggested that Cook might also want to see the UK ambassadors to EU countries before the informal European Council on 23 May and that the ambassadors themselves 'would find it valuable to have from ministers an account of the government's approach to the IGC endgame.' A joint meeting with all the UK ambassadors to the EU member states was pencilled in for 21 May in London for this purpose.

Finally, Cook's initial schedule would involve meetings with some of his key EU colleagues before 20 May. The key players were identified by his officials as van Mierlo (Dutch presidency), Kinkel (Germany), Charette (France), Spring (Ireland) 'particularly because of the Irish interest in frontiers issues' and the foreign ministers of the Nordic countries with whom the UK shared 'a number of common interests.' There would be opportunities for these meetings on 9 May, 12-13 May (in the margins of the WEU ministerial meeting in Paris) and 19 May. Meetings would also be undertaken at minister of state level by the new Europe minister.

Though this represented a demanding and time-consuming agenda for the new foreign secretary, Cook was advised that this was based on the assumption that 'given the weight of domestic matters with which the government will be concerned' (and thus keeping the prime minister occupied) he would feel it necessary himself to drive forward the process of IGC policy preparation. The government would be aiming to have as full and coherent a set of positions as possible in time for the special European Council on 23 May, and, beyond that, for the final run-up to the Amsterdam European Council. In order to take this lead, the formalities of decision-making within government required Cook to clear the proposed FCO positions on the IGC with the prime minister. Hence the letter sent by Cook to Blair on 6 May setting out the government's broad approach to the IGC and a tentative positioning on the key issues. The initial draft letter had been enclosed with the detailed brief awaiting Cook as he assumed his new position. Given its accuracy in reflecting the evolving positions of the Labour leadership in the run-up to 1 May, the letter was likely to have been based on the discreet soundings that FCO officials had taken from Butler, Whitty and Clark in their meetings prior to the election, as well as research of Labour's public statements in opposition.

The letter to Blair stressed that the government 'should reaffirm our commitment to finishing at Amsterdam and not give the impression that it is we who are seeking delay.' Nevertheless, it suggested that given the tight timetable of IGC meetings, it would not be surprising if, due to the complexity of the issues, some points could not be resolved at Amsterdam. In such an eventuality it was suggested that there could be a further European Council under the Luxembourg presidency, possibly on 25/26 July. On the substance of the IGC, Cook identified three key IGC objectives: to bring the EU closer to the citizen, to prepare it for enlargement and to improve its effective capacity for external action. He suggested that all of these objectives would fit well with the government's own priorities and that the achievement of them was likely to represent a success for the UK. This appeared to be a departure from some of the position papers submitted to the LWG in opposition, which derided an obscure institutional reform agenda not of Labour's (or the UK's) own making.

Turning first to the objective of bringing the EU closer to the citizen, Cook suggested that there were a number of achievable reforms consistent with making the EU more relevant and comprehensible to ordinary people. Though unlikely to appeal to those 'viscerally opposed' to more European co-operation, the government could 'rightly present' these reforms as 'positive for this country.' These reforms included new treaty provisions on basic human rights, non-discrimination and sex equality, a new treaty title on employment, the end of the social chapter opt-out, stronger provisions on the environment, strengthened provisions on subsidiarity and on the quality of legislation, measures to enhance the role of national parliaments, more effective anti-fraud measures, animal welfare provisions and improvements to transparency. Cook would also suggest that the new government put forward a proposal to allow greater access for individuals to the ECJ, although there was uncertainty over whether this would win support from other member states. In relation to all proposals, he emphasised the 'need to scrutinise the detail carefully, particularly as regards potential costs either to the exchequer or to business.'

In relation to the second objective of preparing the EU for enlargement, Cook suggested that the following reforms were likely to be achieved: 1) some extension of QMV in the first pillar, though he suggested that this was not expected to be one of the most difficult issues of substance as there appeared to be 'little enthusiasm' for abandoning unanimity in the most sensitive areas (for the UK government) such as treaty change, matters with major implications for national budgets, or derogations from the single market; 2) reweighting of votes in Council - while there would be opposition from many smaller states, Cook suggested that this 'would be a success for us and we should argue for it'; 3) a reduction in the number of the Commissioners - though there was much support for this, Cook suggested that it was not clear whether any proposals would succeed and that the new government should therefore be 'reluctant to surrender the UK's right to two Commissioners - at least unless we get a visible return'; 4) a 'modest increase' in EP powers through extension of codecision (it was not clear why this was categorised among the reforms necessary for enlargement). Cook's letter reflected the pragmatic cynicism now being encouraged by his officials at the FCO. It suggested that there was merit in giving the EP codecision wherever legislation was voted by QMV 'thus excluding those areas which are genuinely sensitive.'

The letter nevertheless emphasised the need for careful presentation of government policy on these institutional issues. It acknowledged that Labour's opponents would seek to depict the extensions of QMV and codecision as a 'weakening of national control over policy decisions' but stressed that the government would have 'strong arguments' on its side: 'in the perspective of enlargement we need more effective decision-making machinery; we can use this machinery to form majorities in the United Kingdom's interest which will not then be subject to obstruction by one or two member states; and it is right that the European Parliament should exert a democratic influence over decision-making to complement that of the Council - which will work to the advantage of the United Kingdom given that Labour MEPs represent the largest national party grouping at Strasbourg.' This last point contrasted with the private FCO view that democracy was good unless it interfered with important decisions.

Cook then turned to the 'several key issues which remained unresolved' in the IGC where 'long-term British interests' were at stake and therefore tough negotiations foreseen. Of these, JHA, flexibility and CFSP/defence had been identified by the Labour leadership prior to the election as the most difficult issues to resolve, while Cook's officials had added to this list an issue that had a particular resonance for the UK: fishing quotas. In relation to JHA, the proposals on partial communitisation were presented positively as an opportunity to secure recognition in the treaty that the UK would retain frontier controls in respect of third-country nationals, even when other member states removed theirs. This was 'something which previous British governments never achieved.' However, it was acknowledged that the pressure for reform from other member states posed difficulties as the UK government did not want these matters to be dealt with in the first pillar, particularly as this would require some form of opt-out or differentiation. Given the sensitivity of the areas covered by the JHA, the government would also oppose QMV or heavy involvement of the EC institutions in these matters. Nevertheless, the government would not wish to be excluded from policies such as police co-operation. Moving on to flexibility, the letter conceded that there might be an argument that an enlarged EU would require some flexibility (in contrast to Butler's earlier assertions that flexibility was not required to facilitate enlargement). However, Cook warned of the dangers of a two-speed Europe and counselled 'a very cautious approach' despite the widespread support the flexibility idea had elsewhere. He thus advocated a continuation of the strategy pursued in opposition, questioning 'the need for flexibility arrangements in the first pillar' while not necessarily committing Britain to opposition to any change to the present position. Nevertheless, the necessity that any flexibility clause should require the consent of all member states and be open to all to use would also be stressed.

On CFSP, Cook proposed that the government should resist any unqualified recourse to majority voting while considering other possibilities such as wider use of majority voting but with a national veto available where key interests were concerned. He also recommended that the government oppose the Franco-German proposals on EU/WEU merger and encourage the neutral member states to do likewise. But the new government would also seek to present a constructive approach in this area. Thus Cook's letter proposed the development for consideration of a range of options falling short of merger, involving increased practical co-operation between the EU and the WEU and arrangements to allow the Petersberg crisis-management tasks to be undertaken within the EU treaty.

Lastly, Cook explained that almost every member state would have on its 'shopping list' some items of particular domestic importance, and that for the UK, the most prominent of these would be fish quota-hopping on which 'a reasonably substantial outcome' was required. The Spanish were 'implacably opposed' to a submission made by the government's Conservative predecessors. It was therefore suggested that the new agriculture minister (Jack Cunningham) quickly bring forward a paper suggesting what alternative might be negotiable.

The letter also provided an opportunity for Cook to seek Blair's approval for the system of government co-ordination on the IGC outlined previously by his officials. Thus Cook would circulate minutes on the main horizontal issues, the Europe minister would circulate papers on less central IGC issues and, where relevant, lead departments would circulate papers on specific 'policy' issues. Cook or the Europe minister would chair meetings where collective discussion was required. A collective government discussion on the IGC would then take place before the informal European Council on 23 May, in order for agreement to be reached on negotiation objectives and strategy. The letter concluded with a stress on the importance of the right presentation of government policy on the IGC. This would be kept fairly general and would balance 'a positive approach to Europe' with 'a determination to protect British interests through constructive negotiation.' In public, the government would stress its commitment to complete the IGC at Amsterdam and its view that the IGC was as an opportunity to make Europe more relevant to ordinary people and to prepare for enlargement. The negotiations would be presented as 'tough but a dialogue of partners, not opponents.' Thus the government would make clear that it would negotiate and argue its case through 'persuasion rather than sulking', though in the end it would have to be satisfied that the negotiation was 'a good deal for the UK.' Accordingly, on some important issues like frontier controls, flexibility and foreign policy and defence the government would acknowledge that there would 'be difficult discussions' and that if it did find itself isolated on a key point 'then so be it.' But it would neither seek such an outcome nor anticipate it.

The government was faced with an immediate decision with repercussions for public presentation of policy during its first weekend in office. This concerned the appointment of a minister of state in the foreign office with responsibility for European affairs (i.e. the minister for Europe), and the related question of whether Wall should be replaced as the foreign secretary's personal representative at the IGC by the new minister before the IGC representatives meeting of 5-6 May. Were a new personal representative to be appointed, he or she would need instructions beforehand. The meeting was viewed as a critical early opportunity for the government to signal the start of a new era in the UK's relations with the EU, making a quick decision on these questions essential. The general expectation within the Labour party was that the post of Europe minister would go to Joyce Quin, given her long tenure in the shadow post under the leadership of both Smith and Blair. There was therefore surprise when Blair instead appointed Doug Henderson to the post while Quin was appointed as a home affairs minister (her responsibilities would include JHA matters). Henderson had been a shadow home affairs spokesman before the election and his appointment came as a particular surprise as he had not been known to utter a public word on European issues in his time as an MP (Anderson and Mann 1997: 113n), though he had been involved in internal party discussion on the possible impact of EU provisions on access to information. Although Cook would have been consulted on the appointment, the final decision rested with Blair, deriving from the vast powers of patronage that he had inherited as prime minister. The idea of appointing Henderson rather than Quin may have been Blair's own or may have come from one of his 'inner circle.'[2] Given both the sensitivity and the high profile nature of the Europe post, various senior figures in and around the leadership may have had an interest in who got it. One highly authoritative source suggests that Peter Mandelson had sought the post for himself but that Blair had decided against this whilst also rejecting all Cook's nominations for the post, probably including Quin (Rawnsley 2000: 1-2, 21-22). Anderson and Mann suggest that Blair had proposed giving the post to the former chairman of British Petroleum (BP), Sir David Simon, but that this was vetoed by Cook (1997: 113n).[3] Pressure may also have come from Gordon Brown who was keen to place his own acolytes (who included Henderson) into key positions. Indeed, Andrew Rawnsely writes that Henderson's 'principal qualification for the post was that he was pushed by Gordon Brown' (2000: 22).[4] Another factor favouring Henderson's appointment was his experience as a trade union negotiator. Negotiating experience would be particularly valuable given the decision to also appoint the new Europe minister as the UK's IGC representative in place of Wall. While the appointment of someone without much knowledge on the subject to the post of Europe minister puzzled some of those involved in Labour's IGC preparations, Henderson's lack of knowledge may have been viewed by Blair and his advisers as a positive attribute. There was a possibility that Quin as Europe minister may have been characterised by the right-wing press as a rabid pro-European negotiating UK interests away to Europe. There may also have been a genuine view within the prime minister's office that Quin might be too soft in the negotiations given her pro-European instincts. Henderson had no record in the area, and could not be characterised as either Euro-phile or Euro-sceptic. Rather he could be presented as a tough pragmatic negotiator.

Henderson therefore went into the personal representatives meeting of 5 May as an unknown quantity among his European colleagues, many of whom had become acquainted with Quin. Though the issues discussed may have been new to Henderson, his statement was nonetheless warmly received by the other representatives (many of whom already had a good idea of the new positions Labour would bring, due to pre-election contacts) and was of critical importance to setting a new tone in UK relations with the EU (McDonagh 1998: 183-184). Henderson's statement more or less corresponded to the draft earlier provided by FCO officials for Cook's approval,[5] though a few new opening sentences had been added, most likely at Cook's behest. While the earlier draft had begun in a rather neutral fashion, the new opening section demonstrated the desire of Cook and the rest of the Labour leadership to make a clearer political statement at the outset, emphasising the break from the government's Conservative predecessors and also once again stressing Labour's practical policy agenda for the EU. The new government's priorities were defined as completion of the single market, enlargement, CAP reform, and 'to tackle unemployment and promote flexible labour markets.' This partly reflected the approach Cook had pursued since the establishment of the LWG in opposition. However, the new emphases on completion of the single market and labour market flexibility were emblematic of the shift in emphasis from the social democratic Keynesian approach, as advocated by Cook, of the earlier policy papers, to a more neo-liberal approach more in tune with the general economic thinking espoused by Blair and Brown. The shift to the latter approach had become more apparent in the run-up to the general election. The emphases on single market completion and labour market flexibility, together with CAP reform and enlargement could also be viewed as representing a continuity in UK government thinking. This continuity was now accentuated by the influence of the Whitehall machine.

As Butler had advised prior to the election, the statement sought to buy the new government some time before it revealed its hand on many of its detailed positions, suggesting that while the Labour party had followed the IGC negotiations over the previous twelve months, it did not have final positions on every detail. Henderson emphasised both the importance the new government attached to the negotiations, and its positive approach:

> I know that we won't agree on every point - like any other member state, we will defend what we see to be our interests with vigour. But we want to work with you as colleagues in a shared enterprise. Not using the language of opponents. Europe, for the new British Government, is an opportunity, not a threat.

The statement placed the new government firmly in the European mainstream as far as first pillar institutional reform was concerned, signalling the government's agreement that enlargement necessitated an 'overhaul of the decision-making machinery' involving 'some extension' of QMV (with EP codecision extended where QMV applied), and a more effective Commission 'without departing from the present balance within.' The latter was a hint that the new government sought retention of two Commissioners for the large states. The statement also sought to link the under-representation of the large states in Council voting with the issue of the democratic deficit by suggesting that a reweighting would 'restore some of the democratic legitimacy which has been lost over the years.' Elsewhere, Henderson signalled Labour's intention to end the social chapter opt-out and its support for an employment chapter, for enshrining in the treaty basic rights (including non-discrimination provisions) and for greater transparency in EU decision-making, greater involvement of national parliaments, a strengthened emphasis on the environment and a more effective application of subsidiarity. Henderson linked the subsidiarity principle to Labour's domestic constitutional reform agenda, describing it as 'important for ensuring the decentralisation which we intend to pursue in Britain as well as Europe.'

Henderson also set out the new government's broad approach on the policy areas that would cause it more difficulty with its European colleagues. He stressed that while flexibility could be tolerated in the intergovernmental pillars, i.e. constructive abstention in CFSP and 'some degree of differentiation in JHA' the Labour government would find it hard to reconcile the need for legal and institutional unity with the idea of flexibility in the first pillar. In relation to CFSP, Henderson stated the government's support for practical measures to improve its effectiveness, such as the enhanced planning capacity, but reiterated the government's belief that policy decisions should represent the views of all member states (notwithstanding its acceptance of constructive abstention). He also made clear the government's opposition to an EU defence function, though he did signal its preparedness to see more effective links between the EU and WEU, particularly in relation to implementation of the Petersberg tasks.

Henderson's statement confirmed that the JHA was probably the area where the new government had the most problems. Stressing the 'differences of geography and traditions' which made this necessary, he suggested that any treaty change agreed by the UK would require explicit recognition of 'its right to maintain frontier controls in respect of third country nationals' combined with arrangements 'which allow us to work together as fifteen member states wherever possible.' Henderson made clear the government's desire for JHA policies to continue to operate on an intergovernmental basis while conveying the government's willingness 'to look constructively' at other ideas for improving the effectiveness of co-operation in this area (Henderson, 5 May 1997).

Policy Co-ordination and Initial Diplomacy in Government

The positions set out by Henderson at this formal debut by the Labour party into the IGC negotiations represented an accurate summary of the positions that the new government would continue to pursue in the short period up to the Amsterdam summit. They also bore a striking resemblance to the positions that had emerged within the LWG by the summer of 1995 as reflected in the policy document adopted by the party conference. This was particularly the case on first pillar issues and also on CFSP and defence. The broad principles of Labour party policy on flexibility and JHA communitisation had also remained pretty much unchanged since the 1995 document, although the details of these had been fleshed out further with Butler's assistance in early 1997. Given the difficulty in reaching agreement on these latter two issues with the new government's European partners, further deliberations would continue within government on refining the details of possible compromise positions that it would take into the negotiations. Following Henderson's speech there followed a period of inter-departmental policy consideration within government to ensure that it was united in its approach to the negotiations, to thrash out the detailed line on the positions already set out and to agree positions on those sometimes highly technical issues that had not been properly considered so far. On the more technical issues, such as legal personality and treaty simplification, the expertise of the FCO would allow it to play a particularly strong influence in guiding the government's policy.

While this process of policy refinement was being undertaken, the new government was simultaneously engaged in the process of swiftly establishing bilateral relations with its key European counterparts, in order to reiterate its general positions, develop a clearer and more detailed understanding of the priorities of these key partners and accordingly sound out its European colleagues in relation to possible areas of compromise and issues on which alliances could be formed within the negotiations. This was a process that itself would feed into the policy co-ordination exercise being conducted within the government. Policy would accordingly be refined to reflect areas of compromise that may have emerged in these bilateral discussions, or indeed from the ongoing formal multilateral IGC discussions. As advised by his FCO officials, Cook therefore made an early start in establishing bilateral relations with his key European counterparts, visiting Paris and Bonn on 7 May for bilateral meetings with the French foreign minister, Charette, and the German foreign minister, Kinkel. He also maintained contacts with his PES colleagues in these countries, meeting with Lionel Jospin, leader of the French PS and Oskar Lafontaine, then leader of the German SPD, both of whom were in opposition. The meeting with Jospin would have particular value due to the imminence of the French national assembly elections in early June, after which he emerged as French prime minister and a key player in the final IGC negotiations.[6] Comprehensive briefs on the range of issues to be discussed, the IGC priorities and positions of both France and Germany, and the internal political situations in both countries were provided for Cook's meetings with his counterparts. In terms of how Cook should present the government's position on the IGC, the briefs for both meetings were almost identical to each other and also closely corresponded to the position set out by Henderson in the IGC representatives meeting on 5 May. Thus the common government line appeared to be an emphasis on drawing a line under the recent past in terms of the UK's relations with the EU and setting out the government's priorities of completing the single market, enlargement, CAP reform, tackling unemployment and promoting flexible labour markets (the briefs for these visits also stressed the need to make a reality of European foreign policy co-operation), before setting out its more detailed attitudes to the IGC, i.e. caution on the awkward issues of JHA, CFSP/defence and flexibility but a more mainstream attitude on first pillar issues. Cook would reiterate the government's arguments on the awkward issues and suggest that both France and Germany worked closely together with the UK on first pillar issues in which the countries had common interests, for example on Council vote reweighting and towards some differentiation between large and small states in the Commission (possibly through larger states having a vice-president). Cook would also seek to work with the French on enhancing the role of national parliaments, signalling the UK's intention to give consideration to the French proposal for a greater role for COSAC[7] in ensuring the maintenance of subsidiarity.

With the machinery of the FCO and the UK embassies throughout the EU now at Labour's disposal, alliances with the PES parties in government had now become less central to Labour's strategy. Seeking compromises and common ground with the centre-right leadership of Germany and France would be critical to a satisfactory completion of the IGC by the Labour government. The reports from the Bonn and Paris embassies on which the briefs for Cook's visits were partly based, provided an insight into how negotiations with the two key member states would proceed. The Bonn embassy described the planned meeting between Blair and Kohl at the beginning of June as the most important event for the UK on the path to the Amsterdam summit and optimistically suggested that there might be 'a deal to cut with the Germans' which would mark a move towards UK interests. The German strategy had so far been 'to make deals with France, then bind in Italy, Spain and the Benelux and bring the rest along in the wake' with the UK 'left to last.' The implicit aim was to isolate the UK and place it 'under pressure in the end game.' However, the view from Bonn was that the Germans were now showing signs of 'wanting to negotiate with us, not freeze us out.' Furthermore, the UK's position vis a vis Germany was better than it might seem for a number of reasons including a German keenness to get the negotiations over and a recognition that some of their proposals, such as those on EU/WEU merger and on a flexibility clause which did not require unanimous approval, would not succeed and not just because of the UK. Moreover, the new government in the UK would obtain some credit for being prepared to incorporate the social agreement and for being prepared to consider the extension of QMV in limited areas, while the Germans would recognise that, even with the election over, the UK still had only limited room to compromise and would not wish to start their relationship with the new government with a major row.

Blair would see Kohl at the special European Council on 23 May and the NATO/Russia meeting on 27 May. However, the formal Blair-Kohl meeting in early June was obviously the most important opportunity to establish a working relationship. The suggestion from the Bonn embassy was that it should be possible in this period to exploit a fresh start to take advantage of Germany's wish to close on time and so to move Kohl in the direction of British interests. Indeed, it was predicted that the Germans would not press the UK on EU/WEU merger, and that it was pretty clear that they would acquiesce in UK retention of a veto on immigration and border controls. A compromise formula would accordingly be possible which would preserve the UK position and allow Kohl 'to tell his voters that there has been a real step forward in the fight against cross-border crime.' Nevertheless, it was suggested that these issues would 'need pre-cooking beforehand' with Kohl's chief foreign policy advisor Bitterlich. Indeed, it was in the chancellory that the key decisions would be taken: 'Kohl will not go into detail with the prime minister, but leave this to personal advisers to work out.'

Discussions with the French had now been complicated by Chirac's decision to call early legislative elections for early June, meaning that the composition of the French government at Amsterdam would be unclear. Nevertheless, it was suggested from Paris that the French would still want to conclude the IGC at Amsterdam though they were no longer demanding a maximalist outcome (which would encounter ratification difficulties whatever the election result). The view from the Paris embassy was that the most likely conflicts between the UK and France would be over third pillar issues (especially QMV extension), QMV in CFSP, EU/WEU merger and flexibility. In order to circumvent these differences, the French would most likely be prepared to support UK retention of border controls and 'be prepared to discuss solutions enabling the UK to opt-in or out of the third pillar.' However, it was expected that in return the French would press for flexibility in the second and third pillars and extension of QMV. There would be common ground between the UK and France on subsidiarity, national parliaments and making the Commission more effective. In terms of tactics, the French had 'until now regarded themselves as having very little alternative but to work closely with the Germans on IGC issues' but would welcome new areas of common ground with the UK as a useful counterbalance to German pressure. Nevertheless, the French would 'tend to pocket any concessions they see and ask for more.' It would therefore be necessary to ensure that 'shifts in their direction be sold hard as part of a satisfactory overall package at Amsterdam.'

In both maintaining diplomatic contacts with the UK's European partners and in compiling the initial minutes outlining the government's IGC policy, the FCO had now taken a firm lead in developing the Labour government's IGC policy. This machinery also put Cook firmly in the driving seat as regards setting out the principles and details of policy and negotiating strategy, with Butler and Whitty now relegated to more peripheral roles. Nevertheless, Butler and Whitty, as well as

Cook's adviser, David Clark, were all brought into the FCO policy apparatus. Clark was appointed as special adviser to the foreign secretary. Cook also asked Butler to continue advising him until after the UK Council presidency in the first half of 1998. Butler would continue to be kept informed on IGC developments and provide Cook with advice wherever he was asked. On top of his appointment as a government whip and spokesman on EU affairs in the House of Lords, Whitty was given an additional post in the FCO as minister responsible for relations with the EP. The structure of cabinet government meant that other Labour party figures, who had hitherto played a peripheral role, now played a more prominent role as government ministers, both in responding to the various IGC minutes sent by Cook and Henderson, and in airing their views in the cabinet European policy co-ordinating committee. In inviting responses from ministers from relevant departmental areas, the process of 'minuting' brought into play a number of newly appointed Labour ministers who had not played a central role in IGC policy formation in opposition. All now had their own departmental machines at their disposal and were able to intervene in order to further their particular departmental interests. Moreover, on some key issues such as JHA and defence, Cook had to share the lead in policy-making and issue joint minutes with the relevant secretaries of state (e.g. George Robertson at defence and Straw at the home office) while in some areas, Cook ceded the lead entirely. For example, in relation to employment and social affairs a joint minute was issued by the secretary of state for education and employment (David Blunkett) and the secretary of state for trade and industry (Margaret Beckett). Differences of opinion between ministers were generally settled either at the cabinet sub-committee on Europe, known as (E)DOP, or through bilateral contacts between the relevant ministers and their officials. Any such differences tended to be minor and related to technical details.

The various minutes sent out by Cook and Henderson elicited a number of responses across the various government departments. There was an obvious overlap between the FCO and other government departments on some issues that made responses from the ministers concerned inevitable. In addition, the minutes on the 'horizontal' issues, which had implications across government departments, elicited responses from a number of ministers. For example, Cook's minute on 14 May on the 'complex horizontal issues' of fundamental rights, external economic relations, treaty simplification and legal personality received responses from Straw (on fundamental rights, treaty simplification and legal personality), the Scottish secretary, Donald Dewar (on fundamental rights and non-discrimination), the education and employment secretary, Blunkett (on sexual equality), the defence secretary, Robertson (on non-discrimination), the trade and industry secretary, Beckett (on external economic relations) and the chancellor, Gordon Brown (on external economic relations). In relation to ECJ jurisdiction in ensuring the EU respected fundamental rights, Straw shared Cook's caution over its application to the second and third pillars, and stated his firm opposition to its application to the third pillar. This was echoed by Dewar who had responsibility for home affairs in Scotland. Dewar also expressed reservations about the potential cost of non-discrimination provisions being used to ensure provision of information in different languages. Robertson expressed concern about the implications of non-discrimination provisions for the armed forces while Blunkett indicated a preference for references to the 'under-represented sex' rather than women in sexual equality provisions. On external relations, Beckett indicated enthusiastic support for the proposal to give the European Commission competence to negotiate on intellectual property, services and investment. This reflected her own departmental interests. Indeed, the former Bennite argued that there were 'strong trade policy reasons for equipping the Community with the means to pursue the most liberal line possible.' Cook had expressed tentative support for the proposal, but suggested that the government reserve its position until later negotiations, in order to join a consensus later 'as part of a wider trade-off.' Beckett and Straw also both firmly endorsed Cook's view that the government should reject the proposals on extending the legal personality of the EC pillar to the EU as a whole, and on merging the existing EU and EC treaties in order to create a consolidated text. The latter was an issue in which exposure to the realpolitik reasoning of the FCO caused a shift by Labour from the policy it had supported in opposition. Though Labour had supported treaty consolidation in opposition, Whitehall lawyers had warned that it would not only weaken the pillar structure but would require domestic ratification of the entire merged treaty.

Cook's minutes on 'horizontal' institutional issues similarly elicited a variety of responses from his government colleagues, including a number of critical interventions by the prime minister. There appeared to be general agreement across government to the position on QMV set out in Cook's minute of 19 May on QMV and codecision although the heritage secretary, Chris Smith, wrote stating his opposition to QMV for culture and for audio-visual aspects of industry provisions. Cook had suggested that there were only 'a small number of areas where the balance of advantage to the UK is such that we should actively pursue QMV' (i.e. research, regional policy, fraud and financial management, sexual equality, possibly some environmental measures) but that even in these areas, this should not be one of the government's 'top negotiating priorities.' In addition, he suggested that there were a number of 'relatively minor policy and institutional areas where there is no key UK interest at stake, but (where) there would be a genuine efficiency gain from QMV.' However, he suggested that 'for now' the UK 'should let others make the running in these areas' though if a consensus emerged in favour 'we might agree to some of them in the endgame.' On codecision, Blair intervened to endorse Cook's view that while Labour's stated position of supporting codecision where there was QMV was a 'good starting point' the government need not 'stick to it rigidly in areas where there are practical disadvantages in codecision.' Blair wrote 'to register that the UK should not stick rigidly to applying codecision to all areas covered by QMV, particularly in the social field.' Cook had suggested exceptions to this principle include some environmental measures (art. 130s.2 relating to planning, water supply and land use) and most areas of the CAP (both Cunningham, as agriculture minister, and Dewar responded to register their opposition to any codecision in agriculture). The exceptions outlined by Cook were areas where it was felt that EP codecision might increase costs (to the EC budget and/or business and industry). On particular treaty articles where QMV extension and codecision was being proposed, Cook recommended opposition to both in relation to freedom of movement (art. 8a) and social security for EC migrant workers (art. 51) but support for QMV extension while opposing codecision (given the cost implications) for structural and cohesion fund framework programmes.

Blair also intervened in response to Cook's minute on the ECJ on 19 May, expressing concern over the idea of an individual right of access to the ECJ. This seemed to result in the proposal being dropped by the government. A later minute from Cook on QMV reweighting and Commission reform on 28 May, received a response from Blair's close political ally, the minister without portfolio, Peter Mandelson, suggesting a tougher line against granting the EP a right of approval over the Commission president and giving the president the power to reshuffle the Commission.

Cook's minute on CFSP of 19 May did not meet with any objections from ministerial colleagues. Indeed, it was notable that Cook's emphasis on the need to retain unanimity in CFSP was strongly supported by Straw, who suggested that any other line would undermine the broadly similar line being taken in relation to the third pillar. The defence secretary, George Robertson, was also demanding a hard line on this issue. While recommending opposition to the Franco-German proposal for the European Council to define CFSP common strategies by unanimity, with subsequent decisions to be taken by QMV,[8] Cook did suggest that the government 'consider if necessary endgame agreement to extend QMV for implementation decisions in tightly controlled circumstances, provided that a national safeguard is included' (as provided by the presidency proposal to allow member states to veto decisions for stated reasons of national interest). Similarly, Cook recommended that the government 'question other member states on the benefits of constructive abstention, but consider endgame agreement to a mechanism which does not damage UK interests' (Robertson agreed that this was a reasonable approach). On practical proposals to improve CFSP machinery, Cook advocated UK support for the proposal for a planning and analysis capacity and 'for a low profile senior official' based in the Council secretariat to act as a CFSP representative (while opposing combining this with the role of Council secretary-general). Straw's response to Cook's CFSP minute also stated strong agreement with Cook's opposition to a role for the Commission in a new CFSP troika, and with his suggestion that in relation to CFSP funding, there should be a solution that gave the Council, rather than the EP, a final say in CFSP expenditure decisions, and did not preclude national funding. Again, Straw noted a 'read-across' with the JHA pillar and drew a parallel to the similar positions being pursued by him in relation to it. However, the position on CFSP expenditure highlighted another policy shift that Labour had made from opposition to government. In opposition, Labour had supported the abolition of distinctions within EU expenditure and full EP scrutiny of all areas (Labour Party 1995: 12, Blair 1995). This position may well have been adopted in opposition through the influence of the EP representatives within the LWG (who perhaps gave the party leadership the impression that there was widespread support for it across the member states) but quietly dropped once Labour was in government both because it realised that no such consensus existed amongst the member states and through exposure to the FCO's cost-based caution towards increasing the EP's powers. Moreover, the policy had been adopted in opposition as a means of giving the EP full scrutiny over CAP spending and with the aim of providing extra leverage to reduce CAP spending. However, FCO officials had argued that giving the EP leverage over CAP spending would more likely lead to increases rather than decreases in spending.

Both Cook's joint minute with Straw on JHA and with Robertson on defence received no objection from other ministers. The joint minute on defence stressed robust opposition to the Franco-German EU/WEU merger proposals and to an EU defence role. Indeed, it was noted that the neutral states and Denmark supported the UK here and would 'not compromise on this if we do not.' In a letter of 4 June, Robertson suggested that the government also reject moves towards a common armaments policy. This was a line subsequently taken into the final negotiations. The joint minute did however suggest that the UK position should not 'simply be negative' and that the government 'be prepared to negotiate flexibly and imaginatively on second order issues, as long as our fundamental interests are protected.' This would involve, for example, closer co-operation between the EU and WEU.

The joint minute on JHA outlined the government's priorities at the IGC, as to achieve 'nothing less than total legal security for our frontiers', retention of national control (i.e. a right to veto) over all JHA policies and a right to participate 'at our own discretion, but not be obliged to do so in EU co-operation on immigration, asylum and visa issues including through whatever arrangements are made for the incorporation of Schengen.' Cook and Straw explained that they could not as yet recommend an eventual bottom line (indicating a lack of confidence in their proposals being accepted by the other governments), but that they would seek to persuade their European partners to accept a package involving the following elements: 1) explicit recognition of the UK and Ireland's legal right to maintain frontier controls (thus establishing two valid common travel areas in the EU); 2) freedom of movement issues: i.e. asylum, immigration and visa policies to be dealt with under a new intergovernmental pillar (pillar 3b) 'in which there would be heavy use of EC institutions and procedures including QMV, but falling short of full communitisation; 3) the new pillar to operate on the basis of flexibility, so that the UK and Ireland (and possibly also Denmark) would not be bound by its provisions but could choose to opt into individual aspects of co-operation as of right (though it was suggested that the UK would rarely want to exercise this right); 4) co-operation on other issues, such as police and judicial co-operation to remain in the existing intergovernmental third pillar, though with a greater role for the EC institutions, e.g. ECJ jurisdiction on disputes between member states, and possibly shared Commission initiative and EP consultation, but not QMV (though provision for 'constructive abstention' was a possibility); 5) provision for Schengen *acquis* incorporation with the relevant elements of Schengen assigned either to the new freedom of movement pillar or to the remaining third pillar, depending on their subject matter.

The minute dealing with subsidiary institutional issues was circulated by Henderson and covered transparency (the line on this had also been set out in a minute from Cook on 16 May), national parliaments, various EP matters, subsidiarity, the Economic and Social committee and the Committee of the Regions. On transparency, he advocated support for IGC proposals providing for a treaty commitment to open decision-making (though the UK would also support a balancing reference to confidentiality, as also supported by France and Germany), for a new right of public access to documents and for publication of all Council votes and minuted statements whenever it acted in a legislative capacity. On national parliaments, Henderson proposed support both for a six week notice period before Council decisions on legislative proposals and for the French proposal on enhancing the role of COSAC. On EP matters, he recommended support for an EP right of assent over the choice of Commission president (though the UK would not press this in the face of clear opposition of others). Henderson also recommended support for proposals on codecision simplification, though the government would not support the proposal for abolition of third reading as this 'would unhelpfully limit the scope to find a mutually acceptable compromise' (opposition to this was shared by a number of member states).[9] In relation to subsidiarity, Henderson proposed support for a draft IGC protocol to incorporate some of the Edinburgh guidelines into the treaty. However, the government would seek further improvements to make the application of the subsidiarity principle more rigorous. Henderson also recommended UK support for proposals to broaden the scope of areas requiring consultation by the Economic and Social Committee (provided that a consensus emerged on which areas should be included) and by the Committee of the Regions (where there was consensus). In addition, support was recommended for various measures to improve the status of the Committee of the Regions, including giving it its own rules of procedure, separate administrative structure and making its membership incompatible with that of the EP.

Many of the more significant IGC policy areas requiring the appropriate cabinet minister to take a lead related to economic policy and provided the new chancellor, Gordon Brown, with an opportunity to shape the direction of policy. For example, Brown issued a minute on financial management and anti-fraud proposals on 9 May, subsequently tabled at the IGC. These proposals were intended to oblige member states to co-operate with the Commission to ensure sound financial management of EC funds and to repay mismanaged funds. Brown had also intervened in relation to the joint minute from Beckett and Blunkett setting out the government line on employment and social affairs. He opposed employment incentive measures[10] and measures on social exclusion, though in relation to the former, (E) DOP subsequently agreed that treaty language on incentive measures would be acceptable if finance was from 'within existing financial envelopes.' As regards other policy areas, the agriculture minister, Jack Cunningham, set out the government lines on quota hopping and on animal welfare in correspondence on 14 May, and this was subsequently agreed within the government, resulting in the UK making an IGC proposal to ensure that animals were classed as 'sentient beings.'

The IGC Negotiations

By early June, the detailed government line on most IGC issues appeared to have been settled. However, in relation to the two most difficult issues, JHA communitisation and flexibility, there still appeared to be some room for modification, due to the difficulties in reaching a compromise and the technical complexities of the negotiation. As the joint Cook-Straw minute on JHA in May had indicated, a bottom line had yet to be decided on this issue. In relation to the most difficult 'horizontal' IGC issue, flexibility, a minute detailing the government's approach was not issued until 9 June. By this point, the government was now conceding that it would not be able to prevent flexibility from appearing in the first pillar altogether. It now seemed clear that a flexibility provision would apply in all three pillars. Thus the government's strategy would be to 'ensure that the scope of any clause and the conditions imposed on it make it as toothless as possible.'

These agreed lines were carried by the government's representatives in the IGC negotiations, which now developed a new intensity following the 'unblocking' of the political situation in the UK and the entry into the negotiations of a UK government that was willing to negotiate constructively (McDonagh 1998: 183-187, Dinan 1999: 178, Laffan 1997b: 30). These negotiations took place at prime ministerial/head of government level, notably at the special European Council in Noordwijk on 23 May and at the Amsterdam summit itself, at foreign minister level and at working-group (IGC representative) level. The less contentious issues were generally resolved at working-group level, with more difficult issues passed on to foreign ministers to attempt to resolve. Both these forums were used to sound out member states on possible areas of compromise in difficult areas, although on the most difficult issues such as flexibility, JHA, defence, extension of QMV and institutional reform (e.g. Commission size and vote reweighting) it was left to the heads of government to thrash out the final compromise package. McDonagh describes the IGC representatives group as the 'core forum in which shape would be given to the emerging package' (1998: 185). Although Henderson was now the official IGC representative, the spadework continued to be undertaken by the UK team of negotiators led by Wall. While the latter paid particular attention to discussions with officials from the Dutch presidency and other member states, Henderson would concentrate on arguing the UK's case and negotiating with his ministerial counterparts in the other member states, developing bilateral contacts and making set-piece statements in the representatives group. Comprehensive reports were provided to Cook on all levels of meetings and on the state of play in the negotiations.

An informal IGC representatives meeting was held at Houthem in the Netherlands on 16-17 May, at which the presidency made available documents setting out its view of the state of play in relation to virtually all of the IGC package (apart from sensitive institutional questions which would be held back until the final endgame) (McDonagh 1998: 185). At this meeting, the UK positions on JHA, CFSP/defence and flexibility were reiterated. However, on JHA, the UK delegation was informed that prevention of JHA communitisation was not feasible.

Moreover, de Bruijn suggested to Wall that the line being taken by Henderson on communitisation was harder than that taken by Blair with Kok. This view was rubbished when discussed within the UK delegation. Identifying this as the most difficult issue to resolve, Wall suggested to Cook that the UK should not budge from its position, though it should not destroy its room for manoeuvre by making a public statement to that effect. The UK was however displaying some openness towards Schengen incorporation. Henderson suggested that the UK would be open to discussion of this provided that the JHA was not communitised. As with JHA, the UK was not budging in its opposition to moves on a EU defence role. The view within the UK negotiating team was that its position on defence was being recognised by the Dutch Europe minister, Patijn, but not yet by the Dutch foreign minister (and Patijn's boss) van Mierlo. Indeed, Patijn suggested that Kok would have no appetite for pressing the EU/WEU merger proposal against UK and other opposition, and that those who wanted merger should rein in their ambitions. This was described as provoking 'a predictable harrumphing reaction from Hoyer (Germany) and Barnier (France).' The UK would therefore seek to play on Patijn's more sympathetic view and the apparent divergence between his views and those of his more senior colleague. Henderson did express cautious government support for extending Commission competence on external economic relations, which was strongly supported by Ireland, Finland and Belgium but strongly opposed by France. Some member states were linking this issue with CFSP, and arguing that if the French wanted progress on CFSP (where they had complained about the inadequacy of the presidency text) then they should be more forthcoming on external relations. Discussion also took place at the meeting on the issue of EU legal personality, with the UK, Ireland and Denmark all opposing the idea. However, a compromise more acceptable to the UK had been proposed, which would give the EU the legal capacity necessary for the exercise of its functions. Wall recommended that the government examine the proposal carefully, though he suggested that it would be preferable to seek to kill the whole idea off altogether.

The informal meeting at Houthem was followed swiftly by a conclave of foreign ministers on 20 May, itself held to prepare for the special European Council on the 23 May. It also constituted Cook's first formal IGC meeting (McDonagh 1998: 186). The meeting saw detailed discussion of draft CFSP provisions, with Cook appearing to join the developing consensus that constructive abstention was the best way forward in order to improve decision-making. This would provide the basis of a compromise package, with the UK government also supporting the proposal for common strategies (to be adopted by unanimity) with QMV for implementing measures and involving a national safeguard clause, allowing member states to veto decisions for stated reasons of national interest. But there continued to be two distinct and divergent views on EU/WEU merger (i.e. for and against). Nevertheless, Wall had suggested following the Houthem meeting that a compromise was possible, with the French possibly willing to move towards the UK position on EU/WEU relations provided that the UK helped the French in their objective of creating a new high representative for CFSP.

The Noordwijk European Council saw continued discussions on JHA communitisation. The occasion also marked Blair's debut on the European summit stage. The 'good atmospherics' of this meeting contributed to a widespread understanding of the UK position on frontier-controls. The backing of the Irish and Danes for the UK position had been useful here. Nevertheless, it was noted that there was no support when the Danish prime minister, Rasmussen, argued that all JHA issues should remain intergovernmental. Furthermore, Patijn had informed Wall that he was under instruction from the Dutch prime minister, Kok, to accommodate the UK on border controls, but under the proposed communitised structure, not the 'pillar 3b' proposed by the UK. Given the already existing common-travel area between the UK and Ireland, any special status applying to the UK would also apply to Ireland. However, the Irish prime minister, John Bruton was concerned that both the UK and Ireland should not be excluded from later joining in with arrangements adopted by the rest of the member states. Reference was made within the UK delegation to an informal quadrilateral involving Blair, Kok, Bruton and Rasmussen, indicating that the four leaders were working closely together within the IGC discussion. The Irish and Danish leaders were certainly working closely with the UK in seeking to resist the JHA communitisation proposals. In this sense, Kok was the weakest link in this 'quadrilateral.' His continuing sympathy for third pillar communitisation was described as the 'main stumbling block' in this area. The Noordwijk meeting was also notable for a tirade by the Luxembourg prime minister, Junker, against the ECJ, accusing it of megalomania in misusing its role and powers to extend its authority and scope. Both Blair and Rasmussen associated themselves with the broad thrust of Junker's remarks on the ECJ, and Rasmussen used them in his arguments against JHA communitisation. Kohl also sympathised with Junker's views on the ECJ, but suggested that this was not a subject for the IGC to discuss, a sentiment with which Chirac agreed.

Noordwijk also saw continuing discussion of Commission reform. This was focused around Kohl's proposal to set a maximum number of Commissioners of twenty, to be reviewed upon enlargement. This would allow the status quo to remain until enlargement, and would possibly be linked to a commitment by the large states to give up their second Commissioner following the first wave of enlargement, thus allowing a review to be delayed until the number of member states exceeded twenty. Wall suggested the UK support this proposal, but only in return for assurances that the UK would always hold a senior portfolio. There was also a large consensus on the need to enhance the role of the Commission president, though there was no detailed agreement on this. Wall suggested that the UK should continue to reject bestowing on the president the decisive say over the appointment of Commissioners and that the language used at Noordwijk (i.e. member states nominating Commissioners in consultation with the president) was the most the UK could accept. Kok had outlined a four stage procedure in relation to the appointment of the Commission and the president: first the European Council would propose a candidate, secondly the EP would approve the nomination, then the member states in consultation with the president would agree on nominees for the Commission which would finally be subject to a vote of approval by the EP.

McDonagh writes that after Noordwijk, the notion that a decision would be taken which would discontinue the right of every member state to nominate a Commissioner was in 'terminal decline' (1998: 185). While this appeared to be a victory for the smaller states, there was divergence on the linked question of vote reweighting, reflecting the cleavage between the larger and smaller states (Moravcsik and Nicolaidis 1998: 18). Blair, Kohl and the Spanish prime minister, Aznar, all spoke in favour of a link between vote reweighting and Commission size. Conversely, this view was rejected by Chirac who stressed the link between reweighting and QMV extension. Indeed, while there appeared to be agreement at Noordwijk on the need for greater use of QMV in the light of enlargement, no such consensus existed on the system of voting. While the larger states appeared to prefer a simple reweighting, many of the smaller states backed a proposal for a double majority system, involving a population criteria. Dehaene (of Belgium), Rasmussen (of Denmark) Junker (of Luxembourg), Klima (of Austria) and Guterres (of Portugal) all spoke in favour of this. However, the Greeks and Finns both opposed reweighting altogether. The link between QMV and codecision extension was also discussed at Noordwijk. Despite his caution on codecision for some areas, Blair also spoke in favour of extending codecision to areas where QMV applied, agreeing with Dehaene, Junker and Simitis (of Greece) on this. In a similar vein, in spite of the UK opposition to abolition of third reading, Blair stressed that if codecision was to be extended then the procedure needed to be simplified first. He won support from Rasmussen on this.

Following on from these discussions, the Dutch presidency produced new treaty texts on 1 June. According to FCO officials, these had made a 'handful of minor moves' in the UK direction but the main problems remained as before. These included continued references to EU/WEU merger, flexibility in all three pillars and JHA communitisation. The text on JHA provided for communitisation of immigration and asylum policy and incorporation of Schengen for thirteen of the member states, but with the 'clearest reference yet to the right of the UK and Ireland to maintain their frontier controls and helpful language on separation of the Schengen *acquis* from the *acquis communautaire*.' The text on flexibility had proposed two different alternatives for its scope in pillar one. The first would leave the scope open and possibly require unanimity to trigger enhanced co-operation. The second would limit the scope of flexibility to about a dozen areas but probably come with a QMV trigger. The presidency text also included proposals on QMV extension, which were largely acceptable for the UK 'with one or two exceptions' and on QMV reweighting which did 'not go quite as far' as the UK would like. In addition, FCO officials referred to proposals on the powers of the Commission president as 'unwelcome' and also to the 'bad texts' which remained on EU legal personality, ECJ justiciability over human rights in the second and third pillars, and codification of the treaties. Greater satisfaction was expressed in relation to the new text on employment, which went 'some way' to meeting UK concerns on flexible labour markets. Changes on subsidiarity, transparency, health and consumer protection and on fraud and financial management (based on the UK proposal) were also described as helpful.

The new presidency texts were produced in time for the foreign ministers meeting of 2-3 June. Unlike previous ministerial meetings, the meeting was intended to be a detailed drafting session with the presidency pressing for agreement on at least some of the issues before Amsterdam. Cook's officials suggested that he use the meeting to flag up UK concerns on awkward 'second order' issues that the government wished to settle before Amsterdam, such as legal personality, treaty codification and justiciability of human rights. Cook would stress that the question of EU legal personality was not up for negotiation as the UK had 'fundamental objections,' viewing any provision allowing the EU to conclude international agreements in CFSP or JHA as having 'profound constitutional' repercussions' and being a 'wholly disproportionate response to a relatively minor difficulty in the workings of the intergovernmental pillars.' The UK would, however, give consideration to a proportionate solution of member states authorising the presidency to conclude agreements on their behalf. Similarly, Cook would make clear that the presidency proposal on treaty codification was 'quite unacceptable.' Although the UK would accept a consolidated treaty with no legal force, the presidency was proposing codification of the various treaties into one consolidated treaty text, which, according to FCO officials would represent a radical legal restructuring of the treaties, fatally undermining the pillar structure and also requiring a further IGC to conclude the work. On fundamental rights, Cook would express surprise that the draft text still proposed ECJ jurisdiction in all three pillars, as the UK government had thought an understanding had been reached that there should be no jurisdiction for CFSP at least.

The foreign ministers meeting also saw continuing discussions of the key issues of CFSP, flexibility and institutional reform. While the UK government was continuing to propose revisions to the presidency proposals on CFSP decision-making, it now appeared to be generally satisfied with the safeguards built into the presidency text, i.e. facilities for constructive abstention from decisions and the right to block QMV in implementing decisions for stated reasons of national interest. Cook would also give the UK's support to a presidency proposal for an inter-institutional agreement on financing. However, Cook would continue to oppose the proposal, supported by France and Italy, to combine the posts of CFSP high representative and Council secretary-general. It was the UK view that this was unfeasible given that both posts comprised full-time responsibilities. Cook would also continue to reiterate UK arguments on flexibility, stressing the need for legal uniformity and the negative signal that this would send on enlargement. But given that flexibility in the first pillar now appeared to be unavoidable, Cook would seek to ensure the conditions for it were extremely tight in order to minimise its potential use. These conditions would include a unanimity trigger and separation from EC law. Cook's officials suggested that if, as seemed likely, the other member states pursued the option of a tightly defined scope with a QMV trigger, then Cook should seek a requirement, at the very least, for a provision similar to that being touted in CFSP, whereby QMV could be over-ruled for stated reasons of national interest.

Discussion of institutional reform at the foreign ministers meeting focused on the issues of Commission size and the role of the president, Council vote reweighting, QMV extension and EP powers. Despite Wall's earlier expression of sympathy for Kohl's proposal to fix the Commission size at twenty, Cook's officials were now advising him to oppose this, as it would take pressure off the small states on the number of Commissioners and remove a key bargaining chip in achieving QMV reweighting. The FCO view was that a solution on Commission size had to be part of a deal on vote reweighting. The government would therefore oppose delaying until enlargement, but would be prepared to give up the second UK Commissioner provided that this was part of a deal on reweighting and that there was a 'real differentiation' between Commissioners of more and less populous member states. On reweighting itself, the UK would express concern at suggestions made at Noordwijk that it might be postponed until enlargement. The FCO viewed this as 'a poor outcome' and indicated a preference for the French reweighting model circulated at Noordwijk, rather than the presidency models put forward. The French model was seen as desirable by the FCO as it would restore the pre-Ioannina situation of two big states and one of the smaller ones together being able to block a decision. However, Cook's officials stressed that this point should not be made in the discussions. The government would argue in concert with the French and Spanish for a simple reweighting, rather than a double majority, and argue its necessity for reasons of greater transparency and democratic legitimacy. On QMV extension, Cook would signal UK agreement in relation to most of the areas suggested by the presidency, except for art. 8a (freedom of movement), art. 51 (social security), art. 128 (culture - where the heritage secretary had opposed) and aspects of art. 130s (environment taxation and choice of energy sources). In addition, Cook would support codecision for all areas proposed apart from art. 8a, art. 51, art. 130d (structural funds) and art. 130s. He would also reiterate the need for a simplified procedure if codecision were to be extended, pointing to the eighteen to twenty-four month average that it took to pass legislation. However, as signalled earlier, the UK would oppose the specific proposal to abolish third reading.

In relation to the appointment of the Commission, Cook would signal general UK assent for the four-stage procedure outlined by Kok at Noordwijk. But he would oppose giving the president the right of veto over member states' nominees, as implied by the reference in the presidency text to selection of the Commission by 'common accord' between the president and the member states. He would also oppose the proposed reference to the president giving 'political guidance' to the Commission, which FCO officials described as ascribing to the president a political leadership role 'inappropriate' for an 'unelected' official. However, the UK appeared to be battling against a general consensus in favour of these modifications to the Commission president's role.

The other main issues on the agenda for the foreign ministers to discuss were employment and environment (McDonagh 1998: 186). In relation to the former, the Germans were attempting to get the presidency to drop proposals for incentive measures. Although the language of the new presidency text on labour market flexibility was welcomed by the UK government, it would continue to support the Germans in resisting incentive measures. Indeed, Blair, Brown, Beckett and Blunkett were all agreed on opposing them. However, of greater concern to the UK and Germany on this issue were the French elections that coincided with the meeting. The elections would lead to a new socialist government in France, led by Lionel Jospin, which would look to re-open the employment issue and push for far more ambitious provisions. In relation to environment, the Nordic countries were pushing for the strengthening of art. 100a.4 allowing individual member states to apply higher environmental standards provided they were not a barrier to trade. FCO officials suggested sympathy for this approach provided that there were adequate safeguards to protect the single market. To this end, the UK was supporting the text put forward by the presidency but were not backing the Danes in their attempts to get this strengthened.

Discussion of these and other issues also continued at the IGC representatives meeting of 5-6 June. Following this meeting, there was a feeling within the UK negotiating team that there had been some movement in the UK direction on the 'second order' issues of legal personality, treaty codification and judiciability of fundamental rights. On the latter, there had been agreement that there would be no ECJ powers over fundamental rights in the second pillar and that the UK had 'secured language for the third pillar which would limit the ECJ role on fundamental rights to those areas of the third pillar where it has jurisdiction already.' On legal personality, where the UK had proposed an alternative text, most member states continued to support the presidency text, though it was reported that the French had 'proposed some useful dilution.' In relation to treaty codification, the UK had resisted attempts to strengthen the presidency text and actually 'succeeded in getting it watered down.' In addition to this, the UK had tabled a text on external economic relations, which was described 'as a wrecking amendment' leading to 'the satisfactory result (to the UK delegation) of a French alternative' leaving the substance of (the proposed text) largely as it was but providing for agreement by unanimity on a fast track procedure for negotiations on services within the WTO. There had also been discussion of codecision simplification, with France and the UK both arguing hard for the retention of third reading to little avail. This led Wall to suggest that if the French continued to fight against, then the UK should support them, but that otherwise the UK should drop the argument as it would 'already have more issues to fight on than anyone else.'

While discussions continued in the representatives groups, and various other working-groups established by the presidency to thrash out the treaty texts, it was clear that the big issues, i.e. JHA, defence, flexibility, would not be settled until the Amsterdam summit itself. Jospin's victory in the French legislative elections would also raise the stakes for Amsterdam and, as feared by the Labour government, re-open the issue of employment just when it was beginning to indicate satisfaction with the text so far agreed (Moravcsik and Nicolaidis 1998: 23-24). Indeed, many of the government's erstwhile allies in PES-led governments would be seeking to claw back concessions that they had made to the UK and the centre-right governments of Germany and Spain in watering down the employment text. Wall recommended that the UK government seek to prevent the issue from being opened up again at working-group level as it would be 'countered by unacceptable alternatives' from the French representative, who since Jospin's victory, had been 'obliged to ask for more things which are unpalatable to us.'

By 9 June, Cook's officials were suggesting that near-agreement had already been reached on a number of key issues, including CFSP, environment, consumer protection, subsidiarity, transparency, fundamental rights and quality of legislation, and that though the UK had 'not won every point of detail', the outcome on these were 'consistent with the objectives set out in correspondence' and could be 'effectively presented as in the UK interest.' The line that Blair, Cook and the UK negotiating team would take in the final week of the IGC on the remaining key issues continued to be refined within the FCO. While the concerns of various government ministers on other non-key areas would be pursued as far as possible, the FCO stressed that it would 'be a matter of judgement' as to how far these could be pursued at the Amsterdam summit. A minute on the remaining issues would form the basis of discussion on the Amsterdam summit in cabinet on 12 June. For those issues yet to be resolved at the IGC, the government would continue to pursue the line set out in correspondence between ministers, modified to take account of particular concerns expressed by ministers in correspondence up to the Amsterdam summit. However, where problems remained at Amsterdam, it would be a matter for the prime minister's judgement as to how far they could continue to be pursued. It was suggested that Amsterdam was likely to focus on 'a limited number of key outstanding issues', most importantly, JHA, defence and flexibility, where the government would continue to pursue the priorities already outlined, though on JHA it was acknowledged that the structure of the text and its exact contents were likely to be 'fluid' right up until Amsterdam.

The other key issues for the UK that would await resolution at Amsterdam were identified within the FCO as institutional reform (most importantly Commission size, vote reweighting and QMV extension), legal personality, treaty codification, quota hopping and the various UK proposals on fraud, transparency and animal welfare. In relation to institutional reform, the UK government would now be prepared to cede its second Commissioner, in the context of enlargement 'but only as part of a package which gives substantially greater voting weight to large member states.' The UK would also continue to pursue the positions already outlined in relation to QMV and codecision extension, and on legal personality and treaty codification. Cook's officials reported that good progress was being made on UK proposals on 'fraud, transparency, and animal welfare' but that a 'further push' might be necessary at Amsterdam to achieve all of the government's objective on the first two of these. Bilateral contacts with the Commission on the quota-hopping issue were also continuing, and optimism was expressed that a 'satisfactory solution' would be achieved at Amsterdam.

Aside from the discussions within the various IGC representative and ministerial meetings, the government was also pursuing its IGC strategy through bilateral contacts with other member states, forming alliances with various member states on a range of issues. Most importantly, the government worked closely with the Irish and Danes in combating the proposals on JHA communitisation. The UK also worked closely with these countries, as well as Austria, Finland and Sweden in opposition to the proposals supported by the other member states on EU/WEU merger. Blair appeared to enjoy particularly good relations with the Irish, Danish and Dutch leaders. Hence the reference within the UK negotiating team to the informal 'quadrilateral' of Blair, Bruton, Kok and Rasmussen. Of all EU member states, the Danes were probably the closest to the UK in terms of their attitude to European co-operation. Not surprisingly therefore, Blair and Rasmussen had agreed to stick together on second and third pillar issues when they met in the margins of the Malmo PES congress in early June. While one of the themes of the UK negotiating strategy was to cultivate alliances with some of the smaller states who were wary of Franco-German domination of the EU, there were some issues on which the Labour government would form more formidable alliances with the larger states. Despite the co-operation it had previously enjoyed with the PES-led governments, the Labour government worked closely with the centre-right German government in seeking to dilute the proposals for an employment chapter (an effort also supported by the centre-right Spanish government). In addition, the UK government found common ground with the French on certain institutional reform issues such as Council vote reweighting, certain aspects of the EP's role and the role of national parliaments (e.g. in seeking to raise the profile of COSAC). Despite conflicting views on CFSP decision-making and defence, the UK and French were also united in fending off Italian and Spanish suggestions that EU members of the UN Security Council be obliged to consult other member states and uphold the interests of the EU within it. Nevertheless, it was from its relationship with the Dutch government that the Labour government appeared to profit the most. Labour had benefited greatly from its close relations with the PVDA government when in opposition. These good relations continued in government, with Blair meeting Kok within days of entering office. Of the PES parties, the PVDA had the closest ideological affinity with 'New Labour' and was the most sympathetic towards its stance on employment. However, it was rather paradoxical that the Dutch minister who appeared to be the most helpful towards the UK positions, Patijn, was a representative of the PVDA's Liberal coalition partners.

Cook and Henderson had a number of meetings with counterparts from other member states to explore possible common ground in the days leading up to Amsterdam. These included Cook's meeting with the Danish foreign minister, Helveg Peterson in London on 10 June and Henderson's meeting with his Spanish opposite number Ramon de Miguel in Madrid on 11 June. Blair also kept in contact with his counterparts, meeting some of his colleagues at the PES congress in Malmo and also keeping in touch with Kok by telephone. Cook's meeting with Peterson followed what the Danes described as a 'very favourable' meeting between Blair and Rasmussen in Malmo on 6 June where they reached agreement to stick together on pillars two and three. Cook used the meeting with Peterson to reiterate the UK position on flexibility, with which the Danes also agreed. Peterson echoed Cook's point on not giving way on the argument for a unanimity trigger. There was also support on this from Finland and Sweden. However, Peterson was also attracted to the suggestion put forward by one of the UK negotiators, that a compromise could be put forward mirroring the national interest clause on flexibility. Cook and Peterson accordingly agreed that they should stick together on unanimity here 'but have the emergency brake (i.e. national interest clause) in our back pocket as a fall back.' Peterson also agreed with Cook on the need to prevent

QMV for art. 51 (social security for migrant workers). However, there was recognition that the UK would not support the Danes on strengthening the environmental guarantee in relation to single market measures. Blair had expressed concerns to Rasmussen at Malmo that a strengthened art. 100a.4 would be used for protectionist purposes, especially by the French.

Cook's discussions with Peterson reflected the link being made by the UK between making concessions on some issues and getting the right result in its priority areas. The government appeared to have already come to terms with flexibility in the first pillar provided that it could be tightly circumscribed, and also now viewed the emergency brake clause as an acceptable alternative to unanimity. Cook indicated to Peterson that the UK was now prepared to also consider a deal on JHA communitisation provided that the right result was achieved on EU/WEU merger. This was a signal that the UK's top priority was to avoid EU/WEU merger and that the government would be willing to make concessions on JHA communitisation to achieve this. Indeed, Blair had informed Kok on the 9 June that the UK was ready to consider whether it could accept a communitised free movement chapter if both the rest of the JHA text and the wider IGC package (notably EU/WEU) were satisfactory. This was a significant shift in the UK position on this key issue. There appeared to be an understanding between the UK and the Danes that they would forewarn each other of any significant shift in position. UK officials accordingly conveyed the UK's conditions for accepting some communitisation. These conditions also met many of the Danish concerns, but Peterson indicated that the Danes would continue to resist communitisation and, if isolated (as the UK shift implied), would seek an opt-out based on the derogations they had negotiated from the TEU at Edinburgh in 1992.

The meeting between Henderson and de Miguel on 11 June provided an indicator of attempts (which would later bear greater fruit) to develop close relations between the UK and Spain as a counterpoint to Franco-German domination. Indeed, de Miguel emphasised the importance of close UK-Spanish links as a counterbalance to the Franco-German-Benelux core. More specifically, the Spanish argued that the two countries should stick together on institutional issues, agreeing with the UK that if the larger states were to give up their second Commissioner then some differentiation in favour of the larger states was required (de Miguel referred to the rather dubious precedent of the UK and Spain sticking together at Ioannina). The Spaniards wanted a result on reweighting that would allow them to block a decision in alliance with one other large state and one small state. This coincided with the French and UK position, though was complicated by the fact that Spain had two votes less than the other large states (ideally the Spanish wanted the same number of votes). The centre-right Spanish government also shared German opposition to the proposal for an employment chapter. De Miguel and Henderson agreed that as a bottom line 'incentive measures' should be tightly constrained. Henderson and de Miguel also agreed on the need to maintain unanimity in those areas of the social chapter where it continued to apply. This confirmed the shift made by the Labour party in the run-up to the election away from its earlier support for QMV extension in social policy. However, the Labour government appeared to be more progressive than the Spanish in other areas of possible QMV extension. De Miguel stated strong opposition to extension in industrial, regional and environmental policy. Indeed, de Miguel was reported to have exclaimed 'you're joking' at suggestions that QMV be extended to industrial policy. But the roles were reversed on the sensitive defence issues, with de Miguel restating Spanish support for EU/WEU merger. Nevertheless, the UK government did take encouragement from de Miguel's hints that Spain would not insist on this to the death. There was similar encouragement on flexibility when, in response to Henderson's suggestion of a national interest/emergency brake clause to accompany a QMV trigger, there were suggestions that the Spanish would not be opposed, though they doubted that it could ever be used in practice. Henderson had suggested that, despite its continuing distaste for the presidency text on flexibility, the UK could go along with it, provided that it included such a clause and that the list of excluded areas was extended to cover taxation and EMU.

The two issues that caused particular difficulties for UK-Spanish relations were 'quota hopping' and the status of Gibraltar. De Miguel had described elements of the Commission's draft declaration on quota hopping as 'impossible.' Discussions would continue on this. The Gibraltar question had implications for two IGC issues: the treaty simplification exercise and Schengen. While opposing treaty consolidation, the UK supported a simplification exercise involving a reordering of treaty articles and deletion of obsolete ones. However, one proposal within this exercise was to bring the 1976 EC act on EP elections into the treaty. This would include an annex excluding Gibraltar from its provisions. Though it would not alter the situation, bringing the act into the treaty would have the politically awkward effect of highlighting Gibraltar's status. Although both the UK and Spain had placed a reserve on this proposal, the Spanish had indicated that they would not hold out against this. Similarly, FCO advice was that Blair should not argue the point at Amsterdam. Incorporation of Schengen created difficulties in relation to Gibraltar because the UK wanted to retain the right to opt-in at a future date. This would similarly bring to the fore difficulties related to the Spanish-Gibraltar border and disputes over sovereignty. The Spanish were therefore likely to want to place conditions on any future UK participation. Despite this, de Miguel expressed some sympathy with Henderson's restatement of the UK need to retain national control over immigration and asylum policy and over border controls in the context of Schengen incorporation. Indeed, de Miguel stressed that it was not the Spanish who were pushing for Schengen incorporation and that they would prefer the status quo to the wrong solution. These sympathetic remarks may have had something to do with the Spaniards' own wariness on JHA issues. They had particular concerns over asylum policy derived from an anxiety to ensure that suspected Basque terrorists could not seek asylum in other EU countries. Indeed, Spain had tabled a proposal at the IGC aimed at preventing a citizen from one member state from claiming political asylum in another (McDonagh 1998: 179, Dehousse 1999: 54-55).

Contacts at the highest level between the key member states continued in the last few days before the Amsterdam summit. The Dutch prime minister, Kok, visited Kohl in Bonn on the 11 June to discuss a number of issues before the presidency finalised a draft text ready for circulation the next day. Jospin's sudden emergence as a key player within the negotiations had upset calculations in a number of member states, and, as predicted, breathed new life into the discussions on employment. This meant that employment would join a list of issues, also comprising JHA, defence, flexibility and institutions, on which the presidency would aim to focus discussion at the summit (McDonagh 1998: 189). The Dutch expressed the hope that member states would not re-open other issues or make new proposals. However, disagreement between Jospin and Kohl on the employment issue resulted in failure to agree a joint position at the Franco-German summit at Poitiers on 13 June, as was the norm between the two countries at previous IGCs, adding a degree of uncertainty to the final summit outcome (Duff 1997b: 64, Fella 1999: 31, *The Observer* 15 June 1997). Nevertheless, reports from UK officials were indicating some optimism that an outcome satisfactory to the UK government could be achieved. A report on Kohl's approach to the Amsterdam summit suggested that if things went 'to the wire' then Kohl was 'likely to give ground on EU/WEU merger' and might 'decide that a QMV trigger for flexibility is not for next week.' Moreover, it was noted that Kohl was 'no master of detail' and that his officials 'always worry about what he will give away when they are absent.' Furthermore, the report noted that Kohl was 'most susceptible to political argument presented in a spirit of mutual trust and mutual endeavour' and suggested that this was 'the best way to persuade him that our move on JHA requires movement on his part.' This was a reference to Blair's indication to Kok that the UK would be willing to accept some JHA communitisation subject to certain conditions and as part of a wider compromise package. Indeed, in discussions with UK diplomats, German officials would indicate that the UK conditions for communitisation were now acceptable to the German government. Prospects for an outcome acceptable to the UK on flexibility and on defence were also improving. The provisions on first pillar flexibility in the presidency text of 12 June had been tightly circumscribed as a result of UK pressure. Reports from Denmark indicated that these conditions were so strong that the Danes were now also likely to accept. Moreover, both the Danes and the Swedes would continue to support the UK on the need for a unanimity trigger. These countries would also continue to support the UK position on defence. In the face of the continued opposition of these and other countries, German officials indicated that the German government was now willing to compromise on EU/WEU merger, instead accepting strengthened treaty language on closer EU/WEU relations.

The Amsterdam Summit and the Final Treaty

In order to prevent the Franco-German dispute over employment and the wider question of European economic governance from overshadowing the Amsterdam summit, a special four hour meeting of EU finance ministers was held just prior to the commencement of the summit proper on 16 June, in order to reach a deal on a package of employment measures to placate the French (McDonagh 1998: 188). Much of this did not require treaty change, relying on an increase in lending by the European Investment Bank for infrastructure investment and related employment creation projects. This represented a face-saving exercise for Jospin, as in relation to the treaty itself, Blair and Kohl combined to ward off the French proposals for an interventionist employment chapter (Moravcsik and Nicolaidis 1998: 24, Dehousse 1999: 36-37). The member states did agree to an employment chapter on the first day of the summit, but it reflected the determination of the UK and German governments among others to ensure that it emphasised co-operation in relation to national policies and did not initiate new pan-European expenditure. Indeed, the UK government successfully ensured a treaty emphasis on deregulation and the adaptability of the labour market (Anderson and Mann 1997: 113-115, Newman 1997: 31-32). Satisfaction was expressed among the UK negotiators that they had 'shifted the direction towards labour market flexibility, employability, training and skills for life.' However, it was suggested that 'Jospin might have got further with his government-must-create-jobs approach had it not been for the linkage with EMU and the determination of governments to avoid higher deficits.'

The Labour government was able to claim even greater satisfaction in relation to the trickier issues of JHA communitisation, flexibility and defence. If the government's primary objectives at Amsterdam were to prevent the development of an EU defence role and secure a legal guarantee for the retention of UK frontier-controls, then the summit outcome could certainly be portrayed as a mission accomplished for the UK negotiators (Anderson and Mann 1997: 115, Young, JW 2000: 179). The agreement of flexibility provisions in the first pillar that were extremely tightly constrained could be portrayed in a similar light. But these outcomes represented the achievement of the government's 'bottom line' on these issues. In reality, the Labour government had, in the week or so leading up to Amsterdam, been forced to concede on two of the three key strategic objectives identified by the party leadership in opposition in the first half of 1997 and adopted within government in its first month in office, i.e. the prevention of JHA communitisation and of provision for flexibility in the first pillar. Butler's prediction that the French and Germans could be persuaded to drop flexibility in the first pillar if the British were constructive in other areas was not borne out (LP Butler, 13 January 1997). Nevertheless, the new treaty title on 'freedom, security and justice', which amounted to a partial communitisation of JHA policies (in immigration and asylum) and provided for the incorporation of the Schengen acquis, would apply to only thirteen of the member states, excluding the UK and the Irish Republic. Both the UK and Ireland succeeded in their objective of ensuring that they could opt-in to any measure adopted under this title. Furthermore, the Danes negotiated a protocol ensuring that any new measures adopted under the Schengen arrangements would not apply to them (Moravcsik and Nicolaidis 1998: 29, Duff 1997b: 27-32). The Germans had turned in a remarkable performance in relation to the newly communitised 'area of freedom, security and justice.' Despite their earlier apparent enthusiasm for it, the Germans insisted on a five year transitional period (rather than the three year period proposed by the presidency) during which unanimity would apply and legislative initiative would be shared between the member states and the Commission. After five years, there would be a move to exclusive Commission initiative. There would also be a possible move to QMV decision-making, but only if the member states agreed by unanimity to do so. The Germans had been anxious to ensure that the member states kept a handle on this decision. This compromise had been advanced by the German government in order to meet demands made by its own interior ministry and its Länder (regional state) governments. Indeed, it appeared that the German interior ministry would have preferred it if the UK had continued to block communitisation. In another move to appease the Länder governments, the Germans also insisted on member states having control of access to health care, social security payments and work for migrants. Kohl would later explain to the German parliament that the German government had insisted on unanimity for immigration and asylum to protect Germany's interests as the EU country with the most asylum applicants (though this had been the original reasoning for German support for communitised policies) and because Germany could not accept migrant workers making claims on its welfare system (Dinan 1999: 181, Dehousse 1999: 30-31).

There had also been a fair degree of wrangling to ensure that the UK delegation was satisfied that it had negotiated a watertight exemption from the new title and its objective of a border-free area. Where the presidency draft had conceded whatever national control 'necessary for the purpose of monitoring immigration' the UK delegation had inserted the phrase 'as it may consider' before 'necessary.' This ensured that responsibility for interpreting the degree of domestic control deemed necessary would rest with the UK authorities (Fella 1999: 37). One of the UK negotiators had described the texts incorporating the Schengen agreements into the treaty as a 'dog's breakfast' but suggested that the changes the UK had secured would prevent the Schengen states from damaging its interests. Before incorporation could proceed, examination of the Schengen acquis would take place in order to ascertain which aspects could be incorporated in the new 'freedom, security, justice' treaty title in the first pillar, and which would have to go into what remained of the third pillar. Provisions on police and judicial co-operation in criminal matters were not communitised and remained in the old JHA pillar. However, there was agreement at Amsterdam on measures to effect closer co-operation between judicial authorities and police forces in the JHA pillar, particularly through Europol, which gained an operational capacity. There was also agreement on an enhanced role for the ECJ here, allowing it to make preliminary rulings on the validity and interpretation of various measures adopted under the JHA. However, this would be subject to individual declarations from member states, stating that they were willing to accept ECJ jurisdiction (satisfying the UK government which sought to limit ECJ jurisdiction). The treaty also stipulated that the ECJ would have no jurisdiction in relation to police/law enforcement operations of member states and the general maintenance of law and order and internal security (Barrett 1997: 123-127).

In a similar vein to JHA, the UK government had refined its negotiating position in relation to first pillar flexibility in the fortnight leading up to Amsterdam. When it became clear that it was not going to be able to dissuade the French and Germans from pursuing the proposal, the Labour government set about ensuring that the provisions were as toothless as possible. This it succeeded in doing by insisting on a number of conditions and a swathe of policy exemptions that would tightly circumscribe the possibility of co-operation being pursued under the clause. Moreover, while the UK government did not persuade enough of its partners of the need for a unanimity requirement to trigger flexibility, it did win the agreement of the other member states to the national interest/emergency brake clause that it had been touting the previous week, despite French and German opposition (Gillespie 1997: 52). Indeed, the UK had strong support from Greece, Denmark, Sweden, Ireland and to a lesser extent Spain and Portugal on this (Moravcsik and Nicolaidis 1998: 20). This had the equivalent effect of maintaining a national veto over the use of the flexibility clause, and led some observers to later reflect that the treaty for the first time had given formal recognition to a form of the Luxembourg compromise (Dinan 1999: 179, Moravcsik and Nicolaidis 1998: 20, 1999: 80).

The prevention of moves to establish a European defence through the merger of the EU and WEU represented the clearest success for the Labour government. But a successful outcome on this issue was always more likely given the solid support the UK had on this issue, for different reasons, from Denmark and the neutral states. The deal that emerged on defence was based on a joint Swedish-Finnish initiative, although it also echoed possible compromises that had been mooted by the FCO in internal government correspondence. It provided for closer institutional relations between the EU and WEU, incorporating the Petersberg humanitarian, rescue and peacekeeping tasks into the treaty (Moravcsik and Nicolaidis 1998: 27). But the treaty also opened up the possibility of integration of the WEU into the EU should all member states at some point in the future agree. Thus the aims and objectives of the CFSP would include 'the progressive framing of a common defence policy...which might lead to a common defence, should the European Council so decide.' This gave all member states an effective veto on future merger (McDonagh 1998: 192, Dinan 1999: 179). Nevertheless, the treaty also reflected the UK government line in stressing that European security arrangements had to be compatible with NATO obligations and that NATO remained the basis of common European defence.

The UK government was also able to declare satisfaction with the general outcome on CFSP, with one UK negotiator suggesting that the extension of QMV was 'more theoretical than real.' The compromise on CFSP decision-making had been sign-posted well ahead of Amsterdam, providing for common strategies to be agreed by unanimity and for implementing decisions within these and within other policy decisions (e.g. common positions, joint actions) to be decided by QMV, but with an emergency brake/national interest clause (which would oblige the Council to refer an issue to the European Council to decide by unanimity). Nevertheless, some observers pointed to ambiguities relating to the precise definition of this categorisation of CFSP acts (Moravcsik and Nicolaidis 1998: 25). A satisfactory compromise was also reached at Amsterdam on the status of a CFSP 'high representative.' The UK had opposed combining this role with that of Council secretary-general given the various existing full-time responsibilities required of the latter post. However, the compromise allowed for the creation of a deputy secretary-general who would be responsible for running the Council secretariat and thus freeing the secretary-general to carry out the 'high representative' duties. Referring to fears that, in this new role, the secretary-general might undermine the role of the member states in CFSP, one of the negotiators suggested that the UK had 'succeeded in structuring the job in a way which minimises that risk.'[11] The treaty made clear that the Council presidency would continue to represent the EU externally and the secretary-general would simply assist in this.

Although there was widespread disappointment across the EU at the failure to resolve some of the key institutional reform issues at Amsterdam, the UK government would plead 'not guilty' in the subsequent blaming exercise. At the most, it could be argued that the UK shared the blame with most of the other member states that were unwilling to compromise their varying national interests. Indeed, the quarrel over institutional reform was described by one of the UK negotiators as the 'biggest barney' of the summit. This was attributed to 'the very divergent interests of the large and small member states' and to the Dutch handling of the issue 'not as a neutral presidency but as a small country.'[12] The presidency had proposed a three stage reform of the Commission based on Kohl's Noordwijk suggestions. This involved the large states giving up their second Commissioners upon enlargement in return for a vote reweighting, and a more comprehensive review once EU membership exceeded twenty. At Amsterdam the Dutch proposed a vote reform based on a new double majority voting system, but the UK, France and Spain 'dug in' against this proposal. It was suggested that a 'deal which would have given us voting by a double majority...in exchange for giving up one of the Commissioners was not much of a deal.' It was notable that the proposed double majority voting system involved a population criterion that would give Germany a greater weight than the other large states. This may have explained the opposition of the UK, France and Spain. The French in particular were unwilling to acquiesce to such a move (Moravcsik and Nicolaidis 1998: 18). The reform was therefore postponed and a protocol attached to the treaty stating that each member state would have just one Commissioner at the date of the next enlargement but only if the weighting system in the Council had been modified in a manner acceptable to all member states. Furthermore, the protocol declared that a further IGC would take place at least a year before EU membership exceeded twenty in order to undertake a more comprehensive review (Dinan 1999: 180-181, McDonagh 1998: 193-194).

Cook later proffered his disappointment that this reform had not been agreed, telling the House of Commons foreign affairs committee that one of the 'most unsatisfactory outcomes' at Amsterdam was 'that one of the largest and most difficult questions about enlargement is now deferred until enlargement is nearer.' Cook appeared to apportion the blame to the smaller states and to Spain, suggesting that the necessary reforms had foundered on the refusal of the former to countenance a reweighting and the insistence of the latter that if there was to be a reweighting then Spain ought to get the same number of votes as the four largest states.[13] Cook recalled that 'at 4.00 am we found ourselves at an impasse' and the compromise protocol was therefore put forward (House of Commons FAC 1997: 12). One of the UK negotiators suggested that 'Aznar's last minute attempt to get the blocking minority in the Council set at 23 (as per the pre-Ioannina situation) provided one of the more bizarre episodes of the Council' and that Kohl and Blair 'were instrumental in finding the formulae which averted a complete bust up.'

Moravcsik and Nicolaidis suggest that both Kohl and Chirac had privately encouraged a postponement of the issue (1998: 19). However, the eventual compromise was described as 'pretty good' from the UK point of view as it meant that there was 'no question of our giving up a Commissioner unless we secure an acceptable deal on reweighting of votes.' Moreover, as the Finns had complained to the UK, the small states might have to pay twice by 'accepting reweighting while having no guarantee they can keep their Commissioner in the long term.'

There was similar disappointment across a number of member states and some anger over the failure to agree significant extensions of QMV. Indeed, the German foreign minister, Kinkel, and the Dutch foreign minister, van Mierlo, were reported to have physically squared up to each other over this issue as the Dutch became increasingly frustrated at the number of 'ifs and buts' being written into their treaty, and as their carefully laid plans for institutional reform turned to dust. Despite the uncharacteristic willingness of a UK government to sanction a number of increases in policy areas covered by QMV, progress in this area was extremely modest, as each policy area invariably found one or other of the member states opposed to QMV (Moravscik and Nicolaidis 1998: 22- 23, McDonagh 1998: 192). This situation meant that the UK government did not have to argue vigorously to prevent extension in those areas that it had identified previously as requiring opposition. Amongst others, the UK position was assisted by the Danes, who had indicated previously that they would veto QMV for art. 8a, art. 51 and art. 130s.2.[14] As indicated by the Kinkel-van Mierlo face off, the presidency was particularly angered by German back-tracking on QMV extension. Indeed, it appeared that Germany actually opposed QMV extension in more areas than the UK. Kohl's hands had become increasingly tied by pressure from the Länder governments in his own country, which opposed QMV extension in those policy areas that corresponded to their own spheres of authority (Moravcsik and Nicolaidis 1999: 68, Dinan 1999: 180). German insistence on unanimity was particularly marked in relation to the new title on 'freedom, security and justice.' The use of QMV was agreed for the new treaty provisions on employment, social exclusion, equal opportunities, public health, transparency, fraud, customs co-operation, statistics, data protection and outermost regions. It was also extended to the existing treaty provisions on research and development, compensatory aid for the import of raw materials and 'right of establishment' for EU citizens (Laffan 1997b: 46). These were all relatively minor areas of policy (Moravcsik and Nicolaidis 1998: 23). Of these areas, the only QMV extension that the UK had opposed was in relation to outermost regions.[15] However, this was not deemed to be an issue worth arguing to the death on. Conversely, the UK government had been prepared to support QMV extension in a number of areas not agreed, i.e. aspects of industrial policy, regional policy and non-fiscal aspects of environmental policy. In addition, no QMV extension was agreed in the areas formerly covered by the social protocol, which were now brought into the treaty proper. The government was no doubt relieved at this, given its ever increasing caution over matters of EU social and employment policy (Larragy 1997: 81).

Though generally successful in maintaining its line in relation to most institutional issues, the Labour government was forced to concede its position as regards the role of the Commission president. Prior to Amsterdam, the government had indicated that it opposed the treaty references to the Commission working under the political guidance of the president and to the president and the member states selecting the other Commissioners in common accord. This implied a presidential veto over nominees (Laffan 1997b: 32, Duff 1997b: 160, Dehousse 1999: 58-60). However, the UK position did not appear to have much support among the other member states and these references were agreed and included in the final text. Indeed, the provisions agreed at Amsterdam reflected the four stage process set out by Kok at Noordwijk. This also included a right of EP assent over the nomination for Commission president. The Labour government had appeared content to endorse this latter proposal, once it won majority support.

Elsewhere, the UK government was able to report success in achieving its objectives in other potentially awkward 'second order' issues such as treaty consolidation, EU legal personality and external economic relations. In relation to treaty consolidation, a compromise put forward by the French (who shared the UK's reservations) was agreed whereby work would continue on drawing up a consolidated text but it would have no legal value and be made public for 'illustrative purposes' only (Duff 1997b: 200, McDonagh 1998: 93-94). The proposal for EU legal personality was also dropped. A compromise was adopted under the CFSP title allowing member states to mandate the Council presidency to conclude international agreements with third countries (though member states would be able to require national ratification before agreements became binding). This addressed the concerns of those who argued that the inability of the EU to negotiate international agreements in areas covered by the two intergovernmental pillars (as only the EC possessed legal personality as an international organisation) required the bestowing of legal personality on the EU as a whole (Keatinge 1997: 100). In relation to external economic relations, the presidency proposal had not been agreed but instead there was a new provision allowing the scope of EC competence to be extended by unanimous agreement in the Council (McDonagh 1998: 192). This was a way of overcoming French objections to an extension of the Commission's mandate to negotiate on the EC's behalf to services and intellectual property (Moravcsik and Nicolaidis 1999: 65).[16] In addition to these satisfactory compromises, the UK government was successful in negotiating an agreement on quota hopping which satisfied its principal concerns, curtailing the ability of non-resident fisherman to exploit national fishing grounds (Young, JW 2000: 179). The UK government was also able to claim success in achieving the adoption of its proposals on animal welfare (classifying animals as 'sentient beings' with welfare requirements), private sector funding in TENs and co-operation on fraud and financial management.

The IGC reform proposals on which the approach of the Labour government appeared to differ the most from its Conservative predecessors were those various measures put forward as a way of bringing the EU closer to its citizens, by enhancing the EU's democratic character and improving the accountability of decision-making (George 1997: 115-116, Newman 1997: 32). It was no coincidence that it was in relation to these proposals, where Labour appeared to be in the EU mainstream in supporting reform, that the summit appeared to achieve its greatest success in reaching agreement on significant treaty change. These changes included a new human rights sanctions clause establishing mechanisms allowing the Council to suspend the rights of membership of any member state in persistent breach of fundamental human rights principles and ECJ jurisdiction to ensure the EC institutions (limiting jurisdiction to the first pillar and those third pillar areas where the ECJ could already act) adhered to art. F(2) referring to respect for fundamental rights as guaranteed by the ECHR (Whelan 1997: 147-151). In addition, a new first pillar article granted the Council the capacity, acting by unanimity, to take appropriate action to combat discrimination based on sex, racial or ethnic origin, religion or belief, disability, age or sexual orientation (Whelan 1997: 152-153). There was also a new treaty commitment to transparency in decision-making with a stipulation that the result of Council votes and reasons for them would be published when the Council acted in a legislative capacity. In addition, a new article provided for universal citizens' access to documents from the EC institutions related to decision-making (McDonagh 1998: 89-90, Duff 1997b: 109). The summit also saw agreement to measures, which had been championed by the UK and France in particular, to improve the participation of national parliaments, including a minimum national scrutiny period of six weeks on all proposals for EC legislation and a protocol providing for contributions by COSAC (Duff 1997b: 177-178, Dinan 1999: 181). The scope for consultation by the Committee of the Regions and the Economic and Social Committee was also broadened (Laffan 1997b: 38). Furthermore, on another issue where it had pressed for action, the UK government could gain satisfaction from the inclusion of a protocol incorporating the Edinburgh guidelines on subsidiarity (Duff 1997b: 104-106).

In terms of democratising decision-making, the changes of government in the UK and France had been integral to agreement reached at Amsterdam to increase the powers of the EP. Unlike its Gaullist predecessor, the new French socialist government, which included Elisabeth Guigou - formerly EP IGC representative - as justice minister, actively promoted increased EP powers (Moravcsik and Nicolaidis 1998: 22).[17] Furthermore, the significant extensions of codecision were generally in line with the position pursued by the new Labour government in the UK. A simplification of codecision was also agreed, as had been generally advocated by the UK. However, the simplification also encompassed the proposal to abolish third reading of the codecision procedure, which the Labour government had opposed. Though the French had also opposed this previously, the change in government in France had left the UK more isolated on this issue and it was decided that opposition was not worth pursuing to the death at Amsterdam. The newly simplified codecision procedure was extended to all areas previously covered by the co-operation procedure (with the exception of measures relating to EMU[18]) and a few areas previously covered by consultation and was also introduced to the new treaty provisions where QMV also applied (Duff 1997b: 142-151).

UK negotiators reported that codecision had not been extended to art. 8a.2 (free movement), art. 51 (social security), and art. 130d (structural and cohesion funds). This was presented as a success for the UK as these were the areas where it had opposed codecision extension. However, differences emerged over whether or not the first two of these had been successfully blocked when the Dutch published the text based on what was agreed at Amsterdam a few days later (McDonagh 1998: 195). According to this text, codecision had indeed been extended to both art. 8a(2) and art. 51 as well as another clause where UK records indicated codecision had not been agreed: art. 57(2) (mutual recognition of professional qualifications). The government was not too concerned about the latter, as it had actually supported both QMV and codecision for it and had only assumed that codecision had not been extended because others had blocked QMV for it. On art. 8a and art. 51, the UK had achieved its objectives of preventing QMV extension and assumed that codecision had not been extended either. According to UK records, Patijn had clearly stated that issues which had been withdrawn from the QMV list would not be subject to codecision. The differing UK-Dutch recollections over what was agreed were taken up by UK officials with the Dutch. However, it was stressed within the FCO that the UK should not make a big issue of it. The dispute needed to be kept low key and confidential in order to avoid public embarrassment. Nevertheless, UK protestations here were to no avail. At a COREPER meeting of 30 June, the Dutch reported that their records confirmed that codecision had been agreed in these articles and that Kok had summed up to this effect at Amsterdam, contradicting and over-ruling Patijn's earlier summing up. The UK was supported by the French at the COREPER meeting in insisting that codecision should not apply where unanimity was retained. Furthermore, France, Sweden and Portugal all backed the UK version of events. However, Germany, Belgium, Italy and Luxembourg all supported the presidency version of events. In the face of this resolute defence of the presidency record of Amsterdam, the UK government was forced to concede on this issue.

Although the dispute over what had been decided in relation to codecision and the subsequent failure to correct the presidency text was an embarrassment to the government, little damage was done to the perceived national interest. Indeed, FCO officials described the extension as 'undesirable but not critical.' It had been of much greater importance to the UK government to ensure that QMV was not extended to the articles in question, and this it had done. The government was able to gloss over the unfortunate extension of codecision to these areas and present them as in line with the general government approach to democratising decision-making. However, the dispute on codecision was overshadowed by a further disagreement on what was agreed in relation to UK and Irish participation in the Schengen arrangements. Indeed, the low-key approach that the UK government took on the codecision dispute can be partly attributed to its desire to concentrate attention on the more damaging dispute over Schengen. The presidency text issued following the Amsterdam summit included a requirement in the Schengen protocol that participation in the existing *acquis* by non-Schengen members should be subject to a unanimous decision by the existing members. This conflicted with the FCO record of Amsterdam, according to which the text had made such participation subject to the new flexibility provisions. Moreover, contrary to what the FCO thought had been agreed, an accompanying declaration calling for the best efforts of member states to allow UK and Irish participation where they so desired had been removed from the final text. Making participation subject to the flexibility provisions would mean that this would only require a QMV decision in favour among the participating states. This would have meant that UK and Irish participation could only be prevented by a blocking minority of states or by a Commission decision to reject an application.[19]

The UK government did not expect to want to participate in the large majority of the Schengen *acquis*, but it did want to retain the option of doing so in areas of interest to the UK. However, making UK participation subject to a unanimous vote would make it possible for just one member state to veto this. Both Belgium and Spain regarded the Schengen *acquis* as indivisible and would therefore be tempted to block UK participation. Moreover, Spain was likely to use the Gibraltar issue as a reason to block UK participation. Indeed, the chief minister of Gibraltar had already expressed anger that the UK had sold Gibraltar out by agreeing to unanimity (and an effective Spanish veto) here. The FCO was not letting the Gibraltar government know that this was not what it thought had been agreed. As with the codecision issue, FCO officials warned that the presidency would be 'very loathe' to reopen the text. It was thus recommended that Blair and Cook take this up with their Dutch counterparts at the G7 meeting in Denver later that month. One of the UK negotiators had already taken up both this and the codecision issue with de Bruijn. According to FCO records, the presidency text on Schengen submitted to the summit contained the flexibility reference, but in response to Aznar's assertions that unanimity was essential here, the presidency had agreed to circulate an alternative Spanish text (containing a unanimity requirement) for examination and discussion. However, the FCO recorded that at no stage did the UK agree to the Spanish text and that, in response to Spanish demands, Cook had reiterated at the summit the UK desire to retain a right to opt-in and expressed concern that UK participation would be blocked for non-Schengen reasons. It was reported that the Irish were also 'hopping mad' about the replacement of the flexibility reference by unanimity, and strongly supported the UK interpretation of what had been agreed and the UK efforts to restore the original text. Cook and Blair would stress at Denver that they had neither seen nor agreed to the Spanish text on Schengen. Nevertheless, UK protestations on this were to no avail. At a private meeting of the Spanish, UK, Irish and Luxembourg permanent representatives called by the Dutch on 30 June (the day before the Dutch handed over the presidency to Luxembourg), the presidency supported the Spanish view of what had happened. According to the presidency record, when Kok had asked at the summit if any of the other member states had objections to the text on Schengen (which, according to the Dutch, included the Spanish amendment) no-one had objected. The presidency did suggest a compromise to the assembled permanent representatives whereby a QMV vote would be required if the UK and Ireland at a future date wished to accept the entire Schengen acquis, but a unanimity vote would still be required if they wished to accept only a part of it. However, the Spanish representative stated this would be totally unacceptable. The Spanish prime minister's instructions were that any changes would have to go back for negotiation at European Council level. This was something that all delegations were anxious to avoid (McDonagh 1998: 195). All that the Spanish would offer was a declaration by the Schengen states to make the 'best efforts' to allow the UK and Ireland to participate in the provisions should they wish to do so. With the Irish unwilling to push the matter further, the UK conceded defeat on this issue.

Though it was later referred to in academic literature (McDonagh 1998: 195, Duff 1997b: 27-28) this embarrassing defeat was, at the time, expertly kept from the public view by the UK government. Indeed, the anxiety of the UK government to keep the dispute from public view explained its unwillingness to take it any further by raising it at European Council level. If publicised, the disputes over what had been agreed on codecision and Schengen could have been caricatured as illustrative of the irresponsibility and untrustworthiness of the Labour government in representing UK interests in the EU (although the Conservative opposition could hardly complain about a situation in which future UK participation in Schengen had been made more difficult). At the least, the affair demonstrated that UK ministers and officials were not always in control of developments in the negotiations and were not always aware of what was going on. But the dispute probably caused more embarrassment to UK officials than it did to UK ministers, given the pride that the former took in their expertise in European diplomacy. The affair may also have shed some light on the negotiating tricks used by the presidency and other member states in order to bounce reluctant member states into accepting treaty compromises, although in the case of codecision at least, the situation appeared attributable more to accident than conspiracy.

The Labour Government and the IGC Negotiations: An Evaluation

Despite its private embarrassment over what had been agreed on codecision and Schengen, the UK government would proclaim success in achieving its negotiating objectives, as set out in Blair's statement to the House of Commons on the Amsterdam European Council: 'to protect our essential interests over immigration, foreign policy, defence...to promote changes of real interest to the British people and to move Europe on to a new positive agenda' (Hansard 18 June 1997). The Labour government would present the role that it played at Amsterdam as a restoration of the UK to a central, and indeed, leading role in the EU (Rawnsley 2000: 73-75, Anderson and Mann 1997: 114-115, Young, JW 2000: 177). The government's communications strategists were able to use Blair's clear victory in the heads of government bicycle race staged as a public relations exercise at Amsterdam as a metaphor for the leading role the Labour government would now play in Europe. This presentation of the role played by the UK delegation at Amsterdam did have some basis in fact. UK diplomats in a number of member states reported praise among the UK's governing partners for the positive role played by the Labour government at Amsterdam. Furthermore, it was reported that there was 'much talk in the corridors' of the way in which Cook and Blair 'were on top of all the issues' and of the role they were playing in brokering deals. The impact of Blair at Amsterdam was described thus:

The atmosphere of the meeting was one in which the old order was fading. Our partners see the prime minister as the leading representative of a new generation of political leaders who could fill the gap left by the old guard, as long as we can develop policies which are as attractive as their presentation.

Referring to the success enjoyed by Cook and Blair in achieving the UK's objectives, and the detailed preparation undertaken for the negotiation, one of the UK negotiators suggested that it 'was not just in yesterday's bicycle ride that the race was to the fittest.' The performance of the UK leaders was contrasted with those of the two leaders who emerged with diminished authority at Amsterdam: Kohl and Chirac. Chirac - his authority shattered by Jospin's victory - had 'intervened when he wanted to, but was otherwise pretty detached (and occasionally asleep).' Kohl had 'played a powerful role' but this was 'mostly negative' calling for more unanimity in dealing with asylum and refugee cases and ending up as the one leader who could not accept the presidency compromise on the extension of QMV because it went too far.

The reported skirmish between van Mierlo and Kinkel illustrated the anger felt by the Dutch presidency at the last minute German back-pedalling over the various treaty texts. The German performance was also met with incredulity among the more 'federalist' inclined countries such as Italy, though such was the nature of the latter's maximalist positions that Kohl was reported as having turned to the Italian prime minister, Prodi, at Amsterdam and voiced doubts about the sanity of the Italian delegation. Indeed, only the Italians and the Belgians appeared to have stood firm in pursuing the maximalist reform options at the summit (Moravcsik and Nicolaidis 1998: 32). The Italian prime minister, Prodi, appeared to have blamed the Spanish for the failure to agree institutional reform, apparently referring to Spain when he mentioned 'flash-points' around 'national interests on which it was not very pleasant to speak.' However, others pointed the finger at the Dutch presidency for leaving discussion of institutional reform until the end and attempting to get agreement in the early hours of the morning. As an Austrian official noted, by this time everyone just wanted to go to bed. On the other hand, an adviser to Aznar was expressing disappointment that the Spanish had been let down at the last moment on institutional reform by the UK and the French. The same adviser had also expressed disgust at the German performance, describing Kohl's preoccupation with national concerns, for example on treatment of public banks in the Länder, as 'indefensible for a country leading the process of European integration.'

Aside from Spanish disgruntlement over institutional reform, the UK government emerged fairly unscathed from the post-Amsterdam recriminations. The replacement of an intransigent Conservative government in the UK by a Labour government willing to accept reform in a number of areas appeared to have wrong-footed a number of member states. Indeed, it appeared that some member states had previously hidden their reservations over a number of reforms, safe in the knowledge that the UK government would do their opposing for them. This was most evident in relation to the scope of QMV, where a new willingness on the part of the UK to accept extensions of QMV forced a number of member states, notably Germany, to come forward with their own reservations (Moravcsik and Nicolaidis 1998: 22-23, 1999: 77, Young, H 1999: 490). Whitty would later publicly claim that the UK was no longer the main obstacle to progress within the EU, citing the government's willingness to move further than the Germans on QMV extension, further than the French in enhancing the powers of the EP and further than the Spanish in strengthening EU environmental policy (Whitty, 28 September 1997). Nevertheless, the UK had remained, under a Labour government, the strongest opponent of moves towards an EU defence role at Amsterdam, and only really had the support of the Danes in opposing JHA communitisation (Moravcsik and Nicolaidis 1999: 74-75). While the new government had received plaudits from a number of European colleagues for its constructive approach to the final negotiations, there were some mutterings that little had changed in terms of the UK attitude on these key issues (*The Guardian*, 30 May 1997).[20]

To the outside observer, the Labour government's performance on EU defence and JHA communitisation appeared to confirm a continuity in the approach of the new government and its Conservative predecessors. In its rejection of an EU defence role and its hardline position on the retention of UK frontier controls, the new government certainly seemed to be taking up where the old one had left off (Young, JW 2000: 179). However, the willingness of the Labour government to countenance imaginative compromises on CFSP decision-making and EU/WEU relations and its willingness to agree to a package on JHA communitisation, which involved the incorporation of the Schengen *acquis* for thirteen of the member states while holding out the possibility of the UK joining in later, and an enhanced role for the EC institutions in the remaining third pillar areas, marked a break from the intransigent posturing of Labour's predecessors. Nevertheless, some may argue that once the election was over, a victorious Conservative government may also have been willing to countenance these compromises. This hypothesis is impossible to prove. However, the increasing presence within the Conservative parliamentary party of MPs (accentuated by the new intake of MPs in 1997) who were openly hostile to any further treaty changes that enhanced the role of the EC institutions, would have made such compromises extremely difficult to achieve (Ludlam 1998: 52-56). Despite this, the briefings provided by FCO officials for the incoming government on 1 May suggest that government officials (if not the government itself) had been preparing for compromises on these issues.

Given that the official policy of the Conservative government had been to not negotiate, there was a strong sense of relief among FCO officials at the entrance of a Labour government with a policy of constructive engagement, thus providing them with an opportunity to deploy their diplomatic skills to the full in the negotiations and pursue the various compromises that they had been exploring in private. Indeed, one UK official remarked of the fresh start provided by the new government: 'You can't imagine how wonderful it is to feel you are actually being listened to' (Young, H 1999: 489). Constructive engagement was certainly a marked change from the obstructive detachment that went before, and provided a more suitable challenge for the FCO's skills. However, while government officials displayed an obvious willingness to engage with the European agenda in order to further British national interests and shape the direction of EU policy, FCO briefings for the new government reflected traditional UK reservations about some of the high flown rhetoric about European integration deployed on the continent (Buller and Smith 1998: 168-169, George 1997: 101). Hence Whitehall suggestions that the new government get their European counterparts to base the discussions on practical objectives rather than theological debate. On the level of EU policy, a number of clear objectives had been developed within Whitehall over the previous decade or so, among which were a stress on ensuring the full completion of the single market and of facilitating enlargement to the east (George 1997: 101-102). Simultaneously, there appeared to be genuine reservations within Whitehall, borne out of a perception of Britain's place in the world and its national interests, towards moves to establish an area of free unimpeded movement in the EU through incorporation of the Schengen agreement (seen as unsuitable for Britain given its island nature), and attempts to transform the EU into some form of defence alliance (based on fears that such a move would undermine NATO and the transatlantic partnership). Flattered by the evident pleasure displayed by Whitehall officials at their entry to government and the new constructive approach that they brought, Labour ministers seemed content to conform to the various reservations that their officials had on these and other issues, and willingly embraced traditional foreign policy approaches to furthering British interests in Europe (many of which had only temporarily been forced into retreat by the Major government's lurch towards obstructionism in the 1990s). Labour ministers were new to government and therefore quite susceptible to the counsel offered by their officials, a perceived 'wisdom' grounded in the attractive combination of technical expertise and diplomatic experience.

Indeed, the extent to which the Labour government embraced a number of traditional UK foreign policy assumptions in relation to the EU is striking. As J W Young suggests, in some fields 'such as the completion of the single market, its enthusiasm for an eastern enlargement, its emphasis on reforming the CAP and, most notably, in its belief that unemployment was best tackled by free enterprise ideas of a flexible labour market, the Blair government seemed the natural successor of Margaret Thatcher.' Furthermore, the emphasis on retaining border controls and blocking European defence developments also reflected traditional British interests (Young, JW 2000: 178-179, Barrett 1997: 121). On some of these issues, such as single market completion, defence, frontier controls and enlargement, Labour had already clearly adopted these traditional UK policies in a spirit of bipartisan consensus in opposition. More belatedly, in the run-up to the election, Labour had also become converted to an emphasis on labour market flexibility and ensuring business competitiveness in matters relating to European employment and social policy, as illustrated by its business manifesto and its sudden reluctance to extend the scope of QMV or to broaden the scope of the social protocol provisions once they were opted into (Labour Party 1997a, Larragy 1997: 81). But following its entry to government, Labour also embraced FCO thinking on issues where its position had not been fully decided in opposition such as the role of the Commission president and EU legal personality. In addition, there were issues where Labour did have a decided policy in opposition, but where it appeared to shift towards the more traditional FCO view once in government. These included treaty consolidation (which it previously supported but now rejected) and the role of the EP, particularly in relation to decisions with implications for the EC budget and expenditure, where the government became quite cautious.

As regards EP powers, exposure to the FCO's cost based caution had led to a shift from Labour's previous support for EP codecision for most legislation, irrespective of implications for expenditure, and for eliminating categories of expenditure in order to give the EP full scrutiny powers over the whole budget. Although the latter position had been adopted in opposition primarily as a means of reducing CAP expenditure, FCO officials persuaded Labour ministers that EP involvement would have the opposite effect and lead to expenditure increases. The hardening of position in relation to the EP was also notable in relation to the abolition of the third reading of the codecision procedure, which Labour had supported in opposition but unsuccessfully opposed in government, and the proposal to give the EP the right to initiate legislation which Labour supported in the 1995 policy document but did not pursue once in government.[21] One LWG participant refers to the rather 'disparaging' attitude UK officials possessed towards the EP (Interview with LWG participant). This was certainly reflected in the policy shifts undertaken by Labour once in government. Nevertheless, the appeal of enhancing the EP's role as a way of allowing its MEPs to exercise leverage over EU policy-making was diminished once Labour moved from opposition to government. Once in government, Labour ministers had a new-found interest in retaining the balance of power within the EU in favour of the Council.

What is clear from examination of Labour's policy-making on the IGC once in government, was that, in terms of structure, it appeared to have been totally taken over by the Whitehall machine. The 'Europeanising' influence played by the EPLP, which had already been downgraded in the months leading up to the election, appeared to be downgraded further. It had not, however, been totally marginalised. There was some recognition that certain figures within the EPLP could continue to provide a valuable source of expertise. Henderson was taken to see Richard Corbett on his first visit to Brussels within days of taking office and they had an hour long discussion in which Corbett explained various IGC issues to him (Interview with Corbett).[22] Henderson also had a meeting with Pauline Green at the FCO on 8 May. Green urged Henderson, and the government generally, to liaise closely with the PES group up to and beyond the Amsterdam summit. It was suggested that this would help in manoeuvring the EP past any difficulties thrown up in the course of the IGC. Henderson would also meet the EPLP leaders, David and Crawley on 13 May, and would meet the EPLP as a whole at the end of May. Whitty also continued to liaise with the EPLP in the course of his new part-time role as FCO minister with responsibility for relations with the EP. Nevertheless, in general, contacts between the new government and the EPLP during the remaining negotiations were a means of ensuring that the government's line was understood and complied with by the latter.[23]

Labour's entry to government also resulted in a similar downgrading in importance and value to the party leadership of its involvement in the PES party confederation. The link with other PES parties in government, and the Dutch PVDA in particular, as a conduit for ensuring a steady and fairly comprehensive flow of information on the IGC and for indirectly influencing the nature of the negotiations, had remained critical to the Labour party right up to the general election, even if Labour's commitment to a convergence of IGC policy positions with its PES colleagues had already diminished since the Madrid meeting of December 1995. However, once Labour had the diplomatic machinery of government at its disposal, the importance of its links to the PES parties also diminished. Although a good relationship with the Dutch presidency remained of critical value and the good relationship and co-ordination of positions with the Danish social democratic government also proved valuable, these relationships were now conducted on a government to government basis rather than one based on party links or secret channels. PES solidarity was no longer necessary. Of greatest importance to the new government was the cultivation of good relationships with the centre-right governments in Germany and France. Of course the sudden and slightly surprising emergence of a PES government in France at the beginning of June 1997 upset calculations somewhat, and for some this briefly opened up the prospect of a new powerful alliance of PES parties in two of the leading member states. However, Blair's refusal to countenance Jospin's proposals on employment, and his implicit chiding of the interventionist approach held by the French socialists in his speech to the PES congress in Malmo on 6 June, clearly demonstrated what Blair now thought about calls for PES solidarity. Blair had lectured his erstwhile PES allies at Malmo on the need to modernise and warned them that 'to be competitive in the modern world, knowledge, skills, technology and enterprise are the key, not rigid regulation or old-style interventionism' (Anderson and Mann 1997: 114). Blair's lecturing tone and the implication that the other PES parties were pursuing outdated policies did not go down well with his PES colleagues, particularly the French, given their recent success (Interview with LWG participant, Clift 2001: 170). Even the Dutch foreign minister van Mierlo was heard to remark after Blair's Malmo speech that some things never changed – 'another British leader telling the Europeans where they were going wrong' (Young, H 1999: 491, Rawnsley 2000: 75).

This is not to say that the PES no longer had any value at all for the new Labour government. While nearly all links with EU governments were now carried out through usual diplomatic channels, the Malmo congress did provide the Labour leadership with a useful forum through which to engage in informal discussions with a number of the PES leaders in governments. Blair had talks with Kok, Persson and Rasmussen at Malmo (with Blair and Rasmussen agreeing to stick together on second and third pillar issues). However, Blair's contacts with Jospin at Malmo were distinctly frosty. Indeed, Blair had assumed Jospin was going to lose in the French election, and had thus resisted suggestions that the two talk. After the French elections, the relationship between the two PES governments went 'from bad to worse' (Interview with LWG participant). The lack of unity between the two new governments on employment and other issues symbolised the limitations of the PES as a forum for agreeing joint party positions. Once ensconced in government, Blair appeared to view it primarily as a forum to proselytise on behalf of the 'New Labour' conception of social and economic policy, and persuade the continentals to follow his lead and ditch the European social model for a neo-liberal Anglo-Saxon economic model (Young, H 1999: 490). The PES was viewed by the Blairites as no more than a useful forum for informal contact, and one that was certainly far more useful to Labour when in opposition.

Although the new government appeared to no longer see much utility in the PES as a forum for co-ordinating party and government positions, the advantages that Labour's membership of the PES had bestowed upon it in opposition were undoubted. The contacts with the Dutch and other PES governments that Labour had enjoyed in opposition had proved decisive in providing the Labour leadership with the capacity to 'hit the ground running' when it entered government and found itself in the midst of the IGC negotiations.[24] In his account of the negotiations, the Belgian IGC representative, Franklin Dehousse, suggests that 'the remarkable preparation' by the Labour party in opposition, together with that of the FCO, made it possible to launch the final phase of the IGC 'more or less immediately' once it took office, and that Dutch draft treaty texts 'took on board the positions of the Labour manifesto' (Dehousse 1999: 13-14). Although the FCO would take credit in likening the government's successes at Amsterdam to a race 'to the fittest', it was the level of preparation that the Labour leadership undertook in opposition that ensured that it would be on top of the issues from day one in government, would not be bounced into an undesirable agreement either by its own government officials or by the other member states and indeed ensured that the other member states had left the negotiations open for them in expectation of a new government with a new approach. With a fair amount of help from the Conservatives' very public divisions on the EU (Young, JW 2000: 167-174, Young, H 1999: 457-468), the level and nature of Labour's preparations in opposition had also denied the Conservatives the opportunity to portray Labour as preparing to sell out to the EU, either by exploiting ambiguities in its positions or exposing inconsistencies with statements by the EPLP or the PES. Although it is difficult to judge whether this level of preparation made any difference to Labour's victory on 1 May, it was certainly decisive in ensuring that Blair and Cook could return from Amsterdam proclaiming triumph on 18 June.

Notes

[1] Because of the sensitivity of the sources used to research this chapter, much of the discussion of government policy development and the final IGC negotiations has been left unreferenced.

[2] Butler suggests that 'Blair's people' had decided that Quin should not get the post and that both he and Cook were taken by surprise by this decision. Butler was not very impressed at this decision given what he viewed as Henderson's lack of knowledge of Europe (Interview with Butler).

[3] This involved bestowing a peerage upon Simon, allowing Blair to appoint him to government from the House of Lords. Although he did not get the post of minister for

Europe, Blair was determined to give Simon a European role, appointing him as minister for trade and competitiveness in Europe at the DTI.

[4] Henderson's removal from the post a year later (when Quin was given the post) and from government two years later was similarly attributed to his closeness to Brown, and Blair's subsequent desire to remove Brown's friends from influential positions (Rawnsley 2000: 162-166).

[5] According to Butler, this statement was based on a rough skeleton draft that he had passed on to FCO officials (Interview with Butler).

[6] In a gamble that would spectacularly backfire, President Chirac had called national assembly elections, a year earlier than necessary, in order to give greater legitimacy to the Gaullist government's planned austerity measures, viewed as necessary to get the French economy in shape for EMU.

[7] The conference of European affairs committees of the national parliaments.

[8] Straw's response to Cook warned that the third pillar experience illustrated that it was 'all very well to seek to draw a distinction between substantive decisions and implementing decisions, but in practice the line between them can often be blurred with some implementation decisions having major policy consequences in their own right.'

[9] In the event of a joint EP-Council conciliation procedure failing to agree on a legislative text, the third reading of the codecision procedure entailed the Council being able to confirm its own text which would become law unless the EP rejected it by an absolute majority within six weeks. According to Richard Corbett, the elimination of this option would underline that it was only by compromise and agreement that the EP and Council could adopt legislation together under the codecision procedure (1998: 40).

[10] Though harmonisation of member states' policies was explicitly excluded, the presidency proposals envisaged that incentive measures would be adopted in the new employment title by QMV, in order to complement member states' own activities and promote best practice and sharing of experience. The main UK objection to this appeared to be that it would create new expenditure programmes.

[11] It was also suggested that the UK government think about putting forward a candidate for the post 'or backing someone else's in return for a key role for the UK in support.'

[12] The Netherlands had demanded that if there was to be a reweighting then they should have more votes than Greece and Belgium, given that each of the latter had a population 50 per cent smaller (Moravcsik and Nicolaidis 1998: 19).

[13] The Spanish demanded that if they were to give up their second Commissioner, then they would no longer accept having less Council votes than the other large states (Moravcsik and Nicolaidis 1998: 18).

[14] Relating to freedom of movement, social security and aspects of environmental policy.

[15] The new provisions on outermost regions, based on proposals put forward by France, Portugal, Spain and Greece, gave member state territories outside continental Europe special status under the structural funds and derogations from state aid provisions.

[16] Moravcsik and Nicolaidis describe the apparent UK stance in opposing an extension of competence to trade in services as a rare example at Amsterdam of a member state acting against its national interest (given the UK competitiveness in services) for ideological reasons (i.e. an unwillingness to support extensions of the Commission's powers) (1999: 77). Nevertheless, the government department with the clearest interest in securing EU-wide liberalisation in trade in services through extending competence, the DTI, actually did argue for such a competence for the expected reasons of national interest. However, the FCO had been more ambivalent on this issue, preferring to hold back possible support for extending competence until the final endgame, only to be used as a bargaining counter in order to

secure other UK goals. In the end, the UK was not required to fully reveal its hand on this issue because strong French opposition killed the proposal.

[17] Guigou reportedly pressed strongly for this change of position within the new French government (Moravcsik and Nicolaidis 1998: 68). The Gaullist president, Chirac, now forced to co-habit with a Socialist government and with his legitimacy severely eroded by his disastrous decision to stage early national assembly elections and subsequent defeat, was forced to acquiesce in this change of French position, though he apparently remarked to his advisers that this was an issue of marginal importance (Moravcsik and Nicolaidis 1998:22, 1999: 68).

[18] EMU provisions were deemed too sensitive to re-open.

[19] Duff suggests that, had the UK-Irish interpretation prevailed, the outcome would have heralded a Europe à la carte, as the two 'would virtually have been able to pick and choose what they wanted from a menu of sensitive items closely affecting the citizen' (1997b: 28).

[20] One Italian diplomat complained that the UK government was storing up problems for itself further down the line. He also suggested that some Americans had told him that the UK was behaving 'more royalist than the king' i.e. more cautious than the USA, on the EU-WEU relationship.

[21] EP legislative initiative was not seriously considered by the IGC. Moravcsik and Nicolaidis suggest that the EP itself held back on its demands here, knowing that a right to legislative initiative would lead to similar demands from the Council, perhaps to the disadvantage of supranational institutions as a whole (1998: 21-22).

[22] According to Corbett, most of this discussion was taken up by an attempt to explain the complex comitology issue to Henderson.

[23] While some of the key figures involved in IGC policy-making in opposition viewed the relationship with the EPLP as something that should be nurtured, this feeling was not generalised across government. In general, most of the people that mattered in government would view the EPLP 'as being a force to be neutered rather than nurtured' (Interview with LWG participant).

[24] Cook himself informed the BBC Radio *Today* programme, the day after Labour's election victory, that the new government was ready to 'hit the ground running' in the IGC negotiations (Anderson and Mann 1997: 112).

Chapter 7

Conclusion: Continuity, Change, Ideological Shifts and Counter-Shifts

Continuity and Change

The UK negotiating position at Amsterdam which, in general substance, was successfully reflected in the treaty outcome, showed strong continuities with the positions adopted by the LWG and reflected in the policy document adopted at the Labour party conference in 1995. On the key IGC issues, the substance of the positions adopted by the Labour party in opposition were retained in government. But a continuity could also be observed in relation to the positions pursued in the IGC by the new Labour government after 1 May 1997 and those held by its Conservative predecessors. This continuity related primarily to the structure of the treaties: i.e. a desire to retain the pillar structure of the TEU, with two intergovernmental pillars operating alongside the EC pillar, and in terms of certain key tenets of the policies pursued within the intergovernmental pillars, i.e. a desire to retain national control over immigration and asylum policies and border controls, and similarly to exercise national control over policies and decisions developed under the CFSP pillar and to prevent the development of an EU defence capacity within it. As Moravcsik and Nicolaidis suggest, in relation to the key areas of border controls, the positions adopted at Amsterdam by the UK government 'reflected structural realities, rather than partisan ideology' (1999: 68).

Nevertheless, the emphasis on Conservative-Labour continuity can be overstated. While the positions adopted in relation to an EU defence capacity and the retention of UK border controls may have reflected certain structural realities, i.e. generalised assumptions of UK national interest, which were reflected in a bipartisan approach to these issues, on several other key IGC issues there was a marked break from the positions taken either implicitly or explicitly by the Major government at the IGC. Most notably, the Labour government supported some extensions of QMV (and would have been prepared to support further extensions in areas not agreed at Amsterdam), significant extensions of the EP's role (both through increased codecision and in relation to a right of approval over the Commission president), broad anti-discrimination provisions, new provisions on fundamental rights which extended the jurisdiction of the ECJ, new provisions on transparency in relation to decision-making and access to documents, a new (albeit vague and limited) treaty title on employment and incorporation of the social protocol of the TEU into the treaty proper. On all these issues, the behaviour of the Major government, as indicated in public statements and positions taken by its representatives in the Reflection Group and the IGC, suggested that real progress in terms of treaty changes would have been prevented. Though a Conservative victory in the 1997 general election might have given the Major government more room for manoeuvre at the IGC, particularly had it significantly increased its parliamentary majority, the increasing predominance of Euro-sceptic opinion within the Conservative parliamentary party would have made compromise on these issues difficult for Major to sell to his party. Indeed, while Major and a number of his senior cabinet colleagues may themselves have been politically inclined to seek compromise at the IGC, the mind-set of much of the Conservative parliamentary party following the Maastricht ratification debacle of 1992-93 was that further 'concessions' in terms of treaty changes to increase the scope of EU supranationalism were unacceptable. Confirmation of the hardening of this uncompromising mind-set would come after 1997, when the majority of what was left of the Conservative parliamentary party following its shattering defeat enthusiastically embraced the increasingly hardline Euro-sceptical platform adopted under Major's successor as party leader, William Hague (Baker 2001: 280-281, Hix 2000: 60).

Thus the evidence presented by the positive approach pursued by the Labour government in relation to the aforementioned issues provides a refutation of rather glib assertions, made both prior to and following its assumption of governmental office, that the positions taken by Labour at the IGC were not significantly different from those taken by the Conservatives. Labour's 'constructive engagement' with the 'mainstream' European agenda could be contrasted with the seemingly wilful isolationism presented by the Conservative government (Hughes and Smith 1998: 94). Moreover, as a number of observers have pointed out, Labour's entry into government effected an 'unblocking' of the IGC negotiations and facilitated the treaty settlement at Amsterdam (McDonagh 1998: 183, Dehousse 1999: 14, Dinan 1999: 177). Though key institutional reform issues were left unresolved at Amsterdam, if any blame could be directed at the UK for this, it would have the company of several other member states in sharing culpability.

Labour's engagement with the 'mainstream' EU agenda for treaty reform was reflected not only in the role played by its representatives in government in the final stages of the IGC negotiation, but also by the unprecedented level of contact undertaken with other governments when still in opposition prior to 1 May. The willingness of other EU governments to deal with the then Labour opposition was an illustration of the broad consensus that existed among the member states that the key to reaching a successful conclusion to the IGC was a change of government in the UK (Dehousse 1999: 13). Furthermore, Labour's membership of the PES provided a formal arena for systematic contact between it and various PES governments, and most importantly, with the Dutch presidency in the critical phase of the IGC in the first half of 1997. Labour's engagement with other centre-left parties in the EU through the PES was in sharp contrast to the disengagement of the Conservative party from its 'natural' centre-right allies in the EU. It was clear that by 1996, centre-right leaders such as Chancellor Kohl and President Chirac, had lost patience with the Major government and shared the belief of centre-left governments in the EU that a change of government was required in the UK in order to proceed to a satisfactory treaty reform in 1997 (Hughes and Smith 1998: 94).

Labour's membership of the PES was integral to providing it with the information on the IGC negotiations necessary for its representatives to prepare for a smooth transition to government and entry into the negotiations. Its contacts with the Dutch presidency also facilitated the capacity of the latter to guide the negotiations in a manner that would reduce the ability of the Major government to exploit the IGC for domestic political purposes and exploit Labour's electoral vulnerability on the Europe issue (McDonagh 1998: 138). This contact also allowed the Dutch presidency to prepare possible treaty compromises ready for Labour's entry into government, while the wider contact with PES parties contributed to a broader understanding within the EU of the domestic constraints that Labour was operating within and of the positions that Labour would bring to the negotiating table. In this way, the Labour party was also able indirectly to influence the direction of the IGC negotiations prior to assuming governmental office. But did this engagement with the PES involve credible attempts by the Labour party to co-ordinate policies with its sister parties and what effect, if any, did this have on the evolution of the Labour party's positions on the IGC?

Though attempts at policy co-ordination in relation to the IGC within the PES were undertaken, culminating in the declaration adopted at the Madrid PES leaders' meeting in December 1995, the results were limited. Indeed, the Madrid declaration appeared to be an exercise in glossing over differences between the PES parties on key institutional issues such as Commission size and Council vote reweighting and in relation to sensitive issues such as JHA communitisation and a possible EU defence capacity (PES December 1995). In many areas, the Madrid declaration reflected a lowest common denominator approach to policy co-ordination and, as Pauline Green suggests, the whole exercise appeared rather half-hearted (Interview with Green). This state of affairs probably suited the Labour leadership, as its prime intention in relation to the PES, as elucidated in Whitty's initial memo on the establishment of the LWG, was to avoid embarrassing differences emerging between it and its PES allies and/or being 'bounced' into taking positions by association, rather than the achievement of a deeper policy co-ordination (LP Whitty, 1 November 1994). Nevertheless, the Madrid declaration did demonstrate a consensus among the PES parties on some institutional changes: i.e. the need to address the democratic deficit through an increase in the powers of the EP and open and transparent decision-making in the Council, and the principle that some extension of QMV was required given the perspective of enlargement (though differences remained on what the precise extent of this QMV extension should be). Furthermore, on policy issues on which a clearer left-right cleavage existed at the IGC, such as employment and environmental policy, the PES parties were in agreement as regards the inclusion of progressive sounding clauses within the Madrid declaration. As was the case regarding IGC proposals related to the theme of democratisation, the positions taken on strengthened employment and environmental provisions were of a kind that one would expect from social democratic or socialist parties. Given the preponderance of PES parties in government in the EU by the time of the Amsterdam summit, it was no coincidence that the final treaty did involve progress in these areas. Indeed, it appears that the PES governments were responsible for ensuring that employment remained on the IGC agenda, despite the reticence of centre-right governments in Germany, France and the UK (Ladrech 2000: 110-115).

It is more difficult to judge the effect that PES involvement had on Labour's own IGC policy formulation. A number of the policy papers discussed by the LWG and much of the internal correspondence within the Labour leadership did indicate a concern to ensure that Labour party policy on the IGC did not stray too far from the PES mainstream. While careful to present an image of strong defence of British interests within the EU, official party documents in the run-up to the general election also stressed that a Labour government would restore the UK to a leading role within the EU and end the isolation of the Major years (Labour Party 1996, 1997a, 1997b). Developing co-operation with its PES partners on various EU policy issues was a key element in this process. This was reflected in the 1995 policy document which referred to Labour acting to promote its positive agenda for reform of the EU 'together with our friends and colleagues in the European Parliament and in the other socialist and social democratic parties in Europe' (Labour Party 1995: 2-3). Interaction with the PES parties enabled the Labour party to identify policy options which had broad support among its sister parties and judge whether or not its own positions were in tune with them and likely to be acceptable to its potential future partners in the IGC negotiations. Moreover, discussions with its PES allies exposed the Labour leadership to possible policy solutions that it had not considered of its own accord. Indeed, the position papers presented by Whitty to the LWG on various IGC issues generally referred to the views and proposals put forward by other PES parties as factors to be taken into account in deciding the Labour position. The relationship of Labour's positions to those taken by the rest of the PES was a factor given consideration as Labour formulated its IGC policy. The positions of the PES generally provided the 'European' parameter to policy options under consideration by the Labour leadership. As Robert Ladrech suggests, involvement in the PES provides opportunities for problem-solving and 'mutual learning' and contributes to a European 'socialisation' (or Europeanisation) (2000: 61). This had an effect on the Labour party's consideration of various policy options in relation to the IGC.

In defining policy options and linking the positions of the Labour party and the other PES parties, a crucial role was played by the parliamentary group of the PES in the EP. The PES group position on the IGC was a great deal more developed than that of the PES 'party' and was a point of reference for the latter, particularly as a number of PES MEPs, including Pauline Green, David Martin and Elisabeth Guigou, were members of the PES IGC working-group. In terms of Labour party policy, the role played by the PES group in the PES 'party' structures was especially significant given Labour's influential position as the largest single national grouping within the PES group, as reflected in the key positions held by its representatives, particularly Green as leader. Furthermore, the influence of Labour party members within the PES group extended to the role played by Richard Corbett, who was responsible for drafting its position on the IGC as well as various other discussion documents. This was in addition to the important role he played as adviser to Guigou. The EPLP representatives exerted an important 'Europeanising' influence within the LWG, ensuring that the London leadership was aware of policy options being discussed within the EU institutions and among the other member states and acting as advocates for 'European' policy solutions. In some policy areas, the EPLP representatives on the LWG (and also on Straw's JHA working-party) and other Labour MEPs consulted by Whitty on his numerous visits to Brussels were able to offer a technical expertise not possessed by the London leadership and thus influence party thinking by facilitating understanding of issues and of the rationale for 'integrationist' solutions. In this respect, the role played by Corbett was of great importance given his frequent discussions and correspondence with Whitty. Given their daily interaction with colleagues from other PES parties within the PES group, the EPLP representatives acted as valuable 'interlocutors' between the Labour leadership and the wider PES and acted as advocates for policy co-ordination within the PES. Green was able to play a particularly influential role in this respect, given her good relationship with the Labour leadership and her presence at PES leaders' meetings as well as meetings of the PES IGC working-group.

The intertwined nature of the relationship between the Labour party, the EPLP, the PES group and the wider PES 'party' therefore gave Labour MEPs an opportunity to exercise a subtle 'Europeanising' influence, while Labour's strength within the PES group allowed it to exercise a strong influence over the formulation of the position of the latter and gave it added leverage within the PES 'party' as a whole. Nevertheless, while some internal Labour party documents on the IGC exhibited a degree of self-consciousness about being isolated within the PES, on issues which were deemed to be politically sensitive for domestic electoral reasons and/or reasons of critical national interest the latter considerations tended to triumph over the need to maintain solidarity with Labour's sister parties. This pattern was apparent in relation to the positions taken on environmental taxation, national border controls and common immigration/asylum policies and EU defence capability. QMV was rejected on green taxes, despite the recognition that there was some political logic to it, primarily because of the likely political capital that the Conservatives would make of the adoption of such a position and also because support for EU-wide green taxes would probably have contradicted Labour's campaign against the Conservative government's domestic imposition of VAT on fuel (LWG IGC3D). Communitisation of immigration and asylum policy and incorporation of the Schengen *acquis* abolishing national border controls was rejected for a combination of factors relating to domestic electoral politics and genuine perceptions of the UK national interest (Labour Party 1995: 15-16, Interview with LWG participant). The proposal to establish an EU defence capacity was opposed primarily for the latter reason: it was viewed as undermining the UK national interest, which lay in ensuring the primacy of NATO in European security (LWG IGC6E, Labour Party 1995: 14-15). Given the existence of NATO, an EU defence role was seen as both unnecessary and undesirable.

The Ideological Context

Labour's policy-making on the IGC should not however be reduced simply to a dialectic between the Europeanising influence of the EPLP and PES on the one hand and the domestic/national concerns which pulled the policy process in an opposite direction. Policy on the IGC needs also to be assessed in the context of the wider ideological and political transformation that the Labour party had undertaken since 1983. Although the platform of withdrawal from the EC was dropped soon after Labour's electoral disaster of 1983, it was not until the policy review established by Neil Kinnock following the 1987 defeat that Labour appeared to fully embrace the then EC as the appropriate arena for the achievement of its policy objectives. Though the policy review led to the abandonment of Keynesian policies of economic expansion at the domestic level, Labour's policy documents at the end of the 1980s and early 1990s seemed to reflect a belief that Keynesian policy models could still be pursued at the European level. The EC was viewed as a possible tool for economic co-ordination among its member states in order to ameliorate the effects of the processes of globalisation that had seemingly rendered nation-states that wished to implement progressive social democratic programmes impotent in countering the power of international capital (Labour Party 1993b: 47-48). Moreover, Labour enthusiastically embraced the development of a European social dimension as a valuable counterpoint to Thatcherite policies in the UK, and in a similar vein, enthusiastically grasped the logic of EC-wide action on the environment. To this end, the Labour leadership was content to endorse QMV in these policy areas as a means to ensure the same effectiveness of policy development that this change in decision-making had facilitated for the single market programme. Furthermore, there was a read-across from Labour's desire to democratise the UK constitution to its view that EU decision-making should be democratised through an enhanced role for the EP (Labour Party 1993a: 34). This combined with a broader political consideration: Labour's strong performances in the 1989 and 1994 EP elections were high points in an otherwise electorally miserable wilderness period. Its strength in the EP offered Labour the opportunity to exercise a leverage over EU policy-making which was denied to it at the national level, particularly given the 'absolutist' nature of parliamentary government in the UK. Labour's continued support for increased EP powers whilst in opposition must be understood in this context.

In sum, the transformation of Labour's policies under Kinnock's leadership, both in relation to the EU and generally, seemed to represent an evolution into a European social democratic party. This transformation appeared to be confirmed when Kinnock was succeeded by John Smith, who was generally perceived as a genuine European social democrat. Though the social democratic discourse of the 1995 policy document which emerged from the deliberations of the LWG was rather pared down when compared to Labour's 1991 and 1993 EU policy documents, key features of this approach, including support for a strong social dimension, economic co-ordination to create employment and a Keynesian sounding counter-cyclical European recovery fund, as well as strengthened EP powers, were retained (Labour Party 1995: 3-6). Labour's EU policies, at least until 1995, therefore reflected this evolution into a European social democratic party, making the alignment of its policies with its PES sister parties relatively unproblematic, at least in matters relating to the social and economic orientation of the EU and the need for democratisation.

Although Labour's apparent evolution into a European social democratic party represented a major ideological shift, it was clear that, upon his succession to the leadership, Blair and his fellow travellers on the 'New Labour' project did not regard the ideological transformation of the Labour party as complete. Thereafter, a further subtler shift occurred in the ideological approach of the Labour party, taking it beyond the European social democratic stance elaborated under Kinnock and Smith, and with clear repercussions for EU policy. Though this was not reflected in the 1995 policy document, it became more apparent in the public pronouncements of Labour spokespersons in 1996 and 1997 and was demonstrated by the hardening of its positions in relation to the social chapter and the proposed employment chapter and a distancing from its previous support for EU wide economic co-ordination to promote growth and employment and redistribute power and wealth. Thus, while Labour continued to support the principle of both a social chapter and an employment chapter, its emphasis shifted from promoting employment rights and creating jobs through an EU counter-cyclical mechanism to avoiding costs to business and ensuring 'flexibility' in the labour market. Labour's rejection of old-style social democratic interventionism was confirmed by Blair's performance at the PES congress in Malmo in June 1997 where he warned his somewhat startled PES colleagues that they should 'modernise or die', and by the key role he played at Amsterdam in killing off the attempts by Jospin to resurrect the kind of interventionist EU-wide policies that Labour had appeared willing to support in 1995 (Rawnsley 2000: 75, Young, H 1999: 490-491, Anderson and Mann 1997: 114-115, Callaghan 2000: 164-165). These episodes illustrated the apparent antipathy of 'New Labour' to notions of the EU being used as a mechanism by which a European social model could be protected and developed. This has been noted by David Marquand:

> The paradox is that, as the Thatcherites correctly spotted, part of the purpose of the EU is to Europeanise a solidaristic model of society and the economy…(and) to defend that model against the pressures of the global marketplace to create a supranational space in which to protect the European social market from creeping Americanisation (1998: 20).

Although this conception of the EU was generally embraced by the Labour party in the early 1990s it is not one with which 'New Labour' under Blair appeared to have any truck. While the EU policy documents produced under the Kinnock and Smith leaderships in 1991 and 1993 seemed to endorse the idea that the protection of the European social model from the excesses of international capital provided a convincing rationale for the existence of the EU, this view was rejected by the Blairites. Indeed, far from resisting 'creeping Americanisation' the Blairites appeared to prefer the deregulatory model favoured by the US Democrats to the interventionist solidaristic model favoured by centre-left parties on the European continent (Callaghan 2000: 165, Kenny and Smith 2000: 244). Nevertheless, it was only in the run-up to the general election, particularly after the LWG stopped meeting in autumn 1996, that this shift in emphasis became more clearly apparent. This had not been reflected in the 1995 policy document, which had stayed true to social democratic formulations on economic co-ordination, employment and the social dimension. The document had generally reflected a conception of the EU shared by its authors, Whitty (responsible for the initial draft) and Cook (responsible for the revised draft). But this did not necessarily reflect the views of the entire Labour leadership. Within the LWG and the Labour leadership generally, a distinction could be made between those that continued to adhere to the social democratic conception of the EU (as outlined by Marquand above) and the true 'New Labour' believers, notably Blair and Brown, who were at best ambivalent about this approach. Whitty and Cook seemed to be clearly within the former camp (at least prior to 1997[1]) and their views were more than likely shared by most of the EPLP. Indeed, Cook's approach to the EU, as reflected in his early strategy paper to the LWG and his speech to the European Policy Institute in January 1995 where he referred to the EU as a 'democratic parallel to the global character of modern capital', appeared to be at one with the conception of the EU enunciated in Labour's policy documents in the early 1990s (LWG IGC3A). But it is puzzling that despite its Keynesian and redistributionist tone, the 1995 policy document was approved by both the LWG and the NEC and therefore presumably had the blessing of Blair and Brown. The support enunciated in the document for an EU counter-cyclical strategy appeared to sit uneasily with the more orthodox neo-liberal strategy being set out by Brown in relation to the UK economy, though the two strategies were not necessarily mutually exclusive and Brown had initially shown some interest in the Euro-Keynesian strategy floated by Coates and Holland in 1992 and developed in the Delors White Paper in 1993 (Anderson and Mann 1997: 93-97, Callaghan 2000: 149-151). Brown and Blair may have consented to the references to this strategy in the 1995 policy document in order to humour Cook and the EPLP, among whom the idea had a high degree of support, and also because they were concentrating their efforts on distancing the Labour party from old-style interventionism at the UK level, whilst leaving Cook with a considerable amount of leeway to shape EU policy. But it was notable that Blair had also expressed support for the Delors initiative in a speech in Brussels in January 1995 and that the economic policy document, *A New Economic Future for Britain*, produced by Brown's treasury team around the same time as the EU policy document also stated support for the EU counter-cyclical strategy (Callaghan 2000: 150).

Nevertheless, by the middle of 1996, as the general election neared and the desire to calm business fears about interventionist policies and labour costs became an increasing obsession, it appears that Blair and his allies had decided that this area of EU policy also required an ideological cleansing to allay such concerns.[2] Moreover, this may have reflected a broader shift in New Labour's economic thinking in 1995-1996. Paul Norris argues that statements on economic policy by the Labour leadership in this period demonstrated a clear break from the German-style 'stakeholder capitalism' that the Labour leadership had previously flirted with and an embrace of the 'unrestrained market capitalism of the Anglo-American model' (1999).[3] The shift in EU policy was reflected in the appointment of a leading Blairite, Stephen Byers, as spokesman on the social chapter. From mid-1996 onwards, Byers sought to distance the Labour party from support for social and employment measures that might impose costs on business. Thus while continuing to support the social and employment chapters in principle, the Labour party had, by the time it entered government, reverted to what one LWG participant describes as a 'Thatcherite position' as regard their contents (Interview with LWG participant). Similarly, Labour's positions on EU environmental policy shifted to a more liberal pro-business position. This was reflected at the PES congress in Malmo, when Blair indicated to Rasmussen that Labour would support strengthened environmental provisions but only if they did not undermine the single market.

The difference in approach between the Blairites and the European social democrats such as Cook and Whitty was also reflected in their respective attitudes to the PES. While recognising its limitations, the latter embraced it enthusiastically as a tool of policy co-ordination in order to work towards a particular social and economic orientation.[4] The Blairites on the other hand appeared more ambivalent. This included Blair himself, who appeared much less interested in networking with other PES leaders and seeking to co-ordinate positions with them. This was particular so when compared to his predecessor, John Smith. Blair was not particularly keen on PES meetings and would usually do his best to get out of them. Indeed, one LWG participant suggests that Blair regarded the PES as a waste of time. Blair was persuaded to engage more with the PES, though he only went to the Dublin PES leaders meeting at the end of 1996 under duress. Blair appeared to have a particular dislike for formal multilateral meetings, though he did see the value of bilateral discussions in order to develop alliances with individual PES parties. In particular, he enjoyed good personal relations with some PES leaders, such as Kok, Klima, Guterres and Persson. However, these could be contrasted with Blair's poor relations with Jospin, with whom he refused to speak prior to the French national assembly elections (Interviews with LWG participants). Moreover, Blair's condescending attitude to what he viewed as the dated policies of PES parties was apparent at Malmo shortly after Jospin's victory. Indeed, Blair's close personal and ideological relationship with the US Democratic president, Bill Clinton, overshadowed his relations with PES leaders (Hodder-Williams 2000). This was reflected in Blair's tendency to proselytise within the PES on behalf of an Anglo-Saxon deregulatory economic model, the dynamism of which was contrasted with the rigidities of the European social model (Clift 2001: 176).

National Interests and Structural Realities

Labour's adoption of a more neo-liberal deregulatory approach to the labour market and broader economic policy at both the UK and EU level, combined with its pursuit in government of certain structural UK interests such as retention of border controls and resistance to EU defence, has led JW Young to suggest that the Blair government was the 'natural successor' to that of Margaret Thatcher (2000:

179). The pursuit of these policies, together with other traditional British prerogatives such as reform of the CAP and the need to speed up the process of enlargement appeared to demonstrate, at least superficially, a striking continuity in the EU policy priorities of Conservative and New Labour governments (Hughes and Smith 1998). But while there was a continuity in terms of the policies pursued, as already discussed, there were in many respects sharp differences in the respective approaches of the Conservative and Labour governments to many of the institutional reforms on the agenda of the Amsterdam IGC. These different approaches reflected diverging political strategies as to how UK interests should be pursued. As indicated by the Labour party manifesto in 1997, the Blair government viewed 'constructive engagement' and the exercise of British leadership in the EU as the best way to secure UK interests. In contrast to this, the Major government had increasingly resorted to isolationism rather than attempting to negotiate constructively in order to safeguard certain UK interests. While Major himself and a number of his cabinet colleagues may also have been personally inclined to negotiate constructively within the EU (as the Thatcher and Major governments had done in relation to previous treaty changes), they were prevented from doing so by the internal politics of the Conservative party. Further concessions to 'Brussels' were close to impossible given the post-Maastricht ratification mind-set of the Conservative party (Baker 2001: 279-281). The Conservative party increasingly appeared to want the best of two worlds: to have the benefits of EU membership such as membership of a vast single market with liberalised trade and the exercise of influence in global trade discussions, but without the 'drawbacks' implied by having a supranational Commission and ECJ to ensure effective and binding implementation of treaty commitments (and the legislation deriving from these), supranational forms of voting (i.e. QMV) to ensure effective decision-making, and certain 'flanking' policies to ensure a 'level playing field' in the single market and to ameliorate market failures. The Conservative party was content for these mechanisms and provisions to apply where UK interests were furthered but not where decisions were taken and enforced which might be inconvenient to the UK government or to broader national interests. On the other hand, the Labour party appeared to recognise that in order for the EU system to function effectively, certain mechanisms were required which, while sometimes working counter to UK interests, would also ensure the effective implementation of key UK objectives, and that the potential advantages of the latter would outweigh the potential disadvantages of the former. According to the liberal intergovernmental model of EU development outlined by Andrew Moravcsik, it is this kind of rational cost-benefit analysis of EU level solutions that characterises the behaviour of national governments in European negotiations (1993).[5] This approach also appears to characterise the thinking of UK government officials and explains the relief felt within the FCO at the fresh start heralded by Labour's entry to government.

Even where there appeared to be a difference between the Conservative and Labour governments as regards the policy priorities to be pursued, such as in relation to the social and employment chapters, a closer analysis indicates that the difference in approach between the two governments related more to the political strategy for achieving UK objectives rather than the policy objectives themselves.

It appears that the Blair government's support for both the social and employment chapters reflected a belief that through shaping and participating in these provisions, the UK could form alliances with like-minded member states (i.e, those with centre-right governments such as Spain and Germany) to dilute their contents and ensure that 'unnecessary' costs to business were avoided. Robert Taylor suggests that Blair had assured the CBI leadership in a private meeting in January 1997 that a Labour government would seek to block the adoption of new legislation within the social chapter once it had signed up to it. This helped to convince the CBI that UK participation in the social chapter would actually be a good thing, as this would increase the chances of new social policy measures (which in any case would affect UK companies operating on the continent whether or not the UK was part of the social chapter) being blocked (2001: 261-263).[6] Indeed, in his statement to the House of Commons, upon his return from Amsterdam, Blair proudly proclaimed that the Labour government had prevented the extension of QMV in the social chapter, and that British business had thus benefited from UK participation in it. This was because an extension of QMV 'would have affected our companies even if we had not been party to the chapter' (Hansard 18 June 1997). Thus the shift in the UK position on the social chapter under the Labour government, did not, as suggested by Simon Hix, simply reflect the Labour party's representation of different economic interests from those of the Conservatives, i.e. the interests of organised labour (2000: 51), but rather reflected a more pragmatic political strategy. Of course, the party's historic link with the labour movement would have made it politically very difficult for a Labour government to oppose these provisions altogether, particularly given the critical role played by the development of an EU social dimension in the party's earlier conversion to pro-Europeanism. However, the government's approach to the social and employment chapters seemed to involve combining symbolic concessions on issues that appealed to the party grassroots and affiliated trade unions (and were likely to elicit broader public support) whilst ensuring that the provisions were deprived of significant substance. Indeed, in terms of defending a particular economic interest, the Blair government would prove to be a more faithful defender of the interests of big business than those of organised labour (Monbiot 2000). One could also argue that the defence of established economic interests by New Labour actually represented a divergence from its strategy of reconciling its EU policies with domestic politics. Support for EU action on social and environmental protection and employment creation had the potential to be electorally popular, yet the Labour party began to distance itself from such notions in the run-up to the general election.

Hix also attributes the divergence in approach between the Labour and Conservative governments as regards the powers of the EP to their differing economic preferences. Noting that the EP's main legislative competences relate to rules governing economic, social and environmental regulation, Hix argues that because the natural coalition of social-democrats and Christian-democrats in the EP was closer to Blair's 'social market' agenda than 'the more neo-liberal agenda of the Thatcher and Major governments', the Blair government 'was willing to see an increase in the EP's powers to counteract either a "corporatist" or a "neo-liberal" majority in the Council' (2000: 50). This rather overlooks the Blair government's tendency, which became ever more apparent after Amsterdam, to seek to develop 'neo-liberal' alliances with centre-right governments in the Council behind deregulatory and pro-business positions. Moreover, examination of the subtle shift in Labour's positions once in government demonstrated that once ensconced in power it became more interested in retaining the balance of power in favour of the Council (rather than the EP) in relation to both legislative and budgetary decisions. Furthermore, it could be argued that the Labour government and the governments of other member states were more willing to make concessions to the EP's demands at Amsterdam because the vast majority of the key legislation regarding the single market and related matters was already in place and the EP's ability to make an impact therefore minimal. Labour's previously strong support for the EP related more to political factors than economic factors: i.e. the strength of the EPLP and the possibility of exercising leverage over EU policy-making, combined with the general commitment to UK and EU democratisation which followed the party's embrace of a more pluralistic attitude to political power in its opposition years. It was notable that just as Labour's enthusiasm for EP powers waned once it was in possession of the trappings of national political power, so too would its enthusiasm for certain aspects of the programme of domestic constitutional reform elaborated in opposition (Fella 2000).[7]

Paradoxically then, Labour's entry to government appeared to herald a new era of constructive engagement within the EU, with a number of notable breaks in policy from the recent past, while at the same time presenting a continuity in terms of the pursuit of certain key UK structural interests and a shift from the 'social democratic' perspective which had been central to Labour's earlier conversion into a pro-European party. As Richard Heffernan writes, the Europeanism of the Blair government would derive 'from the desire that Britain should benefit from membership of an EU that protects and enhances British interests' (2001: 188). In many respects, the Labour party under Blair was perceived as representing the pragmatic perspective that UK interests were best served through active engagement with European institutions that had once characterised the Conservative party of Heath, Howe, Hurd and Heseltine, but from which Conservative governments had increasingly departed since the end of the 1980s. This appeared to be the view within the FCO and among the 'establishment' interests that had previously been associated with the Conservative party. In particular, many business leaders had become increasingly aghast at the isolationism of their natural allies in the Conservative party and had indicated a preference for the European policies of New Labour (Young, JW 2000: 173, Marquand 1998: 24). Blair's words of comfort to the CBI and Chambers of Commerce concerning New Labour's determination to resist costly European social legislation would have increased the attraction of his EU policies to big business. The willingness of a senior former diplomat such as Sir Michael Butler to associate himself so openly with the EU policies of New Labour also symbolised the party's new 'establishment' appeal. Butler's experience of government and European diplomacy was of considerable importance to the Labour party in the run-up to the election in ensuring it was fully prepared for entrance into government and into the negotiations. The sudden emergence of Butler as a central actor in Labour's IGC policy-making in late 1996 accentuated the tendency of its positions to reflect traditional UK interests. At the same time, the social democratic and 'Europeanising' influences of the EPLP and the PES began to wane as the election neared and the Blair leadership sought to provide reassurance that it was both business friendly and would defend certain UK interests in the EU. Labour's EU policy thus became both more business orientated and nationalistic in the run-up the general election. While the latter positioning related more to electoral politics, the former reflected both electoral politics and a broader shift in economic preferences towards a traditional UK 'establishment' position. The shift to a pro-business EU policy orientation would be further demonstrated, once in government by Blair's appointment of the former head of BP, David Simon, to the post of minister for trade and competitiveness in Europe.

Once in government, party policy-making on the IGC became intertwined with that of the Whitehall machine, and Labour's tendency to pursue traditional institutional interests became a striking feature of EU policy. In particular, this reflected structural economic interests. As Hix writes:

> Whichever government is in power, the British economy has a particular position vis-à-vis the core economies of the EU. Britain has lower levels of welfare spending, lower levels of worker protection, generally lower wages, more liberal markets...is more open to the global economy and is stronger in certain economic sectors (such as financial services) (2000: 50-51).

As a result certain economic preferences have been pursued, irrespective of the party in government. Thus the Blair government would continue to press for completion and further liberalisation of the single market, improved labour market flexibility and the related theme of 'economic reform' to eliminate 'structural rigidities' in the EU economy (Stephens 2001a: 70, Heffernan 2001: 185-186, Hughes and Smith 1998: 96-97).

To these traditional economic preferences could be added political preferences deriving from Britain's island nature, leading to a belief that national control of borders and immigration/asylum policy was more effective than EU-wide mechanisms, and from the historic British relationship with the USA, which led to a belief that NATO remained the best framework for European security. However, it was notable that while the approach of the Blair government as regards UK economic preferences would harden during its first parliamentary term (as its relationship to business interests became more entwined), its preferences as regards immigration/asylum and defence would shift (Hix 2000: 50). This related to changing perceptions of the UK's structural interests among government ministers and officials. Large increases in the number of asylum-seekers entering the UK via other EU states would lead to a realisation that a common EU approach on immigration and asylum policies was desirable and to attempts by the Labour government to seek to opt-in to aspects of the 'freedom, security and justice' title in 1999 (though not those aspects relating to the abolition of national border controls). The inability of the EU/WEU to organise effective peace-keeping in Bosnia and its reliance on US airpower to remove Serb forces in Kosovo in 1999 led the Labour government to launch an initiative, alongside the French, to establish an EU rapid reaction force which would take over the Petersberg crisis management tasks (while territorial defence remained the preserve of the WEU/NATO) (Hoffman 2000: 193-195, Roper 2000: 9-10). The latter change of policy was rather unexpected given the primacy attached by the Labour government at Amsterdam to resisting EU defence proposals (Stephens 2001a: 71-72). Indeed, other policy priorities appeared to have been sacrificed to secure this negotiating objective. Nevertheless, the main reasoning behind the stance of the Blair government at Amsterdam was to avoid the functions of NATO and its primacy in terms of the territorial defence of Europe being undermined. The rapid reaction force initiative would later be backed only when the Blair government had become convinced that these long-held UK principles regarding NATO could be maintained and that the functions of this new military entity could be limited to crisis management without any overlap with NATO's territorial defence responsibilities.

In relation to institutional reform, the approach pursued by the Labour government at Amsterdam would remain fairly unchanged at the IGC staged in order to resolve the institutional questions it deferred, i.e. reform of Commission size, Council vote reweighting and QMV extension. This culminated in the Treaty of Nice agreed in December 2000. In relation to the first two of these issues, the approach pursued could be easily explained in terms of the interests of one of the EU's larger states in having its relative size more accurately reflected in EU decision-making. Thus the UK – along with the other large states – agreed to eventually give up its right to a second Commissioner, but only in parallel with a reweighting that would significantly increase its voting strength in the Council (Antola 2002: 76-77).[8] In relation to the scope of QMV, Nice would see its extension to many of the policy areas (such as industrial policy) to which the Labour government had been prepared to agree at Amsterdam, as well as other second level issues (such as appointments) where it perceived an interest in effective decision-making. But it continued to resist QMV in areas that were deemed as too sensitive to jeopardise a national interest by creating a risk of being outvoted, such as social security, taxation, own resources and defence, reflecting its 1997 manifesto commitments (Baker 2001: 285-288). Nice also saw extensions of the scope of EP codecision to those fairly non-sensitive areas to which QMV had also been extended. In general, however, the enthusiasm of the Blair government for the role of the EP would continue to diminish after the Amsterdam summit. Most notably, public statements by both Blair and Cook indicated a switch in emphasis to enhancing the input of national parliaments into EU policy-making as a way of bringing the EU closer to its citizens (*New Statesman*, 14 August 1998, Blair, 6 October 2000).[9] Labour's massive losses in the 1999 European elections[10] (and the consequent fall from grace of the EPLP from its previously influential position in the EP) would accentuate this diminishing enthusiasm.

The Nice summit would also see agreement that a further IGC on the future of the EU be held in 2004 in order to give greater clarity to its constitutional architecture, through discussion of a possible constitutional or political text setting out the role of the EU's institutions, its policy-making mechanisms and competences and the rights guaranteed to its citizens.[11] In opposition, the LWG had rejected the idea of a European constitution. Furthermore, Whitehall wariness as regards the possibility of a consolidated treaty text undermining carefully negotiated treaty compromises had been demonstrated in the development of the Blair government's positions prior to Amsterdam. This approach would be reflected in the government's caution as regards the status of any text emerging from the 2004 review, preferring a political declaration to a judicially enforceable constitutional text. This would also be linked to the government's new found preference for enhancing the role of the national parliaments in European policy development, with Blair suggesting that a chamber of national parliamentarians be established to ensure EU adherence to a political declaration (rather than a judicially enforceable constitution) outlining where it should and should not act (Blair, 6 October 2000, Fella 2002: 2).[12]

As Nice would later demonstrate, New Labour's process of policy formulation in relation to the EU would become more inextricably tied to that of the Whitehall machine once it became further embedded in government. The influence of certain 'institutional' Whitehall interests on the development of EU policy was, however, already apparent in the run-up to the Amsterdam summit. The positions taken by various ministers in the policy co-ordination exercise, as the government refined its negotiating stance for Amsterdam, generally appeared to reflect the departmental interests of their respective government fiefdoms. In some cases this created a divergence of approach between government departments and left ambiguities in the government position. For example, there did appear to be some divergence between the DTI and FCO in the run-up to Amsterdam in relation to the UK position on extending the Commission's mandate to negotiate in trade in services and intellectual property. The DTI appeared to favour such a supranational approach, in line with UK trading interests given its economic strength in these sectors, while the FCO appeared to favour reserving the UK position on this issue in the negotiations. The UK's later negotiating position at Nice would indicate that this dilemma had been resolved in favour of the DTI approach. The vigour with which a minister previously associated with leftist Euro-scepticism (Margaret Beckett) championed the departmental interest of the DTI prior to Amsterdam was particularly noteworthy. In general, the FCO has also in recent decades been viewed as having an institutional interest (in order to enhance its own status) in seeking strong UK engagement in the EU.[13] The treasury, on the other hand, has generally been reticent about any interference in its sphere of authority (Buller and Smith 1998: 167-178). This appears to have been reflected, once Labour entered government, by the increasing Euro-enthusiasm of the foreign secretary, Robin Cook, and the comparatively Euro-sceptical path taken by the chancellor, Gordon Brown, previously viewed as a Euro-phile advocate of UK participation in the European single currency (euro). In the course of the government's first term of office, the perception would develop that Brown was now rather sceptical about the merits of UK euro entry. Cook on the other hand - aware of the political clout that euro membership would give to the UK within the EU (from which the FCO would obviously benefit) - would become one of its leading advocates within the government (Baker 2001: 283-285, Stephens 2001a: 69). Another government department traditionally viewed as wary of any EU interference in its sphere of authority is the home office. The interventions made by the home secretary, Jack Straw, prior to Amsterdam, certainly appeared to reflect this institutional interest, although in this case they also coincided with his own rather Euro-sceptic beliefs. Nevertheless, as already noted, the positions of both Straw and the home office would shift as the logic of closer European co-operation on immigration and asylum issues and in the fight against crime and terrorism became more apparent. Once in office, the difficulties posed by trying to resolve problems arising in relation to these policy issues in national isolation would become clearer to Straw and he would rethink his previous antagonism to closer integration in JHA. Moreover, following the successful re-election of the Labour government in 2001, Straw would replace Cook as foreign secretary, and (along with the new minister for Europe - the former Maastricht rebel, Peter Hain[14]) also find himself espousing the FCO's pro-euro line (*The Guardian*, 15 December 2001).

The Euro and Labour's European Future

The brief flurry of media interest in institutional issues awakened by the Nice negotiations aside, the question of whether or not the Blair government would seek to take Britain into the euro-zone would dominate discussion of Labour's European policy after Amsterdam (Holden 1999, Gamble and Kelly 2000, Baker 2001, Stephens 2001a). Officially, the Labour party line on British membership of the single currency had, under the Blair leadership, more or less remained the one of conditional support inherited from the Smith leadership. Although it had been agreed within the Labour leadership in late 1994 that the party's approach to the EMU issue would be tied to the work of the LWG, it appeared that the LWG did little more than take note of the formulations on the issue put forward by Gordon Brown's then shadow treasury team. These formulations on the EMU question were no doubt discussed privately between the offices of Blair and Brown, but were developed separately from the IGC policy-making process being undertaken by the LWG. Since Maastricht, the Labour leadership had offered support in principle for EMU but had been ambiguous as to whether or not UK participation was as a desirable, feasible and/or realistic possibility in the near future. Thus both the EU policy document adopted under Smith in 1993 and the policy document adopted under Blair in 1995 signalled support for the project but referred to the need for 'real' economic convergence within the EU (rather than a convergence based simply on the monetary indicators of the TEU) and the need for political accountability in the management of the single currency before UK membership could be considered (Labour Party 1993b: 49-53, 1995: 3-7). The need for 'real' convergence was also stressed by Blair in his Bonn speech of May 1995. This speech was notable for Blair's suggestion that for the Labour party there was no 'overriding constitutional barrier' to UK participation in the final stage of EMU. Labour recognised the economic benefits that membership would bring, and its ultimate judgement on joining would be based on economic considerations (Blair, 30 May 1995). The manifesto for the general election in 1997 again stressed the need for genuine convergence but also warned that to 'exclude British membership of EMU would be to destroy any influence we have over a process which will affect us whether we are in or out' (Labour Party 1997b: 37). Labour also went into the election promising to seek the consent of the British people first, through a popular referendum, should it decide in favour of UK entry. Though this pledge has been portrayed as a reaction to the referendum promise made by the Major government in 1996, which forced Labour to follow suit (Deighton 2001: 316-317, Stephens 2001a: 72), such a move by the Labour leadership had always looked on the cards. Indeed, the idea of staging a referendum was flagged up at the first meeting of the LWG at the end of 1994, in a paper circulated by Whitty (LWG IGC1D).

The Blair government was forced to take a decision of sorts in relation to EMU a few months after the Amsterdam summit, being obliged to indicate whether or not it would seek UK entry among the 'first wave' of member states participating in the euro in time for its launch in January 1999 (though there were initial misplaced hopes that the project could be delayed[15]). This would lead to the government - for the time being - exercising the opt-out negotiated by Major at Maastricht, whilst declaring its willingness in principle to join and fleshing out in more detail the conditions which would require positive fulfilment in the future in order for it to stage the promised referendum and recommend entry (Stephens 2001b: 198-202, Gamble and Kelly 2000: 2). Like the five conditions for entry to the EEC set out by the party in 1962 (Newman 1983: 173-178), the five conditions set out by Gordon Brown for euro entry in 1997[16] would be highly subjective and reflect a need to compromise between sceptics and enthusiasts within the Labour leadership (Stephens 2001a: 72-74). Moreover, in spite of the attempt to reduce the question of UK euro entry to one of economics, the importance of political factors in shaping government thinking was clear. As had been the case in the shaping of its positions for the Amsterdam IGC, Labour would be caught between the contrasting demands of the domestic political situation in the UK and its desire to engage constructively and play an influential and leading role in the development of the EU. Given the unpopularity of the prospect of euro membership among the British people and the virulent campaign against it in much of the press, domestic politics appeared to militate against seeking UK entry (Stephens 2001a: 74). Nevertheless, Blair appeared to be personally convinced that in order to be taken seriously as a central and leading player and maintain a strong political and economic influence within the EU, UK euro membership was essential (Stephens 2001b: 203). While the enthusiasm of Blair and his foreign office ministers for the euro would grow, Brown's journey in the other direction has already been noted. Though this increasing scepticism was partly attributed to personal rivalries within the government,[17] it also related back to the original concerns found within the Labour party in the early 1990s relating to the transparency, accountability and deflationary bias of the ECB. This may have seemed paradoxical given Brown's relative economic orthodoxy - as compared to the left-wing critics of the EMU provisions - and his decision to give the Bank of England operational independence within days of Labour taking office in May 1997 (a step initially interpreted as a positive move towards UK euro membership, given the EMU requirement for national central bank independence). Nevertheless, Brown recognised the shortcomings of an excessively monetarist approach. His and the treasury's preference for the more transparent and symmetrical policy-making system established for the Bank of England over that of the ECB would soon become apparent (*The Guardian*, 4 January 2001). The new UK structure put in place by Brown obliged the Bank of England to avoid both excessive inflation and deflation in respect of a target set by the government[18] (allowing the government to continue to exercise overall control over the direction of policy) and provided for the publication of the minutes of the Bank's deliberations on monetary policy. The ECB on the other hand had only an obligation to keep inflation as low as possible and operated in secrecy. Brown and the treasury seemingly recognised the deflationary dangers in this system (and of the inflexibility of accompanying rules limiting the size of national budget deficits even in times of recession[19]) and believed that a system more akin to the UK one would be preferable for the euro-zone (*The Guardian*, 9 November 2001). In launching a national changeover plan for the euro in February 1999 (to prepare the economy logistically should the decision to join be taken), Blair declared that 'as a matter of principle, Britain should join the single currency' provided the economic tests were met (Stephens 2001a: 73, 2001b: 203). But the domestic unpopularity of the euro, continuing concerns about the level of convergence between the UK economy and that of the euro-zone, Brown's cooler approach and treasury reservations about euro-zone monetary policy-making meant that a decision on if and when to stage a referendum had still not been taken by the Blair government as euro notes and coins went into circulation in January 2002. Yet as long as the UK remained outside the euro-zone, seeking to change its policy-making structure would prove a difficult task. British leadership in the EU would have its limits while the UK remained outside of its most ambitious project.

This book has offered a detailed examination of Labour's positions on the key treaty reform issues in relation to the 1996-97 IGC. However, the nature of this policy development and the shifts in emphasis illustrated by this examination offer wider lessons for the study of Labour's European policy positions post-Amsterdam in relation to further treaty reforms, the question of British participation in the euro-zone and the wider debate on the future of the EU. The desire for constructive engagement would be tempered by domestic political constraints but also shaped by the shifts in policy emphasis that characterised the creation of New Labour. New Labour's constructive engagement with the EU would be bound up with a desire to export a 'third way' social and economic model that owed more to Clinton and the US Democrats than to the European social model. This would also have repercussions for Labour's relationships with other PES parties. The potential of the PES as a forum for EU policy co-ordination appeared to gain increased significance in 1998 with the election of a PES (SPD) government led by Gerhard Schröder in Germany, and the emergence of a PES (PDS) prime minister, Massimo d'Alema, within the ruling centre-left coalition in Italy. For the first time, the leadership of the 'big four' EU member states would be held simultaneously by

PES parties. Though this raised some hopes that the four could work together (along with the other nine EU governments with PES representation) to steer the EU in a more pronounced social democratic direction (Ladrech 2000: 116), Blair would continue to proselytise to all who would listen on behalf of his Anglo-Saxon third way vision. Some PES leaders, including Schröder, would attach themselves to the 'third way' banner and most seemed to accept the need for greater flexibility in the European economy (whilst not necessarily wishing to de-regulate to the post-Thatcherite level of the UK[20]). However, this seemed to fall rather short of mobilising the entire PES family behind a distinctive social democratic project for the EU (Clift 2000).[21] Indeed it was more about distancing the EU from social democracy, in its traditional sense. The adoption of a joint PES manifesto for the 1999 EP elections (which - unlike in 1994 - Labour adopted without feeling the need to issue a separate national manifesto) seemed to suggest that the Labour leadership still took the PES seriously as a forum for policy co-ordination, particularly as it was drawn up by a working-group chaired by Robin Cook (Ladrech 2000: 92, PES 1999). However, the PES solidarity implied by the manifesto was somewhat undermined by the launch of a separate joint document on the third way by Blair and Schröder mid-way through the election campaign.[22] Moreover, while Blair would cultivate close bilateral relationships with certain PES leaders, his penchant for bilateralism would also extend to close relationships with centre-right leaders such as Aznar (Stephens 2001a: 70, Taylor 2001: 264), much to the irritation of New Labour's sister party in Spain, the PSOE.[23] Even more controversially, following the defeat of the centre-left coalition in the Italian elections of 2001, Blair would also develop an alliance with the right-wing Italian prime minister, Silvio Berlusconi, in favour of further European liberalisation and against any new initiatives on workers' protection.[24]

Blair's third way as applied both to the UK and the EU as a whole reflected a belief that the answer to the challenges presented by globalisation was to go with the grain of the 'irreversible changes' that it brought and equip businesses with the best possible means to survive in the increasingly competitive global marketplace (Callaghan 2000: 160). Globalisation was thus a fact of life to which there was no alternative, and in relation to which national governments had minimal ability to impose any order. As Stuart Hall suggests, New Labour has accordingly withdrawn from the active management of the economy, instead concentrating on adapting society to the global economy's needs, tutoring its citizens to be self-sufficient and self-reliant in order to compete more successfully in the marketplace (1998). This approach is reflected in the words of Peter Mandelson, Blair's closest collaborator on the New Labour project:

> ...what is the case for the new Europe we are making? If the EU did not exist, we would need to re-invent it. First think of economic realities today in a world of globalisation. We live in a world of mobile capital and rapid technology transfer. Prosperity depends on creating the most favourable environment for business to invest. Governments can help create that environment by offering business unimpeded access to big markets, giving business the capacity to maximise economies of scale and

guaranteeing stable economic conditions throughout a large economic area for investment and growth (Mandelson, 28 June 1999).

This appears far removed from the justification of European institutions provided by Labour's 1993 policy document as necessary to prevent abuses by transnational companies, protect the vulnerable and exploited and exercise 'collective power' to prevent the direction of the European economy being determined by 'international commercial forces' (Labour Party 1993b: 47). It also seems fairly distant from Cook's 1995 description of the EU as a democratic counterweight to global capital (LWG IGC3A) and indeed from the 1995 policy document which suggested that the objectives of the EU include the creation of worthwhile employment for all and better redistribution of the wealth created by the single market (Labour Party 1995: 2-3). Labour's shift away from this approach explains the Blair government's positions in relation to proposals pushed by the German finance minister Oskar Lafontaine (who like much of the SPD was decidedly to the left of Schröder), following the SPD victory in 1998, for greater macro-economic co-ordination at the EU level, stronger employment and environmental protection and EU tax harmonisation. Some form of tax co-ordination was viewed as necessary to prevent a race to the bottom among EU countries seeking to attract investment by reducing taxes (and accordingly the welfare and public service provision funded by them). Lafontaine's proposals, though perhaps rather ill-timed given their coincidence with the launch of the euro, reflected his view - shared with much of the SPD and the French PS - that globalisation was not an ineluctable force and that its liberalising impulses could be resisted through international policy co-ordination at the EU level and beyond (Clift 2000: 63, Callaghan 2000: 163-172). While this approach had support from the French and some other PES governments (Clift 2000: 67-8), the Blair government did not hide its disdain for it or its pleasure when Lafontaine was forced to resign from the German government because of his differences with Schröder.

While there has been a degree of convergence among PES parties around the third way themes of structural reform to ensure greater flexibility in the European economy (Deighton 2001: 318, Stephens 2001a: 70-71),[25] New Labour has diverged from some of its European sister parties as regards the policy options open to the EU in the face of the economic transformations wrought by globalisation (Callaghan 2000: 166-167). This reflects a general shift in Labour's political and economic approach engineered by Blair and his New Labour collaborators prior to the 1997 general election and confirmed by the Blair government's behaviour at the Amsterdam summit. The shift away from a European social democratic perspective made it more difficult for the UK government to find common cause with centre-left governments on the continent that shared its concerns about the asymmetry and lack of transparency in the management of the euro. Nevertheless, the behaviour of the Blair government at Amsterdam and thereafter confirmed the pro-European transformation of the Labour party and signalled the launch of a new phase of constructive engagement with the European continent. Though this reflected continuities in the pursuit of certain traditional British interests it represented a clear break from the troubled history of previous Labour governments in Europe and from the downward trajectory in relations delivered by Conservative governments in the 1990s. Blair would boldly state his aim of resolving 'once and for all...(the UK's) ambivalence towards Europe' (Stephens 2001a: 67). But doubts would continue concerning these aspirations for strong UK engagement and leadership in Europe as long as the UK remained outside of the euro-zone. Until the leap of faith into the euro-zone could be made, the influence of the British contribution to the debate on the future of the EU would have its limits.

Notes

[1] Gamble and Kelly note that even those within the government thought to be sympathetic to a European Keynesian social democratic agenda (such as Cook), would later go out of their way to distance themselves from these positions. They cite a speech by Cook in which he emphasised that the government's 'third way' was based on a rejection of both neo-liberalism and 'corporatist social democracy' (2000: 21).

[2] These Blairite allies included Peter Mandelson and Roger Liddle who would increasingly make their presence felt in the shaping of Labour's EU policy in the run-up to the election and once it entered government. Liddle and Mandelson had collaborated on the publication which was the nearest the 'New Labour' project had to a 'philosophical' elaboration of its policies and values: *The Blair Revolution: Can New Labour Deliver?* (1996). Liddle would be appointed as adviser on EU policy in the No. 10 policy unit following the election. Though Mandelson did not have a formal role in EU policy, either before or after the election, he would seek to carve out a role for himself as the leading enthusiast for British engagement in the EU within the Labour government. He would retain a strong influence over Blair despite between twice forced to resign from the government. His first resignation came in December 1999 following allegations of misconduct over his failure to disclose a personal loan from his fellow minister Geoffrey Robinson, whose financial affairs were under investigation by Mandelson's own (DTI) department. Though he would later make a ministerial comeback as Northern Ireland secretary, Mandelson was forced to resign again in January 2001 after being made the scapegoat for the government's close relationship with the billionaire Hinduja brothers (under investigation for bribery and corruption in connection to the Bofors arms scandal in their native India).

[3] The 'stakeholder' model was associated with thinkers such as Marquand and the former *Observer* editor and economic journalist, Will Hutton. It would have involved state intervention to promote long-term investment in the economy and social consensus, placing obligations on companies that went beyond the short-term interests of their shareholders. Norris suggests that the 'Hutton-Marquand vision' was rejected because it would have involved confronting 'entrenched capitalist interest in the shape of the City and its allies in the Treasury and company boardrooms' (1999: 30). John Callaghan suggests that Brown and Blair distanced themselves from Hutton's ideas because of their association with 'corporatism, labour-market regulation and legal obligations for firms that had been "set free" by the Thatcher governments.' Furthermore, he suggests that the Labour leadership 'did not want the burden of advocating policies that went against the grain of British society and that involved a risky institutional upheaval with no guarantee that the model would succeed on British soil.' However, he notes that they were 'markedly less cautious in their admiration for the economy of the US and less sceptical about Britain's capacity to emulate

it' (2000: 158-159). See Hutton (1999) for a critique of New Labour's failure to offer an alternative to the 'new right' neo-liberal consensus on the economy.

[4] Cook's personal commitment to the PES would be confirmed in early 2001, when he succeeded Rudolf Scharping as president of the PES (though this would hardly compensate Cook when he was demoted from the FCO to the position of leader of the House of Commons following the general election in June).

[5] According to this model, a domestic preference formation process first defines a set of national interests and identifies the potential benefits for national governments of EU level policy solutions, and a process of intergovernmental strategic interaction then defines the possible political responses of the EU system in order to deliver on these preferences. The outcomes of intergovernmental negotiations are therefore determined by the relative bargaining power of governments and the relative importance they attach to particular policy preferences (Moravcsik 1993)

[6] This approach would later be confirmed by the Blair government's attempts to block a proposed EC directive on workers' information and consultation, siding with the German, Spanish and Irish centre-right governments and against the vast majority of PES-led governments (*The Guardian*, 6 April 2001). Indeed, Taylor suggests that Mandelson and Liddle were active in lobbying the German government and the German employers' federation to oppose the directive (2001: 262). Following the German general election of 1998, the new centre-left government of Gerhard Schröder (who was more sympathetic to the Blairite 'third way' than most other PES leaders) also opposed the directive. However, the Blair government abandoned its opposition and agreed to the directive in June 2001 after the German government changed its position and indicated support for it, meaning that the UK would have to find other allies to form a 'blocking minority' against (*The Guardian*, 12 June 2001).

[7] For example, the Blair government severely watered down earlier proposals on a freedom of information act in the UK, and made clear its preference for an appointed rather than elected second chamber to replace the House of Lords. Furthermore, while devolving government to Scotland, Wales and London, it sought to exercise rigid control over the selection of Labour party candidates to the new bodies, most notably in relation to Labour candidates for first minister in Wales, and mayor of London (Fella 2000: 88-89).

[8] The reweighting - coming into effect in January 2005 - nearly tripled the voting strength of the largest states from 10 to 29. The voting strengths of the smaller states however, were (apart from the Netherlands) multiplied by less than two and a half. The leverage of the larger states was also augmented by the eventual increase of the threshold for a qualified majority from 71.3 per cent to 74.8 per cent of the total weighted votes (should all 12 CEE and southern European applicants join the EU) and by the new provision allowing for a request for verification to ensure that states comprising a qualified majority also represent at least 62 per cent of the total EU population. While favouring all the larger states, the latter provision would also give added leverage to Germany over the other large states, given its substantially greater population.

[9] In a *New Statesman* article in August 1998, Cook proposed the creation of a chamber of national parliamentarians within the EU to oversee the proper enforcement of the subsidiarity principle, and ensure that the EU level of governance did not exceed its rightful jurisdiction. Cook argued that the only way to tackle the 'democratic deficit' was through the involvement of 'democratic institutions in which the public have confidence and with which they identify' (with the implication that these requirements were not met by the EP). Blair developed this theme in a speech to the Polish stock exchange in October 2000.

[10] Labour was reduced to just 29 MEPs in 1999 (down from the 62 won in 1994). This reflected a fall in its share of the vote from 44.2 per cent to 28 per cent, although the fall in overall electoral turn-out (from 36.1 per cent in 1994 to 23.1 per cent in 1999) contributed to Labour's poor showing (Baker 2001: 279).

[11] This would include discussion of the Charter of Fundamental Rights adopted at Nice as a non-binding political declaration. The Blair government had opposed attempts to make the Charter legally enforceable through incorporation into the EU treaties. However, it was agreed that the 2004 review would reconsider the status of the Charter.

[12] Blair suggested this in his speech to the Polish stock exchange in October 2000. A commitment for a chamber of national parliamentarians was also contained in Labour's 2001 election manifesto (Labour Party 2001: 38).

[13] Kevin Theakston cites the view given by a Labour minister that the FCO viewed EU policy as a 'way of getting involved in a whole range of other issues' (2000: 125).

[14] Although Hain, like Straw, has often been depicted as a former Euro-sceptic, it is important to note that Hain's Maastricht rebellion was related more to his distaste for the deflationary and undemocratic EMU provisions than to a generalised Euro-scepticism, and that he was sympathetic to a Euro-Keynesian economic co-ordination strategy to counter the negative effects of EMU. Hain would also be appointed the UK government representative on the constitutional convention established in 2002 to prepare for the 2004 treaty review. The convention would comprise representatives of the national parliaments and the EP as well as those of the governments of the EU member states.

[15] Philip Stephens reports that upon taking office in May 1997, Brown raised with his officials the possibility of getting the UK's European partners to delay the euro project by two years, but that Sir Nigel Wicks, the senior treasury official responsible for European affairs advised him that this was impossible (2001a: 72, 2001b: 200).

[16] These conditions related to: 1) the degree of compatibility between the business cycles of the UK and the euro-zone, so that the UK economy could operate comfortably and permanently with euro-zone interest rates; 2) the existence of sufficient flexibility to deal with any economic problems that emerge; 3) whether or not membership of the euro-zone would create better conditions for firms making long term decisions to invest in the UK; 4) the impact that entry into the euro-zone would have on the UK's financial services industry; 5) whether or not joining the euro would promote higher growth, stability and a lasting increase in employment.

[17] Brown was reported to bear a grudge against Peter Mandelson, New Labour's most influential advocate for the euro, because the latter had backed Blair to succeed Smith (rather than Brown) as Labour leader in 1994. It has also been suggested that Brown had extracted a promise from Blair in 1994 that once in government, Blair would at some point step down as prime minister and leave the way open for Brown to succeed him, and that Brown's consent for euro entry somehow depended on Blair keeping to this promise (Stephens 2001a: 74, 2001b: 201-204).

[18] The chancellor set an inflation target of 2.5 per cent. Should the rate vary by more than one percentage point (either above or below the target), the monetary policy committee (MPC) of the Bank of England would have to explain itself to the treasury. The obligation on the MPC was to avoid both inflation and deflation, also taking into account the importance of economic growth. The chancellor would review and possibly reset the target annually in the budget (Stephens 2001b: 190).

[19] The stability pact agreed at the Dublin summit in December 1996 obliged euro-zone members to limit budget deficits to no more than three per cent of national gross domestic product. Member states exceeding this limit could be subject to fines. Brown's view was

that deficits at times of cyclical down-turns were acceptable, but that budgets should be balanced over the course of the economic cycle. What came to be defined as Brown's 'golden rule' was that over the course of the economic cycle, governments should be allowed to borrow, but only to invest, and not to finance current spending (Stephens 2001b: 191-193).

[20] Ben Clift notes that while most European social democratic parties accept the need for some increased flexibility in labour markets, there are widely diverging starting points between post-Thatcherite Britain under Blair and the other far more regulated European economies (2000: 70).

[21] Clift's comparative study of New Labour's third way and European social democracy demonstrates that while most PES parties on the continent accept the need for greater flexibility in their economies, many also continue to have a greater faith in the active interventionist role of the state, through a more balanced mix of demand-led and supply-side measures, and a number of PES parties have shown an interest in initiatives such as the 35 hour working week as introduced by the French PS. Clift also draws attention to the enthusiasm shown by PES governments in France, Germany, Sweden, Portugal and Italy (in late 1998) for stronger EU economic co-ordination to protect the European social model (2000).

[22] The launch of the Blair-Schröder paper: *Europe: The Third Way/Die Neue Mitte* caused some consternation among other PES parties, and particularly irritated the French socialists (Ladrech 2000: 74-75, Clift 2001: 170). It emphasised a liberal supply-side approach while the PES manifesto was more recognisably social democratic, advocating a more balanced mix of demand and supply-side measures.

[23] Alongside an article by Will Hutton entitled 'Now Spanish socialists know how British socialists feel', *The Observer* published an open letter in April 1999 from Manuel Escudero, chief policy adviser to José Borrell, the leader of the PSOE, expressing concern that Blair had collaborated with Aznar on a joint policy declaration on employment and economic reform. Hutton reported that Blair had told Aznar that he wanted as few social democratic EU Commissioners as possible, a weakened EP and a strengthened Council in order to bolster his strategy of moving the EU towards an Anglo-Saxon economic and social model (*The Observer*, 18 April 1999). Hutton also suggested that Blair had opposed the appointment of the former Spanish socialist prime minister, Felipe Gonzales (though he was never a serious contender), to succeed Santer as European Commission president and had successfully pushed the candidature of the former Italian prime minister (and 'third wayer'), Romano Prodi.

[24] Berlusconi's right-wing coalition in Italy included the formerly neo-fascist, National Alliance, and the populist anti-immigrant, Northern League. Blair was accused by the moderate leader of the TUC, John Monks, of being 'bloody stupid' for allying himself with Berlusconi. Blair and Berlusconi issued a joint statement on EU economic reform in February 2002 (*The Observer*, 17 March 2002).

[25] Thus there was general support among the PES and non-PES governments for the economic reform agenda put forward under the UK Council Presidency at the Cardiff European Council in June 1998. This led to a special summit on economic reform in Lisbon in March 2000 which formalised the system put forward at Cardiff of peer review and benchmarking around economic guidelines, stressing employability (i.e. improving skills and knowledge) in the labour market, welfare reform and encouragement for innovation and enterprise, particularly in relation to e-commerce.

Bibliography

Anderson, Paul and Mann, Nytta (1997), *Safety First: The Making of New Labour*, Granta, London.

Anderson, Stephanie B (1998), 'Problems and Possibilities: The Development of the CFSP from Maastricht to the 1996 IGC' in P. Laurent and M. Maresceau (eds), *The State of the European Union, Vol.4: Deepening and Widening*, Lynne Rienner Publishers, London.

Antola, Esko (2002), 'The Future of Small States in the EU' in M. Farrell, S. Fella and M. Newman (eds), *European Integration in the 21st Century - Unity in Diversity?*

Baker, David (2001), 'Britain and Europe: The Argument Continues', *Parliamentary Affairs*, Vol. 54, No.2.

Baker, David and Seawright, David (eds) (1998), *Britain For and Against Europe - British Politics and the Question of European Integration*, Clarendon, London.

Baker, David and Seawright, David (1998), 'Labour Parliamentarians and European Integration' in D. Baker and D. Seawright (eds), *Britain For and Against Europe*.

Baker, David, Gamble, Andrew and Ludlam, Steve (1993), 'Whips or Scorpions? The Maastricht Vote and the Conservative Party', *Parliamentary Affairs*, Vol. 46, No. 2.

Baker, David, Gamble, Andrew and Ludlam, Steve (1994), 'The Parliamentary Siege of Maastricht 1993: Conservative Divisions and British Ratification', *Parliamentary Affairs*, Vol. 47, No.1.

Baker, David, Gamble, Andrew, Ludlam, Steve and Seawright, David (1996), 'Labour and Europe: A Survey of MPs and MEPs', *Political Quarterly*, Vol. 67. No. 4.

Bardi, Luciano (1994), 'Transnational Party Federations, European Parliamentary Party Groups and the Building of Europarties', in R.S. Katz and P. Mair (eds), *How Parties Organize*.

Barker, Elisabeth (1971), *Britain in a Divided Europe*, Macmillan, London.

Barrett, Gavin (1997), 'Justice and Home Affairs Co-operation - An Overview', in Tonra (ed), *Amsterdam: What the Treaty Means*.

Barrett Brown, Michael and Coates, Ken (eds) (1993), *A European Recovery Programme*, Spokesman, Nottingham.

Blair, Tony (1996), *New Britain, My Vision of a Young Country*, Fourth Estate, London.

Bogdanor, Vernon (1992), 'The 1992 General Election and the British Party System', *Government and Opposition*, Vol.27, No.3.

Brivati, Brian (1997), *New Labour in Power: Precedents and Prospects*, Routledge, London.

Brivati, Brian and Jones, Harriet (1993), *From Reconstruction to Integration: Britain and Europe since 1945*, Leicester University Press, Leicester.

Brown Pappamikail, Peter (1998), 'Britain viewed from Europe' in D. Baker and D. Seawright (eds), *Britain For and Against Europe*.

Buller, Jim and Smith, Martin J (1998), 'Civil Service Attitudes towards the EU', in D. Baker and D. Seawright (eds), *Britain For and Against Europe*.

Buller, Jim (1995), 'Britain as an Awkward Partner: Reassessing Britain's Relations with the EU', *Politics*, Vol.15, No.1.

Bulmer, Simon (1992), 'Britain and European Integration: Of Sovereignty, Slow Adaption, and Semi-Detachment', in S. George (ed), *Britain and the European Community*.

Bulmer, Simon (1983), 'Domestic Politics and European Community Policy-Making' *Journal of Common Market Studies*, Vol. 21. No.4.

Burley, Ann-Marie and Mattli, Walter (1993), 'Europe before the Court: a political theory of legal integration' *International Organisation*, Vol. 32, No.1.

Callaghan, John (2000), *The Retreat of Social Democracy*, Manchester University Press, Manchester.

Clarke, Michael (1992), *British External Policy-Making in the 1990s*, Macmillan, London.

Clift, Ben (2000), 'New Labour's Third Way and European Social Democracy', in S. Ludlam and M. J. Smith (eds) *New Labour in Government*.

Clift, Ben (2001), 'The Jospin Way', *Political Quarterly*, Vol.72, No.2.

Coddington, Anne and Perryman, Mark (1998), *The Moderniser's Dilemma - Radical Politics in the Age of Blair*, Lawrence and Wishart, London.

Corbett, Richard (1992), 'The Intergovernmental Conference on Political Union', *Journal of Common Market Studies*, Vol. 30, No. 3.

Corbett, Richard (1996), 'The IGC Reflection Group', *Links Europa*, Vol. 21, No.1.

Corbett, Richard (1998), 'Governance and Institutions', *Journal of Common Market Studies*, Vol 36, Annual Review.

Corbett, Richard, Jacobs, Francis and Shackleton, Michael (1995), *The European Parliament*, Cartermill, London.

Criddle, Byron (1993), 'The French Referendum on the Maastricht Treaty' *Parliamentary Affairs*, Vol. 46, No.2.

Croft, Stuart (1992), 'The Labour Party and the Nuclear Issue' in M.J. Smith and J. Spear (eds), *The Changing Labour Party*

Daniels, Philip (1998), 'From Hostility to "Constructive Engagement": The Europeanisation of the Labour Party', *West European Politics*, Vol. 21. No.1.

Dehousse, Franklin (1999), *Amsterdam: The Making of A Treaty*, European Dossier Series, University of North London: Kogan Page, London.

Deighton, Anne (2001), 'European Union Policy', in A. Seldon (ed), *The Blair Effect - The Blair Government 1997-2001*.

Dinan, Desmond (1999), *Ever Closer Union - An Introduction to European Integration*, Macmillan, London.

Duff, Andrew (1997a), *Reforming the European Union*, Federal Trust, London.

Duff, Andrew (1997b), *The Treaty of Amsterdam: Text & Commentary*, Federal Trust, London.

Duff, Andrew (1998), 'Britain and Europe: the Different Relationship', in M. Westlake (ed) *The European Union beyond Amsterdam*, Routledge, London.

Dunleavy, Patrick, Gamble, Andrew, Holliday, Ian and Peele, Gillian (eds) (2000), *Developments in British Politics 6*, Macmillan, Basingstoke.

Dunleavy, Patrick (2000), 'Elections and Party Politics' in P. Dunleavy, A. Gamble, I. Holliday, and G. Peele (eds), *Developments in British Politics 6*.

Eatwell, John (1992), 'The development of Labour party policy 1979-92', in J. Michie (ed) *The Economic Legacy 1979-92*, Academic Press, London.

Edwards, Geoffrey and Pijpers, Alfred (eds) (1997), *The Politics of European Treaty Reform: the 1996 Intergovermental Conference and Beyond*, Pinter, London.

Edwards, Geoffrey and Pijpers, Alfred (1997), 'The 1996 IGC: An Introduction', in G. Edwards and A. Pijpers (eds), *The Politics of European Treaty Reform*.

Evans, Mark (1999), 'The Constitution under New Labour', in G. Taylor (ed), *The Impact of New Labour*.

Farrell, Mary, Fella, Stefano and Newman, Michael (eds) (2002), *European Integration in the 21st Century - Unity in Diversity?*, Sage, London.

Featherstone, Kevin (1988), *Socialist Parties and European Integration: A Comparative History,* Manchester University Press, Manchester.

Feld, Werner (1998), *The Integration of the EU and Domestic Political Issues,* Praeger, Westport, Connecticut.

Fella, Stefano (1999), *The 1996-97 Intergovernmental Conference and the Treaty of Amsterdam: A Thwarted Reform,* South Bank European Paper, No.1/99.

Fella, Stefano (2000), 'A Europe of the Peoples? - New Labour and Democratising the EU', in C. Hoskyns and M. Newman (eds), *Democratising the EU,* Manchester University Press, Manchester.

Fella, Stefano (2002), 'Introduction: Unity in Diversity - the Challenge for the EU', in M. Farrell, S. Fella and M. Newman (eds), *European Integration in the 21st Century.*

Ford, Glyn, Kinnock, Glenys and McCarthey, Arlene (eds) (1996), *Changing States: A Labour Agenda for Europe,* Mandarin, London.

Forster, Anthony (1998), 'Britain and the Negotiation of the Maastricht Treaty: A Critique of Liberal Intergovernmentalism', *Journal of Common Market Studies,* Vol.36, No.3.

Frankel, Joseph (1975), *British Foreign Policy 1945-73,* Oxford University Press, London.

Gaffney, John (ed) (1996), *Political Parties and the European Community,* Routledge, London.

Gamble, Andrew (1994), *Britain in Decline: Economic Policy, Political Strategy and the British State,* Macmillan, London.

Gamble, Andrew and Kelly, Gavin (2000), 'The British Labour Party and Monetary Union', *West European Politics,* Vol. 23, No.1.

Garry, John (1995), 'The British Conservative Party: Divisions Over European Policy', *West European Politics,* Vol. 18, No.4.

George, Stephen (1994), *An Awkward Partner - Britain in the European Community,* Oxford University Press, Oxford.

George, Stephen (ed) (1992), *Britain and the European Community - the Politics of Semi-Detachment,* Clarendon Press, Oxford.

George, Stephen (1997), 'Britain and the IGC', in G. Edwards and A. Pijpers (eds), *The Politics of European Treaty Reform.*

George, Stephen and Haythorne, Deborah (1996), 'The British Labour Party', in J. Gaffney (ed) *Political Parties and the European Community.*

George, Stephen and Rosamund, Ben (1992), 'The European Community', in M. J. Smith and J. Spear, *The Changing Labour Party.*

Gillespie, Paul (1997), 'The Promise and Practise of Flexibility', in B. Tonra (ed), *Amsterdam: What the Treaty Means.*

Grahl, John and Teague, Paul (1988), 'The British Labour Party and the EC', *Political Quarterly,* Vol. 59, No.1.

Greenwood, Sean (1992), *Britain and European Co-operation since 1945,* Blackwell, Oxford.

Haahr, Jens Henrik (1992), 'European Integration and the Left in Britain and Denmark', *Journal of Common Market Studies,* Vol.30. No. 1.

Haas, Ernst (1958), *The Uniting of Europe: Political, Social and Economic Forces, 1950-1957,* Stanford University Press, Stanford.

Hall, Stuart (1998), 'The Great Moving Nowhere Show', *Marxism Today,* Special Issue on New Labour.

Ham, Peter van (1997), 'The EU and the WEU: From Co-operation to Common Defence?', in G. Edwards and A. Pijpers (eds), *The Politics of European Treaty Reform.*

Heffernan, Richard (2001), 'Beyond Euro-Scepticism: Exploring the Europeanisation of the Labour Party since 1983', *Political Quarterly,* Vol. 72, No.2.

Hix, Simon (1996), 'The Transnational Party Federations', in J. Gaffney (ed), *Political Parties and the European Community*.

Hix, Simon (1999), 'The Party of European Socialists', in R. Ladrech and P. Marliere (eds) *Social Democratic Parties in the European Union*.

Hix, Simon (2000), 'Britain, the EU and the Euro', in P. Dunleavy, A. Gamble, I. Holliday and G. Peele (eds), *Developments in British Politics 6*.

Hix, Simon and Lord, Christopher (1997), *Political Parties in the European Union*, Macmillan, London.

Hodder-Williams, Richard (2000), 'Reforging the "special relationship"; Blair, Clinton and foreign policy', in R. Little and M. Wickham-Jones, *New Labour's Foreign Policy: A New Moral Crusade?*

Hoffman, Stanley (1966), 'Obstinate or Obsolete: the Fate of the Nation State and the Case for Western Europe', *Daedulus*, Vol. 95, No.3.

Hoffman, Stanley (1982), 'Reflections on the Nation State in Western Europe Today', *Journal of Common Market Studies*, Vol. 21, No.1.

Hoffman, Stanley (2000), 'Towards a Common European Foreign and Security Policy', *Journal of Common Market Studies*, Vol. 38, No.2.

Holden, Russel (1999), 'New Labour's European Challenge: from Triumphant Isolationism to Positive Integration', in G.R. Taylor (ed), *The Impact of New Labour*.

Holland, Robert *(1991), The Pursuit of Greatness: Britain and the World Role*, Fontana, London.

Holland, Stuart (ed) (1983), *Out of Crisis: A Project for European Recovery*, Spokesman, Nottingham.

Hughes, Colin and Wintour, Patrick (1990), *Labour Rebuilt - The New Model Labour Party*, Fourth Estate, London.

Hughes, Kirsty and Smith, Edward (1998), 'New Labour - New Europe?', *International Affairs*, Vol. 74, No.1.

Hutton, Will (1999), 'New Keynesianism and New Labour', in A. Gamble and T. Wright, (eds), *The New Social Democracy* (Political Quarterly Special Issue), Blackwell, Oxford.

Jeffreys, Kevin (1993), *The Labour Party since 1945*, Macmillan, London.

Jones, Nicholas (1999), *Sultans of Spin*, Victor Gollancz, London.

Jones, Tudor (1996), *Remaking the Labour Party - From Gaitskell to Blair*, Routledge, London.

Katz, Richard S and Mair, Peter (eds) (1994), *How Parties Organize: Changes and Adaption in Party Organisations in Western Democracies*, Sage, London.

Keatinge, Patrick (1997), 'Strengthening the Foreign Policy Process', in B. Tonra (ed), *Amsterdam: What the Treaty Means*.

Kenny, Michael and Smith, Martin J (2000), 'Interpreting New Labour: Constraints, Dilemmas and Political Agency', in S. Ludlam and M. J. Smith (eds), *New Labour in Government*.

Keohane, Dan (1993), *Labour Party Policy on Defence Since 1945*, Leicester University Press, Leicester.

Keohane, Dan (1992), 'The Approach of British Political Parties to a Defence Role for the European Community', *Government and Opposition*, Vol. 27, No.3.

Ladrech, Robert (1996), 'Political Parties in the European Parliament', in J. Gaffney (ed), *Political Parties and the European Community*.

Ladrech, Robert (2000), *Social Democracy and the Challenge of European Union*, Lynne Rienner, London.

Ladrech, Robert and Marliere, Phillipe (eds) (1999), *Social Democratic Parties in the European Union*, Macmillan, Basingstoke.

Laffan, Brigid (1997a), 'The IGC and Institutional Reform of the Union', in G. Edwards and A. Pijpers (eds), *The Politics of European Treaty Reform.*

Laffan, Brigid (1997b), 'The Governance of the Union' in B. Tonra (ed), *Amsterdam: What the Treaty Means.*

Larragy, Joe (1997), 'Social Policy', in B. Tonra (ed), *Amsterdam: What the Treaty Means.*

Leys, Colin (1997), 'The British Labour Party since 1989', in D. Sassoon (ed), *Looking Left: European Socialism after the Cold War*, IB Tauris, London.

Lightfoot, Simon (1995), *Is the Party of European Socialists a Political Party?'*, EPOP Conference Paper, London.

Lightfoot, Simon and Wilde, Lawrence (1996), 'The 1996 Intergovernmental Conference: what's in it for the left?', *Contemporary Politics*, Vol. 2, No.2.

Little, Richard and Wickham-Jones, Mark (eds) (2000), *New Labour's Foreign Policy: A New Moral Crusade?*, Manchester University Press, Manchester.

Ludlam, Steve (1998), 'The Cauldron: Conservative Parliamentarians and European Integration', in D. Baker and D. Seawright (eds), *Britain For and Against Europe.*

Ludlam, Steve (2000), 'The Making of New Labour', in S. Ludlam and M. J. Smith (eds), *New Labour in Government.*

Ludlam, Steve and Smith, Martin J (eds) (2000), *New Labour in Government*, Macmillan, Basingstoke.

McDonagh, Bobby (1998), *Original Sin in a Brave New World: An Account of the Negotiation of the Treaty of Amsterdam*, Institute of European Affairs, Dublin.

McLeod, Rhoda (1998), 'Calf Exports at Brightlingsea', *Parliamentary Affairs*, Vol. 51, No.1.

Mandelson, Peter and Liddle, Roger (1996), *The Blair Revolution - Can New Labour Deliver?*, Faber, London.

Marliere, Phillipe (1999), 'Introduction: European Social Democracy *in Situ*', in R. Ladrech and P. Marliere (eds), *Social Democratic Parties in the European Union.*

Marquand, David (1998), 'The Blair paradox', *Prospect*, May 1998.

Martin, David (1992), 'Comment on "Assessing MEP influence on British EC Policy"', *Government and Opposition*, Vol. 27, No.1.

Milward, Alan (1992), *The European Rescue of the Nation-State*, Routledge, London.

Minkin, Lewis (1991), *The Contentious Alliance - Trade Unions and the Labour Party*, Edinburgh University Press, Edinburgh.

Monbiot, George (2000), *Captive State - The Corporate Takeover of Britain*, Macmillan, London.

Moravcsik, Andrew (1993), 'Preferences and Power in The European Community: A Liberal Intergovernmentalist Approach', *Journal of Common Market Studies*, Vol 31, No. 4.

Moravcsik, Andrew and Nicolaidis, Kalypso (1998), 'Federal Ideas and Constitutional Realities in the Treaty of Amsterdam', *Journal of Common Market Studies*, Vol. 36, Annual Review.

Moravcsik, Andrew and Nicolaidis, Kalypso (1999), 'Explaining the Treaty of Amsterdam: Interests, Influence, Institutions', *Journal of Common Market Studies*, Vol. 37, No. 1.

Mullard, Maurice (2000), *New Labour, New Thinking - The Politics, Economics, and Social Policy of the Blair Government*, Nova Science Publishers, Huntington, New York.

Newman, Michael (1983), *Socialism and European Unity*, Junction Books, London.

Newman, Michael (1996), *The Party of European Socialists*, European Dossier Series No.41, University of North London, London.

Newman, Michael (1997), *Britain and European Integration since 1945: An Overview*, European Dossier Series No. 49, University of North London, London.

Northedge, Frederick (1974), *Descent From Power: British Foreign Policy, 1945-1973*, George Allen and Unwin, London.

Norris, Paul (1999), 'New Labour and the Rejection of Stakeholder Capitalism', in G.R. Taylor (ed), *The Impact of New Labour*.

O'Leary, Siofra (1996), *European Union Citizenship: Options for Reform*, Institute for Public Policy Research, London.

Petersen, Nikolaj (1997), 'The Nordic Trio and the Future of the EU', in G. Edwards and A. Pijpers (eds), *The Politics of European Treaty Reform*.

Pijpers, Alfred and Vanhoonacker, Sophie (1997), 'The Position of the Benelux Countries', in G. Edwards and A. Pijpers (eds), *The Politics of European Treaty Reform*.

Pilkington, Colin (1995), *Britain in the European Union Today*, Manchester University Press, Manchester.

Rawnsley, Andrew (2000), *Servants of the People: The Inside Story of New Labour*, Hamish Hamilton, London.

Robins, Lynton (1979), *The Reluctant Party - The Labour Party and the EEC 1961-75*, G.W. and A. Hesketh, Ormskirk.

Roper, John (2000), 'Two Cheers for Mr Blair? The Political Realities of European Defence Co-operation', *Journal of Common Market Studies*, Vol. 38, Annual Review.

Rosamund, Ben (1990), 'Labour and the European Community', *Politics*, Vol. 10.

Rosamund, Ben (1993), 'National Labour Organisations and European Integration: British Trade Unions and "1992"', *Political Studies*, Vol. 41, No.3.

Rosamund, Ben (1998), 'The integration of Labour? British Trade Union Attitudes to European integration', in D. Baker and D. Seawright (eds), *Britain For and Against Europe*.

Rentoul, John (1995), *Tony Blair*, Little, Brown, London.

Sassoon, Donald (ed) (1997), *Looking Left: European Socialism after the Cold War*, I.B. Tauris, London.

Seldon, Anthony (1998), *Major: A Political Life*, Phoenix, London.

Seldon, Anthony (ed) (2001), *The Blair Effect - The Blair Government 1997-2001*, Little, Brown, London.

Shaw, Eric (1994), *The Labour Party Since 1979: Crisis and Transformation*, Routledge, London.

Shaw, Eric (1996), *The Labour Party Since 1945: Old Labour, New Labour*, Blackwell, Oxford.

Smith, Martin J (1992), 'A Return to Revisionism?: The Labour Party's Policy Review', in M.J. Smith and J. Spear (eds), *The Changing Labour Party*.

Smith, Martin J (2000), 'Conclusion: the Complexity of New Labour', in S. Ludlam and M.J. Smith (eds), *New Labour in Government*.

Smith, Martin J, and Spear, Joanna (eds) (1992), *The Changing Labour Party*, Routledge, London.

Spear, Joanna (1992), 'The Labour Party and Foreign Policy', in M.J. Smith and J. Spear (eds), *The Changing Labour Party*.

Stephens, Philip (2001a), 'The Blair Government and Europe', *Political Quarterly*, Vol. 72, No.1.

Stephens, Philip (2001b), 'The Treasury Under Labour', in A. Seldon (ed), *The Blair Effect - The Blair Government 1997-2001*.

Story, Jonathan (1997), 'The Idea of the Core: The Dialectics of History and Space', in G. Edwards and A. Pijpers (eds), *The Politics of European Treaty Reform*.

Szukala, Andrea and Wessels, Wolfgang (1997), 'The Franco-German Tandem', in G. Edwards and A. Pijpers (eds), *The Politics of European Treaty Reform*.

Taylor, Gerald R (ed) (1999), *The Impact of New Labour*, Macmillan, Basingstoke.

Taylor, Gerald R, (1999), 'Power in the Party', in G. R. Taylor (ed), *The Impact of New Labour*.

Taylor, Robert (2001), 'Employment Relations Policy', in A. Seldon (ed), *The Blair Effect - The Blair Government 1997-2001*.

Theakston, Kevin (1999), 'Labour and the Civil Service', in G. R. Taylor (ed), *The Impact of New Labour*.

Theakston, Kevin (2000), 'New Labour and the Foreign Office', in R. Little and M. Wickham-Jones (eds), *New Labour's Foreign Policy: A New Moral Crusade?*

Tindale, Stephen (1992), 'Learning to Love the Market: Labour and the European Community', *Political Quarterly*, Vol. 63, No.4.

Tonra, Ben (1997), 'From Maastricht to Amsterdam', in B. Tonra (ed), *Amsterdam: What the Treaty Means*.

Tonra, Ben (ed) (1997), *Amsterdam: What the Treaty Means*, Institute of European Affairs, Dublin.

Tsakaloyannis, Panos (1997), 'The EU and the Common Interests of the South?', in G. Edwards and A. Pijpers (eds), *The Politics of European Treaty Reform*.

Tsoukalis, Loukas (1997), *The New European Economy Revisited*, Oxford University Press, Oxford.

Webb, Paul (1999), 'The British Labour Party', in R. Ladrech and P. Marliere, *Social Democratic Parties in the European Union*.

Westlake, Martin (1997), 'Keynote Article: "Mad Cows and Englishmen" - the Institutional Consequences of the BSE Crisis', *Journal of Common Market Studies*, Vol. 35, Annual Review.

Westlake, Martin (ed) (1998), *The European Union beyond Amsterdam*, Routledge, London.

Whelan, Anthony (1997), 'Fundamental Rights' in B. Tonra (ed), *Amsterdam: What the Treaty Means*.

Whiteley, Paul (1997), 'The Conservative Campaign', *Parliamentary Affairs* (Special Issue: Britain Votes 1997), Vol. 50, No. 4.

Wickham-Jones, Mark (2000), 'Labour Party Politics and Foreign Policy', in R. Little and M. Wickham-Jones (eds), *New Labour's Foreign Policy: A New Moral Crusade?*

Wilkes, George and Wring, Dominic (1998), 'The British Press and European Integration: 1948-1996', in D. Baker and D. Seawright (eds), *Britain For and Against Europe*.

Wincott, Daniel (1996), 'The Court of Justice and the European Policy Process', in J. Richardson (ed), *European Union: Power and Policy-Making*, Routledge, London.

Young, Hugo (1999), *This Blessed Plot - Britain and Europe from Churchill to Blair*, Macmillan, London.

Young, John W (2000), *Britain and European Unity 1945-1999*, Macmillan, Basingstoke.

Newspaper/Magazine Articles

Daily Mail, 16 February 1995: Christopher Bell, 'Labour blows its Euro cover.'

Le Figaro, 30 August 1994: Interview with Edouard Balladur.

Financial Times, 5 August 1996: John Kampfner, 'Labour shift on Social Chapter.'

The Guardian, 16 February 1995: Patrick Wintour and John Palmer, 'Straw tells MEPs to toe Major line on controls.'

The Guardian, 30 May 1997: Ian Black and John Palmer, 'Dutch end EU honeymoon.'

The Guardian, 22 April 1999: David McKie, 'By George! What a con.'

The Guardian, 6 April 2001: Ian Black and Michael White, 'Job losses put new EU pressure on Britain.'

The Guardian, 12 June 2001: Ian Black and Patrick Wintour, 'UK caves in on work directive.'

The Guardian, 9 November 2001: Larry Elliot, 'Don't bank on it.'

The Guardian, 15 December 2001: Michael White and Ian Black, 'Straw changes tack on single currency.'

The Guardian, 4 January 2002: Patrick Wintour and Nicholas Watt, 'Treasury euro doubts revealed.'

New Statesman, 14 August 1998: John Lloyd, 'Interview: Robin Cook.'

The Observer, 15 June 1997: Arnold Kemp, 'All together now.'

The Observer, 18 April 1999: Will Hutton, 'Now Spanish socialists know how British socialists feel.'

The Observer, 17 March 2002: Nick Cohen, 'Tony's new best friend.'

The Sun, 17 March 1997: Tony Blair, 'I'm a British patriot.'

The Sun, 22 April 1997: Tony Blair, 'We'll see off Euro dragons.'

The Sun, 24 June 1998: Front Page Editorial 'Is this the most dangerous man in Britain.'

Documents from EU Institutions, EU Governments and Non-Governmental Organisations

Bertelsmann Foundation (1990) The Shaping of a European Constitution, Bertelsmann Foundation, Gütersloh.

CDU/CSU (1994) Fraktion des Deutschen Bundestages, *Reflections on European Policy*, Bonn, 1 September 1994.

Jacques Chirac and Helmut Kohl (1995) Letter to the President of the European Council, 6 December 1995.

European Commission (1995) Report on the operation of the Treaty on European Union, 10 May 1995.

European Movement (1994) *Reform of the European Union: Proposals of the European Movement for British Policy Towards the Intergovernmental Conference of 1996*, European Movement, London.

European Parliament (1989) Resolution adopting the declaration of fundamental rights and freedoms, 12 April 1989.

European Parliament (1994) Resolution on the constitution of the European Union (Herman Report), 10 February 1994.

European Parliament (1995) Resolution on Bourlanges/Martin report on the functioning of the Treaty on European Union with a view to the 1996 Intergovernmental Conference - implementation and development of the Union, 17 May 1995.

European Parliament (1996) Resolution on the Dury/Maij-Weggen report on the convening of the IGC and evaluation of the work of the Reflection Group, 13 March 1996.

European Parliament, 13 March 1996: DG for Information and Public Relations, Central Press Division, Strasbourg Notebook.

European Policy Forum (1993), *Report of the European Constitutional Group, A Proposal for a European Constitution*, European Policy Forum, London.

FCO (1996), *Partnership of Nations: The British Approach to the European Intergovernmental Conference 1996*, HMSO, London.

Justice (1996) *The Democratic Deficit*, Justice, London.

Reflection Group (1995) Report, 5 December 1995, Brussels.

Public ETUC/Labour Party/PES Documents

ETUC January 1996: *Three Challenges for the 1996 IGC: Employment, Solidarity and Democracy*, Resolution approved by the ETUC Executive Committee, 14-15 December 1995.

ETUC February 1996, *ETUC/PES Joint Approaches to the 1996 IGC*, Joint ETUC/PES Statement, Brussels, 1 February 1996.

Labour Party (1983) *New Hope For Britain*, General Election Manifesto.

Labour Party (1991a) *Opportunity Britain: Labour's Policy in Europe*.

Labour Party (1991b) *Labour in Europe*, NEC statement, 30 October 1991.

Labour Party (1992) *It's Time To Get Britain Working Again*, General Election Manifesto.

Labour Party (1993a) *A New Agenda for Democracy - Labour's proposals for constitutional reform*.

Labour Party (1993b) *Prosperity Through Co-operation - A New European future*.

Labour Party (1994) *Make Europe Work for you*, Manifesto for the European Elections.

Labour Party (1995) *The Future of the European Union - Report on Labour's position in preparation for the Intergovernmental Conference 1996*.

Labour Party (1996) *New Labour, New Life for Britain*.

Labour Party (1997a) *Equipping Britain For the Future*, Business Manifesto.

Labour Party (1997b) *Because Britain Deserves Better*, General Election Manifesto.

Labour Party (2001) *Ambitions for Britain*, General Election Manifesto.

PES Group (1994) *The 1996 Intergovernmental Conference: First thoughts on our aims and objectives*, 29 June 1994.

PES Group (1995) *An Initial Approach to the IGC Treaty Review Conference*, approved by PES group, 29 March 1995.

PES (1994) Manifesto for the Elections to the EP, adopted by the PES Congress, 6 November 1993.

PES (1999) Manifesto for the Elections to the EP, adopted by the PES Congress, 1-2 March 1999.

PES December 1995, *Bringing the European Union into Balance*, Declaration on IGC approved by PES party leaders, Madrid, 14 December 1995.

Speeches/Public Statements

Tony Blair, 30 May 1995, Speech to the Friedrich-Ebert Stiftung, Bonn.

Tony Blair, 18 June 1996, Speech to BDI Conference, Bonn.

Tony Blair, 6 October 2000, Speech to Polish Stock Exchange: *Europe's Political Future*, Warsaw.

Robin Cook, 28 May 1996, Press Statement at launch of 'Labour's Business Agenda for Europe', Westminster.

Robin Cook, 19 June 1996, Press Statement on Beef Crisis, London.

Hansard, 18 June 1997, Statement by Prime Minister on Amsterdam European Council.

Doug Henderson, 5 May 1997, Opening statement by minister for Europe at IGC representatives Meeting, Brussels.

House of Commons, Foreign Affairs Committee 1997, First Report, *The Treaty of Amsterdam*, Session 1997-98: Evidence from Robin Cook, 4 November 1997.

Peter Mandelson, 28 June 1999, Centre for European Reform/Prospect Lecture, Brussels.

Larry Whitty, 28 September 1997, Speech to EPLP fringe meeting, Labour Party Conference, Brighton.

Internal Party Sources

Leader's Working Group on the IGC (LWG)

1) 5 December 1994:
LWG1 Minutes, Chair's Note.
LWG IGC1A: Terms of reference.
LWG IGC1B: Membership and secretariat.
LWG IGC1C: Timetable for IGC.
LWG IGC1D: IGC Issues – background.

2) 9 January 1995:
LWG2 Minutes, Chair's Note.
LWG IGC2A: Labour's agenda for Europe.
LWG IGC2B: Overall approach to changes in EU.
LWG IGC2C: Form of the treaty.
LWG IGC2D: Voting in the Council.
LWG IGC2E: Powers of the European and national Parliaments.
LWG IGC2F: EMU.

3) 20 February 1995:
LWG3 Minutes, Chair's Note.
LWG IGC3A: Press release on Cook's speech to European Policy Institute.
LWG IGC3B: PES Group, reflection document by Elisabeth Guigou.
LWG IGC3C: Summary of positions of PES parties on IGC.
LWG IGC3D: Extension of QMV.
LWG IGC3E: Draft PES Group paper by Pauline Green.

4) 27 March 1995:
LWG4 Minutes, Chair's Note.
LWG IGC4A: Agricultural policy: Council of Ministers procedures.
LWG IGC4B: European Parliament - powers and procedures.
LWG IGC4C: Second draft PES Group Paper by Pauline Green.
LWG IGC4D: Institutional implications of enlargement.
LWG IGC4E: Draft report of EP institutional affairs committee on IGC by David Martin.
LWG IGC4F: EMU.

5) 1 May 1995:
LWG5 Minutes, Chair's Note.
LWG IGC5A: Report of PES working-group meeting, 30-31 March 1995.
LWG IGC5B: Final version of PES Group paper by Pauline Green.
LWG IGC5C: Draft ETUC Congress declaration on IGC.
LWG IGC5E: Role of national parliaments.
LWG IGC5F: Treaty amendment on racism and xenophobia.
LWG IGC5G: Measures on energy, civil protection and tourism.

6) 19 June 1995:
LWG6 Minutes, Chair's Note.
LWG IGC6A: Final version of EP resolution on IGC (Bourlanges/Martin report).
LWG IGC6B: Report of PES working-group meeting, 11-12 May 1995.
LWG IGC6C: Commission paper on the functioning of the TEU.

LWG IGC6D: Reflection Group - initial document.
LWG IGC6E: Foreign, security and defence policy aspects of the IGC.
LWG IGC6G: Final draft of report of PES working-group on IGC.

7) 26 July 1995:
LWG7 Minutes, Chair's Note.
LWG IGC7A: Report of PES working-group on IGC, adopted as discussion document by
    PES leaders meeting, 24-25 June 1995.
LWG IGC7B: Spanish presidency - initial document.
LWG IGC7C: CAP and enlargement.
LWG IGC7D: Draft interim report of LWG.
LWG IGC7E: Report of working-group on free movement and border controls.

8) 14 September 1995:
LWG8 Minutes, Chair's Note.
LWG IGC8A: Re-edited draft interim report to conference.
LWG IGC8B: TUC report to congress on European issues.
LWG IGC8C: Developments on Reflection Group.

9) 5 February 1996:
LWG9 Minutes, Chair's Note.
LWG IGC9A: Reflection Group report (commentary).
LWG IGC9B: PES Leaders' declaration on IGC, adopted in Madrid, 14 December 1995.
LWG IGC9C: Madrid heads of government summit declaration, 15-16 December 1995.
LWG IGC9D: EP report on Madrid summit.
LWG IGC9E: House of Lords European Communities committee report on IGC.
LWG IGC9F: ETUC report on Madrid summit.
LWG IGC9H: New issues arising from Reflection Group and Madrid summit.
LWG IGC9J: Note on Venice conclave of PES Leaders.
LWG IGC9K: House of Commons select committee on European legislation, report on IGC.
LWG IGC9M: Joint PES/ETUC statement on IGC.

10) 1 April 1996:
LWG10 Minutes, Chair's Note.
LWG IGC10A: Government White Paper on IGC (commentary).
LWG IGC10B: EP Resolution on IGC (Dury/Maij-Weggen report).
LWG IGC10C: Regional aspects of IGC.
LWG IGC10D: European Court of Justice.
LWG IGC10E: Extension of QMV - detailed position.
LWG IGC10F: Background briefings on social dimension, QMV, EP powers.
LWG IGC10G: Swedish proposals on employment.
LWG IGC10H: Turin summit communiqué.

11) 10 June 1996:
LWG11 Minutes, Chair's Note.
LWG IGC11B: EP resolution on Turin summit.
LWG IGC11C: Report on IGC proceedings.
LWG IGC11D: Flexibility and variable geometry.
LWG IGC11E: Subsidiarity.
LWG IGC11F: Subsidiarity.
LWG IGC11G: Transparency.

12) 8 October 1996:
LWG12 Minutes, Chair's Note.
LWG IGC12A: Position after Florence summit.
LWG IGC12C: Attitudes on IGC of EU institutions and other member governments.
LWG IGC12D: IGC submissions by the presidency, the institutions and member states.
LWG IGC12E: IGC submissions from the UK government.

Internal Labour Party (LP) Documents/Correspondence

LP (Gordon) Brown, 11 November 1996: Briefing to Labour MPs, MEPs and prospective parliamentary candidates on social chapter.

LP (Sir Michael) Butler, 6 November 1996: Brief for Blair, 'Talk with Chirac.'

LP Butler, 12 November 1996: Note to Clark, 'Private Channel to the Dutch Presidency.'

LP Butler, Undated 1997: List of meetings on behalf of Labour party.

LP Butler, 13 January 1997: Briefing, 'Flexibility, Opt-outs and the Third Pillar.'

LP Butler, 13 February 1997: 'IGC - State of Play.'

LP Butler, 19 February 1997: Note to Whitty, Clark and Quin on QMV.

LP Butler, 4 March 1997: Note to Clark, re: Cook's meeting with Santer.

LP Butler, 6 March 1997: 'Summary Record of Talks with French Ambassador and German Minister on 5 March 1997.'

LP Butler, 19 March 1997: Note to Whitty, 'Summary record of conversation with Dutch Presidency on 18 March 1997.'

LP Butler, 7 April 1997: Note to Whitty, 'Conversation with Dutch Ambassador on 7 April.'

LP Butler, (David) Clark and (Larry) Whitty, 30 April 1997: 'Possible Strategy for the IGC after the Election.'

LP Butler and Whitty, 27 March 1997: Memo to Cook, 'Europe: Co-ordination of Government Policy.'

LP Clark and (Joyce) Quin, 9 December 1996: Note on meeting with Patijn.

LP (Richard) Corbett, 21 March 1997: Note to Blair, Cook and Whitty on IGC issues facing Labour government.

LP (Jack) Cunningham, 9 September 1994: Letter to Blair recommending establishment of 'Leader's Committee' on 1996 IGC.

LP PES Brief, November 1995: Briefing for conclave of PES leaders, Madrid, 11 November 1995.

LP PES Brief, December 1995: Briefing for meeting of PES leaders, 14 December 1995.

LP PES Brief, June 1996: Briefing for meeting of PES leaders, Florence, 20 June 1996.

LP (Sir Robin) Renwick, 31 January 1997: Note to Powell, 'Europe: Majority Voting.'

LP (Jack) Straw, 23 February 1995: Briefing, 'The European Union, Immigration, and Border Controls - The Labour Party Position.'

LP Whitty, 1 November 1994: Memo to Blair, Prescott and Cook on Labour's approach to 1996 IGC.

LP Whitty, 11 April 1995: Note to Prescott, Cook and Sigler, 'IGC: Views of TUC.'

LP Whitty, 16 May 1995: Note to Prescott, Cook, Quin, Powell and (David) Hill, 'Parliament Report on the IGC 1996: EPLP Position.'

LP Whitty, 16 June 1995: Note to Straw, 'Europe and Racism and Xenophobia.'

LP Whitty, 26 September 1995: Note to Cook, Prescott and Sigler, 'European Report for Conference - Swedish Proposals.'

LP Whitty, 25 October 1995: Note to Cook, 'IGC Reflection Group and David Davis.'

LP Whitty, 30 May 1996: Note to Blair, Prescott and Cook, 'Strictly Confidential - Beef Crisis etc.'

LP Whitty, 18 June 1996: Note to Prescott, Cook and Powell, 'European Parliament Resolution: Florence Summit Preview, Beef and British non co-operation.'

LP Whitty, 3 July 1996: Note to Cook on Blair's speech to Chambers of Commerce.

LP Whitty, 30 October 1996: Note to Cook, Quin, David and Powell, 'IGC - Franco-German Submission on Flexibility.'

LP Whitty, 8 December 1996: 'Dublin Draft Treaty - Overall Commentary.'

LP Whitty, 3 February 1997: Note to Byers on 'Leading Britain into the Future' document.

LP Whitty, 14 February 1997: Note to Cook, Quin and Powell, 'IGC - Latest Developments.'

LP Whitty, 18 February 1997: Note to Cook, Quin, Byers, Ian McCartney, Norris and Matthew Taylor, 'Social Protocol: QMV etc. - Commission Document.'

LP Whitty, 19 February 1997: Note to Prescott, 'Europe Issues to Raise with Tony Blair.'

LP Whitty, 1 March 1997: Note to David Blunkett, Cook, Byers and Norris, 'Draft Pronk Report on IGC Changes.'

LP Whitty, 18 March 1997: Note to Cook and Powell, 'European Issues.'

LP Whitty, 23 March 1997: Note to Sigler, Matthew Taylor and Liz Lloyd, 'IGC: Rome Meeting of Foreign Ministers, Tuesday March 25.'

LP Whitty, 25 March 1997: 'Dutch Draft Treaty Amendments - Analysis and Comment.'

LP Whitty, 26 March 1997: Note to Cook, Quin, Butler and Clark, 'IGC Position: French Government.'

LP Whitty, 6 April 1997: Note to Cook, Quin, Powell, Butler and Clark, 'IGC: Presidency Papers, Representatives Group and Foreign Ministers Meeting.'

LP Whitty, 30 April 1997: Note to Cook, 'EU Foreign Ministers Meeting.'

Internal PES Documents/Correspondence

PES IGC Working-Party, January 1995: Unofficial summary of first exchange of views of PES IGC working-party, 12-13 January 1995.

PES IGC Working-Party, May 1995a: First draft report of the PES working-party on the 1996 IGC, 7 May 1995.

PES IGC Working-Party, May 1995b: Second draft report of the PES working-party on the 1996 IGC, 31 May 1995.

PES IGC Working-Party, June 1995: Report of the PES working-party on the 1996 IGC, presented to PES party leaders meeting, Valbonne, 24-25 June 1995.

PES (Dick) Spring, 10 October 1996: Note for attention of leaders of PES parties, re: PES co-ordination meeting in Dublin, 5 October 1996.

Internal ETUC/TUC Documents/Correspondence

ETUC January 1995: Draft resolution on IGC (1), 'For A Strong, Democratic and Open European Union Built on Solidarity.'

ETUC April 1995: Draft resolution on IGC (2), 'For A Strong, Democratic and Open European Union Built on Solidarity', submitted to ETUC Congress, Brussels, 8 May 1995.

TUC November 1994: 1996 IGC: Orientations for ETUC discussions, 29 November 1994.

TUC (Tom) Jenkins, 10 April 1995: Note to Whitty on ETUC draft resolution on IGC.

TUC (David) Lea, 20 September 1995: Note to Whitty on Labour party IGC policy document.

TUC September 1995: General council report to annual congress.

TUC 1996 Group, October 1996: Note on meeting of 1996 group, 31 October 1994.

Index

*For Product Safety Concerns and Information please contact
our EU representative GPSR@taylorandfrancis.com Taylor & Francis
Verlag GmbH, Kaufingerstraße 24, 80331 München, Germany*

T - #0115 - 270225 - C0 - 219/154/14 - PB - 9780815382232 - Gloss Lamination